CORVETTE
America's Sports Car

BEEKMAN HOUSE

BY THE AUTO EDITORS OF CONSUMER GUIDE®

ISBN 0-517-02036-X

**This edition published by Beekman House,
distributed by Crown Publishers, Inc.,
225 Park Avenue South, New York, NY 10003.**

**Library of Congress Catalog Card Number:
89-60926**

CLUBS FOR CORVETTE ENTHUSIASTS

Florida Chapter,
National Corvette Restorer's Society
12734 Pine Acre Lane
West Palm Beach, FL 33414
Founded: 1977
Current membership: 300
Publication: *Fuel Line*, quarterly newsletter

National Corvette Owners Association
P.O. Box 777A
Falls Church, VA 22046
Founded: 1975
Current membership: 25,000
Publication: *For 'Vettes Only*

National Council of Corvette Clubs
P.O. Box 325
Troy, OH 45373
Founded: 1957
Current membership: 10,000

Western States Corvette Council
2321 Falling Water Court
Santa Clara, CA 95054
Founded: 1965
Current membership: 3,000
Publication: Quarterly newsletter

The editors gratefully acknowledge the contribution of the Corvette clubs and club members, Corvette owners and photographers, and other Corvette enthusiasts whose names are listed here. Particular thanks to the General Motors executives and personnel who generously assisted with the research and development of this book.

CONTRIBUTING PHOTOGRAPHERS

Clint Clemens
Alex Gabbard
David Gooley
Sam Griffith
Talbot Hack
S. Scott Hutchinson
Kenn Jeschonek
Bud Juneau
Milton Gene Kieft
Bill Kilborn
Bill Locke
Dan Lyons
Vince Manocchi
John L. Matras
Ron McQueeney
Doug Mitchel
D. Randy Riggs
Richard Spiegelman
Nicky Wright

SPECIAL THANKS TO:

John M. Bolton: *GM Photographic*
Paul Deutschman
Chuck Jordan: *V.P. GM Design*
Floyd C. Joliet: *GM Design Staff*
David S. Kaplan:
    Callaway Engineering
Ed Lechtzin: *Chevrolet PR*
Bill Locke: *Florida Chapter N.C.R.S.*
Suzanne Lull: *Cypress Gardens*
Wayne Morrical: *GM Design Staff*
Jim Pratner
Larry Shinoda

CORVETTE OWNERS

Ron Adams
Vern Alexander
David Anderson
Auburn-Cord-Duesenberg Museum
A.R. Bartz
Paul Batista
William Bauce
Joseph E. Bortz
Bill Carpenter
Joe Cimmino
Eric R. Coleman
Thomas & Mae Crockatt
Leonard Davidson
"T" & Ed DeCamp
Ed Dwyer
Jeff Dzemske
Crystal Endicott
John M. Endres
Jim Engsberg
Sam Feinman
Alexander Gagnon, Jr.
Edward Giacobazzi
Ken Gillamders
Ray Halsey
O.J. Hanna
Bill & Dorothy Harris
Dr. Ernie Hendry
Cassey Hessel
Dean & Carol Hill
Richard Hodgman
John P. Horenci, Jr.
Gary W. Hunt
Jerry Hutter
Dr. J. Bruce Jacobs
Donald Jerie

Gary Jimenez
Warren Johnson
Roger Judski
Merle Kalish
Tom Kelly
Robert Kleckhauskas
William Lankford
Bill & Pat Locke
Phillip & Sandy Lopiccolo
Donald Maich
Steve Marek
Scott Maze
Mike Mikosz
Kenneth Moerer
Edward L. Mueller
Dennis M. Murphy
Robert Paterson
Joe Pendergast
Cynthia A. Rekemeyer
Barry Renaud
John Rikert
Max Rubin
Dave Schanen
Gene Schiavone
Joe Schula
Forrest Shropshire
David Simpson
Dave Stefun
Mike Vietro
Dan Weand
Al Webster
Thomas J. Wilt
Greg Wyffels
Peter Zannis

CONTENTS

THE ANATOMY OF A LEGEND

Given the title of this book, it's fitting to begin with a few thoughts on exactly what qualifies the Chevrolet Corvette as "America's sports car." Certainly few would argue that the legendary Corvette is and always has been a sports car in the accepted sense of that term, and a uniquely American invention. The car also possesses the sort of endurance we tend to associate with legends—in more ways than one. Against occasionally formidable odds, the Corvette has seen more than 900,000 units over nearly four decades of production. Meanwhile, other home-grown sportsters like the Nash-Healey, Kaiser-Darrin, the original Ford Thunderbird and, most recently,

A gathering of Corvettes— "America's sports car"—is enough to stir the blood of any true enthusiast.

the Pontiac Fiero have come and gone like so many flashes in the proverbial pan. At the same time, the 'Vette has consistently proved its mettle in the heat of competition, winning numerous events all over the world.

Equally apt for a legend, the Corvette has long inspired a level of interest and enthusiasm rarely accorded production automobiles, let alone one so relatively common. Indeed, to find cars with similarly wide and devoted followings, you have to look to such comparative rarities as the Porsche 911 Turbo, Lamborghini Countach, and Ferrari Testarossa, all much costlier machines from companies far smaller and more specialized than the Chevrolet Division of giant General Motors. Of course, it hardly hurts that the Corvette has usually been a two-seat convertible, that most romantic of automobiles, or that it's most always been among the fastest and most visually exciting of American cars.

But none of this explains the mythical, larger-than-life quality that surrounds the Corvette, a car that in some ways is not the stuff of which legends are made. As a Chevrolet, for example, it carries a name with somewhat less prestige than the aforementioned European marques. It also suffers in some eyes by lacking their long factory-competition heritage. While there's been no shortage of Corvette victories, they've come mainly from the efforts of private drivers and teams with no overt factory support—though sometimes with a lot of under-the-table assistance.

It's also true that while today's Corvette is much more technically advanced than the first one, Chevrolet has so far resisted the march of technology by retaining the original front-engine/rear-drive format and a V-8 engine very much like the one introduced for 1955. For some latter-day critics, this makes the Corvette too traditional, if not downright old-fashioned, next to cars like the mid-12-cylinder Countach and Testarossa, though arguably no more so than the

equally hidebound rear-engine 911.

More telling is the fact that most every one of the six Corvette design generations seen to date has not been completely "right" as introduced. In fact, America's sports car was born to controversy, dismissed by many in 1953 as an underpowered, overstyled "plastic bathtub." This may explain why the smooth and powerful 1956-57 Corvette, perhaps the one exception to this rule, garnered such high praise. But the 1958 model was greeted as a chrome-laden step backward, and even the exciting, vastly superior Sting Ray of 1963-67 — still regarded by many as the best Corvette ever—had a few "teething" problems. The fifth-generation "Shark" design of 1968 was perhaps the most troubled birth of all: poorly built and begadgeted in the extreme. The current sixth-series 'Vette has also taken a fair amount of time to sort out since it went on sale in 1983.

But few cars are anywhere near perfect at first, and it's one of the singular constants of Corvette history that each new design has been steadily improved as it went along. In this, Chevy has followed Porsche's admirable pattern with the 911. Thus was the '58 swiftly tidied up for its second year and handsomely restyled for its fourth, the Sting Ray progressively relieved of needless styling frills, and the Shark dramatically transformed into a more solid, better balanced, less contrived *gran turismo* over what would turn out to be a remarkable 15-year run. The current Corvette has seen a number of corrections in its first six years and will likely see several more before it yields to the very different seventh generation scheduled for around 1993.

Major roles in the Corvette story have been played by legendary GM figures whose person-alities have always shone through in the finished product, and who have advanced their own reputations as a result. 'Vette aficionados know their names well: Harley Earl, the "father" of Detroit styling and the first Corvette; Ed Cole, the brilliant engineer who contributed so much to the milestone small-block Chevy V-8 that's been the heart of Corvette power for some 35 years; Bill Mitchell, Earl's hand-picked successor as head of GM Design and who was, if anything, even more passionate about the 'Vette; and Zora Arkus-Duntov, who may have influenced the Corvette more than any other single person over some 20 years as its chief development engineer.

Today, 'Vette lovers take comfort in knowing that their car is in equally capable and caring hands. There's the youthful and talented Dave McLellan, who became "Mr. Corvette" when Duntov retired in 1974; Jerry Palmer, the astute designer who spearheaded sixth-generation styling as head of Chevrolet Production Studio Three; enthusiastic engineer John Heinricy; and, last but not least, Chuck Jordan, installed in 1986 as GM design chief. In the pages that follow, these and other Corvette luminaries, past and present, describe why they did what they did, and what they might have done differently. Along the way, they provide valuable insights into the shaping of America's sports car legend.

Two more constants in Corvette history bear mention here. One is high performance value for the money, a reflection of the dedication and spirit of those who've created the cars, and a big factor in Corvette's consistent popularity. The other is continuing high interest in forthcoming Corvette developments, a preoccupation with the future unusual even among jaded journalists and rabid enthusiasts. In particular, a mid-engine model has been a persistent vision—and just as persistently stillborn—almost from the Corvette's inception. The various efforts along this line, as well as other Corvettes-that-never-were, are fully chronicled here. And fascinating stories they are, especially since it appears that the mid-engine dream will finally become a showroom reality in just a few years.

When all is said and done, however, the Corvette legend begins and ends with the car itself—a true sports car of distinctly American character offering vivid performance, superb roadability, rugged reliability, and "dream car" style at realistic prices. If not always state-of-the-art, the Corvette has most always been worthy of comparison with the world's best sports and GT cars, yet it has always been far more accessible to far more buyers. At the same time, it's a car that allows people to keep on dreaming even after they take the keys, lending itself to all manner of appearance and performance modifications in the great "shade tree" tradition of American hot rodding—appropriate for a machine born as a "dream car."

The Corvette's birth and the significant design and engineering developments that followed are what this book is all about. Of course, the sports car idea didn't originate with the Corvette, so Chapter 1 charts the course of this notion over the half-century that preceded Chevy's interpretation in 1953. Chapter 2 covers the Corvette's inception and harried gestation—including the decision to construct its body of fiberglass, another feature retained to this day.

Then it's on to separate sections for each design generation save the fifth, which gets two chapters (9 and 10) because it lasted so long, and the sixth, which is split into 1984-89 (Chapter 11) and 1990 and beyond (Chapter 12). The latter includes full details on the significant ZR-1 model, the most exciting performance Corvette in a decade, and necessarily sketchier information on what should be the next Corvette: the dramatically different 1993 model based on the mid-engine Indy prototype. In Chapter 13 we highlight the Corvette's illustrious competition career, from the brief but glorious factory efforts of the Fifties to today's Corvette Challenge Series, the ultimate racing tribute to America's sports car legend. Special attention is given to a pair of significant Corvette racers, the Super Sport (Chapter 5) and the Grand Sport (Chapter 8). Chapter 14 looks at the fabulous Corvette show cars.

Sprinkled throughout the book are handy reference tables covering model-year production, major specifications, original list prices, engine availability, serial-number spans, and other information of interest to collectors and restorers. You'll also find a number of "sidebar" features on "concept cars" and other one-of-a-kind Corvettes, as well as interviews with the key Corvette figures mentioned above. The glamorous color shots of original and restored Corvettes speak for themselves, and we're indebted to the owners for making their cars available for photography. We're also indebted to Chevrolet Motor Division and the GM Design Staff for their assistance with interviews and original factory photography.

In a world where the rate of change is inexorably accelerating, it's nice to observe that the Corvette, for all its many changes over the years, remains much the same sort of car it was in the beginning. That, too, is part of what makes this American sports car the legend it is—that and the fact that this particular American car has somehow managed to remain exciting and captivating when most others couldn't. Perhaps it only goes to show that the really *good* ideas are indeed timeless.

Certainly the pleasure of owning, driving, or just contemplating these cars is timeless, which may be why it's so often been said over the years that the automotive world would be a much poorer place without the Corvette. That's still true even though there are cheaper and arguably more modern sports cars around, and even though the 'Vette has, of necessity, become a lot more sophisticated and expensive than it used to be. It is this more competitive market that partly explains why the Corvette is now suffering one of the few prolonged sales slumps in its history, despite the recent widespread renaissance of traditional Detroit performance.

Yet 'Vette fans need not fear for their car. For as long as there are those who like to go fast and corner securely in great-looking all-American style, there will always be a place for the Corvette. To them and car lovers everywhere, we dedicate this book with its fond memories of the past, and offer a happy prediction about the Corvette of a not-too-distant future: You ain't seen nuthin' yet.

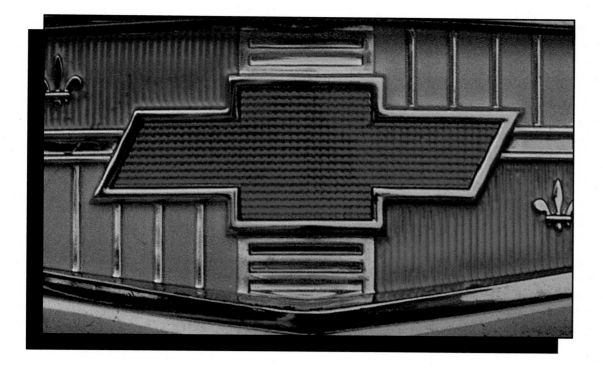

CHAPTER 1

COUNTDOWN TO CORVETTE: THE SPORTS CAR'S FIRST 50 YEARS

What exactly *is* a "sports car"? An apt question when it comes to America's most successful example of the breed, especially since Chevrolet once advertised the Corvette as "America's Only *True* Sports Car."

Enthusiasts have long argued the point, but the most widely accepted definition of a sports car is an auto that's suitable for road travel yet equally capable of winning in race-track competition with only minimum modification. In other words, it's a *dual-purpose* device, the twin functions being neatly expressed by the now-common term "race and ride."

Traditionally, a sports car has been thought of as an open car with two seats and, typically, a folding top of canvas, leatherette, or some other flexible material. Usually, it has some luggage space, if perhaps less than a *gran turismo*. A GT, by contrast, is generally a closed car able to carry at least two people and a decent amount of luggage quickly over long distances. However, not all GTs, especially modern ones, are suitable for out-and-out competition.

Implicit in the notion of "sports car" is driving fun, if not outright ability. A GT may corner like crazy, stop like a jet on an aircraft carrier, and be pleasurable to drive, but it is engineered to emphasize passenger comfort. A "true" sports car is often thought of as *sacrificing* comfort—even to the extent of basics like weather protection—in the interest of minimum weight, maximum acceleration, and engineering features intended to provide the best possible handling, roadholding, and braking.

This explains why so many sports cars have very stiff springs and shock absorbers, which tend to provide maximum roadability at the expense of ride comfort. Likewise the lighter, thinly padded seats found in many sports cars, not to mention the lack of weighty amenities like carpeting, wind-up windows, and power accessories are certainly due to the attempt to achieve ultimate

speed. Understand, though, that this is a more traditional view. With a century of automotive progress behind them, today's sports cars, including the Corvette, can be GT plush and civilized, yet achieve levels of performance and handling once found only in racing machinery.

Though they weren't known as such, sports cars date from the very dawn of the automobile, a logical and vital result of the highly publicized competitive events that were staged to help win public acceptance of the infant "horseless carriage." Chassis and drivetrain design were paramount in those early years. A consensus on the "correct" power source did not exist by any means, with electricity, steam, and internal combustion all having their adherents. Fledgling automakers therefore designed their engines first, then chassis, and finally bodies.

Ultimately, of course, internal-combustion power won out, namely spark-ignition designs running on gasoline, though the compression-ignition diesel engine, which came along a bit later, remains quite popular in many places (if not the United States in the late Eighties). Bodies have evolved from rickety, square-rigged designs of wood, fabric, and metal to sleek, mainly all-steel structures, many of which are welded integrally with a chassis instead of being bolted to it, though even some modern cars retain the more traditional body-on-frame construction.

In the beginning, car bodies tended to be sparse, open affairs. The cars were largely hand-built and thus expensive—novel "toys" for the very rich. But by the early Teens, there were far more companies building far more cars by more efficient means, which brought the automobile within the financial reach of vast numbers of less well-to-do folks. In addition to lower cost, the advent of a growing national network of paved roads and the introduction of closed sedan, limousine, and town car body styles all contributed to the rapid growth in the automobile's popularity. Henry Ford did the rest, making the automobile universal—and universally affordable—by using a moving assembly line to turn out his simple little Model T by the thousands and, eventually, by the millions.

Meantime, high-priced prestige cars like Locomobile, Simplex, Lozier, Chadwick, and the legendary "Three Ps"—Packard, Peerless, and Pierce-Arrow—continued to attract moneyed types able to go motoring strictly for the sheer pleasure of it, as opposed to the more practical purpose of simply getting somewhere. Some of these upper-crust owners soon began replacing their cars' original, heavy, closed bodywork with lighter, more spartan, open two-seater designs. Though the results were still big brutes that were hellish to handle, with none of the agility that would mark the future Corvette, they were certainly more capable than their closed "parents" in the speed runs, durability trials, and cross-country marathons that were the main forms of competition in those days.

This trend inevitably led to the idea of the dual-purpose, race-and-ride sports car. One of its earliest and best-known expressions was the historic Mercer Type 35 Raceabout of 1911, with the T-head-engine models built through 1914 being the most fondly

remembered. A direct forebear of the Corvette to come, the Raceabout was light, fast, and responsive for its time. A big four-cylinder engine designed by Finley Robertson Porter supplied the power, though there wasn't much of it by today's standards: just 58 horsepower at 1700 rpm. But since curb weight was only some 2400 pounds, the Raceabout was a relative rocket. Right from the factory it could top 75 miles per hour, and racing versions came close to the magic 100-mph mark, amazing for that time.

The Raceabout also anticipated many later sports cars by being relatively easy to drive and shift, even though synchromesh was years away. Its chassis was quite modern. The rear axle was a full-floating type located by radius rods, and semi-elliptic leaf springs of vanadium-alloy steel were used at each corner. There was even a pull-up handbrake acting on the rear wheels, supplementing a mostly ineffective foot-actuated service brake operating on the transmission.

At $2150, more than twice the price of the costliest Model T Ford, the Raceabout was obviously not for everyone (another sports-car characteristic that persists to this day). But its jaunty air and jackrabbit quickness captivated the country. It is still one of the most sought-after models among antique-car collectors.

The Raceabout quickly proved its mettle in competition, winning the important San Francisco-Panama Pacific Light Car Race in February 1911. Later that year, two Mercers that were literally driven in off the street ran flat out to finish 12th and 15th in the inaugural Indianapolis 500, averaging 63 mph. According to many reports, they proved so trouble-free that their hoods didn't have to be opened once during the race. Afterward, in what would later become something of a tradition in production sports-car racing, drivers Hughie Hughes of England and Charles Bigelow (who'd won at San Francisco) simply wheeled the Raceabouts off the track and on home. It was a spectacular showing for an unmodified automobile. The next year, Hughes drove a Raceabout to third at the Brickyard, averaging a little over 76 mph.

Raceabouts went on to score many more victories at the hands of speed merchants like Ralph DePalma, Eddie Pullen, and Spencer Wishart, but production didn't continue long: The last ones were built in 1915. Just before that, however, a rival company introduced a new model that would be even more celebrated: the Stutz Bearcat, the car synonymous with sheiks and flappers and all of the other razzmatazz of the Roaring Twenties.

Conceived as a "sportsman's car," the Bearcat was the roadgoing equivalent of the famous T-head Stutz racers that had scored many wins of their own against the Mercers. Its chassis and four- and six-cylinder engines came from Stutz's F-Series passenger models, a kind of "derivative" engineering that would be commonly employed for many later sports cars, including the Corvette. Wheelbase, however, was considerably shorter than on the F-Series and stance rakishly lower. Though far less graceful and athletic than the Raceabout, which it resembled, the Bearcat had superior roadholding, and its overall performance was thrilling.

Besides an attractive restyle in 1917, the Bearcat received a more powerful, 80-bhp, 360-cubic-inch, four-cylinder engine with a 16-valve cylinder head. (The last may surprise those younger readers who think four-valves-per-cylinder engines—including the high-tech LT5 unit of the 1989 Corvette ZR1—are strictly a modern phenomenon.) In this form it was capable of an astonishing 85 mph. The car was reworked again for 1920 and continued to sell well for another couple of years. The final 88-bhp version with 3.00:1 rear axle could hit close to 90 mph, but even this wasn't enough to counteract a sales slide, and the Bearcat was phased out in 1923.

American automakers created a number of memorable, sporty-looking models in the years between the world wars. By and large, though, these automobiles were not the sort of compact, nimble, dual-purpose machines we now think of as sports cars. To be sure, there were a number of romantic roadsters and

Although not "true" sports cars as defined today, many early sporty models were based on their more mundane passenger car siblings. They were really "sports tourers"—comfortable and fast, large and heavy. Their sporty lines can be seen on this '31 Pierce-Arrow Model 42 (opposite) and a 1933-34 Auburn Twelve boattail speedster (above).

convertibles; some, like the elegant Auburn 856 boattail speedster and futuristic Cord 810 Sportsman, have long been considered among the greatest cars of this automotive "golden age." But such cars were more *gran turismo* or "sports tourer" than out-and-out sports car—comfortable and fast, but too large and heavy to be completely at home on a challenging country road. Others, like the Millers and early Duesenbergs, were more competition cars than road machines—too powerful, too unwieldy to be practical in everyday use for the vast majority of motorists. Besides, they were built in tiny numbers and cost a fortune. The same was true of the later SJ Duesenbergs, except that they were pure luxury tourers. America, it seemed, had given up on the sports car.

But not completely. The late Twenties witnessed the birth of a very different type of "sports car": the hot rod. These homebuilt contraptions reflected the dreams and enthusiasm of backyard mechanics blessed with a certain native intelligence but not much cash: they transformed old, worn-out wrecks into very personalized automobiles. Hot rods were supposed to look good on the street and be fast on something called a dragstrip.

Model T and Model A Fords were the favored starting points because they were cheap and plentiful, and their simple basic engineering was amenable to all manner of modifications. The most common changes were discarding the fenders and running boards, lowering the body, maybe bending some sheet metal, fiddling with the suspension, and, naturally, adding horsepower, either by wringing more from the original engine or junking it for something more potent.

In a way, the pioneer hot rodders were after the same things that early automakers sought in their racers: more speed, more agility, more distinctive appearance. Their approach was certainly different—low-budget, one-of-a-kind machines built from a crazy-quilt of production-car pieces—but they were nonetheless quite faithful to the race-and-ride ideal, sports cars in the best sense.

Meanwhile, the sports-car idea was being pursued in Europe along several different lines. Bugatti in France put the emphasis on small, almost delicate, open-wheel racers and two-place road cars built unhurriedly, one at a time. From Germany came the imperious bellow of the heavy, super-expensive supercharged Mercedes-Benz—the imposing S/SS/SSK roadsters of the late Twenties/early Thirties and the more civilized 500/540K sports tourers of 1935-39. In Italy, companies like Maserati and Alfa Romeo were building agile road burners, combining race-bred performance and technical sophistication with curvaceous, open, two-seat styling that marked a new peak in coach-building artistry. But it was England that would define the "classic" sports car we think of today: lithe, lovely roadsters like the Squire, the four-wheel Morgan, the sleek SS 100 (forerunner of the Jaguar), and most of all, the cars from Morris Garages (MG).

MG has long been credited as the marque that introduced sports cars to America (as the company itself once boasted). However arguable the claim, one MG undeniably helped kindle the sports-car fever that swept the country in the early postwar years, the fascination that would be an impetus for the development of the Corvette. It was, of course, the TC, introduced in 1945.

American writer T.C. Browne once characterized the MG TC as "one of the most beloved British exports ever to reach these shores, rivaling Scots Whiskey in its popularity among Americans...[But it became] admired all out of proportion to its numbers (few) or its technical virtues (fewer). In fact, the TC was all but indistinguishable from its immediate prewar predecessor [the TB], and a typical British enthusiast regarded the [even] earlier PB as a measurably superior motorcar. Legends are seldom born of logic." True enough. Still, GIs stationed in England fell in love with this humble little piece of ironmongery, brought some home, and the legend was born.

What made it so special? Charm, for one thing. The TC was cute to American eyes, but it also looked *right*—nifty and sporty. Then there was its appealing quaintness: vintage Thirties styling, diabolical folding-top mechanism, cozy two-seat cockpit, conveniences notable by their absence—the whole package. The flexible ladder-type chassis and crude solid-axle suspension were anachronisms a decade before, and the ride was stiff and joggly. Yet the TC's agility was a revelation to Yanks raised on workaday Fords and Chevys. With an implausibly small 1250-cc four-cylinder engine producing just 54 bhp, the TC was hardly fast—well under 80 mph tops—but it showed power-hungry colonials that a car needn't have a big-inch engine to be fun. And like the Model A Fords so popular with hot rodders, it was as complicated as an anvil.

But perhaps the TC's greatest contribution was that it combined all the basic elements of the sports-car idea that had evolved over the previous 50 years. That it had a folding top and only two seats seemed almost superfluous. The stage was set for the sports-car revolution in the postwar era.

That revolution took a long time to get rolling, as no Detroit producer rushed to build sports cars. Not that they didn't have good reasons. The end of World War II brought the promise of prosperity unknown since before the Depression. Gas was still cheap. The public mood was expansive. Most of all, four years without civilian goods had created a pent-up demand for 15 million new cars. As a result, consumers began snapping up most anything and everything Detroit turned out. Who cared if the cars were only warmed-over 1942 models? They were *new*.

Most returning GIs started to raise families; for them, tiny two-seaters just didn't make sense. When most U.S. automakers issued their first completely new postwar models, for 1949, the cars mirrored the state of the nation perfectly—the longest, lowest, widest, flashiest cars in history. Naturally, they sold like crazy. So, though a great many people may have

One of the ultimate sports cars of its day (and all time), the 1927 Mercedes-Benz SSK (below) boasted a rousing 170 horsepower, 225 with supercharger, but was a handful to drive. In America, the front-drive, V-8 powered 1937 Cord 812 (opposite) claimed a more modest 190 horsepower with supercharging, 115 without.

been *intrigued* by sports cars in the late Forties, not many were actually willing to buy one.

The late Ken Purdy, long-acknowledged "father" of modern automotive journalism, had a description for America's early-postwar cars that summed up what might be called the first buyer backlash against Detroit. "A turgid river of jelly-bodied clunkers," he called them. A small but sturdy handful of buyers agreed, most of them sporting drivers who had brought back or at least experienced a European sports car like the MG TC—people who knew that driving didn't have to be dull. But such enthusiasts were a tiny minority. In 1952, for example, registrations of what by even the broadest definition could be called "sports cars" came to a grand total of 11,000—a mere 0.26 percent of the 4.2 million cars registered in the United States that year.

But by then, the sports-car phenomenon couldn't be stopped. The Sports Car Club of America (SCCA) had already been formed, organizing road races as well as something called a "rally," a motorsports event new to the United States. On highways, sports-car drivers began waving and honking at one another to signal their kindred interest, and many enjoyed playing tag with larger, more powerful American cars.

A steady stream of new models from overseas only fueled their enthusiasm. As if to announce its postwar recovery, England sent over the exquisite Jaguar XK120 in 1949, a curvy, envelope-bodied roadster and coupe motivated by a 160/180-bhp twincam six and capable of flying at up to two miles a minute. They were quite costly—$3500 or so—but the XK120 was the car every MG owner aspired to. In 1950, MG itself issued an improved TC, the TD. Three years later, the MG/Jaguar price-and-performance gap was bridged by the winsome Triumph TR2, offering 90 mph for around $2300, and the handsome

Austin-Healey 100-4, a genuine 100-mph roadster priced about $500 higher.

The nation's motoring press had been quick to spread the sports-car gospel and kept urging Detroit to keep the faith. Purdy set the tone early in a 1949 article for *True* magazine titled "The Two-Seater Comes Back," predicting that sports-car engineering would soon filter down to ordinary family models, which would offer not just greater speed and style but also safety and—something new—driver enjoyment.

Though Purdy was a bit premature, a few people in the industry were sympathetic. One was a Belgian-born engineer newly arrived at the Chevrolet Division of General Motors. Said Zora Arkus-Duntov at a 1953 meeting of the Society of Automotive Engineers (SAE): "Considering the statistics, the American public does not want a sports car at all. But do the statistics give a true picture? As far as the American market is concerned, it is still an unknown quantity, since an American sports car catering to American tastes, roads, ways of living, and national character has not yet been on the market."

Duntov was exaggerating. Even in the late Forties, the booming seller's market had encouraged a number of enterprising individuals to try their luck in the auto business, many of whom did so with a sports car. And why not? In those heady days, offering something a little different, something buyers couldn't get from Detroit, seemed the sure path to success. What better than a sports car? And Detroit itself soon spotted an angle. If average Americans couldn't afford a sports car or the garage space for one next to the family hauler, perhaps having one in the local showroom might at least inspire them to buy one of the "turgid, jelly-bodied clunkers" that were making millionaires of so many Detroit executives.

Would-be millionaires were behind most of America's

Most of the early postwar sports cars came from England, where they had been "discovered" by American servicemen. The MG TC (below) was indeed "The Sports Car America Loved First." Jaguar stunned sports car fans in 1948 with the sleek and fast XK120 (opposite bottom). Triumph debuted the TR2 (top) in 1953, a $2500 high-value sportster.

16

early-postwar sports cars—starry-eyed creations that were typically little more than a swoopy two-seat body clapped onto an existing production-car chassis stuffed with the hairiest engine that would fit. Limited knowledge and shoestring budgets precluded most of these dreams from going beyond the prototype stage, if that far, while others saw only minuscule production, due to small facilities and/or lack of manufacturing expertise. The casualties were legion: the Kurtis Sport and its later derivative, the Muntz Jet; the Boardman and the Brogan; the Edwards and the Gadabout—in fact, a whole slew of names that are now mere historical footnotes.

However, there was one small company that managed a highly respectable effort: Cunningham. The man behind it was wealthy California sportsman Briggs Swift Cunningham, who not coincidentally also engineered the most successful American onslaught on international sports-car competition up to the early Fifties. The cars that carried his name ranged from svelte *gran turismos* to all-out sports-racers. One of the latter, the 1952 C-4R, finished fourth in the annual 24-hour grind at Le Mans in France. Its 1953 successor, the C-5R, finished third behind two D-Type Jaguars, which had the main advantage of disc brakes. Cunningham had tried to buy disc brakes from their British manufacturer, but was stonewalled in his effort.

For power, Cunningham relied on the best American powerplant of his day: the efficient 331-cid Chrysler hemi-head V-8, good for 180 bhp in street tune and up to 300 bhp for competition. His one roadgoing "production" model, the 107-inch-wheelbase C-3 of 1953-54, carried handsome but expensive Italian bodywork (by Vignale) and was painstakingly crafted, so it rarely sold for less than $10,000. That's approximately $40,000 in today's money, about what you pay for a loaded Corvette convertible. But though

the C-3 would be the most numerous Cunningham, production came to a mere 19 fastback coupes and only nine convertibles, reflecting the car's highly specialized character and the meager capacity of Briggs' Florida factory.

Without doubt, though, the Cunninghams were genuine American sports cars: fast on any road and able to compete with Europe's best on any racing circuit in the world. Briggs quit building cars when continued losses forced him to either give up or declare his business a "hobby," but he deserves vast credit for proving the capability of American engineering to an international audience.

More important and directly influential in the Corvette story were the sports-car efforts of two major manufacturers, albeit independents much smaller than General Motors. These were Nash-Kelvinator, imaginative producer of the Anglo-American Nash-Healey, and Kaiser-Frazer, which employed such luminary talents as Howard A. "Dutch" Darrin and Brooks Stevens as design consultants.

Nash president George Mason had a size 52 frame and felt more at home in a Michigan duck blind than behind the wheel of a sports car. But he was a forward-thinker, so Nash was the most progressive of the independents. For example, he made an early bid to merge his company with Hudson, Studebaker, and Packard, correctly reasoning that these four would have to come together following World War II if they hoped to survive against the mighty Big Three. The plan might have been completed had Mason not died in late 1954, as Nash had already cast its lot with Hudson, and Studebaker had been absorbed by Packard (to the latter's ultimate misfortune).

Mason was a visionary in other ways. We hear a lot about "niche marketing" these days, the practice of designing products targeted at small, very specific groups of buyers. Mason would have understood the term, for he was looking at niches as early as the late Forties and was out to beat the Big Three in filling them. For example, he spearheaded the pioneering Rambler, America's first successful compact, then turned to *sub*compacts with the cute British-built Metropolitan, today something of a "cult" collector car.

Mason was also behind one very impressive sports

car, the Nash-Healey, which emerged in 1951 as a sort of embryonic "joint venture" with England's Donald Healey, a one-time racing driver. By the late Forties, Healey had turned to designing his own cars, which he built in small numbers at Warwickshire. In 1949, Healey was thinking about a new roadster powered by Cadillac's just-announced overhead-valve V-8, which led him to book passage to the States on the *Queen Elizabeth*. As fate would have it, he ran into Mason, who was returning from Europe with visions of sports cars dancing in his head. After a few drinks at mid-ocean, Mason convinced Healey that the engine he *really* needed was the Nash Ambassador ohv six. This was duly installed in a 102-inch-wheelbase chassis Healey had already designed, and topped by a smart, if slab-sided, British-built aluminum body. Suddenly, George Mason had his sports car.

Nash's 234.8-cid straight six was hardly modern, and no paragon of power even in heated-up, 125-bhp Healey tune. Nevertheless, the N-H was a strong track competitor. A prototype finished fourth at Le Mans in 1950; the following year, a stock '51 model ran sixth overall and fourth in class. In 1952, the year Cunningham placed fourth, a Nash-Healey came in third overall behind two much more powerful Mercedes-Benz racers. By that time, it seemed as though America was becoming a sports-car power to be reckoned with. But the reckoning was short-lived as far as the Nash-Healey was concerned. Prices were always high—$4000-$6000—so sales never were robust; even a steel body with nicer Pinin Farina styling (for 1952) and the addition of a long-wheelbase

closed coupe (for '53) didn't help. When Nash joined Hudson to form American Motors in 1954, the N-H was forgotten in the corporate rationalization, and AMC went on to greater things with its Ramblers.

Meantime, the 100-inch-wheelbase chassis of Kaiser-Frazer's compact Henry J became the basis for two very different machines that furthered the evolution of the postwar American sports car: the Kaiser-Darrin and the Excalibur J. Each was unique, but their concept was basically the same one that Chevrolet would employ in creating the Corvette: production-line passenger-car parts combined with a beautiful two-seat body and the best engine available. In Kaiser-Frazer's case, as initially in Chevrolet's, that engine wasn't very impressive.

Designated DKF-161, for its 161-cid F-head Willys six, the Kaiser-Darrin was a sleek two-seater with three novel features: a fiberglass body, a three-way folding top that could be left half-up for a landau or town-car effect, and sliding doors that looked a lot better on paper than they ever worked in practice. The latter two ideas as well as the overall styling were pure Dutch Darrin, who'd created the outstanding 1951 Kaiser.

Darrin's sports car went into production after a hard sell to Henry J. Kaiser, but not for long: just 435 production examples were completed, all for model year 1954. High price was a problem here, too: upwards of $3700, well into Jaguar territory and too steep to attract more than a handful of buyers. But the main limitation was the fast-failing fortunes of Kaiser-Frazer, or Kaiser-Willys as it had become by then, which made such products peripheral, if not perilous. When

The Austin-Healey 100/4 (opposite top) debuted in 1953, and was built through 1956. This '52 Muntz Jet (bottom) once belonged to Earl "Madman" Muntz. Total output reached 394 units. Wealthy sportsman Briggs Cunningham built the fastest sports machines in America from 1951-55. The 1953-55 C-3 (above) was a grand touring $10,000 "production" car, of which 27 were built.

K-W fled the U.S. market after 1955, the Darrin died. Though mightily disappointed, Dutch bought about 100 factory leftovers, fitted some with Cadillac V-8s, and sold them at his Los Angeles showroom for $4350 apiece.

Some have questioned whether any Darrin was a true sports car, perhaps because it was quite well-equipped. All had lush upholstery and the obligatory full instrumentation, for example, and most were fitted with a three-speed manual gearbox with floorshift, another expected "sports car" feature. With the thrifty 90-bhp Willys engine, fuel economy could approach 30 mpg, yet the 2200-pound Darrin could do 0-60 mph in about 13 seconds and near 100 mph flat out. Caddy V-8 power made for a 140-mph car with similarly vivid off-the-line acceleration.

And the Darrin did race, so it obviously passed

technical inspection, thus qualifying under the "dual-purpose" definition. The most successful Darrin driver was none other than Mrs. Laura Cunningham, wife of the famous Briggs, who scored a few fair performances in SCCA West Coast regional events.

Brooks Stevens' trim little Excalibur J embodied more of the true sports car spirit than the Darrin. Though the Excalibur employed the same chassis and an overhead-valve version of the Willys six, it was far more spartan, in line with Stevens' hope of keeping retail price to around $2000 or so. Several prototypes were built for SCCA racing, and an Excalibur could lead a group of Jaguar XK-120s and—an occasional Ferrari—down the straights at Elkhart Lake. But once again, Kaiser-Frazer's epic financial problems precluded anything approaching volume production.

We should also not forget Crosley, which got into the sports-car business in 1949 with a spare little roadster called the Hot Shot. This was followed a year later by the Super Sports, the same car with opening doors instead of bodyside cut-outs. Weighing only about 1200 pounds, these were tiny two-seaters built on an 85-inch-wheelbase chassis with Crosley's primitive solid-axle suspension at each end. The firm's equally curious 44-cid four had but 26.5 bhp, but it was enough to make these bantamweights quite quick, and a number of accessory manufacturers offered enough hop-up equipment to turn them into vest-pocket racers. Even in stock form they cornered roller-skate flat, and one modified car showed its ruggedness by winning the Index of Performance at the 1950 Sebring 12 Hours of Endurance in Florida.

But the Hot Shot and Super Sports were doomed by sagging sales of their economy-car sisters, which had no place in the "bigger is better" atmosphere of early-Fifties America. Founder Powel Crosley, Jr., abandoned carmaking soon afterwards, in 1952.

Still, these Crosleys, the Kaiser-Darrin, and Excalibur J all proved that plug-ordinary passenger-car components could work in a sports car, and work well. As Brooks Stevens later recalled of his first Excaliburs: "Barney Roos, chief engineer of Willys, told us we'd put a piston through the hood if we turned that engine any further than 5500 rpm. [But we] consistently turned them at 6500 rpm and never blew so much as a freeze plug." And the Darrin proved the worth of another technological breakthrough that would be crucial for the Corvette: production bodywork made of that versatile new "wonder" material, fiberglass.

Fiberglass, or glass-reinforced plastic (GRP) as it was originally known, was developed during World War II. One of its first applications was in housings for certain military installations, which tended to be rendered invisible to enemy radar owing to GRP's radio-wave "transparency." (This explains why Corvettes and other fiberglass-bodied cars are so resistant to police radar.) When peace returned, it didn't take long for a number of individuals and firms to find new uses for the stuff.

Among the vanguard were Dutch Darrin and Henry Kaiser, who were already thinking of plastic-bodied cars. Kaiser had conceived a tiny $400 economy job made entirely of GRP as early as 1942, and Darrin built a full-size fiberglass-bodied convertible in 1946. That same year, the Owens-Corning Company, one of the country's first postwar fiberglass manufacturers, also applied GRP to an automobile, one of the Scarab experimentals designed by Bill Stout, an engineer sometimes associated with Kaiser-Frazer. So the material obviously worked.

Even better, GRP lent itself easily to low volumes, thus appealing to builders of one-off or limited-

production specials. Manufacturers knew that interest in sports cars was high; at least dealer interest in "line leaders" was. Inevitably, a raft of custom GRP bodies designed to bolt onto everyday chassis began appearing, the start of the "kit car" industry that represented an extension of the hot-rod tradition. The earliest of these were mainly sporty two-seater bodies supplied with all the necessary hardware for an adept do-it-yourselfer who had a suitable chassis to build a complete car at home.

The most successful and influential supplier of GRP kit-car bodies in this period was Glasspar, founded by a young California boat builder named Bill Tritt in 1950 to fabricate fiberglass hulls, a field it soon dominated. Tritt was approached one day by Air Force Major Kenneth B. Brooks with a request to design a body in fiberglass that would fit a standard Detroit chassis, thus creating a possible substitute for the rugged Jeep.

Tritt accepted, and his design appeared at the Los Angeles Motorama alongside three other proposals for plastic bodies compatible with production-car frames. These were Eric Irwin's "Lancer," for big luxury-car chassis; the "Skorpion," designed by Jack Wills and Ralph Roberts with the Crosley in mind; and the "Wasp," another economy-car idea. But Tritt's design, called "Brooks Boxer," was the only one sized for wheelbases of 100-110 inches, exactly the same as those of Detroit's most popular cars.

Glasspar was doing business at the time with U.S. Rubber Company, which supplied some of the raw materials used to make GRP. Tritt's Boxer was introduced to some of the firm's engineers and executives by one of its West Coast sales engineers, Bud Crawford. Ultimately, Glasspar and U.S. Rubber's Naugatuck, Connecticut, division agreed to joint production of GRP car bodies sized for 100-inch-wheelbase car chassis and priced at about $650 each. All would be two-seaters with provision for folding-fabric or vinyl tops.

U.S. Rubber's public-relations pro managed to interest *Life* magazine in this story, which ran it as a feature titled "Plastic Bodies for Autos" in its February 25, 1952, issue. Response was tremendous. Soon, Glasspar bodies were being hung on all manner of chassis,

everything from Crosleys to Henry Js to Fords. Auto-industry people sat up and took note.

So did one prosperous Willys dealer in Downey, California, B.R. "Woody" Woodill. The new-for-'51 Aero-Willys would be a great basis for a sports car, he thought, especially its solid, reliable F-head six. Woodhill contracted Tritt, who agreed to design a new body and supply a separate chassis (the Aero used unit construction).

The result was the "Wildfire," a slinky two-seat roadster appearing in 1952 with Willys drivetrain and suspension. As it was offered fully finished right off Woody's showroom floor, the Wildfire is technically the first "production" fiberglass-bodied sports car, beating both the Corvette and the Darrin by at least a year. Initial price was $2900, though it later rose to as high as $4500. But the Wildfire was also sold as a kit for between $1000 and $1200. Some 300 were built through 1956, though Woodhill said that only 15 were "factory assembled" at his small shop. Undoubtedly the number would have been higher had Willys-Overland not gone down with Kaiser-Frazer.

Woodhill used a variety of sources for such minor components as instruments, bumpers, steering wheels, mirrors, and seats, so few Wildfires were built exactly alike. He also engaged freelance engineer and hot rodder "Shorty" Post to design a frame that would accept Ford/Mercury flathead V-8s, for which dozens of easy bolt-on modifications were available. In this form the Wildfire was very fast, though even the Willys-powered versions were quick.

By the early Fifties, then, a number of diverse but essential influences were in place to spark creation of the Corvette: the reborn interest in genuine sports cars, at least among a handful of enthusiasts; dealer demands for showroom traffic-builders, which reached a crescendo after the initial postwar seller's market was satiated in 1950; the practical development of GRP bodywork for low-production automobiles.

One day in 1952, representatives of U. S. Rubber received an invitation to visit Chevrolet Division, which had expressed interest in how glass-reinforced plastic could be applied to mass-production cars. The Corvette was at hand.

CHAPTER 2

GETTING STARTED: TWO MEN AND A BABY

Credible though they were, the postwar sports cars of independent automakers like Nash and Kaiser made little impression on Ford and Chrysler. The reasons weren't hard to divine. As we've seen, the market for such cars in the early Fifties was far too limited to be worth pursuing, and each company faced problems where it deemed its monies were better spent.

Ford, for example, was busy recovering from the severe damage done in the elder Henry's last years of command. The firm had sunk virtually all its resources into the all-new postwar Ford, Lincoln, and Mercury of 1949, on which its future so desperately depended. Fortunately, the cars sold as well as Dearborn needed them to. By 1952, bolstered by another corporate-wide product overhaul undertaken well in advance of its Big Three competitors, Ford had regained its position as the industry's number-two producer.

Chrysler, of course, had its hands full staving off Ford—and an accelerating sales slide—falling to number-three mainly because of deadly dull styling that kept buyers away in droves. Help arrived in 1950 in the person of Virgil Exner, who began churning out interesting "dream cars" in collaboration with the Ghia coachworks in Italy—an attempt to convince the public that jazzier showroom models were on the way. Many of these exercises were sporty two-seaters and 2+2s: the Chrysler K-310, C-200, and D'Elegance (the last used by Volkswagen of Germany as the pattern for its little Karmann-Ghia coupe); various Chrysler "Specials"; the DeSoto Adventurer I; the Plymouth Belmont roadster; and the Dodge Firearrow series (which evolved into the 1956-57 Dual-Ghia). But

Chrysler was in no position to put any of these into production. Not that it would have helped much. What Chrysler needed was more glamorous mainstream cars, which it finally accomplished for 1955, when it was almost too late.

Things were far different at General Motors Corporation. Thanks to fat government contracts, the mighty colossus had emerged from the war mightier than ever, and though temporarily eclipsed by Studebaker and its all-new 1947 models, GM reclaimed its position as industry styling leader with the tail-finned Cadillacs and Oldsmobile 98s of 1948. For 1949, GM outpaced its competition twice more, introducing modern, high-compression ohv V-8s at Olds and Cadillac, and the jaunty hardtop-convertible body style at those two divisions and for Buick as well. With the overwhelming acceptance of these and other innovations, GM sales seemed headed only one way as the Fifties opened: straight up. So if anyone in Detroit was going to make a serious attempt at a homegrown sports car, GM was the most likely candidate.

A key figure in GM's high success during these years was Harley J. Earl, founder and head of the firm's Art and Colour Section, the American auto industry's first in-house styling department. Earl not only loved cars but was very imaginative. He also had the good sense to surround himself with equally talented assistants, for whom he provided the most stimulating and creative work environment possible.

It was Earl who had almost single-handedly "invented" the dream car with his prophetic Buick Y-Job, a long, low, two-seat convertible first displayed

The Motorama show car (opposite) was very close to the production Corvette. Stylist Harley J. Earl poses with his '38 Buick Y-Job "dream car" (below).

in 1938. It not only set the tone for company styling themes in the years immediately preceding and following World War II, it proved the value of giving the public a "sneak preview" of things to come. This, in turn, led to the Motoramas, those exciting extravaganzas of chrome and choreography that thrilled visitors in cities and towns all over the country between 1949 and 1961.

Earl was eager to return to experimental projects after the war. And once the corporation's new 1949-50 models had been wrapped up, he did. Significantly, his first postwar dream cars were two-seaters: the aircraft-inspired LeSabre of 1951 and the Buick XP-300, shown a year later. Both boasted ideas that were advanced for their day: wraparound windshield, a folding top hidden beneath a metal cover just aft of the cockpit, sculptured rear deck with prominent tail fins, and a low, ground-hugging stance.

But Earl had something else on his mind. Writer Karl Ludvigsen tells it this way: "As an antidote to post-LeSabre creative depression, Earl began thinking seriously about a low-priced sporty car during the late fall of 1951. He'd do this in his office on the 11th floor of the anonymous-looking brick structure on the south side of Milwaukee Avenue, opposite the imposing GM Building. Then he'd wander...down to the ninth floor. There, in a small enclosure adjacent to the main Body Development Studio, Earl could work privately with a personal crew on projects—like this one—that he wanted to shield from premature exposure. Earl was well aware of the perishable quality of a new idea." His new idea was the genesis of the Corvette.

Initial sketches and scale models for Earl's pet project were, as Ludvigsen describes, "most like an amalgam of the classic British sports cars and the [Willys] Jeepster, for Earl had in mind a very simple car, one that could be priced at only $1850—about as much as a Ford, Chevy, or Studebaker sedan in 1952. Such a moderate price meant that the design had to be based on a more or less stock chassis, and that's the way the first tentative studies went."

Then came new inspiration from a car that was displayed for a time in the GM Styling auditorium. Called "Alembic I," it was essentially the original Bill Tritt design for U.S. Rubber Company, which had purchased it and loaned it to GM. Earl now stepped up the pace, and work proceeded as "Project Opel." That name was likely chosen to confuse outsiders, as Chevy frequently did advanced studies for GM's German subsidiary at the time. It was all very hush-hush in any case, with access limited strictly to those with a "need to know." Employees who were not directly involved would probably have never even heard of the "Opel" project.

It was at about this time that Edward N. Cole was transferred from Cadillac Division to Chevrolet, where he took over as chief engineer. Cole would be another key figure in Corvette history, but his list of credits was already impressive. He'd begun working at Cadillac in 1933 after taking part in a work-study program at the GM Institute. His first assignments involved designing military vehicles, such as light tanks, for the Army. After the war, he worked on rear-engine prototypes for both Cadillac and Chevrolet, then concentrated on engines, helping Cadillac's John Gordon develop that division's milestone short-stroke ohv V-8 for 1949. Cole then managed Cadillac's Cleveland plant for 30 months before moving to his new job at Chevy. Once installed, he tripled the engineering staff—from 850 to 2900—then turned to designing a new engine, the landmark 265-cubic-inch small-block V-8 that would appear for 1955.

Meantime, Earl tapped Robert F. McLean, a young sports-car enthusiast with degrees from Cal Tech in both engineering and industrial design, to come up with a basic layout for Project Opel. McLean started from the back of the car, not the front, as was usual practice, though he was assured he couldn't do it this way.

With the rear axle as a reference point, he placed the engine and passengers as close to the rear axle as possible, the goal being the balanced 50/50 weight distribution desirable for optimum sports-car handling. The final figure was a still-creditable 53/47 percent. Wheelbase was set at 102 inches, the same as that of the Jaguar XK-120, one of Earl's favorites. At 57 inches front, 59 inches rear, track was wider than the Jaguar's, but not as wide proportionally as that of the funny-looking little rear-engine Porsches, which were as much an anathema to GM Design then as they are today.

Art and Colour soon coordinated its efforts with those of GM engineers, while leaning rather heavily on LeSabre and XP-300 styling. A panoramic windshield, toothy oval grille, "definition" at the rear fenders, and shadow-box rear license-plate frame certainly indicate the influence of those showmobiles on the designers' work, so the end product was perhaps inevitable. It was certainly controversial, though *Road & Track* magazine, surprisingly enough, found the Corvette "clean and functional...[reflecting] the fact that this is a genuine sports car, a refreshing contrast to the pseudo sports cars being shown by other divisions of GM."

It's important to remember that Earl's sports car was only a proposal in mid-1952—a dream for the Motorama perhaps, but still a long way from production. Yet as Ludvigsen notes, Earl "envisioned new popularity for sports-car racing throughout America with [his] car readily available, saying expansively that people would soon forget about those English cars as soon as these sporty Chevys were on the market."

That chant has since been heard many times, not only from GM but Ford and Chrysler too. Here, Earl figured he could undersell the foreigners by offering far more sports car for the money, with the added benefit of local dealer sales and service.

Having examples like the "Alembic I" at hand, he looked to fiberglass as the best means for holding the line on body tooling costs. As for the chassis, McLean's layout would somehow have to be realized with existing Chevy hardware, some of which would have to be modified to suit. There was simply no other choice.

There were still two, big, unanswered questions about about fiberglass: Would it provide the requisite structural strength, and would it work in series production? The second couldn't be resolved without a production go-ahead, of course, but the first was answered dramatically in "accidental" fashion. Chevy had built a full-size convertible with a GRP body strictly for investigative research and development purposes in early 1952. During high-speed testing at the proving grounds, the driver unexpectedly rolled the car but escaped uninjured. The car's body suffered no major damage, with doors, hood, and decklid all intact. Earl was now more convinced than ever that fiberglass was the way to go.

With Earl aiming for completion in time for the first 1953 Motorama, to be held at New York's Waldorf-Astoria Hotel in January of that year, McLean and the Chevrolet engineers redoubled their efforts to find production chassis and drivetrain components compatible with the developing plastic body. Time was short, so off-the-shelf hardware was crucial. Of course, Chevrolet had quite a bit of hardware available. Ultimately, though, the chassis had to be designed from scratch, owing to McLean's designated engine positioning behind the front axleline instead of directly over it, and the fact that "the open body would contribute nothing to rigidity," as *R&T*'s John R. Bond pointed out in June 1954.

Bond's report quoted extensively from a technical paper delivered to the Society of Automotive Engineers in October 1953 by veteran Chevy engineer Maurice

Opposite page: The Buick Y-Job set the tone for General Motors styling themes during the years immediately before and after World War II, particularly for Buick. The dashboard, however, looks rather old fashioned (bottom). This page: The '51 LeSabre show car was a long, low, and sporty two-seater with a "Panoramic" windshield and a metal cover to hide the folded top.

Olley, who outlined the design criteria that dictated the Corvette's engineering. These included the assumptions that a sports car must have a cruising speed of 70+ mph, a weight/power ratio of better than 25 to 1, and "ample brakes and good handling qualities." The last were said to mean "quick steering with light handling, a low center of gravity, minimum overhang with a low moment of inertia relative to wheelbase, smooth yet firm suspension, and a quick steering response, but no oversteer." By most accounts, Chevy met these goals, and then some.

The foundation was the aforementioned new chassis, a special X-member design with sturdy box-section siderails. Weighing just 213 pounds, it boasted, as Bond noted, an X-member "low enough to allow the driveline to run above it, giving a very strong, solid junction at the 'X.'...The front crossmember appears to be stock and retains the excellent bolt-on sub-assembly feature used by Chevrolet since 1934."

The Corvette's rear-end arrangement was also unique. For the first time in Chevrolet history, an open or Hotchkiss drive was used instead of the traditional torque-tube drive. The reason, as Bond noted, was the Corvette's shorter wheelbase, which "would have required a torque tube so short as to produce excessive change of wheel speed on rough roads." Conventional leaf springs were located on the rear axle, but again breaking with Chevy tradition, they were positioned outboard of the main frame rails for added stability, a feature picked up for the division's all-new 1955 passenger cars and dictated by the low-slung frame.

As for the engine, there was only one available: the tried-and-true 235.5-cid ohv six, which produced 105 horsepower in standard tune. This power was deemed inadequate for the new sports car, so extensive modifications were carried out to find more. Efforts began with a high-lift, long-duration camshaft, similar to that of Chevy's 261-cid truck engine; solid valve lifters instead of the hydraulic type; and dual valve springs, to cope with the higher engine speed.

Chevy specified aluminum pistons on its 1953 engines hooked to the optional Powerglide automatic transmission, but the Corvette unit would have the usual cast-iron jugs to avoid the sort of reliability problems that could occur in a car that was bound to

be driven much harder than the typical family sedan. The head casting was modified to produce an 8.0:1 compression ratio, versus the 7.5:1 squeeze of top-line Chevy passenger cars. Water pump flow capacity was increased, and the pump itself was lowered at the front of the block so that the large, four-blade fan could clear the anticipated low hoodline.

The induction system underwent the most serious alteration: triple Carter "YH" sidedraft carburetors mounted on a special aluminum intake manifold at the engine's left side (as installed). The carbs worked together instead of via a progressive linkage, each feeding a pair of cylinders through a separate choke. Automatic chokes were initially used, but tests showed that all three couldn't be synchronized because they didn't warm at the same rate. Thus, only the Motorama Corvette carried automatic chokes; production models used a manual setup.

Contrary to popular belief, these carburetors weren't created by Carter especially for the Corvette but were ordinary production items. A dual setup had already been used in the Nash-Healey and worked fine with automatic chokes, though that was because it only needed two.

Another unique but simpler change on the Corvette engine was a redesigned rocker-arm cover, necessary because the standard passenger-car item wouldn't clear the low hoodline. Though it looked similar, the Corvette cover was lower at the front, and the "hat sections" for its two through-bolts were turned inside out. The oil filler was repositioned to the rear, thus eliminating the final obstruction.

Equally effective was the special dual exhaust system that reduced back pressure for more power and better sound. Olley's technical paper provides an amusing quote in this regard: "A requirement in the minds of many sports-car enthusiasts is that the exhaust should have the right note. They don't agree what this is. Some prefer 'foo-blap' while others go for 'foo-gobble.' It is impossible to please them all. We hope we have achieved a desirable compromise."

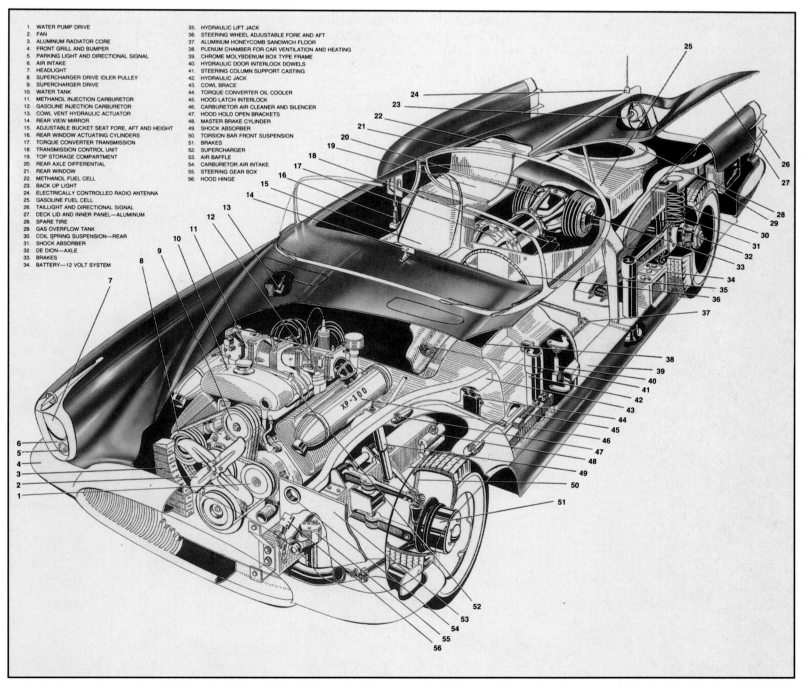

1. WATER PUMP DRIVE
2. FAN
3. ALUMINUM RADIATOR CORE
4. FRONT GRILL AND BUMPER
5. PARKING LIGHT AND DIRECTIONAL SIGNAL
6. AIR INTAKE
7. HEADLIGHT
8. SUPERCHARGER DRIVE IDLER PULLEY
9. SUPERCHARGER DRIVE
10. WATER TANK
11. METHANOL INJECTION CARBURETOR
12. GASOLINE INJECTION CARBURETOR
13. COWL VENT HYDRAULIC ACTUATOR
14. REAR VIEW MIRROR
15. ADJUSTABLE BUCKET SEAT FORE, AFT AND HEIGHT
16. REAR WINDOW ACTUATING CYLINDERS
17. TORQUE CONVERTER TRANSMISSION
18. TRANSMISSION CONTROL UNIT
19. TOP STORAGE COMPARTMENT
20. REAR AXLE DIFFERENTIAL
21. REAR WINDOW
22. METHANOL FUEL CELL
23. BACK UP LIGHT
24. ELECTRICALLY CONTROLLED RADIO ANTENNA
25. GASOLINE FUEL CELL
26. TAILLIGHT AND DIRECTIONAL SIGNAL
27. DECK LID AND INNER PANEL—ALUMINUM
28. SPARE TIRE
29. GAS OVERFLOW TANK
30. COIL SPRING SUSPENSION—REAR
31. SHOCK ABSORBER
32. DE DION—AXLE
33. BRAKES
34. BATTERY—12 VOLT SYSTEM
35. HYDRAULIC LIFT JACK
36. STEERING WHEEL ADJUSTABLE FORE AND AFT
37. ALUMINUM HONEYCOMB SANDWICH FLOOR
38. PLENUM CHAMBER FOR CAR VENTILATION AND HEATING
39. CHROME MOLYBDENUM BOX TYPE FRAME
40. HYDRAULIC DOOR INTERLOCK DOWELS
41. STEERING COLUMN SUPPORT CASTING
42. HYDRAULIC JACK
43. COWL BRACE
44. TORQUE CONVERTER OIL COOLER
45. HOOD LATCH INTERLOCK
46. CARBURETOR AIR CLEANER AND SILENCER
47. HOOD HOLD OPEN BRACKETS
48. MASTER BRAKE CYLINDER
49. SHOCK ABSORBER
50. TORSION BAR FRONT SUSPENSION
51. BRAKES
52. SUPERCHARGER
53. AIR BAFFLE
54. CARBURETOR AIR INTAKE
55. STEERING GEAR BOX
56. HOOD HINGE

The engine was certainly a compromise, but a desirable one; the various changes yielded a freer-breathing "Blue Flame Six" with 150 bhp at 4500 rpm and maximum revs considerably higher than that. By contrast, 1953 passenger Chevys offered 105 bhp with manual shift or 115 with Powerglide.

Chevy's two-speed automatic was selected for the original Motorama show car and would prove one of the most controversial features of the eventual production Corvette. Engineering didn't believe it had a manual gearbox that was strong enough for the fortified engine, and it had no time to tool one, so it was Powerglide or nothing. And despite what the purists would say, the choice wasn't entirely bad, for Powerglide was simple, rugged, and reliable. It just wasn't very exciting.

The transmission was installed essentially unchanged from its passenger-car specifications except for shift-point rpms, which were raised to match the new engine's 11-percent increase in torque. Tests showed that the stock oil cooler wasn't necessary in this lighter car with sprightlier acceleration, so all oil lines normally running forward to the cooler were plugged. Shift control was floor-mounted for both practical and aesthetic reasons.

A rumor persists that the Corvette's front suspension was identical to that of contemporary Chevy passenger cars. This is true as far as geometry goes, for the Corvette used the same coil-sprung upper-and-lower A-arm arrangement the division had been using since 1949. However, shock rates were recalibrated, and a larger-diameter anti-roll bar was fitted with an eye to the Corvette's reduced weight and enhanced performance. Bond observed that spring rates appeared to be stock, but that less sprung weight gave "the effect of

'stiffer' springs with a faster bounce frequency." He also pointed out a center of gravity "only 18 inches above the ground. This in conjunction with a heavier stabilizer bar and stiffer, non-symmetrical rear springs contributes to greatly reduced roll angle when cornering."

Steering was basically off-the-shelf Saginaw recirculating-ball, but with ratio quickened to 16:1. According

Edward N. Cole (above right) was Chevy's chief engineer when the Corvette was developed. Although the famed 265-cid V-8 was under development, early 'Vettes had to make do with a fortified 150-bhp version of Chevy's Blue Flame Six (opposite top). A cutaway (below) shows the layout of mechanical components.

to Bond, the steering idler arm was redesigned "because of the lower engine mounting and is carried on a double-reverse ball bearing." Also, the Corvette steering wheel was an inch smaller in diameter than that of passenger Chevys.

On the subject of steering gear, Olley's technical paper contains this interesting aside: "We are aware of a preference in some quarters for a rack-and-pinion steering on cars of this type. However, this involves a steering ratio on the order of 9 or 10 to 1. We regard this as too fast even for a sports car...." How times change.

As the Motorama show car neared completion, Ed Cole, by virtue of his new position, was one of the first within Chevrolet Division to see it. Ludvigsen records that he "literally jumped up and down" and promised

to support Earl in his efforts to win production approval—all the way to the GM Building's 14th Floor executive suite.

To the top they duly went, to pitch company president Harlow Curtice. A few weeks after Cole saw the full-size plaster model, Earl had it set up in the Styling auditorium to show Curtice and Chevrolet Division general manager Thomas H. Keating. The curtain flew up with a flourish, after which Earl took Curtice and Keating on a walkaround tour, explaining enthusiastically that here was not only a profitable new product but one that would add much-needed sparkle to a Chevrolet image that was staid at best.

His persuasiveness worked, and the car was okayed as part of the first 1953 Motorama. At the same time, it was decided that engineering work with a view to eventual production would proceed as Project EX-122, with the final go/no-go decision based largely on show-goers' reactions.

Finished in gleaming Polo White with a bright Sportsman Red interior, the Motorama Corvette was a hands-down sensation, and the inevitable inquiries soon started pouring in from all over the country: When will it be at my dealer's, and how much will it

cost? From drawings and production dates, it's clear that Earl and Cole never had any doubts that a production version would be offered. Sure enough, Chevy decided to start building Corvettes as soon as possible—and as 1953 models.

Except for its cowl-mounted fresh air scoops (which reappeared in non-functional form for 1956-57), the Motorama Corvette was one of the few show cars to reach production with its styling virtually intact. The fact that Earl's pure original was retained, unsullied by committee modifications, enhances the appeal of early Corvettes among collectors and enthusiasts. And that styling has aged well, turning as many heads now as it did more than 35 years ago.

But the Corvette had significance far beyond show-car styling, and it was recognized even as the first production models appeared. *R&T*, for example, concluded its 1954 report by opining that in its specialized engineering, innovative fiberglass body, and obvious devotion to sports-car ideals, the Corvette "heralds a new approach, offers new hope, for the individualist."

Chevy's great sports-car experiment was about to begin.

CHAPTER 3

1953-55: TRUTHS AND CONSEQUENCES

The enthusiastic reception accorded the Motorama Corvette has perhaps been overrated as a factor in the birth of Chevrolet's future sports-car legend. The decision to proceed with a production model was actually taken well before January 1953, when GM president Harlow Curtice and Chevy Division chief Tom Keating gave their blessing to Harley Earl's mock-up. No doubt they'd have had second thoughts had show-goers turned up their noses, but that would have been surprising in those sports-car-conscious days. Chevy thus duly scrambled to tool up, announcing that the Corvette would soon be available at local dealers for a suggested retail price of $3513.

Myron Scott of Chevy's public relations staff explained the origins of the name. A "corvette" was a type of small, agile 19th century warship, though the term more recently applied to small wartime convoy vessels and subchasers. Interestingly, one early press release introduced the car with the British spelling "Courvette."

GM engineer Maurice Olley was quick to answer those who wondered whether anything worthy of the name "sports car" could have an automatic transmission: "...The typical sports car enthusiast, like the 'average man' or the square root of minus one, is an imaginary quantity. Also, as the sports car appeals to a wider and wider section of the public, the center of gravity of this theoretical individual is shifting from the austerity of the pioneer towards the luxury of modern ideas....There is no need to apologize for the performance of this car with its automatic transmission."

Olley's use of the word *luxury* is significant. As *Automobile Quarterly* observed in a 1969 retrospective: "During 1952 the Corvette evolved entirely away from the simple roadster originally visualized by Earl [and] by January 1953...had become a 'luxury' machine." This evolution, along with the rigid time and cost targets imposed on the development program,

go a long way toward explaining why the Corvette emerged as a curious combination of the crude and the civilized.

Take, for example, that Powerglide transmission. Though not at all accepted by sports-car purists, its popularity with consumers pleased Chevy's marketing people as much as it saved time and money for the engineers. Earl's body design, though clean and

appealing, was still gimmicky for some tastes. Coming under particular scrutiny in some quarters were the rocket-like rear fenders with their tiny fins, the dazzling vertical grille teeth, and the sunken headlights covered by mesh stone guards. The top, which folded neatly beneath a flush-fitting cover, could be managed with fair ease by one person. But the clip-in side curtains, perhaps favored over roll-down windows as a cost-cutting measure, were every bit as anachronistic as they were on British roadsters of the period. The shadow-box license-plate housing was covered by plastic that tended to turn cloudy. The Motorama car's exterior door pushbuttons were eliminated in the transition to production, which meant that the only way to open a door from the outside was to reach inside for the release. In short, as a fully "finished" car, the first Corvette wasn't.

Though most 'Vette fans tend to assume otherwise, the decision to go with fiberglass body construction was made quite late in the game. GRP was expeditious for having the Motorama showmobile ready in time, but steel was seriously considered throughout most of the Corvette's harried gestation. Said engineer Ellis J. Premo at a meeting of the Society of Automotive Engineers: "At the time of the Waldorf show, we were actually concentrating on a steel body utilizing Kirksite tooling for the projected production of 10,000 units for the 1954 model year."

But though Kirksite dies were faster and cheaper to

Opposite page: The 1953 Corvette. This page: The 30-millionth Chevy was built on December 28, 1953. Chevy brass marking the occasion (top) were T.H. Keating, general manager, at the wheel, and (from left) E.H. Kelley, general manufacturing manager; W.E. Fish, general sales manager; E.N. Cole, chief engineer; and J.W. Scott, executive assistant. Meanwhile, future designs were being discussed (left) by GM president Harlow H. Curtice (seated) and Harley J. Earl, GM vice president, Styling Staff.

make than conventional ones, their more limited life would have made them unsuitable had that volume been achieved. They were thus never cast. Besides, as *Road & Track*'s John Bond reported in early 1954: "As experience was gained with the new [fiberglass], so also did confidence increase...."

Fiberglass also made it possible to mold very complex shapes that would have been prohibitively expensive to stamp in steel, an advantage often noted at the time but frequently forgotten now. The result, as shown in a widely circulated GM press photo, was a body composed of only nine major sub-assemblies: floorpan, trunklid, top cover, the two doors, hood, front fenders/nose, front gravel pan, and rear fenders/gravel pan.

"Chevrolet sums up the experiment this way," *R&T* reported: "'What we get for all this is a very usable body, somewhat expensive, costing a little less than a dollar a pound, but of light weight, able to stand up to abuse, which will not rust, will not crumble in collision, will take a paint finish, and is relatively free from drumming noise.'" Chevy, however, was indulging in a bit of hyperbole. Corvette paint finish wasn't that good at first, and creaks and groans as well as drumming plagued most every Corvette built through 1962.

The GRP used for the Motorama show-car body was ²⁄₁₀-inch thick, hand-laid into a mold taken directly from Earl's pre-production plaster styling model. Fiberglass molding techniques were still far from perfected, and more experimentation was needed before actual production could begin. Ultimately, improvements in process chemistry allowed the production body to be only ¹⁄₁₀-inch thick, with no loss in surface quality or structural strength. However, Chevy had to build several interim bodies as trials before it was convinced that fiberglass was really feasible.

After months of frantic activity, Corvette production got underway in a small building adjacent to Chevy's main plant in Flint, Michigan, on the last day of June

This page: The early Corvette boasted bucket seats, floor-mounted shift lever, and a 5000-rpm tach. Opposite page: Chevy PR was quick to point out that "This first American-built sleek sports car was the result of GM experiments in building bodies of laminated fiberglass reinforced with steel." The lightweight body required fewer pieces than steel construction.

1953. According to a much-later press release, it was a day the "division made automotive history. Amid shouted instructions and with flashbulbs popping to record the event, Tony Kleiber, a body assembler, drove a car off a Chevrolet assembly line."

And that *was* a grand accomplishment. Corvette had traveled from Motorama dream to roadgoing reality with remarkably few alterations [see box] and in an amazingly short time. General manager Keating was on hand to emphasize the point: "This occasion is historic in the industry. The Corvette has been brought into production on schedule in less than 12 months...."

Still, the sporting Chevrolet wasn't quite "real" even at this point—not really *ready*. "The engineers want to keep on testing these first cars for a few thousand more miles," Keating continued. "It may be important to Chevrolet's future plans to learn the amazing flexibility that is demonstrated here in working out new design ideas in plastics." Had he wanted to be more specific, he could have mentioned that all the 1953 models were to be essentially handmade cars; indeed, photographs indicate much improvisation.

Road & Track was more succinct, noting in its August 1953 issue that the year's entire contemplated production is "sold." That was a nice way of saying that Chevy didn't really intend to sell Corvettes to the general public, at least not just yet. Indeed, the division's Central Office issued a dealer notice on July 10 listing the Corvette's wholesale net price as $2470, a delivery and handling charge of $248, and a suggested retail figure of $3250. But, said the bulletin, "no dealer is in a position to accept firm orders for delivery of a Corvette in 1953."

In essence, Chevrolet was employing what we'd now call a "controlled production start-up," which made sense. Given the newness of fiberglass manufacturing techniques and Chevy's lack of experience with them, the quality of the finished product was very much in doubt. And as ever, GM was loath to risk making a blunder in public should things not go according to plan—especially with a brand-new "image" car that had already attracted so much attention.

Accordingly, the Corvette's initial production schedule was set at just 50 cars a month—a maximum of 300 units for the balance of calendar '53. All would be built the same way so workers could concentrate on putting the bodies together properly without being rushed and without the distraction of trim and equipment variations. In the mid-Eighties, Pontiac would employ the same go-slow approach with its mid-engine Fiero—like the first Corvette, an innovative design concept with few manufacturing precedents.

As a result, all '53 Corvettes were painted Polo White and had Sportsman Red interiors, black tops,

6.70 × 15 four-ply whitewall tires, Delco signal-seeking radios, and recirculating hot-water heaters. (The last was a considerable improvement on the ineffective devices of period British sports cars.) Also standard was a complete set of needle instruments, including a 5000-rpm tachometer and a counter for total engine revolutions (a feature that would continue through 1959).

Quality wasn't Chevy's only concern, though. It's quite likely that as production began, some managers had second thoughts about the newfangled sports car and decided it needed an extra dose of that magic elixir—publicity. Again quoting that press release on the car's history: "An estimated four million persons had seen the [Motorama] Corvette....In the fall of '53, Chevrolet sought to double this number by using the first production cars produced in Flint as dealer display attractions. Each of the eight Chevrolet wholesale regions was assigned a car to send from dealer to dealer for one- to three-day showings during the last three months of the year. In an effort to enhance the new Corvette's image as a prestige car, dealers restricted sales to VIPs in each community— mayors, celebrities, industrial leaders, and favorite customers. This system continued into 1954 as Corvettes, now being built in St. Louis, began to come off the line at a faster rate."

Dealers had heard all about it in July: "Only 300 of these cars can be built during the entire balance of 1953," said a division missive. "Some of these, necessarily, will be used for further engineering and

The Corvettes negotiating Chicago's infamous Lake Shore Drive S-curve (right) were part of a dealer driveaway and publicity stunt. The cars wear 1954 Illinois dealer plates. A '54 Corvette (opposite) enters the body-drop in Chevy's St. Louis plant, which took over production from Flint in late '53.

experimental purposes, and many will be retained for display, publicity and show purposes in connection with our regular regional trailer shows and exhibits around the country. In view of the fact that we have received urgent requests, both from dealers and directly from the public, totaling many times the few Corvettes available in 1953, we have not been in a position to accept from anyone or make any commitments as to delivery at retail to date."

It was just as well, because quality problems surfaced early. Predictably enough, they involved the fiberglass body. Chevy proudly described the Flint assembly line as a "miniature...its bins filled with all the nuts and washers and trim pieces necessary for continuing

production...only six chassis long but with every place...filled with additional chassis and component parts of the subsequent bodies to keep assembly rolling. However, the line is big enough for the initial rate of production which Chevrolet has established for pioneering in a new field of plastic bodies."

Actually, the pace *had* to be slow. Each body began as 46 separate pieces, supplied by the Molded Fiber Glass Company of Ashtabula, Ohio. Workers had to fit all these into wooden jigs, then glue them up into the larger subassemblies, all of which took time and left vast room for error. Worse, some pieces didn't fit together very well as delivered, the result of molding flaws that required still more hand labor to correct.

Visual Differences—Motorama vs. 1953 Production Corvette

Motorama Car	Production Car
Chrome-plated engine parts	Many plated parts now painted
Shrouded fan	No shroud
"Corvette" name script front and rear	No name script front and rear
Hydraulic door and hood opening	Manual door and hood opening
Exterior door pushbuttons	No exterior door controls
Small front-fender chrome molding	Full-length chrome fender molding
Chrome inside door knob	White-plastic inside door knob
Two dash knobs, right side	No knobs
No windshield end seals	Windshield end seals
No drip moldings and seals	Drip moldings and seals
Upper front fender scoops	No front fender scoops
Narrow headlamp bezels	Wide headlamp bezels
Oversize wheel spinners	Smaller spinners
Upper dash edge painted	Upper dash edge vinyl-covered
Automatic choke	Manual choke

Not surprisingly, then, the fit-and-finish of early Corvette bodies was variable to say the least, with judgments on the fiberglass ranging from fair to excellent compared to steel construction.

Of course, such teething problems are hardly uncommon in the first year of a new car design, especially if it's the first to employ some new material or engineering idea. The first Corvette was no exception. And in view of the way things went, Chevy must have been glad that it had decided to use proven running gear. Most of the body bugs would eventually be worked out, of course, but those first months in Flint were surely a trial-and-error experience quite exasperating—and foreign—to a big outfit like Chevrolet.

This may explain why division publicists worked hard to maintain the public's high initial interest in the Corvette, which hardly seemed necessary until you recall what the standard '53 Chevys looked like. The 'Vette was glamorous and exciting, and the publicists played it up for all it was worth.

Coming right after the big pre-launch buildup, this extra hoopla had an unintended effect. With the cars not genuinely available, yet with ads and stories appearing everywhere, some began to wonder whether Chevy was pulling a fast one. After all, automotive flimflams and pipe dreams were nothing new (the Tucker was still fresh in many minds). Was this "dream car" still just a dream after all? No, but it would take a good many months before people realized it.

In retrospect, Chevy's marketing plan backfired. It was all very well to favor VIPs and the "beautiful people" as opinion leaders. Trouble was, they didn't like the car as much as Chevy had hoped. And the growing suspicion that the 'Vette was only a flash in the pan undoubtedly deterred some buyers even in 1954, when the cars *were* available. Others went looking at MGs, Jaguars, and Triumphs.

The slow sales start seems to bear out this discontent. Coinciding with the production shift to St. Louis, Chevrolet announced that 1954 volume would be upped to 1000 units a month. But the actual number built for the model year was only 3640—less than a third the projected total—and at year's end

1953 Corvettes: Nonconformity and Forgeries

There are a number of variations among the 300 Corvettes built for 1953. The National Corvette Restorers Society notes that early cars lacked, for example, the Guide Y-50 outside rearview mirrors that became standard on later '53s and would remain so through 1962. The first 25 or so were equipped with '53 Bel Air full wheel covers; after that the Motorama-like (but not identical) dummy knock-off covers were adopted. On the other hand, all '53s had signal-seeking Delco radios and recirculating hot-water heaters, as well as a 5000-rpm tachometer with total engine revolutions counter. The latter would be retained through 1959.

Because the 1953 Corvette is not only rare but the first of its kind, it leads the 1954 model in value by a considerable margin. This has prompted a number of forgeries—1954 models "converted" to '53 specifications. However, the perpetrators of these conversions usually overlook a number of minor points:

1. The frame always bears a number corresponding to that on the body number plate. The number appears twice on '53s and can be seen with a flashlight and a small mirror without removing the body.

2. The fuel line exits from the bottom of the fuel tank outboard of the right main frame rail, not true for '54s.

3. Some early '53s carried knock-off wheel-cover hubs mounted at 90 degrees from the standard location.

4. All '53s had two inside hood releases, one at each bottom end of the dashboard. This is not a conclusive point, however, as some early '54s were also built this way.

5. The first 175 cars had foot-activated windshield washers, replaced from serial number 001176 by a dashboard-controlled vacuum system.

6. Some cars lack the standard stainless-steel headlamp stoneguards and/or the Plexiglas rear license-plate cover, but this doesn't necessarily indicate a forgery, as certain states required they be removed.

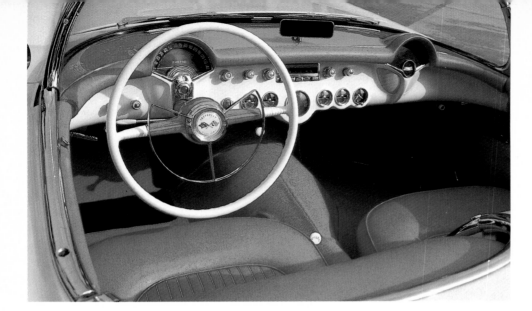

mongrel mechanicals, and high price. MG and Jaguar partisans condemned the car as nonfunctional and faddish. To them, the presence of even the fake knock-off wheel covers meant that the rest of the car was no good at all.

Such judgments were superficial, of course. More thorough inspection proved that, on the whole, the Corvette was quite a good sports car—definitely worthy of being raced as well as being used for daily transport. Even with Powerglide and the six-cylinder engine, a well-tuned example could do 0-60 mph in 11 seconds and notch up to 105 mph flat out. That may seem tame today, but it was hardly bad for 1954.

Road testers judged the ride/handling balance excellent. Said Walt Woron in *Motor Trend*: "Chevrolet has produced a bucket-seat roadster that will hold its own with Europe's best, short of actual competition and a few imports that cost three times as much." *Road & Track*, ever more critical, wondered if the Corvette really was a sports car, then reversed itself by saying it made "a favorable impression immediately on the score of clean lines with a minimum of chrome trim. It looks like a sports car, a very modern one at that....

"[The Corvette's] outstanding characteristic," *R&T* continued, "[is probably its] deceptive performance. Sports car enthusiasts who have ridden in or driven the car without benefit of stopwatch seem to have been unimpressed with the performance. This is an injustice, as the figures shown in our data panel prove.

the division found itself with a surplus of some 1500 cars. It wasn't long before rumors began drifting through GM corridors that the 'Vette was on the verge of extinction.

In light of the car's blend of the sensible and the silly, it was inevitable that the Corvette would have detractors, but it's interesting that the press was far kinder than most of Chevy's selected opinion leaders. To be sure, both groups criticized many of the same things: the "jet-age" styling, clumsy side curtains,

"The second most outstanding characteristic of the Corvette," said *R&T*, "is its really good combination of riding and handling qualities. The ride is so good that few American car owners would notice much difference from their own cars. Yet there is a feeling of firmness about the car, and none of the easy slow-motion effect of our large, heavy sedans. The biggest surprise is the low roll angle—actually less than two of the most popular imported sports cars. The Corvette corners flat like a genuine sports car should...." The magazine also praised the brakes, the roomy trunk, and the easy-to-use folding top and its effectiveness in coping with a Southern California downpour. "Chevrolet may have committed some errors in presenting and merchandising a sports car [but] frankly, we like the Corvette very much."

With such favorable comments, it's amazing Chevy didn't make Corvettes available to the press a lot sooner. As it was, the first few '53s went to project engineers. (Production cars 001001 and 001002 are believed to have been destroyed.) The balance, as noted, went to GM managers and other visible people. Chevrolet didn't begin addressing "civilian" orders until the new St. Louis plant was geared up for '54 production, though the first 14 or 15 were actually built in Flint, as were all engines (suffixed F54YG).

Not surprisingly, the '54 Corvette differed little from the '53, though running refinements occurred throughout the model year. Gas and brake lines were better

protected by being moved inboard of the right-hand main frame rail, and tops and top irons changed from black to tan. The storage bag for carrying the side curtains in the trunk was mildly reshaped and newly color-keyed to the interior.

Speaking of colors, GM now offered a choice. Pennant Blue, mated to a tan interior, accounted for

Opposite page: The '53 Corvette twin-pod dashboard was symmetrical in design, and attractive enough, but it spread the instruments across its width. This made at-a-glance readings difficult, particularly for the center-mounted tach. Bumper protection was minimal (bottom). This page: Sporty-looking crossed flags adorned the Corvette emblem.

Comparison: American Sports Cars 1954

	Corvette	Kaiser-Darrin	Nash-Healey
Price (NADA list):	$3523	$3668	$4721
Model year production:	3640	435	90
Dimensions and Capacities			
Wheelbase (in.):	102	100	108
Overall length (in.):	167	184	180
Curb weight (lbs):	2705	2175	2990
Drivetrain			
Engine type:	ohv I-6	L-head I-6	ohv I-6
Displacement (ci):	235.5	161	252.5
Brake horsepower @ rpm:	150 @ 4200	90 @ 4200	140 @ 4000
Transmission:	2-speed Powerglide automatic	3-speed manual with overdrive	3-speed manual with overdrive
Axle ratio:	3.55:1	4.55:1	4.10:1
Performance*			
0-60 mph (sec):	11	15	10
Top speed (mph):	106	98	105

* Corvette figures are taken from *Corvette: America's Star-Spangled Sports Car*, Karl Ludvigsen (1972). Darrin figures are averaged from contemporary *Motor Age* and *Motorsport* road tests. Nash-Healy figures are taken from a September 1951 *Motor Trend* test, the only one available, though weight and horsepower were approximately the same in 1954.

Comments: Despite the Darrin's low weight and numerically high axle ratio, the Corvette easily had the better of both it and the Nash-Healey, although the latter weighted considerably more. Thanks to its 108-inch wheelbase, the Nash-Healey was the roomiest of this trio, but the Corvette was almost as spacious and had the best space utilization as well as the least overhang. Where the Nash product suffered was in price—well over $1000 more than either of these rivals—styling (especially the unpopular inboard headlamps of 1952-55), and certain bizarre features like an accelerator located between the brake and clutch pedals and overdrive operated by the horn ring. Besides being clearly the most competitive, Corvette had the advantage of being a Chevrolet. It was a relatively hot performer (Powerglide notwithstanding), a good-looker, the least costly, and the only one produced by a Big Three manufacturer, which meant continued parts availability, good trade-in value, wider distribution, and, usually, a choice of showrooms. Corvette demand was initially brisk, and volume handily outpaced that of America's other two 1954 sports cars.

about 16 percent of production. Sportsman Red, selling at about four percent, and the original Polo White, at about 80 percent, were teamed with red interiors. A very small number of cars—as few as six—were painted black and also carried a red interior. Some '54 'Vette owners claim to have original paint in colors other than these four, though they're not shown in factory records. However, paint bulletins are known to have listed a Metallic Green and a Metallic Bronze.

The 1953 Corvette had two short stainless-steel exhaust outlets protruding inboard of the rear fenders. When it was found that air turbulence tended to suck exhaust gases back against the car, soiling the lacquer, the outlets were lengthened and routed below the body. But even this alteration didn't entirely solve the problem, which would persist until the 1956 redesign, when the tips were shifted to the rear fender extremities.

Some initial inconveniences *were* remedied on the '54s. For example, the original two-handle exterior hood latch was replaced by a more manageable single-handle mechanism after the first 300 or so units. The choke control was moved from the right to the left of the steering column, swapping places with the wiper switch. This correction eliminated the hassle of having to reach across or through the steering wheel to operate

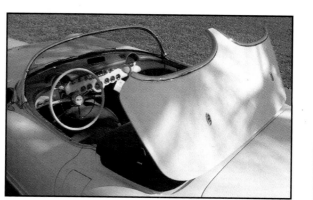

Left, far left, above: *Styling features of the early Corvette included a toothy grille, mesh-covered headlights, fake knock-off wheel covers, and jet-pod taillights capped by dual fins. The Blue Flame six (opposite bottom) propelled the 'Vette from 0-60 mph in 11 seconds. Buyers liked the hinged lid that hid the top (below) but would have preferred wind-up side windows (bottom).*

the choke with the left hand while turning the ignition key with the right. Moisture in the rear license plate recess tended to cause its plastic cover to fog up, so Chevy threw in two little bags of a desiccant material to keep the area dry.

Under the hood, a new camshaft gave the Blue Flame Six an extra five horsepower, boosting the total to 155 bhp, though the increase wasn't announced until the following year. Other alterations included a new-style rocker-arm cover (about 20 percent of which were finished in chrome—serial numbers 1363 through 4381), a tidier wiring harness, and more plastic-insulated wire (replacing fabric). The three bullet-shaped air cleaners were replaced by a two-pot type after the first 1900 cars.

Another niggling problem concerned the top mechanism. On early cars, the main irons had to poke through slots in the chrome moldings behind the seats and were capped with spring-loaded flippers. Beginning with serial number 3600, the irons were redesigned with a dogleg shape that allowed them to slip between the body and the seat back. Unhappily, this led to

continued on page 46

Profile: Harley J. Earl

Enthusiasts generally agree that the impetus for the first Corvette came from Harley Earl, pioneering automotive stylist and founder of GM's Art and Colour Section. Some observers consider him to be more the Corvette's "father" than even engineer Zora Arkus-Duntov.

To be sure, the fiberglass-bodied two-seater could not have progressed from Motorama dream car to production reality without Earl's backing. He fought for the Corvette from the very first, against some fairly stiff odds, and for a reason: It was just his sort of car. Of course, Earl carried considerable clout with GM management, the kind that comes from a swift, sure rise to fame and a winning track record.

Harley Earl was born to be a stylist. His father had designed horse-drawn carriages in Los Angeles, and by the time young Harley had graduated from Stanford, he was a genuine car buff. In the early Twenties he secured a job designing dashing custom bodywork for Don Lee, a Cadillac dealer who catered to the Hollywood elite. While at the Lee shops, Earl was discovered by Lawrence P.

Fisher, then general manager of Cadillac, who hired the 32-year-old as a consultant.

One of Earl's first assignments on arriving in Detroit was the body design for the 1927 LaSalle, the first edition of Cadillac's companion make. It would be the first mass-produced car to be styled in the modern sense. Its lines were gracefully handsome, reminiscent of the contemporary Hispano-Suiza—not much of a surprise, since Earl was quite familiar with European design trends of the day.

That first LaSalle was an instant hit, and many attributed its success to styling. The connection wasn't lost on GM's astute managers, and Earl was soon invited by president Alfred P. Sloan, Jr., to work for the company full time, with the specific task of setting up an in-house styling department. Earl organized it as the Art and Colour Section; the English spelling for *color* was his way of denoting prestige. It was an industry first, and from here on, the professional hand of the stylist would be increasingly evident in American automotive design.

Earl's approach to his work

was impressive. To evolve the form of various body components, he pioneered the use of modeling clay, then considered a highly unusual material for the purpose. Earl also created complete automobiles. Main body, hood, fenders, lights, and other elements were conceived in relation to each other so as to blend into a harmonious whole. This contrasted with most custom body builders, who worked from the cowl back, leaving a car's stock front end pretty much intact.

Quick to realize that one person couldn't hope to carry the styling workload at GM, Earl surrounded himself with talented designers, many of whom would owe him their careers. For example, Virgil Exner, destined to win fame with Chrysler Corporation's "Forward Look" in the mid-Fifties, trained under Earl and headed the Pontiac studio in the Thirties. Other luminaries like Frank Hershey, Art Ross, Ned Nickles, and William L. Mitchell learned their craft from Earl, making their marks at Cadillac and Buick. (Mitchell, in fact, succeeded his mentor following Earl's retirement in 1958.) Clare MacKichan, who helped create the classic 1955 Chevy, was yet another pupil.

Needless to say, Earl's impact on the shape of GM cars was enormous. In fact, for most of his 31 years with the company, the GM design philosophy and Earl's philosophy were one and the same.

An exuberant artist, Earl was unexpectedly playful, often elfish, which contrasted sharply with his physical stature. He was a large man standing over six feet tall with a visual perspective most of his designers lacked. Accordingly, they'd often work while standing on wooden boxes to view their efforts the way he'd see them—though they never did so in his presence. Earl's way of seeing things explains the distinctive ribbed or fluted roof of the 1955-57 Chevrolet Nomad, as well as the use of brushed

aluminum—one of his favorite materials—on the roof of the 1957-58 Cadillac Eldorado Brougham and, before that, a variety of show cars.

Show cars were Earl's favorite projects. Nothing pleased him more than personally designing many of the Motorama experimentals, including the original Corvette. His very first "dream car" may well have been his most influential. The Buick "Y-Job" of 1938 literally defined the shape of Detroit cars for the next two decades with its dramatically low body, absence of traditional running boards, strong horizontal lines, and long boattail deck. Though it doesn't look so modern now, the Y-Job boasted features that still aren't that common today, such as hidden headlights.

Earl's other show models were equally striking. Instead of a rear bumper, the experimental Oldsmobile F-88 of 1954 had seven nerf bars nestled between twin tail pieces. The Olds Cutlass, shown that same year, carried a fastback roofline severely tapered in plan (overhead) view, plus twin chrome-accented tailfins and a louvered backlight that predicted today's popular accessory rear window slats by almost 20 years. The two-seat LaSalle II of 1955 featured abbreviated cycle-style rear fenders, as on an early-1900s runabout, along with exhaust pipes routed through the sills to exit immediately ahead of the rear wheels. The Cadillac Cyclone of 1959, Earl's last show car, was a wild-looking concoction—more fighter plane than car.

Aircraft design influenced much of Earl's work. For example, the trend-setting tailfins that first appeared in production on the 1948 Cadillac were inspired by the twin-tail Lockheed P-38 Lightning, a World War II pursuit plane powered by GM-built Allison engines. During the war years, Earl took his designers to see the plane, then under development at the Lockheed plant in California. They then returned to their studios, where Earl had them adapt several of the fighter's design elements for GM's first postwar cars. According to Irwin W. Rybicki, who succeeded Bill Mitchell as head of GM Design Staff in 1977, Earl favored rounded, massive forms like the P-38's, and these showed up in the pontoon fenders, fastback roofs, and heavy chrome accents that came to characterize GM's early postwar look. Even the first Corvette sported rocket-like vestigial fins.

Harley Earl liked to do things his way, and he usually had the wherewithal to accomplish them. He never lost his enthusiasm for cars during his long GM career, which helps explain the long and hard fight for the production Corvette that came toward the end of that career—a car he kept fighting for throughout its difficult infancy. Right up to his retirement, Earl continued looking for new ways to keep his cars exciting, yet always within the bounds of public acceptance.

As chief designer for the world's largest automaker, Harley Earl put his personal stamp on more different cars than any other individual up to that time. History has already recorded the first Corvettes as some of his best efforts.

**Harley Earl
on Harley Earl:**

The following quotati s n-clude excerpts from 54 interview conducted Arthur W. Baum:

ad Colour
" r to 'myself,' I am n ising a short cut to talk a my team. There are 650 of us, and collectively we are known as the Styling Section. I happen to be the founder of the section and the responsible head, but we all contribute to the future appearance of GM automobiles. . . ."

On Work
"We work informally and, of course, secretly. Since our job is to generate and present design ideas, we have methods of keeping new ideas popping and stirring. To help keep us young, we introduce a freshman squad every year, mostly from two design schools on the East and West coasts. We have contests and idea races."

On Inspiring Designers
"I often act merely as prompter. If a particular group appears to be bogging down over a new fender or grille or interior trim, I sometimes wander into their quarters, make some irrelevant or even zany observation, and then leave. It is surprising what effect a bit of peculiar behavior will have. First-class minds will seize on anything out of the ordinary."

On His Office
"It is a hidden room with no telephone. The windows are blacked out and a misleading name is on the door. . . . In it is a scale model of the first sedan I ever designed for the company, a 1927 LaSalle. I have a great affection for the old crock, but I must admit it is slab-sided, top-heavy, and stiff-shouldered. [Still] there is something on it that explains wha' I have been trying to . On the line we now call beltline, running around body, there is a decorative strip like half a figure eight fastened to the body. This strip was placed there to eat up the overpowering vertical expanse of that tall car. It was an effort to make the car look longer and lower."

On Longer-Lower-Wider
"My primary purpose . . . has been to lengthen and lower the American automobile, at times in reality and always at least in appearance. Why? Because my sense of proportion tells me that oblongs are more attractive than squares, just as a ranch house is more attractive

than a square, three-story, flat-roofed house or a greyhound is more graceful than a bulldog."

On Responding to the Public
"There are always some indignant critics. The most amusing brickbats I get accuse me of being a shrimp and wanting to squash passengers down to the ground to suit my own anatomy. . . . I am six feet four inches tall and weigh over 200."

On Government Regulation
"Highway regulatory bodies keep us fenced in. If we wanted a single headlight on a car, the states would prohibit it, since many of them control the number, brightness, position, and height of headlights. They exercise similar control over tail and stop lights."

On Other Limits to Design
"The engineers quite properly will not let us interfere with the efficiency and soundness of their powerplants. If we wanted to try our hands on a three-wheeled car, I am sure the engineers wouldn't encourage us. They think three-wheel cars are inherently dangerous. They won't give us a rear engine either, until problems like weight distribution are solved, and only then if there is a compelling advantage to the owner."

On Chrome
"I am not particularly committed to chrome. . . . But when chrome arrived as a decorative trim for the industry, it was imperative that I find out how people felt about it. . . . I dispatched my staff to key cities to pose as reporters. They asked hundreds of questions about customer response to or rejection of chrome trim. The conclusions were in favor of chrome, more so on used-car lots."

On Looks
"American cars have always

had a comfortably blunt, leonine front look. This is good as long as the car as a whole is poised right. There was a time when automobiles tilted down in front as if they intended to dig for woodchucks. Subsequently, they went tail-heavy and appeared to be sitting up and begging. Now I think we have them in exactly the right attitude of level alertness, like an airplane at take-off."

On the Motoramas
"A Motorama is more than a good show with good promotion. Frankly, it makes my styling job easier, as visitors express themselves vividly, and by the time hundreds of thousands of these critics have examined your show and commented on your exhibits, you have a firm idea of their likes and dislikes. And it is hardly necessary for me to say that it is vital for us to keep in tune with American thinking about automobiles."

On Color
"The public's greater tolerance has already been expressed in color. Have you recently looked down from a tall building onto a large parking lot? People are also making up their minds that all American cars are good, so why shop for anything more than attractive, pleasant lines and an established worth in the trade-in market? I can't quite go along with that, considering my preference for GM cars and since one color on the road today strikes me as something that belongs on the underside of a railroad bridge."

Summing Up
"Most of our thousands of hours of work every year are small refinements and revisions to improve the comfort, utility, and appearance of our automobiles. But we also need explosive bursts of spanking-new themes, and somehow we get them. I have enjoyed every minute of both kinds of this labor for 28 years. . . . I hope designing is always like that."

The '54 Corvette (both pages) looked the same as the '53, but came in colors other than white. Chevy built 3640 units, but some were unsold at year's end. Dealer driveaways drummed up excitement, as on the Los Angeles Harbor Freeway in March 1954 (far right).

another annoyance: The top irons rubbed the upholstery. Because the preferred top-folding procedure was not that obvious, the factory began sticking explanatory decals on the underside of the top cover.

Corvette pricing had been a sore point with critics and would-be customers. In a ploy to make the car appear more competitive, Chevy dropped the advertised base figure from $3498 to $2774 for 1954. The catch was that the Powerglide automatic now technically cost extra. Since a manual gearbox was not yet available—and since nobody wanted a transmissionless car—a safe assumption would be that all 1954 models had this $178.35 "mandatory option." When all the legitimate options were added—directional signals,

heater, radio, whitewalls, parking brake alarm, courtesy lights, and windshield washer—the sticker was still about the same: precisely $3254.10. As you might guess, this marketing sleight of hand did nothing to spark sales.

The early Corvette may have had its faults, but unreliability wasn't one of them. It wasn't a temperamental beast prone to breaking down like a Jaguar, nor did it demand constant attention like a Ferrari. Not that the 'Vette didn't display a few quirks: Synchronizing the triple carburetors for smooth idle and throttle response was tricky at best; and water leaks were a problem, mostly from around the top and side curtains, though the leading edges of the door openings were

suspect on some units. But these problems were hardly major, and Chevy issued service bulletins to cover them. Running gear? As boringly reliable as in Chevy's everyday passenger models, which was expected but pleasant nonetheless—especially in a sports car.

For all that, the Corvette arrived at a crucial crossroads by the end of 1954. Chevrolet's bold sports-car experiment had laid a considerable sales egg despite the initial huzzahs of the Motorama crowd, favorable press reaction (even from the purists at *Road & Track*), and steady product improvement. Worse, everybody at GM knew it. "We needed and expected 20,000 sales a year," said one manager at the time. "When we got 3600—well, what more could be said?"

Perhaps this, to quote Robert C. Ackerson in the April 1979 *Special-Interest Autos:* "In effect, the early Corvette, while being a better car vis-a-vis its con-temporaries than is generally recognized, tried to be too many things to too many people. In the process, it became a car without a firm base of support. Thus, GM, viewing any expenditure geared toward the Corvette's continuation as being a prime example of throwing good money after bad, could have, in 1955, simply dropped the whole idea. This didn't happen,. and American automotive history is far better for it."

But how close the Corvette came to extinction at the tender age of two, and the reasons aren't hard to divine with hindsight. Buyers were frustrated by that ill-conceived "teaser" marketing approach, which amounted to "look, but don't touch." Additionally, the 'Vette was not a "pure" sports car but a cross between a boulevard tourer (like the Kaiser-Darrin and the then-imminent Ford Thunderbird) and an out-and-out sports-racing roadster (like the Triumph TR2 and Jaguar XK-120). We've also seen how sporting types sneered at some features (mainly the Powerglide automatic and nonfunctional cosmetic items like the dummy knock-off wheel covers), while comfort-lovers objected to others (like the clapped-on side curtains, manual folding top, and a recirculating heater that didn't allow for windows-up ventilation). That there were fit-and-finish problems on top of all this was superfluous.

But perhaps the real problem was a sports-car market that remained tiny at best. Though adequate to support imports like Jaguar or even Triumph, it was still ridiculously small by Detroit standards. One traditional industry notion didn't help—the one that says a car is a

"success" only if it sells in the tens if not hundreds of thousands every year. Two final nails in the Corvette's coffin: a stiff price and the fact that multi-car ownership was still far from common.

The Corvette would have ended right there were it not for three timely developments that would ultimately make the 'Vette a permanent fixture in the Chevy line. Perhaps the most crucial from the standpoints of sales and corporate pride was the introduction of Ford's Thunderbird on September 23, 1954. Although a two-seater like Corvette, it was a "personal car," a comfortable steel-bodied *boulevardier* with handsome lines, expected amenities like roll-up windows, and a standard V-8 engine that made it quite quick. Ed Cole was not unprepared, and his new powerplant was the second key development: the brilliant new 265-cubic-inch small-block V-8 he'd been working on for Chevy's totally redesigned 1955 passenger cars.

The third lucky break for the Corvette's future was the arrival of 45-year-old Zora Arkus-Duntov, a German-trained enthusiast, race driver, designer, and engineer. Duntov had been "fiddling" with Corvettes

The '54 Corvette (opposite top) weighed 2705 pounds, 500 more than the Kaiser-Darrin, 300 less than the Nash-Healey. It cost less, though, and easily outran the Darrin and kept up with the Healey. But competition got tougher in 1955 when Ford unleashed the T-Bird (bottom row); it had great looks and V-8 go. Meantime, engineer Zora Arkus-Duntov (above) began to "fiddle" with the Corvette, giving it performance and handling the T-Bird would never see.

in his spare time since joining the GM Research and Development Staff in 1953. As a racer, he not only knew what serious drivers demanded of sports cars but how to achieve it, and he was appalled by the Corvette: "The front end oversteered; the rear end understeered. I put two degrees of positive caster in the front suspension and relocated the rear spring bushing. Then it was fine—very neutral."

Those slight changes were typical Duntov, whose seat-of-the-pants feel for what was right—and wrong—with Corvettes would make him a legend among GM insiders and, a bit later, Corvette enthusiasts. So respected was he that when it came to management showdowns over suggested changes, the white-haired wizard usually won. "Fiddling" with Corvettes would be Duntov's life's work for the next 20 years. In 1954, however, he was simply another booster for a car that needed all the friends it could get.

"There were conversations...about the Corvette being

dropped," Duntov recalled later. "Then the Thunderbird came out and all of a sudden GM was keeping the Corvette. I think that Ford brought out the competitive spirit in Ed Cole." The Thunderbird certainly challenged GM's resolve, its timing prompting the Corvette's reprieve. What would people think if the world's largest automaker fled this specialized market?

Harley Earl was still the Corvette's biggest booster. For 1955 he proposed a mild facelift, with a wide eggcrate grille similar to that of Chevy's forthcoming new passenger cars, plus a functional hood scoop, dummy front-fender vents, and a redesigned rear deck with the aforementioned outboard exhaust tips. But with sales in the cellar and the high cost of tooling the standard '55 models, there was simply no money. Nor was there much interest for a time, as management debated the Corvette's commercial viability.

Lack of funds also precluded two other Earl ideas seen at the 1954 Motorama. One was a lift-off hardtop

that made the 'Vette into a pretty, thin-pillar coupe. It was a natural, but it would have to wait until 1956. The other concept, a closed fastback coupe, wouldn't make production until much later still, with the advent of the Bill Mitchell-designed 1963 Sting Ray generation. Interestingly, the Motorama fastback was dubbed "Corvair," a name that had actually once been favored over Corvette. (It would, of course, resurface for Chevy's radical rear-engine compact of 1960.)

A third '54 Motorama concept was the handsome Corvette-based Nomad sports wagon. A running exercise on a standard 1953 Chevy wagon chassis, it led directly to the production 1955 model built on that year's new passenger-car chassis and bearing the same lower-body lines, not Corvette styling. Though a few customizers have since made "sportwagons" out of various Corvettes, there's no evidence that GM ever seriously considered this "line extension" for volume production.

As for the car that *was* in production (however meager), the '55 looked to be just a repeat of the 1953-54 Corvette, but was much improved in many respects. The biggest improvement was Ed Cole's superb small-block V-8, fitted to all but six of the '55 models and identified externally only by exaggerated gold "V's" overlaid on the existing "Chevrolet" name script on the lower front fenders. "I had worked on V-8 engines all my professional life," Cole said in a 1974 interview with *Special-Interest Autos*. "You just *know* you want five main bearings—there's no decision to

49

The fastback Corvair (right and above) toured with the 1954 Motorama. Counting the show cars, there were four Corvettes that year (below): regular Corvette, with hardtop, Nomad, and Corvair. Opposite page: The legendary 265-cid V-8 (top) found its way into the '55 Corvette (bottom). Styling was the same, but the big "V" in CheVrolet stood for V-8 go-power.

50

make. We knew that a certain bore/stroke relationship was the most compact. We knew we'd like a displacement of 265 cubic inches, and that automatically established the bore and stroke [3.75 × 3.00 inches]. And we never changed any of this. We released our engine for tooling direct from the drawing boards— that's how crazy and confident we were."

One of the many outstanding features that made the 265 such a pivotal development was the lack of a common rocker shaft. Each rocker arm was entirely independent of the others, so that the deflection of one had no effect on the rest. Each was assembled over a valve stem and pushrod, retained by a fulcrum ball and lock nut. Regardless of whether mechanical or hydraulic lifters were used, the valves were lashed by turning the lock nut. In addition, the arrangement reduced reciprocating weight, which allowed higher rpm and cut down on raw materials.

Other innovations included an intake manifold that provided a common water outlet to both heads, which were die cast with integral valve guides and were completely interchangeable. A short stroke meant short connecting rods, another aid to high-rpm capability. Pressed-in piston pins eliminated the need for split rods and the required locking bolts. Five main bearings of equal diameter carried maximum loads in their lower halves. Weight was saved by circulating the oil through hollow pushrods, providing splash lubrication to the rocker arms and valve stems, thus eliminating the need for separate and costly oil feeder lines. Pistons were modern slipper-type "autothermic" aluminum units with three rings; a circumferential expander for the single oil ring provided axial and radial force to control oil burning. Instead of iron, the crankshaft was forged of pressed steel because of its higher specific gravity and modulus of elasticity. Because the new engine had better heat rejection properties than the old

six, a smaller radiator could be used, which not only saved some more weight but also reduced frontal area. In fact, the V-8 actually weighed 30-40 pounds *less* than the six yet produced over 25 percent more horsepower.

Though only the second V-8 in Chevy history (the first was a disastrous 1917 engine), the 265 was nearly perfect—truly a milestone design. Some 43 percent of all 1955 Chevys were so equipped, putting Chevrolet into the performance field with Ford where it had never been before. So good was the small-block's basic

1953-55 Serial Spans, Production Figures, and Base Prices

Year	Serial Prefix	Serial Span	Prod.	Price
1953	E53F	001001-001300	300	$3,513
1954	E54S	001001-004640	3,640	$3,523
1955	E55S*	001001-001700	6	$2,799
1955	VE55S**	001001-001700	668	$2,934

* 6-cylinder   ** V-8

concept and execution that it still powers production Corvettes more than 35 years later, though with numerous improvements made possible by technology that didn't exist in the mid-Fifties.

The V-8 certainly did wonders for Corvette performance in 1955. Though basically the same engine newly optional in that year's passenger Chevys, the Corvette version ran a special camshaft that raised horsepower 33 above standard tune—to a total 195 bhp at 5000 rpm. Replacing the finicky multiple carbs was a single Rochester four-barrel. Final-drive gearing remained at 3.55:1, but the V-8's higher rev limit prompted a revised tachometer redline of 6500 rpm. Because the engine was lighter, fore/aft weight distribution improved, though the benefit was slight (52/48 percent).

There was no doubting the V-8's performance improvement: It was stunning. The benchmark 0-60-mph sprint now took just 8.5 seconds; the standing quarter-mile only 16.5 seconds. Top speed was up to nearly 120 mph. Despite this, gas mileage was actually better too. *Road & Track*, for example, recorded 18-22.5 mpg with Powerglide, some 2-3 mpg better than the six. The magazine's editors were also impressed by the V-8's greater smoothness and refinement, rated the brakes "more than adequate for ordinary usage" (if not for racing), termed ride quality excellent, and called stability at high speeds near-perfect.

As in 1953-54, the Corvette received several running changes during 1955 production. Soon after start-up, the Pennant Blue color option was replaced by Harvest Gold, with contrasting green trim and dark green top—a popular combination. Metallic Copper also became available, and Sportsman Red was replaced by Gypsy Red. The latter came with white vinyl interior, red saddle stitching, and tan carpet and top. Besides this extra dazzle, the '55s had smoother bodies of slightly thinner section than the 1953-54 models. Fit-and-finish was tidier and tighter. Early '55s retained holes in the frame rails for mounting the six-cylinder engine, but these were soon plugged once it was realized they'd probably never be used again. The X-brace on

Gypsy Red replaced Sportsman Red on the '55 Corvette. The fiberglass bodies, smoother and a bit thinner in section, showed better workmanship. The fussy twin-fin rear fenders would disappear after 1955.

the underside of the hood was replaced by a lateral brace to clear the V-8's air cleaner.

Other changes made to accommodate the V-8 included an automatic choke for the first time since the Motorama show Corvette, and a 12-volt electrical system as on most other '55 GM cars, though the older six-volt setup was retained for the few six-

cylinder Corvettes built that year. The previous vacuum-operated wiper motor gave way to an electric unit, and a foot-operated windshield squirter returned.

Alas, Powerglide remained the only transmission, though its vacuum modulator was dropped (as on other '55 Chevys) so that kickdown was governed solely by speed and throttle position. But very late in

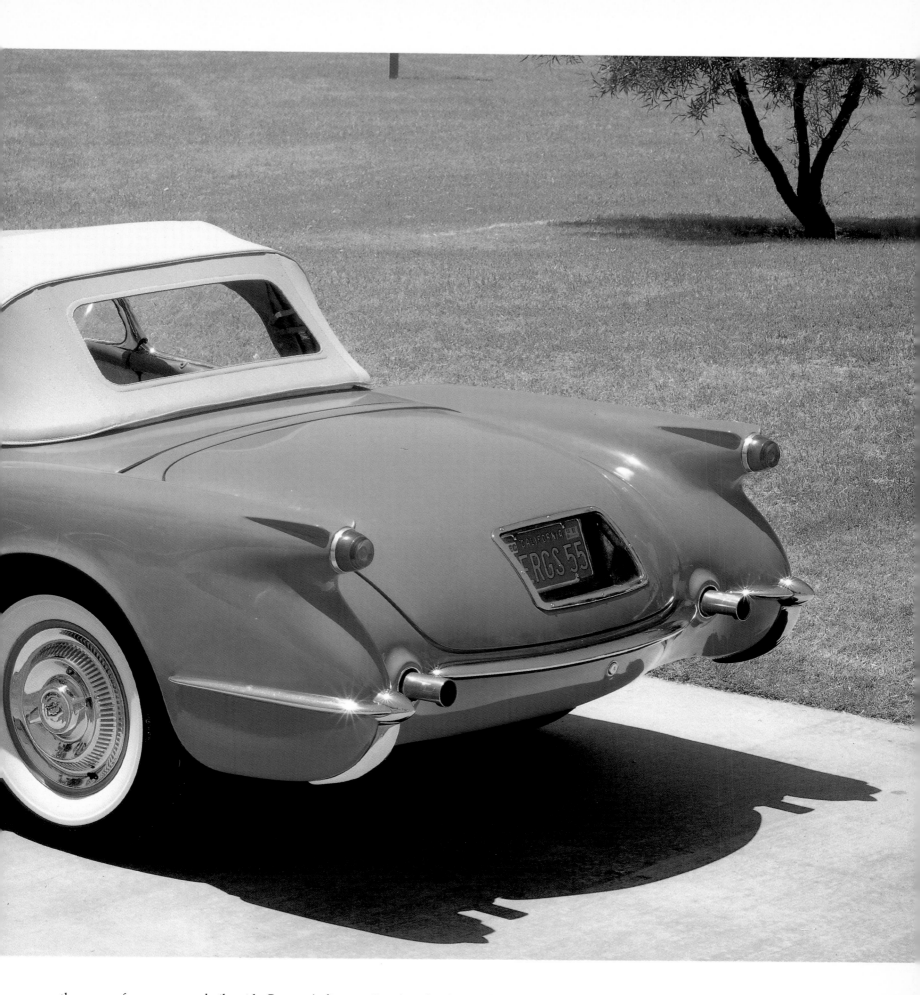

the run, a few cars were built with Corvette's first manual gearbox, a new close-ratio, three-speed manual. It was too late for testing by the monthly car magazines, but it was a harbinger of the future. Drivers swapped cogs via a stubby chrome stalk rising from the side of the transmission tunnel, capped by a small white ball and surrounded by a boot that was clamped to the floor by a bright metal ring showing the shift pattern. Final drive was shortened to 3.7:1, which combined with the lighter gearbox and that potent V-8 to make for the fastest 'Vette yet.

On balance, 1955 marked a great leap forward for Corvette engineering, but not even genuine high performance, improved workmanship, and more pizzazz could turn things around, at least not right away. In fact, sales headed down: only 700 units for the model year, though that would prove to be the all-time low. Chevy was still wrestling with problems that kept production from being either efficient or significant, and the market was still dubious and elusive. Despite 1955's vast improvements, the overall package still wasn't completely right. Said *Road & Track*: "The Corvette comes so close to being a really interesting, worthwhile, and genuine sports car—yet misses the mark almost entirely." Apparently some people were embarrassed about liking this particularly Detroit product, let alone buying one.

With hindsight, then, it's clear that the Corvette was saved from an early grave not by Ed Cole's V-8, welcome though it was, but by Ford's sales success with the Thunderbird. And that was considerable: 16,155 for the model year—a rousing 23 to 1 margin over the plastic-bodied Chevy.

But at least the Corvette had a future again, and it couldn't have been in better hands. Harley Earl, Ed Cole, and Zora Arkus-Duntov were about to transform the awkward two-seater of 1953-55 into a true sports car—"America's *only* true sports car," as Chevy would proclaim. The Corvette's renaissance was at hand.

The '55 Corvette, the last of the first generation models, boasted vastly improved performance and handling. It laid the groundwork for the exciting 'Vettes to follow and gave truth to Chevy's claim that it built the only "true" sports car in America.

Major Specifications: 1953-55 Corvette

Body/Chassis

Frame:	Box-section steel, X-braced
Body:	Glass-reinforced plastic, 2-seat roadster
Front suspension:	Independent; upper and lower A-arms, coil springs, anti-roll bar, tubular hydraulic shock absorbers
Rear suspension:	Live axle on semi-elliptic leaf springs, tubular hydraulic shock absorbers
Wheels:	15-inch bolt-on steel
Tires:	6.70 × 15 4-ply whitewalls

Dimensions

Wheelbase (in.):	102.0
Overall length (in.):	167.0
Overall height (in.):	51.3
Overall width (in.):	72.2
Track front/rear (in.):	57.0/59.0
Ground clearance (in.):	6.0
Curb weight (lbs):	2850

Engines

Type:	ohv inline six-cylinder (1953-55)/ohv V-8 (1955); water-cooled; cast-iron block and head
Main bearings:	4/5
Bore × stroke (in.):	3.56 × 3.95/3.75 × 3.00
Displacement (ci):	235.5/265
Compression ratio:	8.0:1/8.0:1
Carburetion:	3 Carter sidedraft/1 Carter 4-barrel
Exhaust system:	Split cast-iron manifolds, dual exhausts
Brake horsepower @ rpm:	150 @ 4200/195 @ 5000
Torque @ rpm (lbs/ft):	223 @ 2400/260 @ 3000
Electrical system:	6/12-volt, Delco-Remy ignition

Driveline

Transmission:	2-speed Powerglide torque-converter automatic (3-speed manual fitted to a few late '55 models)
Gear ratios:	First—3.82:1
	Second—1.00:1
	Reverse—3.82:1
Rear axle type:	Hotchkiss drive, semi-floating
Rear axle ratio:	3.55:1
Steering:	Saginaw worm-and-sector, 16:1 ratio, 3.7 turns lock-to-lock
Turning circle (ft):	37.0
Brakes:	4-wheel hydraulic, internal-expanding drums, 11-in. diameter; 154.5 sq. in. effective lining area

Performance (Six/V-8)*

0-30 mph (sec):	3.7/3.2
0-40 mph (sec):	5.3/4.4
0-50 mph (sec):	7.7/6.4
0-60 mph (sec):	11.0/8.7
0-80 mph (sec):	19.5/14.4
Standing ¼-mile (sec):	17.9/16.5
Top speed (mph):	107/120
Fuel consumption (mpg):	14-18/18-22.5

* *Road & Track*, June 1954/July 1955

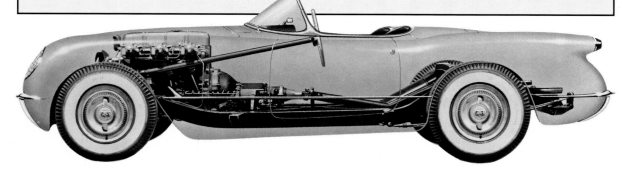

CHAPTER 4

1956-57: GETTING SERIOUS

Why would a low-volume product like Ford's first Thunderbird affect General Motors' decision to continue its equally limited—and costly—Corvette? Actually, it didn't, at least not completely. GM's actions and the Corvette's dramatic turn from plastic plaything to serious sports car after 1955 resulted as much from the Ford-Chevy rivalry of the time as the fact that the T-Bird appeared at the historic pinnacle of that annual sales battle between America's two most popular makes.

Beginning in mid-1953, Ford waged an 18-month production war against Chevrolet in a determined bid to be first in overall sales, a position that had eluded Dearborn since the early Thirties. Ford flooded its dealers with thousands of cars regardless of whether they'd been ordered; dealers were expected to sell them by whatever means. GM naturally responded in kind, and the battle commenced.

Ford and Chevrolet both publicly proclaimed victory at the end of 1955, each trotting out statistics to support its claim. Still, the winner was ultimately less important than the losers, of which there were plenty. Ford's "blitz" not only left Chrysler critically wounded but accelerated the demise of independents Kaiser-Willys, Hudson, Nash, and Packard, all of which were gone by 1958. But it also hardened attitudes at Chevrolet, where the unwritten goal became beating Ford in *every* market segment—including the sporty-car arena.

That the T-Bird overwhelmed Corvette in 1955 model-year sales was more than a slap in Chevy's face. It was a direct challenge to Chevy's supremacy. Electing not only to continue the Corvette but to make it a superior performer in every way became a symbol of meeting the Ford challenge. Besides, everybody at Chevy Division knew that the 1953-55 Corvette had lost sight of its original objective. Neither serious performance sports car nor a small, fun-to-drive runabout that everyone could afford, it had instead become a puffy, well-equipped showboat priced close to $3500—a hefty $1500 more than a "Low-Priced Three" sedan.

It's a great irony of automotive history that Chevrolet would decide to make the Corvette a genuine sports car just as Ford was deciding to go after more sales by transforming the Thunderbird into a four-seater (which bowed for the 1958 model year). The fact was that the T-Bird's 1955 sales mark of 16,000 was no more satisfying to Ford than 700 Corvettes was to Chevrolet. Of course, Chevy would have been mighty happy to sell 16,000 Corvettes, but that seemed a mere pipe dream in 1955. For now, it would be enough merely to recover from what had become a sales embarrassment.

Chevy's landmark 265-cubic-inch small-block V-8 had been greeted with high enthusiasm, and its extra performance was as welcome in the Corvette as it was in Chevrolet passenger cars. Even so, the "buff" magazines weren't all that enthusiastic about the 1955 Corvette. *Road & Track* snidely suggested that it might fill the need "for an open roadster the lady of the house can use as smart personal transport"—not exactly the macho image the Corvette would later embody. *R&T* did concede the benefits of V-8 power, but brought up

the same old complaints about creature comforts—or rather the lack thereof, especially those pesky side curtains. Clearly, what America's sports car needed was a more up-to-date body to match its hearty new small-block soul.

Harley Earl, who'd been taking Corvette criticisms to heart, had been working on that very thing. After

all, he still doubtless considered it *his* car. On February 1, 1955, just as Thunderbirds were beginning to be seen in serious numbers, Earl had all but finalized a full-scale clay model of a new Corvette body. With minor trim changes, it was shown to GM management in mid-April and approved on the spot. The result was a '56 Corvette and a near-identical '57 model that are still regarded by many as the epitome of Corvette styling, at least before the 1963 Sting Ray design.

This second-generation styling was rooted in three 1955 Motorama exercises: the Chevrolet Biscayne and two dreamboats dubbed "LaSalle II" (a nostalgic touch undoubtedly made at Earl's insistence). The Biscayne was a compact four-door hardtop in light green with a color-keyed interior. Appearance features included "bugeye" headlamps set high and inboard of fender-mounted parking lights, and a grille made up of a series of vertical bars. Shallow air-intake slots were positioned in the cowl just ahead of and below a huge compound-curve windshield, and there was a flat cabin floor level with the bottom of the frame. The LaSalle IIs, a similar hardtop sedan and a jaunty roadster, were also carefully color-keyed and had prominent vertical-bar grilles but sported a feature the '56 Corvette would inherit: an elliptical concave section on the lower bodysides. Swept back from the front wheel wells, it recalled the pretty "LeBaron sweep" color inserts of the Classic era.

Opposite page: The 1956 Corvette bowed with new styling, being squarer up front and rounder in the rear. Also new were "coves" on the sides; they were usually painted a different color than the rest of the car. **This page:** *The dashboard was mainly a carryover, but the shift lever was new.*

lifted directly from the production-based prototype seen at the 1954 Motorama.

One of the last GM production cars to be designed before the Styling Staff moved from Detroit to the new corporate Technical Center in Warren, Michigan, the '56 Corvette was not only fresh but a vast improvement over the first generation. It was, in essence, only an evolution but with all the bad elements removed and the good ones emphasized.

A definite "face" was perhaps the most appealing element of the first-generation design. The second generation's was even better. Wire screens had made the "eyes" seem veiled on the 1953-55 models—hardly appropriate for a "man's" car—so the headlamps were uncovered and moved forward out of their recesses. "Many of us will deplore this change," *Motor Life* predicted, though you have to wonder just who they were thinking of. Complementing this was a larger version of the round Corvette nose emblem, with the racy crossed-flags motif that survives to this day. As mentioned, the original "mouth" and its magnificent chrome "teeth" were left alone.

Rear-end revisions were just as tasteful. The old finny fenders and jet-pod taillamps were trimmed down to artful French curves contoured to match rear deck curvature, and new taillights were neatly "frenched" in above a vertical bumperette on each fender. The trunklid "shadow box" was discarded and the license plate moved to below the trunk opening, where it was flanked by horizontal bumperettes with little inboard bullets. The result was a smooth, gently curved tail, with the fenders protruding slightly—but only just. Earl's staff thankfully resisted an impulse to have the dual exhausts exit through the sides of the rear fenders, routing them instead through the rear bumper guards. Incidentally, *R&T* complained about both front and rear bumpers still being *guards* and not "real bumpers," but you could get away with that in those distant days

Author Karl Ludvigsen has cited one other influence, "...the Mercedes 300SL, the production version of which had been shown early in 1954. It was responsible for the 1956 Corvette's forward-thrusting fender lines to more conventional headlights, and the twin [longitudinal] bulges in its hood panel. These changes blended admirably with the Corvette's horizontal grille concept and gave the new car a very handsome 'face.'"

That grille, as *Road & Track* observed, was essentially the same as the 1953-55 affair. The magazine also noted that "the windshield is new," though it looked much the same, and that "the standard cloth top has more bows and is power operated." Literally capping the new design was an extra-cost detachable hardtop

This page: A February 1955 proposal for the 1953-55 Corvette replacement wore a bizarre bullet-nose front end. It also left the front wheels partially exposed, a la the 1955 Buick Wildcat II show car. It had coves on the sides, a theme that would be seen on the '56 Corvette. Opposite page: A clay mock-up (same date) had sculptured indents behind front and rear wheels, but otherwise looked much like the '56 'Vette (top two rows). Another mock-up (bottom two rows) looked like the final '56 design, save for trim and exhaust.

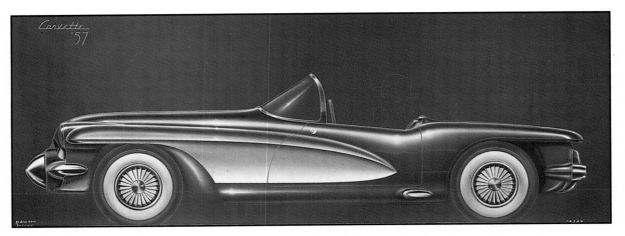

before government-required barrier tests.

The bodyside "coves," as they came to be called, gave the '56 Corvette a styling personality all its own. They also helped relieve the slab-sided look that had led some to term the first-generation design a "plastic bathtub." Even with the coves' narrow chrome outlines—one of the few last-minute trim changes made to the production prototype—the flanks were clean and attractive.

As was the entire car. "There are few unnecessary gimmicks or trim," *Motor Life* reported, "fake knock-off wheel covers and vent scoops excepted." The latter, perched atop the front fenders near the windshield, were supposed to be functional—for cowl ventilation—but cost considerations ruled that out. Wheel covers were new and more ornate. They remained standard issue until 1963 and have become some of the best-known wheel covers in automotive history.

Even the convertible top looked better: tighter, more integrated, and rounded at the rear to echo the aft quarters. The new factory hardtop was also obviously curved and, with its rear side windows, afforded much better over-the-shoulder vision than the soft top.

Despite a few period clichés, the '56 Corvette still looks good more than 30 years later. Furthermore, it passes the real test: It still draws admiring glances. It's one of those rare automobiles with nary an awkward line anywhere.

Like many other enduring designs, the '56 Corvette didn't just look better than its predecessor; it worked better, too. The fussy side curtains were gone forever, replaced by proper roll-up door glass. Even power window lifts were available at extra cost. And proper outside door handles ended the hassle of reaching in through the side curtains on a rainy day.

Except for new waffle-pattern upholstery and revised door panels to go with the wind-up windows, the cockpit was much as before. Unfortunately, that meant

retention of the existing "twin cowl" dashboard with its awkward, near full-width spread of instruments. *R&T* approved of the 'Vette's new spring-spoke steering wheel for looking "as if it came from Italy," even if it made the instrument panel "a little dizzy." But "the floor-mounted 'stick-shift' is nicely done and has an ashtray alongside it on the tunnel." Seats remained separate, flat-bottomed affairs that only hinted at buckets. A transistorized signal-seeking radio was another new feature, though it wasn't yet called a "Wonder Bar."

There was more good news under the hood, where the small-block V-8 was now standard. And it had even more muscle: a rated 210 horsepower at 5200 rpm with a single four-barrel carburetor and higher 9.25:1 compression. That was 15 bhp more than the '55 unit and a big improvement over the 155-bhp six of just two years earlier. Special camshaft, cast-aluminum intake manifold, and dual four-barrel carburetors were available to increase output to 225-240 bhp. Premium fuel was mandatory, of course. The special cam, developed by Zora Arkus-Duntov, helped raise torque on the 225-bhp powerplant to an impressive 270 lbs/ft at 3600 rpm. As for the six, it was gone for good, and *Motor Life* probably expressed the feelings of many by asking, "who cares?"

Running gear was beefed up to handle the extra power, and "buff books" were quick to catch the racing implications. Like the V-8, the three-speed manual gearbox was now standard but with much closer ratios than the '55 version. "At first glance only three forward speeds may appear as a disappointment," *Road & Track* almost apologized to its readers, "but...2nd gear, for example, [is] much closer to high than [in] most 4-speed sports cars. Low, or 1st gear, is approximately similar to 2nd gear in an imported sports car—exploiting the advantages of ample cubic inches." For the record, the spread was 2.2:1 (1st), 1.31:1 (2nd), and 1:1 (3rd). *Motor Life* simply termed all this "a boon for buyers who plan to indulge in any kind of competition." It also lauded a shifter that now attached directly to the transmission housing. "Much of the linkage used on previous models has been eliminated to give more positive shifts."

Drive was taken through a stronger 10-inch-diameter clutch with 12 heat-treated coil springs, replacing the previous diaphragm-spring unit. Final drive was still 3.55:1, but a 3.27:1 cog was newly available. The differential itself was new too, shared with '56 passenger Chevys. Powerglide at last became a true option, listing for $189 and available with either axle.

R&T took note of two other '56 options: extra-wide (5.5-inch) wheels and "four-ply high-speed racing tires, which certainly will be necessary if the top speed potential of this car is ever used." Potential there was. "At the engine's peaking speed of 5200 rpm, the 3.55 axle gives [a calculated] 117 mph, the 3.27 axle 127

Opposite page: *By May 15, 1955, the final design of the 1956 Corvette had been locked up, although this full-size clay lacked chrome trim around the side coves. This page: Front and rear views of the May 1955 car show the more conventional headlight treatment and the frenched-in taillights (bottom left). Note the waffle texture of the upholstery and door and kick-panel trim (bottom right). The real '56 had a tighter-looking top and wind-up side windows (top).*

mph," the magazine reported. "True timed top speeds should be slightly above these figures....The front suspension is unchanged," *R&T* continued, "since the Corvette frame is designed to use the 1951-54 Chevrolet suspension with its 'integral' front crossmember. Brakes, too, remain as before, 11-inch Bendix [drums]."

With all this, the Corvette now shed its image as a half-finished also-ran. The '56 was a genuine screamer with svelte styling and all the amenities any sporting motorist could want. *Road & Track* showed the extent of the metamorphosis in a July 1956 "twin test" of the manual and automatic versions. Both carried the 3.55:1 final drive, making comparisons with earlier test cars easy and straightforward:

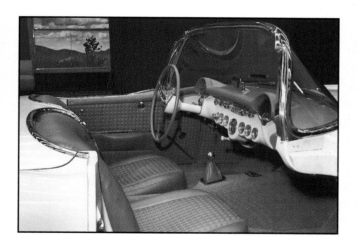

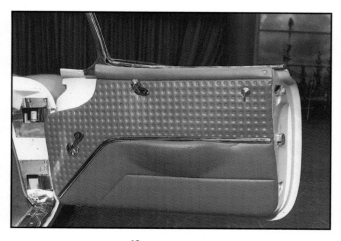

But *R&T* had more to say in its first report on the manual transmission that arrived too late for Corvette testing in 1955: "In the first place, it is somewhat noisy, and we are told that the gears are all 'straight-cut' (not helical), which seems plausible. Secondly, although first gear is not synchronized, it can be engaged at 50 or 60 mph without double-clutching. The technique requires only that the engine speed be brought up during the downshift *while the clutch is depressed.* Such shifts are almost foolproof and require very little finesse, but the same procedure at 25 or 30 mph doesn't work so reliably, and in this case the usual double-clutching process is safer. The advantage of being able to use first gear while slowing down for a corner (as in a race) is, of course, considerable, and is a feature of the new Corvette which was certainly not expected...."

The '56 was a more dynamic Corvette in other respects. *R&T* judged handling "good to excellent compared to other dual-purpose sports cars," though understeer was ever-present. At least the steering was quick—just 3.5 turns lock-to-lock—and weight distribution nearly perfect at 52/48 percent front/rear. Brakes remained a weak point. With just 158 square inches of total lining area, they "faded into oblivion," as one tester said after a hard application. In all, though, road behavior was greatly improved.

As for ride, *Motor Life*'s Ken Fermoyle reported in May 1956 that "those accustomed to American sedans will find [it] hard....Suspension is firm, meaning you definitely feel bumps, tar strips, etc. It also means that you can really barrel a Corvette thru [*sic*] corners with no body lean or heeling. The ride smooths out as speeds increase and always has a solid, glued-to-the-road feel. I drove it hard over a series of gravel back roads, and though it bounces a bit, it always feels

Road & Track
1954-56 Corvette Performance Comparison

	1954	1955	1956	1956
Trans.	Pwrgl.	Pwrgl.	Pwrgl.	Stick
bhp	150	195	225	225
curb wt. (lbs)	2890	2880	3080	2980
test wt. (lbs)	3210	3200	3410	3330
top speed (mph)	104.4	116.9	121.3	129.1
0-60 mph (sec)	11.0	8.7	8.9	7.3
0-80 mph (sec)	19.5	14.4	14.4	12.4
0-100 mph (sec)	41.0	24.7	24.0	20.7
0-1/4 mi. (sec)	18.0	16.5	16.5	15.8

The results, as they say, speak for themselves.

under control—more so than a softly sprung passenger car. Using the punch you get in second gear makes it easy to power around tight turns using the accelerator to 'steer.'"

Still on the subject of refinement, R&T noticed "for the first time a certain amount of body and cowl shake over 100 mph....The more powerful engine is smooth all the way to nearly 6000 rpm, but it did seem a trifle noisier under full throttle than last year's car, which had a much larger air cleaner-silencer. The interior treatment is impressive, but the new winding windows and the power-operated top have forced some curtailment in elbow and leg room. The top, incidentally, is only semi-automatic, for it must be released and partially collapsed before pressing the fold button."

Corvette continued with the 265-cid V-8 for '56, now rated at 210 bhp, although a special camshaft, cast-aluminum intake manifold, and dual four-barrel carbs could boost output to 225-240 horses (opposite). The new top (above) was best described as semi-automatic because it had to be partially collapsed before pressing the fold button.

Karl Ludvigsen, in those days a staffer at *Sports Car Illustrated*, echoed many of these gripes and added a few of his own. He disliked the near-vertical, non-adjusting steering wheel; wished for more rearward travel on more "buckety" seats; bemoaned the cockpit's "dearth of storage space"; and judged the secondary instruments difficult to read "even if you can take your eyes from the road long enough to find them." But in his overall assessment, Ludvigsen was enthusiastically adamant: "In my opinion, the Corvette as it stands is fully as much a dual-purpose machine as the stock Jaguar, Triumph or Austin-Healey. Without qualification, General Motors is now building a sports car."

Since *SCI*'s test car was a three-speeder with the longer-legged 3.27:1 final drive, its performance stats are worth noting. It ran 0-60 mph in 7.5 seconds, covered the standing quarter-mile in 15.9 seconds at 91 mph, and averaged 12 miles per gallon. Ludvigsen praised its gearbox for "well-chosen ratios and effective synchromesh," but found that "the synchro can be

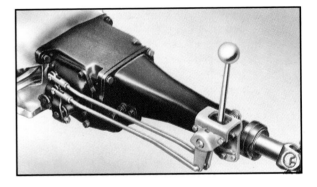

beaten by a very quick move from first to second....Due to the high ratios, the standard-shift Corvette is not really at home in town, and Powerglide might be better for urban use. [Take *that*, sports-car purists!] Out on the road, though, as second gear takes over from first at around 60 and keeps the seat in your back 'til over

Road & Track

1954-56 Corvette Performance Comparison

	1954	1955	1956	1956
Trans.	Pwrgl.	Pwrgl.	Pwrgl.	Stick
bhp	150	195	225	225
curb wt. (lbs)	2890	2880	3080	2980
test wt. (lbs)	3210	3200	3410	3330
top speed (mph)	104.4	116.9	121.3	129.1
0-60 mph (sec)	11.0	8.7	8.9	7.3
0-80 mph (sec)	19.5	14.4	14.4	12.4
0-100 mph (sec)	41.0	24.7	24.0	20.7
0-¼ mi. (sec)	18.0	16.5	16.5	15.8

100, you learn what this car was made for."

But performance didn't tell the whole story. "It is in the handling department," Ludvigsen continued, "that the Corvette proves itself the only true American production sports car. The steering is far from perfect, but it is fast enough to allow right angles to be taken without removing the hands from the wheel, and this virtue will make up for many vices. The latter include an inch and a half of free play....Once the wheel has been set for a bend and the car assumed an initial roll angle, the steering and throttle response are fast and consistent enough to allow very precise control....The stock rear-end damping is a little weak....Cornering speeds and behavior were markedly improved by tire pressure five psi higher than the standard of 25 psi front and 27 psi rear. Raised pressures plus stiffer rear shocks could combine with an already broad track, good weight distribution, and low center of gravity to make the Corvette a real fiend on corners. These criticisms, it will be noted, are minor and apply equally

to many imported machines."

No doubt about it: America's sports car had come of age. No one knew that better than Zora Arkus-Duntov, who believed that a race-winning image was vital to Corvette sales. He would be proven correct. As Carroll Shelby, the man whose Cobra would be the Corvette's

Chevrolet Press Release
CORVETTE AT SEBRING 1956

Sebring, Florida—5.2 miles of slick straightaways and treacherous curves—is one of the world's toughest road courses, calling for the utmost in every phase of automobile performance. The ruggedness of the course and the demands it makes on the machines are illustrated by the fact that of the 60 cars entered (including such famous European marques as Ferrari, Jaguar, and Maserati) only 24 finished. Three of the finishers were Corvettes—a magnificent tribute to the cars' overall competitive performance.

Particularly significant was the completion of the 12-hour endurance race by a stock Corvette, entered by a private individual with a team of two amateur drivers. This Corvette, the owner's personal car, received no special preparation for the race and ran with such un-racing-like equipment as a radio, heater, and power-operated top. The car was still in the race—and running well —long after many of the specially built, expensive European race cars had dropped out.

Of the other two Corvettes entered, one won its class in the Production sports car division and a modified Corvette won the title for its class.

Also significant was the fact that the Corvette was the only American production sports car entered in the race. The Corvette proudly carried American colors into international competition at Sebring and proved conclusively it is America's hottest sports car.

nemesis in the Sixties, later observed: "Racing was the thing that actually saved the Corvette." Duntov had developed his high-lift cam specifically with an eye to competition. If the 'Vette could set a few speed records and win some races, Chevy advertising would do the rest.

Accordingly, the Duntov cam was slipped into a modified '56 Corvette specially prepared at GM's Arizona proving grounds. The car was then shipped to Florida, where Betty Skelton and John Fitch would drive it at the Daytona Speed Weeks trials in January. The goal was 150 mph. Though beach conditions weren't favorable, the car managed an impressive two-way run of 150.583 mph—with Duntov at the wheel.

Development work continued, yielding a new high-compression head that raised the 265's output to a claimed 255 bhp—nearly one horsepower per cubic inch. At the Speed Weeks trials, a Thunderbird prepped by ex-racer Pete DePaolo and driven by Chuck Daigh bested the 'Vette in the production standing-mile contest, but the plastic Chevy proved fastest in the modified class, as Fitch won with a two-pass average of 145.543 mph.

By September, ads were touting this feat. "The 1956 Corvette is proving—in open competition—that it is America's only genuine production sports car," said one—a swipe at the *boulevardier* Thunderbird, which Chevy had already started calling a "scaled-down convertible." Another ad proclaimed: "Bring on the hay bales! The new Corvette, piloted by Betty Skelton, has established a new record for American sports cars at Daytona Beach. But that's only the start. Corvette owners may enter other big racing tests in the months

ahead—tests that may carry America's blue-and-white colors into several of the most important European competitions."

They did. A modified car made a decent showing at Sebring in 1956, finishing ninth in the grueling 12-hour run. Out at Pebble Beach, California, a Corvette finished a strong second behind a Mercedes-Benz 300SL.

Pebble Beach really marked the Corvette's emergence on the world competition stage, but its triumph was far from easy. Arthur B. "Barney" Clark, who wrote many of the memorable Corvette ads of the Fifties and Sixties, described it 22 years later in the new *Corvette Quarterly* magazine: "As [Chevy advertising agency] Campbell-Ewald's director of racing, I had waged a long, secret campaign inside Chevrolet to get us entered in the '56 Pebble Beach races. My reputation was hanging out so far you couldn't see it with 8 × 10 binoculars—but there we were.

"First disaster: Walt Hangsen, the great East Coast driver who was supposed to pilot our entry, phoned to say he was sick but was sending us a replacement.

"Second disaster: Dr. Dick Thompson [a Washington D.C. dentist] arrived. Totally preppie—pink-striped shirt, Brooks Brothers jacket, looking about 18, rosy-cheeked—and so gentle and deferential [he'd make] Mr. Rogers look like Dirty Harry.

"Third disaster: Dr. Dick had campaigned a Porsche 356. He had never driven a Corvette in a race. And we had one half day for practice. However, Dick did pretty well in practice....He finished up somewhere in the first two rows.

"Fourth disaster: Our Corvette had carburetors

approximately the size of hot tubs. Dick had never made a racing start in it, even in practice. The flag dropped and Dick buried the throttle. The Corvette went 'chug'—and stopped! Drowned in gas. Six or seven cars swarmed past before he fired it up. All of them disappeared in the trees.

"Kind friends told me later I looked like there had been a death in the family. You could hear the cars ravening out of Turn Two, through the sweeper, hooking around the top hairpin and wailing down the long twisty drop to the final corner. But you couldn't see anything. I prepared to beat my head on a fence post.

"The mob hammered through the trees, into the final dogleg. The first was...the first was...MY GOD, THE CORVETTE'S IN *FIRST*!

"You talk about pure, unbelievable, exultant joy. That was the day, the hour, the second that Corvette became a genuine first-rank sports car...and I was there!

"That thing came bellowing past like a rhino in heat, vacuuming up the pavement...and I realized I had horribly misjudged Doctor D. Under that mild preppie exterior lurked Atilla the Hun, and heaven help anyone who was ahead of him!

Engine shots (opposite top and above) show off the '56 Corvette V-8's dual four-barrel carbs, air cleaners, specific valve covers, and other related items. Road & Track tested two 225-bhp versions, one stick, the other with Powerglide. Results for the 0-60-mph dash came in at 7.3 and 8.9 seconds, respectively, and top speeds were 121 and 129 mph. Among the more subtle styling changes to be noted on the '56 were a new windshield (it didn't look it) and a larger Corvette nose emblem (bottom).

"Okay, so about three-quarters of the way through those ridiculous drum brakes departed this life, and Rudy Cleye's factory-assisted Mercedes gullwing slipped past. But we still finished first in class and second overall.

"The rest of the afternoon I spent in the pits, greeting my old friends and paying back all the previous remarks about 'plastic toys,' 'prehistoric three-speed gearboxes' and 'Midwestern drum brakes.' I was insufferable...but then I've always been pretty good at that."

Clark's description of "Dr. D." is right on. Thompson had run a Corvette in the Sports Car Club of America's C-Production class only since the spring of '56, yet he won that year's national championship—with a little help from Duntov and other friends. Here was yet another boost to the "competition-proved" image Clark

and Chevy managers were after, an image that Clark's ad copy would play up for years to come.

The Corvette also began doing better in the race that mattered most to GM—the production race—volume rising to about a fifth of the Thunderbird's level for 1956. That may have disappointed the bean counters, but it heartened those car nuts at Chevrolet who'd been fighting to keep the 'Vette alive. After all, 3467 units *was* progress—certainly a lot better than 700. In fact, it represented better than one Corvette for every two Chevy dealers. Even more important, the Corvette was again boosting dealer floor traffic while enhancing Chevrolet's newly won performance reputation. And now that Corvette was beginning to be taken seriously, its supporters argued, it should sell even better in 1957. It did—by almost double.

Nevertheless, the Corvette was still miles away from making money, something Chevrolet Division was rather used to on all its products. Performance imagery, free publicity, and spiffy cars for big dealers and division brass were fine. But sooner or later, any Chevrolet, no matter how esoteric, either made money or died.

Still, it was apparent that GM had changed its attitude about the Corvette as model year '57 dawned; Chevrolet managers seemed quite happy to sustain the car despite modest sales. In fact, there'd been no talk about dropping the Corvette since 1955. Then too, the car was better than ever for '57, with a larger V-8 and, as a mid-year addition to the options list, a four-speed gearbox that had long been demanded by purists. Appearance didn't change—not that it needed to—except that the bodyside "coves" could now be finished in a contrasting color, another new option.

The 283-cid V-8 has since become one of Chevy's most revered engines—the definitive small-block enshrined by a generation of car enthusiasts and all the collectors who followed. It was, of course, the existing 265 engine bored out ⅛-inch (to 3.875 in.; stroke remained a short 3.00 in.). In Chevrolet passenger cars, the 283 delivered 185 bhp in base form, but the standard Corvette version with a four-barrel carburetor developed 220 bhp at 4800 rpm. Dual four-barrels took it to 245 and 270 bhp, and GM's newly developed "Ramjet" fuel injection yielded 250 or 283 bhp. The last was the magic "1 h.p. per cu. in.," and Chevy ads blared the news. It wasn't a first, though. Chrysler had actually exceeded that ideal the previous year—and by more conventional means—with its 355-bhp

This page: The '56 Corvette placed the gauges on the lower part of its twin-cove dashboard: fuel, temp, tach (center), battery, oil, and clock (right). Kids loved 'Vettes, too (below), but the chassis under this one looks a bit underwhelming! Opposite page: As before, exhaust exited through the rear bumpers (top left), but the license (bottom) rested at bumper level in 1956 rather than inside a decklid recess. This engine (top right) has the standard four-barrel carb.

354-cid hemi V-8 in the mighty 300B.

Though almost universal today, fuel injection was a concept alien to American automakers in the Fifties. Chevrolet's system originated in 1955, the same year the division struck a marketing and performance blow with the 265 small-block. Ford, of course, had already had experience with two generations of V-8s, and Plymouth fielded its own new V-8 for '55. Just two years later, the two-year-old Chevy engine, exciting though it was, had stiff new competition. Worse, Ford and Plymouth had prepared larger new cars for 1957, while Chevrolet had to make do with another facelift of its existing two-year-old bodyshell. With memories of the Ford blitz and the hot rivalries of 1955 still fresh in mind, GM management worried that the '57 Chevys would be outpaced. But performance had

already helped Chevy sales once, and it was about to do so again.

The obvious key to higher horsepower was to first enlarge the V-8 and then give it better breathing—i.e., more carburetors—both of which were duly done. GM then considered supercharging, a path Kaiser had followed for 1954-55 and one Studebaker would briefly tread for 1958. But as with the turbochargers of a later era, the supercharger brought with it higher internal stresses deemed undesirable for a make that had built its reputation on reliability. So the engineers took a page from the European performance book and settled on more horsepower via more precise fuel metering than a carburetor allowed: fuel injection.

Model year '57 was closing fast, so a development team was formed—and hustled. The key figures were

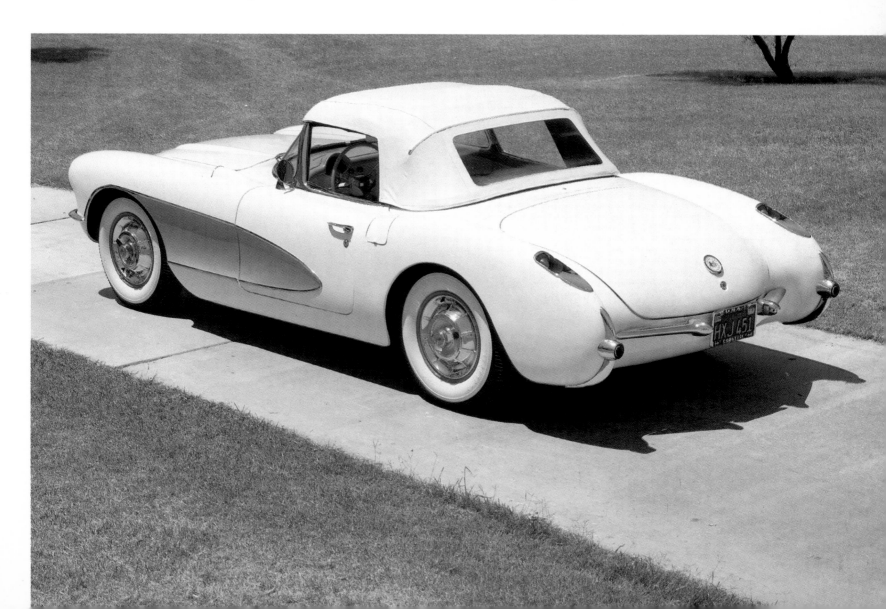

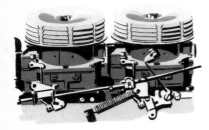

Ed Cole, who'd been promoted to Chevy Division chief in 1955; Harry Barr, Cole's one-time collaborator on the 1949 Cadillac V-8 and now his successor as Chevy chief engineer; John Dolza, head of fuel injection development for the GM Engineering Staff; and Zora Arkus-Duntov.

Duntov had been working on a fuel injection system since early 1956, and under unusual circumstances. In April he'd hit the GM Proving Grounds with a prototype Corvette hardtop equipped with experimental disc brakes but no seat belts. At a good rate of speed, he lost control, left the track, and hit a drainage ditch. Duntov was thrown up into the roof, and the impact broke a vertebra in his back. For the next six months, he worked standing up, confined by a body cast. But he continued pushing because the fuel-injection program was a top priority.

With almost superhuman speed, the engineers put together a fuel injection system that appeared to be relatively inexpensive to manufacture and promised significant power gains. Yet initial dyno-testing showed the fuelie to be no more powerful than a dual-carb V-8. Cole, however, was a believer who wanted nothing less than to offer fuel injection across the entire '57 Chevy line. He got his way and for good reason. Corvette volume was but a fraction of Chevy's total business; "Win on Sunday, Sell on Monday" was still a cherished marketing maxim; and with merely facelifted '57s to sell, Chevy as a whole needed the extra boost that stock-car racing victories would provide—never mind the image enhancement of an exotic "high tech" feature. So it was back to the lab for more feverish research.

Ultimately, Chevrolet and GM's Rochester carburetor division came up with a workable system (see box) that not only increased top-end output but spread power over a wider rpm range. Alas, reliability problems surfaced quickly, which together with the base option's high surcharge—$500, a hefty chunk of change in those days—rendered fuel injection very scarce even among Corvettes. Installations ran to only 240 in a total '57 production run of 6339 units.

Despite its problems, fuel injection provided the necessary performance magic. *Fantastico!* began one ad that pictured a Corvette being loaded off a freighter, a half-covered Ferrari just visible in the background. "Even in Turin, no one has fuel injection!" Ironically, in view of all the hubbub about "1 h.p. per cu. in.," the top fuelie actually delivered closer to 290 bhp—more than the advertised 283. This higher bhp was on 10.5:1 compression, shared with the dual-carb 270-bhp engine. The milder 250-bhp fuelie ran a lighter 9.5:1 squeeze, same as that of the 245-bhp twin-carb unit. Some historians think that in its zeal to promote Ramjet, Chevrolet deliberately *under*rated power on the dual-carb engines—certainly unusual for the day—so they may have actually had more power.

The 283/283 carried the EL order code and should not be confused with the EN racing version, which was sold as a package complete with column-mounted tachometer and a cold-air induction system. Chevy warned potential buyers that the EN option was not for the street, and actually refused to supply heaters on cars so equipped.

In the long run, the four-speed manual gearbox option announced in May 1957 was probably more significant than fuel injection for Corvette performance. Priced at only $188, Regular Production Option 685 was essentially the existing three-speed Borg-Warner transmission with reverse moved into the tailshaft housing to make room for a fourth forward speed. Ratios were again closely spaced: 2.20:1 (1st), 1.66 (2nd), 1.31 (3rd), and 1.00 (4th). "Positraction," Chevy's new limited-slip differential, was a separate option available with four different final-drive ratios to help get the most out of the new engines and gearbox in each particular driving or competition situation.

Answering complaints about handling and braking deficiencies, Chevrolet also issued RPO 684. This was a $725 "heavy-duty racing suspension" package comprising heavy-duty springs, a thicker front anti-sway bar, Positraction, larger-piston shock absorbers

with firmer valving, a faster steering ratio that reduced turns lock-to-lock from 3.7 to 2.9, and ceramic-metallic brake linings with finned ventilated drums. Add the 283-bhp fuelie V-8 (RPO 579E), and you had a car ready to race right off the showroom floor.

And race it did. At Sebring, two production examples finished 12th and 15th overall and 1-2 in the GT class. Just as impressive, the lead car, driven by Dick Thompson and Gaston Audrey, crossed the line some 20 laps ahead of the nearest Mercedes-Benz 300SL. Back at SCCA, the larger V-8 had bumped the 'Vette into the B-Production category, but it didn't matter. Dr. Thompson took the national championship.

But that wasn't all. Corvette took an early-season contest down in New Smyrna Beach, Florida, besting the likes of Jaguar XK-140, Thunderbird, and the vaunted Mercedes 300SL. Chevy's sports car also swept the first four places at that year's Nassau Speed Weeks and dominated C-Production at Daytona, finishing 1-2-3 in both standing-start acceleration and the flying mile. There may have been doubts about the Corvette's saleability after 1957, but there was certainly no doubting its "winability."

In almost any form, the '57 Corvette had absolutely staggering performance. *Motor Trend*'s Walt Woron clocked a 250-bhp fuelie at just 7.2 seconds in the 0-60-mph sprint. The 283-bhp version was even more incredible. *Road & Track*'s four-speed example with

Opposite page: *This General Motors Design Staff photo of a '56 Corvette (with Illinois license plates) is interesting because of the narrow-band whitewalls, which later debuted on the '59 Cadillac Eldorado Brougham. Obviously, GM already had narrow whites in mind.* **This page:** *Chevy's use of fiberglass kept the Corvette's weight down and was ideal for low-volume production.*

75

the short 4.11:1 final drive needed only 5.7 seconds in the same test, breezed through the quarter-mile in 14.3 seconds at better than 90 mph, and sailed on to a maximum of 132 mph. An *MT* car with the 283-bhp engine, dual exhausts, special cam, and solid lifters reached 134 mph, and Woron wasn't convinced that it was fully extended at that. *Sports Car Illustrated* termed its Corvette "the fastest accelerating genuine production car [this magazine] has ever tested." As *Road & Track* headlined its test: "Add fuel injection and get out of the way."

Barney Clark's Corvette advertising copy continued to push performance, with such headlines as "Lesson from Lombard Street" and "FI = 1 H.P. per CU. IN. ×

283." The former showed a 'Vette winding down San Francisco's serpentine Lombard Street hill and stressed the car's handling abilities. The second ad's cryptic headline referred to "the formula...for the most significant advance yet recorded in American sports cars. It means: The 1957 Corvette V-8 with fuel injection turns out one horsepower per cubic inch of displace-ment— and there are 283 cubic inches on tap!

"To anyone who knows cars," the ad continued, taking direct aim at sports-car enthusiasts, "that fact alone is a warranty of significant engineering. But the driver who has whipped the Corvette through a series of S-turns really knows the facts of life: This sleek powerhouse handles! Matter of fact, you can forget the

77

price tag and the proud names—no production sports car in Corvette's class can find a shorter way around the bends!"

There was certainly little to touch one of the hotter '57s in straightline acceleration. Yet as *Motor Life's* Fermoyle had said of the '56, the Corvette remained "a two-faced automobile...more suitable for duty as a high-speed touring car than earlier models [yet] closer to being a true sports car than ever before."

Road & Track praised the fuelie 283 as "an absolute jewel, quiet and remarkably docile when driven gently around town, yet instantly transformable into a roaring brute when pushed hard. It idles at about 900 rpm and pulls easily and smoothly from this speed even in high gear. Its best feature is its instantaneous throttle response, completely free of any stutter or stumble.... The throttle linkage has a certain amount of backlash and friction, but there are no flat spots such as we described in last year's [1956] test of two Corvettes with twin 4-barrel carburetors."

SCI agreed: "We were looking mainly for flat spots— the transition points in the fuel/air metering that are often among the defects of the carb-fed, rather than injected engine. There were none. The beef in the FI engine permits you to take off from standstill in top gear [three-speed transmission] just by revving up to 1500 or so and letting the clutch out slowly. Our zero to 60 (actual) time *in top gear alone* was 13.8 seconds."

Flash ahead 26 years to the eerie similarity in the comments of *Special-Interest Autos* editor Dave Emanuel on a restored '57 fuelie: "With the exhaust pipes reverberating to the engine's 750-rpm staccato idle, the whistle of air flowing through the fuel injection and the rat-a-tat of pushrods rapping against rocker arms, anyone who appreciates the beauty of a highly tuned powerplant is immediately enraptured. As you spend more time behind the wheel, the

Ramjet fuel injection proved troublesome; only a few hundred '57 Corvettes came with it, and all are highly prized collectibles now (bottom). The '57 continued with the waffle-pattern upholstery (top); note the lack of a radio in this car. The scoops in the tops of the fenders (center) are fake; cost considerations precluded making them functional as was originally intended.

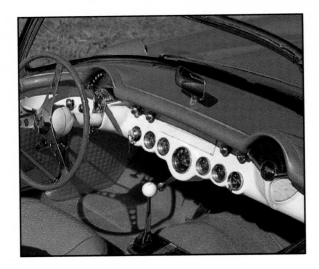

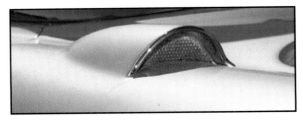

captivation grows greater, prompting you to forget the world of emissions controls and emasculating government regulations.

"Pulling away easily from a dead stop, the engine's responsiveness and eagerness to accelerate leaves no doubt that the true performance potential has been

continued on page 83

Ramjet and the 283: "1 h.p. per cu. in."

Chevy's great small-block V-8 reached its second plateau for 1957, when it was enlarged to 283 cubic inches and offered with optional Ramjet fuel injection. So equipped, it pumped out 283 horsepower and was teamed exclusively with the close-ratio three-speed manual transmission.

All Chevy V-8s featured a number of internal changes that year. Longer-reach spark plugs had metal deflection shields to protect wiring and plug caps from manifold heat, while upper blocks employed thicker castings to prevent cylinder wall distortion from overtightening of the hold-down bolts. Fuel passages were newly tapered, increasing in cross-section toward the intake ports and in the "ram's horn" exhaust manifold for improved scavenging and volumetric efficiency. There were also new carburetor fuel filters, larger ports, wider main bearings, stainless-steel expanders for piston oil-control rings, and a relocated choke to improve hot starting. Dual-exhaust engines received balance tubes that equalized flow so that both mufflers would have approximately the same service life.

"The biggest auto news of 1957" was Ramjet fuel injection, manufactured by GM's Rochester carburetor division and developed by John Dolza, E.A. Kehoe, Donald Stoltman, and Corvette chief engineer Zora Arkus-Duntov. A mechanical system, it was what we'd now call a continuous-flow multi-point type with a separate injector for each cylinder, plus special fuel meter, manifold assembly, and air meter replacing the normal carburetor and intake manifold.

Chevy's 1957 dealer sales book described Ramjet's operation this way: "The basic principle of fuel injection is to deliver fuel directly to [the] cylinder in just the right amount and under precisely controlled conditions. . . . [The injectors, or nozzles] atomize the gasoline, aiming it directly at the intake ports in a pressurized spray. The amount of fuel delivered depends on the air flow, which in turn is controlled by the accelerator. Outside air . . . flows through a special chamber which divides into separate tubes, called ram tubes, one leading to each cylinder. As the air approaches the cylinder, it mixes with fuel being continuously sprayed from the nozzle, carrying the atomized fuel directly into the cylinder in a precisely controlled air/fuel ratio. [A] fuel pump delivers fuel to each nozzle by a pressurizing pump from the fuel reservoir through a regulating system that meters it to the cylinders." A special two-piece aluminum manifold casting carried the air passages and air/fuel metering bases in its upper half, while the lower half contained the ram tubes and covered the top center of the engine.

Several advantages were claimed for Ramjet: "increased power, instant accelerator response, faster cold starts, smoother engine warm-up, elimination of carburetor icing . . . and better overall fuel economy." Volumetric efficiency was undoubtedly superior, fuelies having about five more horsepower than a comparable twin four-barrel engine with no other changes. Since there was no carburetor, of course, Chevy also claimed that fuel injection reduced stalling tendencies from momentary fuel starvation. To handle their extra power, fuelies got mechanical instead of hydraulic lifters, thicker front and intermediate main bearings (by 0.063-inch), and a special distributor with breaker points directly above the shaft bearing to help reduce gap fluctuations.

A major engineering development is seldom simple and almost never bug-free. Ramjet was no exception. Aside from the system's sheer complexity, Chevy engineer Vince Piggins noted that the injectors were "very prone to dirt, clogging, dirty fuel, and what not." Initially, they also absorbed enough heat to cause rough idling, later cured by extending them further into the air stream.

Price was another problem. At $675, Ramjet was prohibitively expensive for a late-Fifties option, especially one whose merits even the experts debated. Another problem, ironically enough, was an early announcement that sparked a sizeable demand for injectors from sister GM divisions and even other automakers, which limited Chevy's own supply and thus fuelie installations. Sometimes, it doesn't pay to be first.

Only a few hundred Ramjet engines were built for '57. Most ended up in Corvettes, where the option not only made more sense but was more palatable, given the two-seater's higher base price. Yet for all its teething troubles and slow public acceptance, Ramjet was improved. Though abandoned for Chevy passenger cars after 1958, it continued as a Corvette option all the way through 1965.

1956-57 Serial Spans, Production Figures, and Base Prices				
Year	Serial Prefix	Serial Span	Prod.	Price
1956	E56S	001001-004467	3,388	$3,149
1957	E57S	100001-106339	6,339	$3,465

The fuel injected Corvette ran a 283-cubic-inch, 283-horsepower V-8 (with 10.5:1 compression), thus good for "1 h.p. per cu. in." This achievement was shared with the '57 DeSoto Adventurer— 345 bhp from a 345-cid Hemi.

By 1957, the Corvette was finding better acceptance in the marketplace, in spite of carryover styling (opposite page)—production nearly doubled to 6339 units. This page: Features like fuel injection (bottom left) were adding a bit of glamour to the 'Vette, and although this car has a three-speed manual (bottom right), a four-speed became available during the model year. Left and below: Good lights help win rallies.

barely tapped. Moving the shift lever through the gears as you accelerate, the feeling of power diminishes only slightly thanks to the closeness of gear ratios....The engine, transmission, and rear axle seem to enjoy a symbiotic relationship, all working in harmony to yield a result that's greater than the sum of its parts."

Perspective, of course, changes with time. Emanuel credited the early Corvettes for their relative simplicity, fine throttle response, and the "raw feel of horsepower that is characteristic of a Chevy small-block fitted with a mechanical-lifter camshaft." However, he judged newer Corvettes "more enjoyable to drive. They offer more room in the cockpit, demonstrably superior handling and ride comfort and significantly better braking capability....Much of the 1957 models' handling potential is compromised by the original-equipment bias-ply tires. The car does go around corners well,

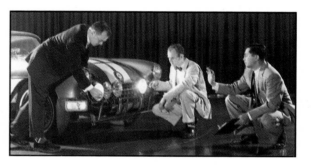

albeit with more lean that should be present in a sports car, but a set of [modern] high-performance radials... would make a world of difference....Then again...the fact that the '57 Corvette comes so close as to invite comparison [with today's Corvette] is testimony to the high caliber of its design."

Undoubtedly, 1957 marked the Corvette's arrival as a sports car respected as much by the *cognoscenti* as by the kids on the street. As one European writer put it: "Before Sebring, where we actually saw it for ourselves, the Corvette was regarded as a plastic toy. After Sebring, even the most biased were forced to admit that the Americans had one of the world's finest sports cars—as capable on the track as it was on the road. Those who drove and understood the Corvette could not help but reach that conclusion."

Corvette's great progress, both mechanical and social, was reflected in model-year 1957 production: 6339—a new record and almost double the 1956 total. Thunderbird's withdrawal from the two-seater market, which Chevrolet saw well in advance, promised at least 10,000 units for 1958, which was almost achieved despite one of the most dismal sales years in postwar Detroit history.

The 283 fuelie Corvette (both pages) was described by Road & Track *as "an absolute jewel, quiet and remarkably docile when driven gently around town, yet instantly transformable into a roaring brute when pushed hard.... Its best feature is its instantaneous throttle response."*

But there was a cloud on the horizon, and it involved racing—just when the Corvette was beginning to show its mettle. In June 1957, the Automobile Manufacturers Association, responding to critics of the Detroit "horsepower race," adopted a two-point resolution that required members to cease performance-oriented advertising as well as competition sponsorship, including technical assistance. GM president Harlow Curtice was among those voting solemnly in favor of the measure, which effectively banned all factory-sponsored racing activities.

The AMA declared that racing "oversells speed and power and undersells safety." The National Safety Council, which had been advocating just such an edict, hailed it as a "big step toward a safer America." The AMA urged buyers to "evaluate cars in terms of useful power and ability to afford safe, reliable and comfortable transportation, rather than in terms of capacity for speed," noting offending ad campaigns like Chevy's "The Hot One's Hotter" and Ford's counterclaim, "It Cools Off The Hot One."

continued on page 86

Evidence suggests that Detroit went along with this out of sheer self-interest. One unnamed executive said that competition support was costing everyone millions, and "the whole thing got to be a monkey on everybody's back." Whatever the whys and wherefores, the AMA decision threatened to kill the Corvette's blossoming competition effort. Duntov called it "a tremendous shock," though he'd never paid much mind to such executive decisions at General Motors.

continued on page 92

Show With Go:

Super Sport and SR-2

Show cars have always loomed large in Corvette history. Perhaps it's because the Corvette was born as one (the original Motorama prototype was officially GM experimental EX-122), more likely because designers and engineers find conjuring up sports cars a lot more fun than doing sedans and station wagons. (Who wouldn't?) In any case, production Corvettes down through the years—"dream machines" all—have inspired many of GM's most memorable one-of-a-kind dreams—including a few conceived mainly to gauge public reaction to plans for a new production Corvette.

That was certainly true of the three Corvette-based experiments shown at the 1954 Motorama, one of which, as mentioned elsewhere, provided a sneak preview of the optional hardtop being planned for 1956. The next Corvette show cars were a bit wilder: a pair of race-inspired designs reflecting the competition prowess of the redesigned 1956-57 production models and presented concurrently with them.

The lesser of these was the Super Sport or SS of 1957. Essentially a mildly customized version of the standard issue, it carried that year's new fuel-injected 283 V-8, four-speed manual gearbox, and heavy-duty racing suspension package. Exterior differences were confined to a low "double-bubble" windscreen, broad dorsal racing stripes, and forward-facing scoops built into the aft portions of the body-side "coves," which were finished to contrast with the otherwise all-white body. Overall, the SS looked a lot like the competition-prepped Corvettes that had appeared at Sebring and elsewhere beginning in early 1956.

Road & Track spotlighted the Super Sport in an April 1957 feature with Jaguar's then-new SS competition car, the implication being that the two might soon meet on some race track. They wouldn't, mainly because Chevy had some-

thing even better: the slinky but ultimately unsuccessful Sebring SS (see Chapter 13) and an open job designated SR-2.

One of the first projects completed at GM's new Warren, Michigan, Technical Center, the SR-2 was originally built for Harley Earl's son Jerry in March 1956. Though recognizably related to the production Corvette, it was far more aggres-sive, with a longer snout, a wider and "toothier" grille, and a huge "shark" fin capping a racing-style driver's headrest, faired into the bodywork just aft of the cockpit on the left. "Cove" scoops and double-bubble windscreen were also featured (and would be picked up for the aforementioned '57 show car). Chassis design and drivetrain components borrowed heavily from the Sebring SS.

The SR-2 looked ready to race, and it did. Bill Mitchell, who'd soon succeed Jerry's father as head of GM Styling, put white paint scallops on the front, making the racy red roadster look something like a racing airplane. He also fitted headlight domes and flat wheel discs for better aerodynamics and added small, quadruple side-exit exhausts just aft of the front wheels. For cold-weather events, there was a special canopy running forward from the headrest to mate with a higher, single-bubble windscreen.

The canopy arrangement was unnecessary at the 1957 Daytona Speed Weeks, where the SR-2 turned in a creditable performance despite inadequate preparation time. Buck Baker averaged 93.047 mph to win the modified-class standing mile and placed second in the flying mile at 152.866 mph, bested only by a D-Type Jaguar. The car was better prepared for Sebring on March 23, where Pete Lovely brought it home 16th after 12 hours of time-consuming pit stops.

There was also a second SR-2, constructed at about the same time for GM president Harlow Curtice. It carried similar side and nose treatments, plus a more modest shark fin mounted centrally, but was otherwise a standard '57 Corvette hardtop. Wheels were chrome Dayton wires with genuine knock-off hubs. The Earl car rolled on Halibrand magnesium rims.

Though the fate of the Curtice car is unclear, the original SR-2 passed briefly into Bill Mitchell's hands. With his personal sponsorship, it raced for several more years at places like Daytona, Sebring, and Road America, though with no notable success. It was ultimately acquired by race-driver Jim Jeffords (who'd driven the 15th-place Corvette at Sebring '57, along with Dale Duncan and John Kilborn).

Mitchell, meantime, got hold of the "mule" chassis left over from the abortive Sebring SS effort, on which he built the racing Stingray that inspired the production 1963 Corvette. That, however, is a story for another chapter.

The Corvette SR-2's most prominent styling features were the aerodynamic-looking fin behind the driver, which doubled as a headrest, and the low-cut racing windshields. The dash panel (top) was much modified from stock.

Needless to say, the SR-2 utilized Chevy's new fuel injection system (above). The car (right) was seen, not only at auto shows, but also on the road and in competition on the track at Sebring, Daytona, and Road America. Jerry Earl's SR-2 racing special (far right) utilized a Corvette Sebring competition chassis.

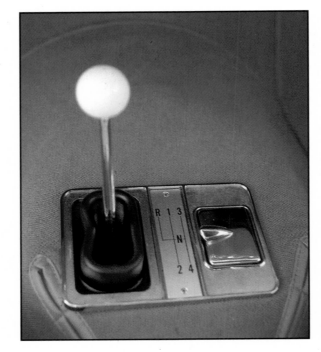

To no one's great surprise, the industry's self-imposed "ban" was soon being circumvented as easily as thirsty drinkers had gotten around Prohibition. Racing development at Chevrolet and elsewhere continued unabated. The only real change was a turn from open to under-the-table assistance to drivers and car owners. Duntov himself saw to it that anyone who wanted a racing Corvette could have one by checking the right options, and he began working on new goodies. He also continued to appear "casually" at numerous races, where other GM executives could also be spotted in or near the pits.

While GM did downplay competition in the years immediately following the AMA edict, Duntov's enthusiasm for the Corvette never waned. Nor did his desire to make the Corvette a winner—not only in America but worldwide. And of course, the ban hardly disconnected his busy telephone, through which he reportedly dispensed priceless technical advice and (it's said with a chuckle) made the occasional arrangement with promising racers for "back-door" parts.

The last major Fifties event at which an American production car ran as an official factory entry was the

Major Specifications: 1956-57 Corvette

Body/Chassis

Frame:	Box-section, X-braced
Body:	Glass-reinforced plastic, 2-seat convertible
Front suspension:	Independent; unequal-length A-arms, coil springs, tubular hydraulic shock absorbers, anti-roll bar
Rear suspension:	Live axle on semi-elliptic leaf springs, anti-roll bar, tubular hydraulic shock absorbers
Wheels:	15-inch bolt-on steel
Tires:	6.70 × 15 4-ply

Dimensions

Wheelbase (in.):	102.0
Overall length (in.):	168.0
Overall height (in.):	51.9
Overall width (in.):	70.5
Track front/rear (in.):	57.0/59.0
Ground clearance (in.):	6.0
Curb weight (lbs):	2730-2850

Engines

Type:	ohv 90-degree V-8, water-cooled, cast-iron block and head	
Main bearings:	5	
Bore × stroke (in.):	3.75 × 3.00	3.875 × 3.00
Displacement (ci):	265	283
Compression ratio:	9.25/9.5:1	9.5/10.5:1
Brake horsepower @ rpm:	210 @ 5600—240 @ 5200	220 @ 4800—283 @ 6200
Induction system:	1 or 2 4-barrel Rochester carburetor, Ramjet continuous-flow fuel injection (1957 only)	
Exhaust system:	Single or dual	
Electrical system:	Delco-Remy 12-volt	

Driveline

Transmission:	3-speed manual	4-speed manual (late 1957 only)	2-speed Powerglide automatic
Gear ratios:	First—2.20:1	First—2.20:1	First—1.82:1
	Second—1.31:1	Second—1.66:1	Second—1.00:1
	Third—1.00:1	Third—1.31:1	
		Fourth—1.00:1	
Rear axle type:	Hypoid semi-floating		
Rear axle ratio:	3.70:1 (4.56, 4.11, and 3.55 optional)		
Steering:	Saginaw worm-and-ball, 16:1 ratio		
Turning circle (ft):	37		
Brakes:	4-wheel hydraulic, internal-expanding drums, 11-in. diameter; 157 sq. in. effective lining area (121 sq. in. with optional sintered-metallic linings)		

Performance (283 bhp/3-speed)

0-60 mph (sec):	5.9—8.9
0-¼-mile (sec @ mph):	15.8 @ 88—14.2 @ 95
Top speed (mph):	121-135
Fuel consumption (mpg):	10-16

Opposite page: By 1957, the Corvette (top and center) had evolved into a true race-and-ride machine in the traditional sense. Yet, its styling was uniquely American, and so was its gutsy V-8. Refinements to the suspension resulted in handling that even hard-nosed Europeans had to respect, and the fuel injection was a state-of-the-art touch. The arrival of the four-speed gearbox in 1957 (bottom) completed the maturation process of the fledgling Corvette.

Grand Prix of Endurance at Sebring on March 23, 1957. Two Corvette Supersport test cars were in the race, which was won by a 4.5-liter Maserati. "The Corvettes were the latest creation of Chevrolet Division of General Motors," reported *The New York Times*. "They were described as the first real threat to European sports car supremacy."

It was one of those rare occasions when the *Times* was late with the news. Recall the use of "dual-purpose" by *Road & Track* and *SCI*'s Ludvigsen to describe the '56 Corvette. Yet if Chevy's sports car had become a genuine race-and-ride machine in the time-honored tradition, it was still unmistakably American in its styling, performance, and sheer visceral appeal. It had taken five years, but the Corvette could no longer be accused of trying to imitate anything from Europe. From here on, it would seldom be confused with anything else on the road.

Personality
Zora Arkus-Duntov

The postwar automotive world has been characterized as one of companies run by anonymous "yes men" in gray flannel suits carrying briefcases. No longer are cars designed by gifted individuals working alone. Today they're the products of committees—compromises that some say show all too clearly how too many cooks spoil a broth. To a large extent, this view is correct. After World War II, automobiles became too complicated and the business of building them too vast for successful one- or two-person efforts like those of Ettore Bugatti, W.O. Bentley, the brothers Duesenberg, and other prewar legends.

The Corvette has been no exception. Though its impetus came mainly from two individuals, Harley Earl and Ed Cole, it's always been very much a "committee car." Still, its evolution and commercial success reflect the fact that the Corvette committee has most always been composed of very talented individuals who've worked well together.

That said, Zora Arkus-Duntov emerges as the original "Mr. Corvette." Certainly, no one like him had ever been employed by Chevrolet Division, and it's doubtful anyone like him will ever be again. Like the car itself, Duntov is one of a kind—the man who above all others made the Corvette a respected sports car at home and abroad.

Duntov did not participate in the Corvette's birth, though he was on the scene. Not that there was much in his background to suggest that he even had a place at Chevrolet Division, an outfit that had built comfortable, reliable, workaday transportation for three generations.

Born in Belgium, Duntov had worked for that British "blacksmith," Sydney Allard, collaborating in the development of the appropriately named Ardun cylinder-head conversion used to soup up the flathead Ford V-8. He came to Chevrolet's attention shortly after Ed Cole became division chief engineer, when Duntov submitted a paper on high-performance engines for Cole's review. Was there a place for Duntov on the new tech-oriented Chevy engineering team? There was, but not until he'd dickered long and hard over salary and benefits. Chevrolet had not been in the habit of employing expensive European high-performance engineers. But Cole had carte blanche from Tom Keating and Harlow Curtice for a massive upgrade and enlargement of Chevrolet Engineering. Duntov came aboard.

Duntov's initial judgment of the 1953 Corvette reminds one of the way that Ken Richardson viewed the prototype 1953 Triumph TR2: "I think that it's the most bloody awful car I've ever driven." Duntov has since been publicly kinder to the '53 Corvette than Richardson was to the TR2, but it's no secret that GM retirees tend to have kind thoughts about their old company. In fact, the first Corvette's handling was abominable, and Duntov immediately set about correcting it—unofficially at first. He was hired to work on the full Chevrolet line, where the Corvette was but a peripheral product.

Duntov was not only a superb engineer but a capable racing driver. In 1956, for example, he and Betty Skelton drove modified Corvettes at better than 150 miles per hour at the Daytona Speed Weeks. The feat marked the birth of the famous "Duntov cam," which enhanced the performance of Chevy's new small-block V-8—and its reputation among hot-rod types. In 1957 he became involved with track-testing of the futuristic Corvette-based SS racer at Sebring, although the car retired after only 23 laps.

When the Automobile Manufacturer's Association agreed that its members should cease all racing activities and performance advertising in the spring of 1957, Duntov advocated violating the edict in secrecy. He was soon involved with GM's "closet" NASCAR program and other under-the-table competition efforts, which helped end the impractical and ill-conceived AMA ban by the mid-Sixties.

Zora Arkus-Duntov retired in 1974 after almost 20 years as chief Corvette engineer. But his energy is that of a much younger man and he remains very close to the company and to the car. His product accomplishments are too numerous to recount in full, so we'll confine ourselves to highlights. Duntov created the prototype mid-engine Corvette Q-model of 1960, and he still regrets that it was never produced. He designed the 1963 Sting Ray chassis, which remained in production essentially unchanged for 20 years. More recently he lent his name to the Duntov Corvette, a conversion that turns a stock, post-1975 coupe into a rip-snorting powerhouse with full roadster bodywork.

What follows is the result of several interviews with Zora Arkus-Duntov over the years. The authors, editors, and Mr. Duntov covered all aspects of the Corvette—a vivid experience, reflecting his remarkable drive and personality.

Editor: Why did you leave Allard and join General Motors?

Zora Arkus-Duntov: I wished to return to America. I had talked to an American general who was stationed in England, and he told me to write to Ed Cole at Chevrolet. I did, but it was not promising. I found a position with Fairchild Aviation, and after I had been in the States for some time, I sent to Ed Cole a copy of a research report on high-performance engines which I had written. We discussed salary and benefits for some time before I accepted. I came to GM in May 1953.

Ed: What did you think of the new Corvette at that time?

Duntov: That it was the most beautiful car I had ever seen. The engine was a letdown, but the proportions and aesthetics were right. I borrowed one in May, when I first joined GM. The handling was not good. I took it upon myself to give this car better handling. This was not part of my normal assignment—just fiddling on the side.

Ed: When, then, did you formalize the Corvette relationship?

Duntov: On the '55, when I was assigned to investigate exhaust staining on the rear of the fenders, which was connected with fumes in the passenger compartment. I attached streamers to a test car and took motion pictures of the air flow. If you opened the vent pane, the exhaust was carried from the rear to the front and into the passenger compartment. Moving the exhaust tips to the very rear of the fenders on the 1956 model corrected both problems.

Ed: Tell us about the Duntov cam.

Duntov: I wished to start building a racing image and to exceed 150 mph at the Daytona Speed Weeks. I calculated that I needed an additional 30 horsepower from the 265 V-8 in high-performance trim. I changed the camshaft design to hold the valves open longer, but not to lift them higher. This provided a fuller valve-opening curve. Engine speed rose to 6500 rpm, and I had the horsepower I needed. But the Corvette was still too heavy for racing, and we were not ready yet.

Ed: So you kept testing and had that terrible accident?

Duntov: Yes, in April 1956. It was my own fault. I arrived at the Proving Grounds to make carburetor tests and found that this car had no seat belts. It had experimental disc brakes. There were many things wrong with this car. Still, I drove it. Sure, like hell. I got sideways and went off the track. I was in a cast for six months. I couldn't bend. I had strings to lift my dress in the rest room. I was quite a sight.

Ed: But you kept working, especially on fuel injection.

Duntov: The fuel-injection project had top priority, because we needed it on both the 1957 Corvette and Chevrolet passenger cars.

Ed: Why didn't the fuel injection work out?

Duntov: It was too expensive. In 1965, when it was dropped, the option cost almost $500 extra. For only $150, we could offer the big-block with more power and torque at lower speeds. The fuel-injection engine had to be wound up first. The big engine was superior. It was not the bugs that killed fuel injection. They could have been worked out.

Ed: How did the Sebring Corvette SS come about?

Duntov: Harley Earl had a D-Type Jaguar and wanted us to fit it with a Corvette V-8. This was absurd, and I said that if Chevrolet wanted to go racing, we should build an entire car. The SS was the result—a combined project between Styling and Engineering.

Ed: Did Styling influence aerodynamics?

Duntov: No. I had them build a full-size model for aerodynamic testing, so that I could have some input on this body. I had them use considerable tuck-under to achieve maximum air velocity under the car. They did not want to do this at first. I could see that they would not have the car ready in time for testing, so I put the test body on a spare chassis.

Ed: And that was the famous "mule"?

Duntov: Yes. It was not a beautiful car, but Juan Fangio and Stirling Moss beat the Sebring track record with it.

Ed: But Fangio did not drive it in the actual race?

Duntov: As the race got closer and Styling failed to complete the car, Fangio feared that it would not be ready and asked to be released from his contract. Carroll Shelby was also signed and released. Finally, the drivers were John Fitch and Piero Taruffi, but that over-tight bushing failed after 23 laps.

Ed: Were there long-range plans for the SS?

Duntov: Yes, I was preparing four SS cars to compete at Le Mans, under a fictitious name. But it really was a terrible lifter. Right away I lost interest in this car. It's beautiful all right, but [it has] the profile of a wing. I drove the Corvette SS racer at the proving grounds at 183 mph, and I ran about 155 mph at the opening of the Daytona track in 1959. But the AMA ruling in 1957 was a tremendous shock. Until 1961, I promoted racing in secrecy.

Ed: Why did the AMA ban finally come apart at GM?

Duntov: Bunkie Knudsen replaced Ed Cole as general manager of Chevrolet in 1961. Both wanted to see Corvettes winning races. Knudsen approved a plan for another pure-racing Corvette. I wanted to build at least 100 specials that would weigh only 2000 pounds and which would have powerful new engines. That was the start of the Corvette Grand Sport.

Ed: What happened to the Grand Sport program? Why was it cut?

Duntov: Higher management.

Ed: Didn't Carroll Shelby approach Chevrolet with the Cobra idea before he went to Ford?

Duntov: Yes. He got two chassis from us and had them

bodied in Italy, but nothing ever came of that project. He settled with Ford instead.

Ed: When did work begin on the first Sting Ray?

Duntov: Both chassis and engine work began in 1959. I had by then been named director of high-performance vehicles. I took pride in the small-block Chevrolet engine.

Ed: What do you recall about designing the Sting Ray chassis?

Duntov: Mainly that everything worked as designed—it lasted up to the 1982 model. In 1962 we produced the Grand Sport with the disc brakes, vented in front, solid at the rear. In '64 we had the Girling Brake Company throw their hands in the air and say they couldn't make discs because Corvettes have too much weight for their performance. I worked with Kelsey-Hayes, and they succeeded in providing excellent brakes for the Corvette.

Ed: But the brakes were by Delco, weren't they?

Duntov: Kelsey-Hayes did not get the contract because Delco Division [of GM] used their leverage. Delco produced a brake identical to Kelsey-Hayes'. For '65 we produced four-wheel disc brakes, and they were so good they stayed until 1982. With the mid-engine Corvette we used a Bendix brake identical to the Delco brake—four pads per caliper.

Ed: Overall, how did you view the '63 Sting Ray?

Duntov: The ergonomics were very good. It was quite adequate as an envelope, with such things as a shift lever location that would fall into the hand readily, good legibility of the gauges, and performance that was nonpareil overall.

Ed: Did you like Mitchell's styling?

Duntov: Overall, we were on the same wavelength. I only remember one disagreement— the split window on the '63 Sting Ray [coupe]. We took it out [of the '64 model].

Ed: What was your opinion of the 1968 Corvette styling?

Duntov: As a whole, design-wise, it was a very good car. Something got lost in the ergonomics, though. You had to move to operate the gearshift. At that time, Bill Mitchell was

impressed by supersonic jets. The first thing I did was to provide more shoulder room. It was so pinched you couldn't drive it without leaning. To gain a half-inch per side, I spent $120,000 retooling door inners. This half an inch was very significant. Another consideration: The '63-'67 car was a terrible "lifter" aerodynamically. The subsequent design was also a lifter, but not to that extent.

Ed: How important was racing?

Duntov: At that time, very important. I considered that it was necessary. To establish the sports car, you have to race it. After a car gets established, like in the mid-Seventies, the racing is second place. We had all the optional items to enable people to race. CERV 1 [an experimental open-wheel single-seat racer] was the progenitor of the Sting Ray suspension-wise.

Ed: Did you like GM's experimental rotary engine?

Duntov: Not at all. But as things began to shape up in '71, I had either a mid-engine car and a rotary engine or not at all. Therefore, I had to accept the rotary engine. Ed Cole [by then, GM president] was enamored with the rotary engine. Therefore, I showed him the two- and four-rotor Corvettes. The four-rotor engine was interchangeable with a reciprocating engine; it could easily be replaced with the small-block V-8. When GM got off the Wankel kick, they went back to a reciprocating engine. The Aerovette [the four-rotor design] got a 400-cid small-block engine. It also had the space to accept four-wheel drive. I told them . . . four-wheel drive [would be important in the future]. First with rear-wheel drive and, two years later, four-wheel drive. If you look at the Aerovette, you see a big tunnel to fit four-wheel drive. But it was just a styling exercise. The mid-engine Corvette minus energy-absorbent bumpers was under 3000 pounds with the 400 or 350 small-block. Torsional stiffness was in the area of 6000 pounds-feet per degree. It was a very good car. It had good luggage space. When I think about it, it's a pity it did

not come about.

Ed: Who killed the mid-engine design?

Duntov: In '74, I had a conversation with the chairman of the board [Thomas A. Murphy]. He said, "Let's wait. Right now we cannot build enough cars to satisfy the demand. When we see the demand will slacken, we'll bring the mid-engine car out." I disagreed with him. I thought Chevrolet should be at the forefront, but he had the last word.

Ed: What do you think of the newest Corvette, and what would you have done differently with it?

Duntov: Very good. I tried to promulgate the mid-engine car. If I was not forced to retire, [the 1984 model] would probably be a mid-engine car. The mid-engine design in '69 and '73-'74 was in the picture on and off. I think I would have won the fight given time, but, unfortunately, I was forced to retire. Styling-wise, aerodynamic-wise, [the '84 generation] is excellent. It is ergonomically well thought out. The chassis is not as good as I wish it were. But second guessing is unfair. . . . Digital gauges I don't care for at all. They're good for slow-moving processes, like fuel gauge, clock, or oil level. But the speedometer and tach should have round faces to show where you have been and where you are going. Instantaneous readouts have no place in a sports car.

Ed: What do you think the next Corvette will be like?

Duntov: By the time they get the money I will be already dead and buried. . . . Chassis-wise, the previous Corvette [Duntov's own design] lived from 1963 to 1982. The amortization of the tooling happened in one year. In subsequent years, it was gravy. The [current] Corvette will live maybe 20 years—I don't know. As for product costs, the '63 Corvette [came in] less than the '62 Corvette. It sounds incongruous with independent rear suspension and everything, but with the front suspension I made up the cost of the independent [rear] suspension. Using suspension pieces of earlier cars was very cost-effective.

CHAPTER 5

CORVETTE SUPER SPORT: DREAMS OF GLORY

hevrolet was riding high in 1956. Though barely a year old, Ed Cole's brilliant 265-cubic-inch small-block V-8 had already won performance laurels for the division in NASCAR stock-car racing and in events like the annual Pikes Peak Hill Climb. Now the newly V-8-powered Corvette sports car began adding to this growing performance reputation with slick new '56 styling, courtesy of General Motors design chief Harley Earl, and a more competent chassis engineered by Zora Arkus-Duntov.

The payoffs were dramatic. As recounted in the previous chapter, Dr. Dick Thompson, in the first of what would be many Corvette drives for him, took a near-stock '56 to a surprising first-in-class and second overall at Pebble Beach against the best racing hardware Europe could muster. Perhaps even more impressive was the ninth-place finish by Walt Hansgen and John Fitch at the 1956 Sebring 12 Hours of Endurance.

But Cole, recently promoted from chief engineer to Chevy general manager, knew that there was no way a stock Corvette could ever win Sebring outright. The competition was just too strong. Chevy's sports car might do well in the production classes or even the Modified category, but sophisticated, purpose-designed racers like the birdcage Maserati, 3.0-liter Ferrari, and Jaguar D-Type would inevitably cross the finish line first.

Cole, however, was a great believer in the old Detroit maxim, "Race on Sunday, Sell on Monday." So was Harley Earl, who'd been afflicted with racing fever ever since the Collier brothers exposed him to it. Both executives were big Corvette boosters, and from the sales standpoint, the Corvette needed all the boosting it could get in '56. Encouraged by the stock car's strong showing at Sebring, Earl set in motion a series of events that led to an all-out assault on the Florida enduro with one of the most singular cars GM would ever build: the Corvette Super Sport.

In retrospect, the SS was one of those expensive indulgences for which GM was so often criticized in the mid-Fifties. Though the company possessed some of the best design and engineering talent anywhere, GM was relatively new to the production sports-car business, let alone experienced with purpose-built long-distance racers. But for Cole and Earl, the lure of Sebring was irresistible.

Other than the fabled 24 Hours of Le Mans, Sebring was the most important international sports-car race of those days. Run on a bumpy old airport course near the central Florida town, it attracted competitors from around the world, with the most prestigious marques usually well represented, all vying for the acclaim and notoriety associated with a Sebring win. Duntov also knew that a good showing at this one event would be a tremendous boost to the Corvette's image—and sales. More than anything, he wanted his car to be respected, not regarded as a mere plastic toy the way some had viewed the 1953-55 models.

Ironically, though, Duntov was nowhere near as eager as Cole and Earl to mount a full-fledged factory-based Corvette competition program. "I was not the driving force in 'Let's Go Racing,'" he told writer Karl Ludvigsen many years later. "I was reluctantly pushed into it."

That was not the impression he gave in public. Consider these comments from Duntov's address to the Society of Automotive Engineers in September 1953, only a few months after Corvette production began: "All commercially successful sports cars [have been] promoted by participation in racing with specialized or modified cars....Even if the vast majority of sports car buyers do not intend to race them, and most likely will never drive them flat out, the potential performance of the car, or the recognized and publicized performance of its sister—the racing sports car—is of primordial value to its owner. The owner of such a car can peacefully let everybody pass him, still feeling the proud king of the road, his ego and pride of ownership being inflated by racing glory."

Dreams of glory must have occupied Harley Earl in the spring of 1956, for he managed to borrow the Jaguar D-Type that had placed third at Sebring just weeks before. Owned by Jack Ensley of Indianapolis, who'd driven it in Florida with 1955 Indy winner Bob Sweikert, the bright-yellow machine was brought to Earl's Styling Staff area *sans* engine, which had been removed, the victim of overrevving. Earl's idea was to slot in a new Chevy V-8, modify the British bodywork, and race the Jag at Sebring '57 as an "experimental Corvette."

The Corvette SS (opposite) was built specifically to go racing at Sebring, Florida. Zora Arkus-Duntov (below, to the left) and other Chevy engineers worked long hours at the Chevrolet Engineering Center to make the SS race-ready for the '57 contest.

This page: The Corvette SS was developed as project XP-64. Styling at first borrowed much from the D-Type racing Jaguar, but the first full-scale clay model looked more like the production 1956 'Vette. The SS, however, was distinguished by a long bullet-style headrest, hidden headlamps, modified side "coves," a toothy Corvette-style grille, and an elongated snout. Opposite page: The SS underwent wind tunnel tests in December 1956 (top row), which showed that lift was moderate and drag about the same as the D-Type Jag. A tubular space frame was utilized, as was a de Dion rear axle and 1956 Chrysler Center-Plane front-wheel drum brakes. The rear brakes were mounted inboard.

To that end, the D-Type was first sent to Bob McLean's Research Studio for evaluation. Then, in June '56, it went to "Studio Z," which was assigned to devise the actual conversion. As Bob Cumberford, one of the designers there (and today a columnist for *Automobile* magazine), later told Ludvigsen: "We were supposed to figure out how to install a Corvette engine, convert the steering to left-hand drive, and disguise the body so no one would ever guess it was a Jaguar—all without changing the aerodynamic qualities!"

These tasks were accomplished, but all for nought. The reason was Harry Barr, Cole's replacement as Chevy chief engineer. When Barr got wind of Earl's project, he hurriedly called Duntov, then vacationing in New York City. "Harley Earl wants to put one of our engines in a Jaguar and run it at Sebring," he told Duntov. "What do you think about it?" Evidently not much, for Duntov rushed back to Detroit and drew up his own proposal for a special all-Chevy sports/racing Corvette, which Ludvigsen says may have been what Earl was angling for all along. Regardless, management approved Duntov's persuasive proposal, and the yellow D-Type was returned to its owner.

By July, Chevy designers and engineers were hard at

work on what had been designated project XP-64. Styling, evolved under Clare MacKichan, was initially much like the racing Jaguar's in sketches, with the same swoopy cigar-like profile and a prominent driver's headrest capped by a large trailing fin. The first full-scale clay model looked more like the production '56 Corvette, but sported a long bullet-style headrest, twin exhaust pipes exiting each bodyside "cove," hidden headlamps, and a wider rendition of the toothy Corvette grille in an elongated snout. This basic design would persist through XP-64's completion, though the original fully open rear wheelarches were made

semi-enclosed, and the external exhausts were moved down a bit and the coves given detachable covers to hide them.

Dimensionally, XP-64 was quite compact. Wheelbase was initially pegged at 90 inches, but this was eventually trimmed to just 72 inches—a full 30 inches shorter than on the production Corvette. For long-distance events, MacKichan designed a clear bubble canopy of the sort then common on GM show cars, with a rear cutout for the headrest. With this in place, the SS stood just 48.7 inches tall; without it, overall height was a mere 36 inches.

This page: The Corvette SS required many unique parts (top). The brakes were of the two-leading-shoe type. They gave better response than the duo-servo units fitted to most American cars. Opposite page: The transmission case was made of aluminum to save weight (top left). The 283 V-8 boasted fuel injection; output came to 307 bhp at 6400 rpm (top right). The SS used variable-rate coil springs at all four corners (bottom left). The tubular steel exhaust system (bottom right) saved weight and added about 20 bhp.

There was no time for working out the intricacies of the Jaguar-style full monocoque structure that Duntov wanted for reasons of strength and minimum weight. A separate frame was desirable anyway, since body changes to fine-tune aerodynamics might require major under-skin alterations. Accordingly, a Mercedes-Benz 300SL tubular frame was selected as the starting point for the SS chassis. In final form, however, the revised platform resembled its German parent only in having a pyramidal cowl structure and a truss-type latticework beneath each (conventional) door. Square instead of tubular sections were used to facilitate the mounting of brake servos, suspension, and other components, and the use of chrome-moly steel held total frame weight to a reasonable 180 pounds.

Weight-saving measures figured extensively throughout the SS. For example, the body was made of sheet magnesium rather than the 'Vette's highly touted fiberglass. (GRP was used for the fuel tank, however.) Magnesium also appeared in the engine's special oil pan, whose finned bottom cover contained a maze of cooling passages. The sump itself was cast with two one-way lateral baffles, or doors, to prevent oil starvation in hard cornering, a feature later to be incorporated on production Corvettes. Aluminum was used for the specially designed cylinder heads, stock water pump, the clutch housing, transmission case, and radiator. The last included a separate oil-cooling

section and, because of its steeply raked-forward mounting (necessary to clear the low nose), a cylindrical coolant header tank.

Suspension was fairly straightforward, with the usual upper and lower A-arms in front, a semi-independent de Dion rear axle, coil springs all-round, and an anti-roll bar at each end. All components, including bushings and mounting hardware, were specially crafted, however, and the springs were wound so that the coils "collapsed" over each other on upward wheel deflection —an early example of what we now call variable-rate springing. Duntov would have ordinarily preferred all-independent suspension for the bumpy Sebring course, but settled for the de Dion axle as sturdier for long hauls—mainly the 24-hour go at Le Mans in June '57, where he hoped the SS might compete after a successful Sebring debut. GM's Saginaw Division supplied a special recirculating-ball steering gear with a fast overall ratio of 12.0:1. This was linked to a height-adjustable steering column with a quick-release steering wheel mechanism to speed entry/exit and thus driver changes during a race.

Duntov wanted disc brakes to counter the racing Jaguars. But though GM's Delco-Moraine Division had been experimenting with discs, there was no time to develop a sufficiently reliable system for Sebring. This left conventional drum brakes the only choice. Trouble was, the usual American duo-servo type was deemed less desirable than a twin-leading-shoe mechanism, and Chevy had no such parts on its shelf. But Chrysler did, so Highland Park's beefy 1956 "Center-Plane" front brakes—a foot in diameter and 2.5 inches wide—were used at all four wheels of the XP-64. Rear binders were mounted inboard to minimize unsprung weight. Brake cooling was provided via a heat-dissipating aluminum "muff" around each drum, plus transverse fins on the outer surfaces of the front brakes and strategically placed body air ducts fore and aft. All braking surfaces were cast iron, carried on sheet-steel face plates.

The SS brake system also incorporated two rather predictive features. One was separate front and rear servos and hydraulic lines, anticipating a federal requirement for production cars in the late Sixties. The other was a kind of primitive anti-lock braking system (ABS)—completely mechanical, of course, rather than electronic as on today's various ABS setups. A special air link was employed to keep rear braking effort proportional to front braking force in a fixed ratio of 30 to 70. Deceleration triggered a cockpit-mounted mercury switch linked to an electric valve in the rear brakes' servo cylinder; when closed, the valve left the cylinder in a predetermined position, which prevented delivery of any further hydraulic assist to the back wheels, thus helping to forestall lockup. The mercury switch was angled slightly forward, and its degree of

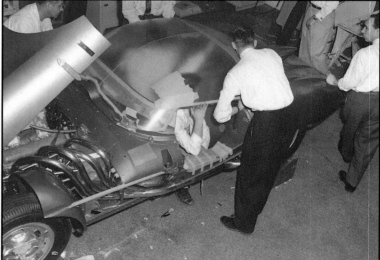

tilt could be altered to compensate for changed fore/aft weight distribution caused by fuel usage during a race, as well as for the onset of slippery track conditions or changes in tire characteristics.

Mechanically, there was no question that the XP-64 would carry the enlarged 283-cid small-block V-8 slated for production 1957 Corvettes, and its new Rochester "Ramjet" fuel injection system. However, Duntov envisioned more complex intake manifolds, with straighter ram pipes that crossed each other to feed separate plenum chambers, each with its own air-metering venturi; the manifolds, in turn, would connect to a special hood air intake. But wind-tunnel tests of the prototype SS body at the GM Tech Center showed

Opposite page: *The de Dion rear axle was curved to go around the Halibrand quick-change rear differential casting (top left). The dash featured a huge tach and a novel rear-view mirror. The body can be seen on both pages in various states of completion. A plastic top was devised to meet Sebring rules, which called for a roof on every sports car entered. This page: The SS, which weighed just 1850 pounds dry, approaches completion. Note the side-mounted exhausts.*

that the hood intake was ineffective due to unfavorable aerodynamic flow at the proposed location, so Duntov had to settle for production-stock manifolds. However, these were fed from special ducts in the grille, which provided enough "ram effect" to add 10 horsepower at 150 mph. Valve sizes were stock 283, as was the rest of the SS engine except for the special aluminum cylinder

heads, whose ports were given a mild "tulip" shape that further improved output. Exhaust valves received heat-dissipating aluminum inserts. For long-distance reliability, compression was kept to a modest 9.0:1.

All this resulted in a rated 307 horsepower at 6400 rpm, versus 283 bhp for the production '57 fuelie, which ran on 10.5:1 compression. Because final curb

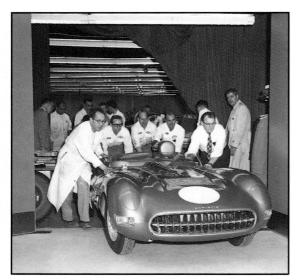

weight came in at a satisfactory 1850 pounds, about 100 pounds lighter than the Jaguar D-Type, the SS promised to be competitively fast.

The rest of the drivetrain was fairly orthodox. A heavy-duty single-spring clutch with hydraulic actuation took drive from the engine flywheel to a four-speed manual gearbox with special ratios (1.87:1, 1.54:1, 1.22:1, and 1.00:1), then back to a conventional differential with racing-type Halibrand quick-change case. A limited-slip differential was planned but, again, there was no time to have it fully ready for Sebring. The driveshaft was open, as on the production Corvette. With the de Dion axle, the differential was frame-mounted, which further reduced unsprung weight. Chevy made its own ring and pinion gears and quick-change final gearsets, which ranged in ratio from 2.63:1 to 4.80:1. The final drive chosen for Sebring was

3.55:1, deemed appropriate for that circuit given the internal transmission ratios.

Duntov had planned to use the March 1957 Florida race as a shakedown for the SS before contesting Le Mans in June. Chevy's futuristic racer was thus entered in the prototype class, along with a brace of production models again running in the GT category. John Fitch was selected as team manager, but Duntov was on hand to supervise the entire operation, which got underway with preliminary track testing in mid-February.

Because development had been so frenzied, Duntov deemed this pre-race testing vital. Without it, the SS would surely make a poor showing. GM officials had approved construction of only one car, but Duntov, ever the corporate conniver, managed to get approval for enough spare parts to construct a second, if

Opposite page: Zora Arkus-Duntov drives and looks over the SS (top row). It is shown (bottom) lapping the track at Sebring in March 1957. The interior (center) featured thin-shell bucket seats and complete instrumentation. This page: The finished SS shows off its sleek lines in this overhead view, which highlights the sculptured look of the hood and fenders as well as showing the air vents in the hood.

incomplete, SS for testing purposes. Karl Ludvigsen records that this second SS was hardly a "real" car: "Its interior was a mass of tubes and mismatched instruments; its body was rough fiberglass with no doors and no rear-deck cover, mounted over a one-inch plywood firewall. The 'Mule,' as it was known, was 150 pounds heavier than the race car and was down on horsepower, but had its full quota of Chevrolet/Duntov engineering."

The Mule proved to be a very shrewd move on Duntov's part—perhaps prescient. As Ludvigsen notes: "Construction of the actual race car took so long that without the Mule, little would have been learned about the [SS] design before Sebring. The Mule disclosed some faults in the cooling and braking systems, in time to rectify them in the race car. At one point, its aluminum cylinder heads were cooked by overheating caused by an incorrectly made radiator header tank, and were replaced by stock iron heads. All in all, some 2000 test miles were put on the Mule in Florida, most by Zora himself."

Meantime, continuing delays in completing the actual racing SS forced a change in drivers. Understandably seeking to give its new showcase sports/racer the best possible chance for outright victory, Chevy had signed the incredibly talented Juan Manuel Fangio to drive the SS at Sebring. It seemed a smart move, especially when the Formula 1 ace made a practice run and nipped his own lap record, set the previous year in a Ferrari—this with the overweight, underpowered Mule. Suddenly, the pits were abuzz about the new Corvette special. The great Stirling Moss, late of Mercedes-Benz fame and Fangio's choice as co-driver, turned in similarly promising practice laps. Despite the Mule's incomplete nature, both drivers commented favorably on its dynamic behavior, but both still ended up in Maseratis on race day. The reason was that Fangio's contract with Chevy was conditional on his approving the car. With no race-ready SS in sight, Fangio begged off and Chevy released him (and Moss) to Maserati. Fitch agreed to take over as lead driver, and suggested Piero Taruffi as his relief. The Italian veteran dutifully answered the call despite having to travel some 6000 miles on very short notice.

Soon the race car was traveling, too—being trucked to Florida at last. It arrived, in Ludvigsen's words, "at the absolute last minute, the men of Styling and Chevrolet laboring inside the van on the way down, in the tradition of the cars for the Motoramas, to ensure that it met 'GM standards of appearance.' The SS was a beautiful machine by anybody's standards, but when it arrived it was still not a finished racing car." Despite overtime work by Duntov and the pit crew, Fitch was still trying to sort out inconsistent braking behavior almost up to the moment of the running Le Mans-type start. Sizzling heat within the magnesium-clad cockpit had already prompted some last-minute body alterations that looked very un-Motorama.

"Waiting anxiously there, on the line," as Fitch would later write in *Adventure on Wheels*, "I felt we had somehow been cheated, that if we had only been allowed another month the bugs would have been ironed out of the SS. Now, with its malfunctioning brakes and many non-race-tested components, I was

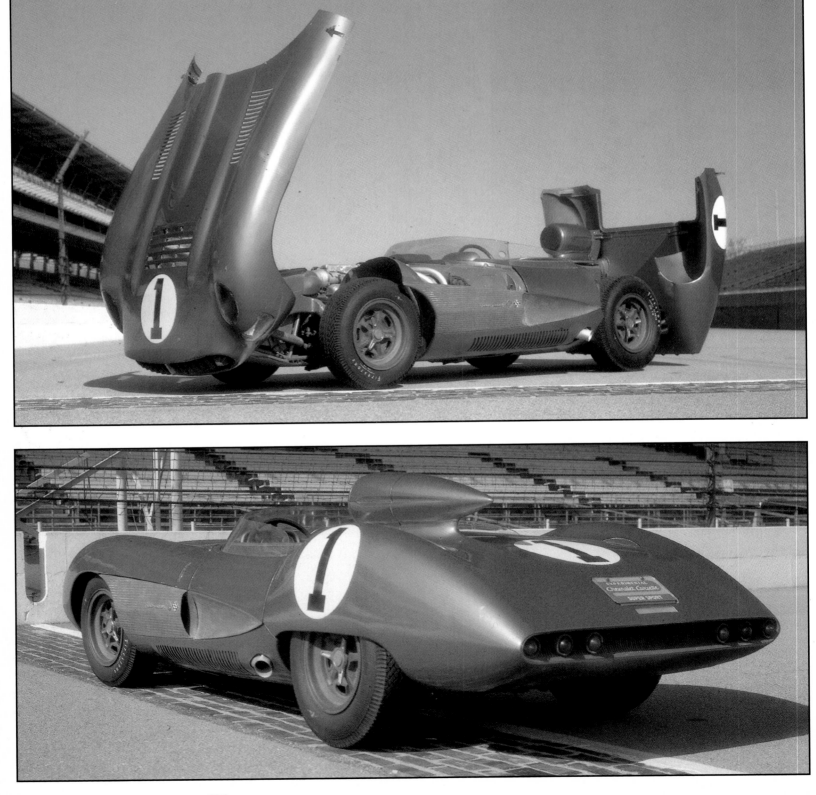

very much afraid of failure—in fact, it was almost a certainty. The huge crowd was solidly behind this 'supreme effort' on the part of Chevrolet—as evidenced by their wild cheers for us during practice. They wanted to see a Detroit car in the circle of champions, and the sleek-looking SS seemed to hold immense promise."

But the fans would not get their wish on that or any other day. During the first few laps, the SS proved even faster than the Mule and was more than up to the D-Type Jags and 3.5-liter Ferraris, but it lagged behind the big 4.5-liter V-8 Maseratis. Then the troubles started. The last-minute brake testing had flat-spotted the tires, causing bad vibrations, so Fitch pulled in on lap three for two new tires. After a few more laps, the engine began sounding terminal. Fitch pulled in again, and the

crew spent 15 minutes tracking down a faulty coil connection, only to watch him replace the coil out on the track soon afterwards. "By this time," notes Ludvigsen, "the rear suspension began to feel distinctly odd, to the extent of letting the tires touch the body and chattering uncontrollably after bumps. Undrivable and overheated, the Corvette SS retired officially after its twenty-third lap, turned in by Piero Taruffi following a conference in the pits with Zora Arkus-Duntov and Ed Cole."

The culprit, as Ludvigsen explains, was "failure of a rubber bushing at the chassis end of one of the lower rods that provided the de Dion tube with lateral location. As Duntov later said, 'It was doomed to fail.' If the fitter was not familiar with the installation procedure for these bushings, he could split them during assembly of the joint. This one had been split in just this way and thus became a built-in focal point for failure. The design itself had not been to blame."

Despite this discouraging debut, Cole had ambitious plans for the future, including a three-car SS team for Le Mans, an improved SS for the 1958 season, and special racing (SR) versions of the production Corvette. But it all came to an abrupt end with the racing "ban" enacted unanimously by the Automobile Manufacturers Association in June 1957 (see Chapter 4). Actually, GM had issued its own cease-and-desist order about a month before. As part of that, Chevy was told to scrap every aspect of the SS project except the race car itself. The division complied, though the Mule would also escape the corporate crusher, thanks to designer Bill Mitchell, who would soon give it a glorious new lease on life. But the SS would never race again.

Both the front and rear bodywork of the Corvette SS lifted way up for easy access to the engine and other components. The SS clearly needed more development time to work out the inevitable bugs. It entered the Sebring 12-Hours with erratic brakes. During the race, the coil had to be replaced, and then the rear suspension acted up. The SS retired after 23 laps. Still, it was competitive in terms of speed and power.

A peculiar irony is that the Super Sport would have died when it did anyway. As Ludvigsen observes: "Even if Chevy had still been racing, the Corvette SS wouldn't have been eligible to run at Le Mans after 1957. In 1956 and 1957 there'd been intense controversy over the high speeds the prototype sports cars were reaching on the classic French track, and in 1958 and 1959 a displacement limit of three liters, 183 cubic inches, was imposed. Duntov, reflecting on the events of those years, is certain that the failure of the three-car Corvette team to run as promised in 1957 was the final straw that provoked the Automobile Club *de l'Ouest* to ban the big-engined cars." As so often happens, though, the authorities would flip-flop and allow GT entries above 3.0 liters for 1960, when the Corvette would finally have its day in the international sun.

The production 'Vettes didn't win Sebring '57 either, but both finished respectably enough. In fact, Dick Thompson and co-driver Gaston Andrey managed 12th overall and first in the GT class. The second entry, piloted by Bill Kilborn and Jim Jeffords, took the checkered flag 15th overall and second in class. These finishes were actually more significant for the Corvette's reputation than an outright SS win would have been, because they came with *production* cars that race-goers could more readily identify with. Said one European writer: "Before Sebring, where we actually saw it for ourselves, the Corvette was regarded as a plastic toy. After Sebring, even the most biased were forced to admit that the Americans had one of the world's finest sports cars—as capable on the track as it was on the road. Those who drove and understood the

Corvette could not help but reach that conclusion." So it was the showroom car and not the hastily devised SS that accomplished Duntov's original goal.

Nevertheless, the Corvette SS (sometimes termed Sebring SS) remains one of the most memorable and consistently intriguing cars in General Motors history. That's largely because it came from GM, a giant outfit which once admitted that its main concern was "making money, not cars"—certainly not sleek, specially designed long-distance race cars. Considering that, it's remarkable that the SS had the potential it did, never mind that it came together with a promptness uncommon to such a huge organization. Then too, the SS dates from that now-nostalgic decade when Detroit thought it could do anything and succeed. That the SS would likely have been a winner with further develop-

ment only enhances its "what if?" fascination today.

But the story doesn't quite end with Sebring: The SS was the first car to officially circle the new Daytona International Speedway, driven by none other than Zora Arkus-Duntov at the track's formal opening in February 1959. Two months earlier, the car had recorded an amazing 183 mph on the five-mile high-speed track at GM's Mesa, Arizona, proving grounds.

Happily, the SS is still around—and still GM property, of course. Looking almost as fresh as the day it arrived at Sebring, it most recently appeared at the 1988 Monterey Historic Races in California—a center-stage attraction in a long weekend saluting Chevrolet performance. The Corvette SS remains a vivid symbol of that tradition, which is why it will always be revered despite its shattered dreams of glory.

The Corvette SS remains one of the most memorable and intriguing cars in General Motors history. Besides being seen at Sebring, it was the first car to officially circle the new Daytona International Speedway. And earlier, it had recorded an amazing 183 miles per hour at GM's Mesa, Arizona proving grounds. The flight of the SS might have been short, but it is still remembered as a symbol of the Corvette tradition.

CHAPTER 6

1958-62:
PROPHETS WITH HONOR

A prophet is without honor in his own land, and so it was with the third-generation Corvette. The inaugural 1958 model was hooted by many as a hokier, heftier version of the memorable second generation—mainly because it *was*—and even Corvette enthusiasts would overlook it for years afterward.

Lately, however, the 1958-62 models have come to be appreciated as prophets *with* honor, and for very sound reasons. Not the least of these is the fact that they forecast the Corvette's shift from spartan, all-out sports car to civilized *gran turismo*. Though totally unappreciated in the late Fifties, this was the format the Corvette had to adopt in order to become a lasting commercial success. It did, and the result was a permanent place in the Chevrolet line for "America's Only True Sports Car."

The third generation is also historically significant because it spanned a period of vast and fairly rapid change for General Motors and the American auto industry in general. These were the years that ushered in Bill Mitchell to replace Harley Earl at GM Styling, gave us the last Corvettes in the original mold, and witnessed the breakdown of the largely monolithic Fifties market in favor of the much more highly segmented and competitive arena that persists to this day. In all, 1958-62 would be some of the most exciting years in Corvette history.

That history has been replete with "near misses" —advanced concepts for future production models ultimately precluded by lack of time, technology, budget, or some combination thereof. The first significant example of these Corvettes-that-never-were crops up in connection with the 1958 model, which GM began thinking about in September 1955.

Despite the Corvette's then-dismal sales, management was sufficiently impressed by what Harley Earl had wrought for '56 to allow preliminary work toward a 1958 model. At the time, GM engineers were entertaining thoughts of unit construction, while Styling Staff was still enamored of the Mercedes-Benz 300SL Gullwing coupe that had burst on the scene in 1954. So strong was the Gullwing's influence, in fact, that it inspired a futuristic show car for the '56 Motorama.

This was the Oldsmobile Golden Rocket, a tight two-seat coupe with a slim vertical grille on a protruding proboscis—sort of a cross between the forthcoming Edsel and the old bullet-nosed Studebaker. Matching front fenders swept in an unbroken line to a torpedo-like rump topped by small fins running about halfway back from the rear roof pillars. Gullwing-like "flipper" sections were cut into the roof to assist entry/exit in this low-riding showboat. The roofline tapered boattail-fashion, with a large rear window wrapped down and around. Intriguingly, the backlight was split on its vertical centerline by a body-color bar—a remarkable forecast of the treatment Bill Mitchell would use on the Corvette Sting Ray coupe of seven years later.

According to author Karl Ludvigsen, the Golden Rocket became the starting point for work toward the '58 Corvette: "The clay model that was completed [in the winter of 1955-56] retained the Golden Rocket's general lines and proportions but had a completely different front end, with four headlights—the rage that

was then sweeping the industry, led by GM—above two large oval nostrils as air inlets."

Ultimately, it all came to naught. A fiberglass styling model was completed by March 1956, but as Ludvigsen records, "Much more engineering work remained to be done...before such a radically changed [Corvette] could be readied for production. A crisis in the manufacturing development of a new Chevy truck line drew away the needed engineers, as did the heavy workload demanded by the all-new 1958 [Chevy passenger-car line]. Corvette as Son of Golden Rocket was shelved for 1958, and as it turned out, for good."

With it went the idea of a switch from fiberglass to aluminum body construction and the idea of a unitized chassis to provide the necessary rigidity. Unit construction was nothing new. GM had long experience with it at its Opel and Vauxhall subsidiaries in Europe, and Chevrolet had envisioned it for a stillborn compact, the Cadet, back in 1946. GM thought unit construction would permit lower unit cost and higher volume, two things the Corvette desperately needed to begin paying its own way. "At one time, we thought it was possible to produce fiberglass for just 10,000 cars," Zora Arkus-Duntov recalled—not nearly enough for making serious money.

In time, of course, Chevrolet learned how to produce more fiberglass—much more. For now, the goal was to get even with Ford, which had edged out "USA-1" in

Opposite page: Although the '58 still looked very much like a Corvette, it had undergone many styling changes. This page: GM displayed the Oldsmobile Golden Rocket dream car at the 1957 Paris Auto Show, claiming that, "GM in its first 50 years has gained a worldwide reputation for using the showman's wand to draw attention to the public's dream and stimulate purchase of new products." Some of the Rocket's features were considered for future Corvettes.

the 1957 production race. That was the job of the all-new '58 passenger-car line. Corvette would just have to get along with a facelift.

It emerged as a fairly heavy-handed one, though there was a reason for it, as Ludvigsen explains: "Carried out in the Chevrolet Studio [as a backup to the proposed all-new design] this was clearly aimed at giving the Chevy sports car more external glitter and gloss, which would allow it to exert the kind of superficial appeal that was felt, at that time, to [be vital for] the successful selling of cars."

Still, a good many Corvette enthusiasts judged the '58 as a big step backward, much as Chevy's blowsy '58 passenger cars seemed a step backward from the last of the "classic" 1955-57 models. As facelifts go, this Corvette wasn't very successful, likely because Earl was going through what might be said to be his "rotund period." The front seemed to take some cues from the SR-2 prototype racer (see Chapter 4), but the overall package was far glitzier than any previous

Corvette. The basically clean, rounded lines of 1956-57 were still evident, only hammered up with simulated hood louvers, dummy air scoops on either side of the grille and in the bodyside "cove" areas, and twin chrome bars running down the trunklid. Quad headlights were on hand as expected, with thick chrome bezels meeting bright strips that continued back atop the fenders. Stylists considered replacing the distinctive grille teeth but wisely thought better of it. The '58 grille did have fewer teeth, though: nine instead of 13.

It's interesting to note where the extra flash came from. Ludvigsen records that the "two nostrils that had been the sole air inlets of the original planned new car became smaller inlets flanking the main opening, which kept the characteristic Corvette oval outline. All three openings had heavy chrome surrounds. Simple grille patterns were tried, honeycomb designs and fine mesh, but...the familiar 'teeth' were again featured....

"These were the main changes planned until the spring of 1956, when the car's quota of nonfunctional

112

styling features was suddenly elevated." Hence the aforementioned gimcracks like those trunklid "suspenders," though that gimmick had been used once already—on a customized '57 built for Prince Bertil of Sweden. Quad lights apart, the '58 front might have looked much like the SR-2's, the idea progressing as far as a full-scale clay that Ludvigsen says "may have been a proposal for a special show car or [a front-end] option for the factory racing programs that were then still flourishing."

But lean, clean, and racy wouldn't do anymore—or so management believed. As Ludvigsen wrote: "If the objective was, as one designer said at the time, to make the Corvette look like a Cadillac, that aim was certainly achieved." Then again, those were the days when GM was trying to make *all* its cars look more like Cadillacs—including Cadillacs!

Inevitably, the '58 Corvette not only looked heavier but *was*. Curb weight exceeded 3000 pounds for the first time, about 200 pounds up from the '57 model, thanks to 9.2 inches in added length and 2.3 inches in added width, bringing the respective overall dimensions to 177.2 and 72.8 inches.

In a December 1957 preview story, *Road & Track*

derisively described the '58 Corvette as "the subject of sundry improvements, including the corrosive influence of the 'stylists.'" Yet beneath the new hoke and heft lurked some genuine improvements. Bumpers, for example, were no longer attached to the body but to the frame, secured by long brackets providing significantly greater protection. Paint was switched from enamel to acrylic-lacquer.

Revisions inside were just as substantial but more successful. Stung by criticism of the original instrument panel layout, interior designers made sure every dial (except the clock) was right in front of the driver. Dominating the new arrangement was a large, semi-circular, 160-mph speedometer; perched ahead of it on the steering column was a round, 6000-rpm tachometer. The customary four engine gauges were arrayed in pairs on either side of the tach. A vertical console dropped down from dash center to present heater controls, clock, and the optional "Wonder Bar" signal-seeking radio. *R&T* snidely termed this "the first mass-production use of a central 'control tower'...haltingly pioneered. No true car controls are mounted in this spot, which has the advantage of their not being reachable, on purpose or accidentally, by a passenger." A grab bar in front of a semi-circular cutout made up the passenger's side of the dash. A locking glove compartment nestled between the seats just below the release button for the integral convertible-top tonneau. Door panels were again restyled, with reflectors added at armrest level for nighttime safety. Upholstery was changed to a new "pebble-grain" fabric.

Bigger and plusher the '58 may have been, but it was a vivid performer—no surprise, as the '57 engine lineup returned with few changes. Top dog, as before, was the high-compression, Duntov-cam 283 "fuelie" with a now-official 290 horsepower at 6200 rpm. A similar arrangement with twin carbs and 9.5:1 compression continued at 270 bhp. Not that most buyers opted for this much. In fact, the base 230-bhp V-8 accounted for nearly half of '58 engine installations, and only 1500 cars were fitted with fuel injection—1000 with the 290-bhp setup, 500 with the 250-bhp version.

Nevertheless, determined speed freaks could still order a near race-ready Corvette from their local Chevrolet dealers, and its price was right. Even the hottest engine, ($484.20), Positraction ($48.45), heavy-duty brakes and suspension ($425.05), four-speed transmission ($188.30), and "Cerametallic" brake linings ($26.90) added only about $1200 to the '58's reasonable $3631 base price. That was remarkable value considering that the 'Vette was more than a performance match for the likes of Jaguar, Porsche, and other big-bucks Europeans. Even exotics like Ferrari weren't far beyond it in performance, if at all.

Car magazines were mostly positive about the '58's mechanical changes. Said Stephen F. Wilder in the December 1957 *Sports Cars Illustrated*: "We were able, in a very short time, to discover how the 1958 Corvette behaves in nearly every conceivable road situation. It may be summed up as 'very well indeed.'" The optional four-speed gearbox received special praise:

Opposite page: By early 1956, the general shape of the '58 Corvette had been pretty well established, although alternatives to the toothy grillework were being considered and the bumpers weren't finalized (top row). The rear end design, however, was close to production. This page: A mock-up from August 1956 had an SR-2 theme (bottom). A new dash (above) put the gauges directly in front of the driver.

This page: *The '58 Corvette in its finalized form (top) translated later into the production car (bottom), equipped in this case with fuel injection. Opposite page: It's probably little known that the basic shape of the 1963 Sting Ray had been developed by December 1957. The Q-Corvette, different on each side, poses (top) with a '58 'Vette; note the similarity to the Sting Ray from front and rear views.*

"It is at least the equal of any box we've ever tried, not only with respect to the suitability of ratios to the engine performance, but the smoothness of the synchromesh, [which] brings to mind the old metaphor about a hot knife and butter."

SCI reported a 0-60-mph time of 7.6 seconds and top speed of around 125 mph for its 250-bhp fuelie/four-speed test car, which was also equipped with the optional "Cerametallic" brake linings. While admitting that the latter "stood up to *SCI*'s severe brake test very well indeed," Wilder made a point that showed Corvette brakes still weren't all they might be: "...Although the drum diameter remains at 11 inches and the shoes are a full half-inch wider, the total braking area is actually reduced 20 percent [from 1956-57] because the forward shoes are lined over only half their length. To reduce the amount of braking done by the rear wheels, the brake cylinders there are only [5/8-inch] diameter instead of one inch, whereas the front ones remain at 1.125. The drums have cooling fins cast on the rim, and as a further option, vented backing plates with air scoops are available. Those large holes up front...may then be opened up and a duct will carry air back, not just to the front brakes but under the door sills all the way to the rear ones, too.

"The Cerametallic brakes are definitely not intended for all types of driving," Wilder warned. "Corvettes so equipped are delivered...with a placard on the windshield which reads, 'This car is not for street use.' Until warmed up, they are quite apt to pull strongly to one side or the other—not the thing for Grandma on her way to the grocery store!"

Indy- and midget-car veteran Sam Hanks tested four '58 'Vettes for *Motor Trend* and came up with some interesting performance comparisons. It would appear that fuel injection was the way to go for fuel efficiency as well as all-out speed—just what Chevy had been saying—though, of course, fuelies were seldom bought for their "economy." Regardless, Hanks definitely liked all the 'Vettes he drove: "Any way you look at it, I think the Chevrolet designers ought to be proud of the style of the Corvette and their engineers should be proud of a fine sports car. It's real great to have an American-built production car that's available to the public as a combination cross-country, city traffic, competition sports car. I'm impressed."

So, apparently, was the public. Despite the somewhat overblown '58 styling, the Corvette turned a profit for the first time in its brief existence. Model-year

continued on page 118

Unfinished Business: The Intriguing Q-Corvette

Although the Corvette has always been a *bona fide* sports car and a unique entity in the Chevy line, it has always shared some parts with the division's high-volume models, a practice that has enabled Corvette to be one of the real values in its field. The intriguing Q-Corvette would have been no different—had it gone into production. The difference would have been in the parts it borrowed.

Beginning in 1957, when planning was underway for 1960-62, Chevrolet contemplated a radical departure from its traditional design and marketing: a separate line of cars featuring a rear transaxle with integral inboard disc brakes and independent suspension. The transaxle, which carried the code "Q," would enable engineer Zora Arkus-Duntov to finally realize his dream of a Corvette with all-independent suspension. Not only that, it was slated to be offered in both manual and automatic versions, some with an integral starter motor and provision for a built-in hydraulic-retarder brake.

Faster than you can say "exoticar," Chevy engineers and stylists began drawing up Corvette proposals around "Q" componentry. One of the cleanest designs looked like a slimmed-down version of the eventual 1963 Sting Ray split-window coupe, with a very pointy nose so slim and wide that it could not accommodate fixed quad headlights. Hidden lights were duly devised, designed to pop up from recesses.

The Q-Corvette envisioned two more departures from Chevy convention. One was dry-sump lubrication, deemed

necessary to permit the lowest possible engine mounting and center of gravity. The other was all-steel unit construction, long debated but finally deemed more practical than a fiberglass-body-on-steel-frame for annual production anticipated at more than 10,000 units. Even so, the Q-model would have been quite light and, with its all-independent suspension, promised

good if not sensational handling.

But even as this "European-inspired" Corvette was being developed, car sales as a whole remained in the doldrums brought on by the 1958 recession. With the market showing few signs of strong recovery—and with the compact rear-engine Corvair already a top priority—Chevy abruptly halted work on the

Q-Corvette.

A similar transaxle setup with swing-arm rear suspension would appear in production on the 1961 Pontiac Tempest, but it proved to be one of the wickedest handlers in Detroit history. In retrospect, then, perhaps Corvette lovers should be relieved that the Q-model never materialized, innovative though it would have been.

of losses were Rambler, Lincoln, and Ford's new four-seat Thunderbird.

Critics have tended to scoff at the '58 Corvette, feeling that Chevy was beginning to move away from the race-and-ride concept as quickly as it had embraced it with the 1956-57 design. Yet the styling changes and the added bulk were appropriate for the late Fifties, and although they detracted from the car's agility, they didn't do irreparable damage. As noted, the heavy-duty handling package was still available, and the 'Vette remained one of the quickest volume-production cars in the world.

Thanks to the efforts of Jim Jeffords and his "Purple People Eater," Corvette again won the SCCA's B-Production crown in 1958. Jim Rathmann and Dick Doane took the GT class at Sebring that year, and veteran Ak Miller won the sports-car class at the Pikes Peak Hill Climb with a time of 15 minutes, 23.7 seconds.

None of these triumphs were mentioned in Corvette advertising, however, because Chevy soft-pedaled performance in the wake of the AMA's "anti-racing"

production was well above 1957's level, totaling 9168 units. As a result, the 'Vette was one of the few domestic models to score increased sales in that recession-wracked season — a fact usually ignored by automotive historians. The only other cars registering gains instead

Although the rear end was the least changed part of the '58 Corvette (right), it sported revised bumpers and exhaust outlets, new taillight lenses, and dual chrome strips on the decklid. Fuel injection remained an option on the 283-cid V-8 (top left), churning out 290 horsepower at 6200 rpm in its most potent form. The revised interior was more user-friendly (top right).

edict of the previous year. Barney Clark's ad copy now emphasized things like a "silken cyclone of a V-8," a "beautifully compact body," and "a chassis that clings to the road like a stalking panther." Headlines asked, "What's as effortless as a Corvette?" and "What happened to gravity?" The latter led to a spiel about handling virtues. "Corvette Does America Proud" was the somewhat nationalistic tone of one ad picturing a two-tone roadster at the famous Pebble Beach, California, *Concours d'Elegance*, surrounded by an array of vintage automobiles.

Another ad showed a Corvette in full stride with a sailplane floating overhead. The florid copy made the obvious comparisons: "...acceleration as easy as a giant's stride, a liquid grace in motion, steering as sharp and precise as a scalpel. In plain truth, a Corvette travels in a way no other American car can equal." Apparently, it was all right to *talk* about performance so long as the word wasn't used or race results listed.

Bill Mitchell once admitted that he and his associates at GM Styling in the Fifties were too willing to "ladle on chrome with a trowel." That's undeniably true, but

they were more sparing with the Corvette than any other car in the corporate fleet. It's to Chevrolet's everlasting credit that the '58 styling was cleaned up considerably for the little-unchanged '59.

Road & Track now put aside its previous snideness to headline its test of the '59 "a pretty package with all the speed you need, and then some." The editors went on to observe that "trim on Corvettes, like all GM cars, is extremely well executed whether it is functional or mere decoration," then lauded appearance that had been "improved by the simple expedient of removing the phony hood louvers and the two useless chrome bars from the decklid." *Sports Cars Illustrated* simply said, "Good riddance."

Interior alterations were just as minor and just as effective. There were repositioned armrests and door handles, a shelf added beneath the passenger grab bar for extra small-item stowage space, and reshaped seats that *R&T* reported "adequately do the job of holding [occupants] comfortably in place during all but the most violent action. We do feel, though, that safety belts would be desirable if much hard driving is to be done." (Did they really wonder?) Speaking of safety, *R&T* felt that the new package shelf "should be removed...as this badly placed receptacle also presents

a safety hazard to the passenger's knees." The editors also recommended junking "the grab rail itself; the thinly padded bar would probably do more harm than good in most cases." Changes the editors would have likely left alone included sunvisors as a first-time option; concave instead of flat instrument lenses (to cut down on reflections); and a T-handle lockout for the manual transmissions in order to prevent accidental engagement of reverse.

Powertrain choices were again unchanged, but the '59 featured a minor mechanical alteration of major benefit: the addition of rear-trailing radius rods. "Running forward [from the axle above each spring] to the boxed frame, they are merely shortened versions of the Panhard rod which will be standard on '59 Chevy passenger cars," explained *SCI*'s Wilder. "Thus relieved of a burdensome additional duty [axle location], the rear shock absorbers are now mounted straight up and down and are recalibrated. Result: a slightly softer ride and noticeably less rear-end steering on irregular surfaces." The rods also helped counteract rear-axle windup, a problem with the bountiful torque of the most powerful engines, and the RPO 684 chassis option was given even stiffer springs—all the better for handling.

Major Specifications: 1958 Corvette

Body/Chassis

Frame:	Box-section steel, with five crossmembers
Body:	Glass-reinforced plastic, 2-seat convertible
Front suspension:	Independent; upper and lower A-arms, unequal-length wishbones, coil springs, tubular hydraulic shock absorbers, anti-roll bar
Rear suspension:	Live axle, semi-elliptic leaf springs, tubular hydraulic shock absorbers
Wheels:	15-inch bolt-on steel
Tires:	6.70 × 15 4-ply

Dimensions

Wheelbase (in.):	102.0
Overall length (in.):	177.0
Overall height (in.):	51.0
Overall width (in.):	73.0
Track front/rear (in.):	57.0/59.0
Ground clearance (in.):	6.0
Curb weight (lbs):	2912

Engines

Type:	ohv V-8, water-cooled, cast-iron head and block
Main bearings:	5
Bore × stroke (in.):	3.88 × 3.00
Displacement (ci):	283
Compression ratio:	9.5:1 (10.5:1 with Duntov cam)
Induction system:	Ramjet fuel injection
Exhaust system:	Split cast-iron manifolds, dual exhaust
Brake horsepower @ rpm:	250 @ 5000
Lbs/ft torque @ rpm:	305 @ 3800
Electrical system:	12-volt Delco-Remy

Driveline

Transmission:	3/4-speed manual, optional 2-speed Powerglide automatic
Gear ratios:	First—2.20:1
	Second—1.66:1
	Third—1.30:1
	Fourth—1.00:1
Rear axle:	Hypoid semi-floating; Positraction limited-slip differential optional
Rear axle ratio:	3.70:1 (4.11:1, 4.56:1, 3.55:1 with Powerglide optional)
Steering:	Saginaw recirculating ball; 17:1 overall ratio, 3.7 turns lock-to-lock
Turning circle (ft):	38.5
Brakes:	4-wheel hydraulic, 11-in.-diameter, internal-expanding drums; 157 sq. in. effective lining area

Performance*

0-30 mph (sec):	3.3
0-40 mph (sec):	4.5
0-50 mph (sec):	5.8
0-60 mph (sec):	7.6
0-80 mph (sec):	12.2
0-¼ mi. (sec @ mph):	15.7 @ 90 mph
Top speed (mph):	125 (est.)
Fuel consumption (mpg):	15-18

* *Sports Cars Illustrated*, December 1957

Opposite page: The grille on the '58 Corvette had nine teeth, compared to 13 in '57. The glitzy front end included dummy air scoops aside the grille, quad headlights with chrome bezels, and simulated hood louvers. The fake vents in the fender coves were not appreciated by purists (this page).

Brakes also came in for attention, with newly optional sintered-metallic linings (RPO 686) developed by GM's Delco-Moraine Division. Priced at a mere $26.90, same as the Cerametallic brakes, the option comprised three pairs of lining segments riveted to the primary brake shoes and five pairs of slightly thicker segments for the secondary shoes. Drums were finless with this option, but were flared at their open ends to enhance cooling. The sintered linings made braking less harsh than the Cerametallic material and needed far less warming up to provide maximum braking effectiveness.

Despite its largely carryover nature, the 1959 Corvette was a very desirable car, cleaner looks and strong powerplants combining to make an appealing package even more so. Most examples could shoot through the quarter-mile in under 15 seconds, and 0-60-mph times of less than eight seconds were typical. By now, *fast car* and *Corvette* had become synonymous.

Auto writer Ray Brock used nothing but superlatives to describe his '59 test: "Handling and brakes are plenty good in stock trim. There is absolutely no need for any of the heavy-duty racing extras unless the car is intended for sports car racing." *Road & Track* was only slightly less exuberant: "Taking everything into consideration, the Corvette is a pretty good car. It probably has more performance per dollar than anything you could buy, and parts are obtainable without sending to Italy, Germany, or England." *R&T* loved the 290-bhp fuelie engine in its test car, which blasted from rest to 60 mph in 6.6 seconds and on to the quarter-mile mark in 14.5 seconds at 96 mph. Top speed was listed at 128 mph with the short 4.11:1 final drive.

In an April 1959 comparison between a 'Vette and a Porsche 356 Convertible D, *Motor Trend* reported respective 0-60 times of 7.8 and 15.2 seconds. The Corvette also beat the Porsche in the quarter-mile—by more than four seconds—and was a big winner in the handling contest, too. The Porsche was superior only in fuel economy, returning 24.5 mpg against 14.3 mpg. Of course, the matchup had something of an "apples-and-oranges" quality to it, as *MT* implied: "If getting performance from a precision-built, small-displacement engine is intriguing, then Porsche is the answer. If you like the idea of having one of the world's fastest accelerating sports cars, then pick the Corvette....The truth is that both are excellent buys. They're sturdy, reliable, comfortable, and, above all, fun to drive. What more can you ask of a sports car?"

The aforementioned *R&T* test of January 1959 broadly hinted that another dramatic transformation was in store for the Corvette: "The changes...in the last six model years are not so great as we think will come about in 1960. We predict that this will be the year of the big changes...most of them for the better."

R&T was both right and wrong. Chevy had indeed been working on a new and far more radical concept for America's sports car—the so-called Q-Corvette. This was a much smaller and lighter two-seat coupe with very streamlined styling, independent rear suspension, and a rear transaxle derived from the one being developed for Chevy's new rear-engine compact. Although the Corvair would arrive on cue for 1960, the Q-model would be another near miss (see sidebar).

Still, demand for the current Corvette, though far from outstripping Chevrolet's ability to supply, was healthier than ever: 9670 units for the model year. Granted, that wasn't much more than the '58 total, and most every Detroit car sold better in '59, but it was heartening nonetheless. Chevy still wasn't making much money on Corvettes, but it wasn't losing any, either.

Sales continued their steady, if modest, climb for

1960, exceeding the psychologically important 10,000-unit level by exactly 261 cars. With the Q-model in abeyance, the 1960 Corvette was virtually indistinguishable from the '59, but minor power increases on the top two engines meant you had to be faster to spot some '60s on the move. Solid lifters and higher, 11.0:1 compression lifted the most potent 283 fuelie to 315 bhp at 6200; a second version with hydraulic lifters for easier maintenance pumped out 275 bhp at 5200 rpm. Because of these gains, Powerglide was no longer available with fuel injection; it simply couldn't take the torque. Carbureted engines remained much the same. The tamest was still the 230-bhp unit with single four-barrel carburetor, followed by a dual-quad 245-bhp hydraulic-lifter version and the solid-lifter 270-bhp engine with twin four-barrel carbs.

Mechanical refinements for 1960 included new aluminum clutch housings for manual transmissions, which saved 18 pounds, and aluminum radiators for cars running the Duntov cam. A power-saving thermostatically controlled cooling fan was a new option, as was a long-range, 24-gallon fuel tank. The RPO 684 heavy-duty suspension package was erased from the options list, a casualty of the AMA's edict, but there was compensation in a larger-diameter front anti-roll bar, matched by a new rear bar as standard. These changes, plus an extra inch of rear wheel travel in rebound, yielded a smoother ride and more neutral handling.

Despite the shift in marketing emphasis toward smooth, no-fuss touring, there were still plenty of

reasonably priced performance options for 1960. Aside from the 315-bhp engine at $484.20, you could still order Positraction ($43.05) and the four-speed gearbox ($188.30). The ceramic-metallic brake linings (RPO 687) returned at $26.90, as did the sintered-iron linings. The 6.70 × 15 nylon tires cost only $15.75 (standard rubber remained 5.50 × 15).

Road & Track reported that the 1960 "high-performance engines (intended primarily for racing) are given very special treatment. In addition to customary inspection, many critical parts are now routed through a special department for a very painstaking examination of dimensions, flaws, finish, and quality of materials. Included in this group are valves, rocker arms, pushrods, pistons, connecting rods, and crankshafts. Just a few years ago, Chevrolet would have laughed at such a suggestion. This certainly shows how serious they are about the sports-car side of the business."

Another indication was yet another "experiment" that never quite got going. Early in the 1960 model year, Chevy offered cylinder heads cast from a high-silicon aluminum alloy as an option for the two fuelie engines. Based on a design first tried with the Corvette SS racer from Sebring 1957, they maintained the stock 11.0:1 compression but featured improved intake and exhaust manifolding. The high silicon content prefigured the block construction of the four-cylinder Vega engine of a decade later, which proved just as troublesome. The aluminum heads were fine in theory but tended to warp if the engine overheated, and

Chevy had quality-control hassles with the castings. The option was quickly withdrawn, but Duntov was far from finished with aluminum-head engines.

By now, most everyone acknowledged the Corvette's on-road abilities. And Chevy hadn't abandoned sports-car competition despite the AMA decision. In fact, the Corvette had one of its finest hours—or rather, 24 of them—that year. Renowned yachtsman and one-time car-builder Briggs Cunningham entered three Corvettes in the 1960 running of the fabled 24 Hours of Le Mans, where Bob Grossman and John Fitch finished a respectable eighth overall in a field of very hairy sports-racing machinery.

Perhaps more than any other group of one-model enthusiasts, Corvette fans always have been interested in the future. It was around 1960 that rumors of an entirely new Corvette began to be whispered. Lending credence to these rumors was the track debut of a dramatic special called Stingray, "privately" campaigned by GM design chief Bill Mitchell. The fact that Mitchell had succeeded to that position upon Harley Earl's retirement in 1958 convinced many 'Vette watchers that the Stingray was the shape of things to come for America's sports car. In some ways, it was.

Meanwhile, Mitchell had been moving to put new life into existing Corvette styling, which had been around in basic form since 1956. But though his studios had no shortage of ideas, the Corvette would see relatively few changes through 1962. Aside from sales that remained peripheral, the main reason for this lack of change was that Chevrolet had other priorities—the

This page: The Corvette cleaned up its act in 1959 by throwing out the chrome strips on the decklid. Opposite page: Shed also were the fake hood louvers (bottom), to which Sports Car Illustrated *said, "Good riddance!" Serious drivers appreciated having the tach right in front of them.*

Corvair for one. Ed Cole's technically advanced compact was the most interesting of the Big Three's new 1960 small cars, but it was beset with service problems—oil leaks, thrown fan belts, and tuning difficulties, among others. When it failed to outsell the conventional Ford Falcon, money was set aside for the development of a more conventional compact, which emerged for '62 as the Chevy II. Once more, the Corvette would have to soldier on with relatively little change.

Even so, the 1961-62 models stand as arguably the best Corvettes since the "classic" '57, which explains why they now tend to be more coveted than the 1958-60 editions. Bill Mitchell made it happen via a tasteful, carefully considered exterior makeover that provided a vast relief from the chrome-laden 1958-60 models. Accompanying this body redesign were numerous mechanical modifications aimed at improved efficiency and higher performance. The result was a back-to-back pair of vintage 'Vettes—the ultimate expression of the original 1953 concept and so refined that they almost qualified as all-new.

A fresh new rear end was the most pronounced change external for 1961, a kind of "ducktail" design lifted virtually intact from Mitchell's Stingray racer and also used on his XP-700 show car. The latter had a certifiably insane front end, with a huge loop-style bumper/grille protruding well forward of the quad headlights set above it, and was rightly dismissed as just so much whimsy. (Except by *Sports Cars Illustrated*, which in early '59 mistook the XP-700 as the template

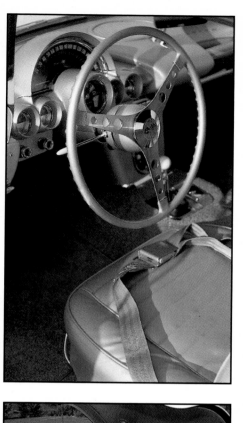

for the all-new Corvette then being rumored for 1960.) But the rear portion was wholly satisfying—a simple flowing shape that just happened to mate well with Harley Earl's production '58 front. Besides improved aesthetics, the ducktail brought a practical bonus: luggage space increased by perhaps 20 percent.

Complementing this change was a pair of small round taillights on each side of the central license-plate recess, plus a modest longitudinal trunklid creaseline running through the traditional, big, round Corvette medallion. Simple chrome bumperettes bracketed the

license plate, which itself gained a little "arch" bumper. And for the first time, the dual exhausts exited below the body, rather than through it or the bumper guards as before.

Up front was a considerably tidier version of the existing four-lamp nose. Headlight bezels were now body color, and the trademark vertical teeth were jettisoned in favor of a fine, horizontal-mesh insert of

continued on page 131

The 1960 Corvette was virtually indistinguishable from the '59, but detail improvements underneath gave it a smoother ride and more neutral handling characteristics. This would be the year that Corvette production cracked the 10,000-unit barrier.

129

Opposite page: The 1960 Corvette listed at $3872 without options, $3 less than in 1959. The standard engine continued to be the 230-bhp 283. This page: GM design was busy in April 1959 working on a space buck for a retractable hardtop for the Corvette. It looks much simpler than the 1957-59 Ford Skyliner mechanism, but if it started to rain it appears as though the trunk would have to be unloaded before the top could be raised—not too practical, perhaps. Note the pop-up headlights.

the sort once planned for '58. The round medallion above gave way to separate block letters spelling out the car's name, topped by a larger version of the Corvette's crossed-flags insignia. The '61 would be the last Corvette available with bodyside coves in a contrasting color, a mere $16.15 option that most buyers ordered.

A heater was still optional for '61—and outrageously priced at $102.25 over the suggested $3934 base figure.

Air conditioning, power steering, and power brakes still *weren't* optional, but you could again order a Wonder Bar signal-seeking AM radio, whitewall tires, Positraction limited-slip differential, and the all-important four-speed manual transmission. More than 7000 lusty souls—nearly three-quarters of all Corvette customers for the year—paid the four-speed's $188.30 asking price. Electric windows and power top were still on the list, while standard equipment was bolstered by

131

This page: *Often discussed in the press was a mid-engine Corvette, and indeed Chevy did experiment with that configuration (top) in 1959. Rear styling of the '61 Corvette was inspired by Bill Mitchell's XP-700 and the Stingray racing car. Opposite page: The 1961 Corvette lost its toothy grille and chrome headlight bezels (top left). The rear (top right) sported a ducktail theme, a flowing shape that mated well with the 1958 front end design.*

the addition of windshield washers, sunvisors, thermostatically controlled radiator fan, and parking-brake warning light.

Mechanically, the 1961 Corvette was much like the '60, though substitution of an aluminum radiator for the previous copper-core unit was fairly significant. The new unit not only improved cooling capacity some 10 percent but weighed half as much as the previous radiator, reflecting Chevy Engineering's continuing quest for minimum poundage. Side-mount expansion tanks were added as a running change.

Engine choices were basically carryovers. There were still five versions of Chevy's renowned 283-cubic-inch small-block V-8: 230, 245, 270, 275, and 315 bhp, the last two being fuelies. The manual three-speed remained the standard gearbox but was now offered with a wider choice of axle ratios. Powerglide automatic continued to be available at extra cost, but was now

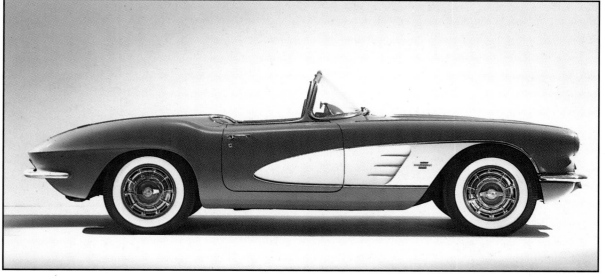

barred from the three hottest engines. As mentioned, most buyers shunned the manual three-speed for the four-speed, which was newly encased in aluminum, saving 15 pounds.

Within the two-seat cockpit, the only change for '61 was a narrower transmission tunnel that opened up needed room. Four interior color schemes were available: black, red, fawn, and blue.

Even with the mildest 283 and Powerglide, the 1961 Corvette was quick by any standard: "Buff book" testers recorded 0-60-mph acceleration of just 7.7 seconds. A fuel-injected/four-speed model tested by *Sports Cars Illustrated* knocked another second off that, making the '61 'Vette one of the fastest cars in the history of stoplight speed duels. Top speed with Powerglide was listed at 109 mph, limited mainly by transmission gearing. The fuelie/four-speed lacked the long-legged overdrive ratio of most modern five-

speed manuals; even so, many of the fuel-injected and twin four-barrel models could see the far side of 130 mph.

Although Corvette still didn't have an independent rear suspension like some costlier Europeans, that didn't seem a drawback on either street or track. Testers sang the praises of the '61's handling virtues, and almost no one found any particular vices. By the standards of that day at least, the Corvette was now one of the most roadable cars built anywhere in the world. Perhaps as proof, it turned in another fine performance at this

year's running of the Sebring 12 Hours of Endurance, a near-stock model finishing eleventh overall.

Lest we forget in all this talk of handling and horsepower, the Corvette had been improving in less dramatic but more practical ways. Fit-and-finish, for example, was the best yet. *Road & Track* carped about "quite a lot of wind noise" and drafts from around the door windows with the hardtop on, but described body quality as "generally excellent, although we did find a few minor flaws on our '61 test car, mostly in obscure places. Panel fit and fairing from one panel to another were good and showed Chevrolet's great attention to the Corvette molds"—quite something for a big outfit that had gotten into building such a specialized product only by degrees.

In the comfort category, *R&T* was also "greatly impressed by the combination of a very good ride coupled with little roll on corners. Most cars with riding qualities approaching those of the Corvette can't match its sticking ability on curves. And those that match or beat its handling usually ride like the proverbial truck."

Overall, as *SCI* observed: "Comparing the 1961 Corvette with a 1957-vintage car, one is surprised at how complete a change has been effected over the years....[The '61 is] one of the most remarkable marriages of touring comfort and violent performance we have ever enjoyed, especially at the price."

If the '61 was good, the '62 was better. With still more power and even cleaner looks, it ranks as perhaps the most desirable Corvette from between 1957-63.

The big news was under the hood—literally, since the 283 got the hot-rodder's traditional bore-and-stroke job, which brought cylinder dimensions to 4.00 ×

3.25 inches and displacement to 327 cubic inches. In this form, the small-block would continue as the Corvette's main muscle through 1965. The emphasis was definitely on power. Even the most docile 327 pumped out a rated 250 bhp, and rabid acceleration fanatics could opt for up to 360 bhp—more than enough to nail you to the seats in "banzai" takeoffs.

But there was more to all this than simply extra cubes. Heavier-duty bearings, larger ports, and a longer-duration camshaft were fitted to all but the base 250-bhp engine, and the solid-lifter Duntov cam was specified for the top-dog fuelie as well as the most potent of the three carbureted mills, now at 340 bhp. Both of these ran tight 11.25:1 compression, versus 10.5:1 for the base and step-up 300-bhp engines. The

latter were perhaps the best choices for all-around use, offering more than enough power plus the simplicity and easy maintenance of hydraulic tappets and a single four-barrel carburetor.

In fact, the troublesome twin four-barrel carbs were now gone altogether, replaced by big, single four-barrel Carters. Peak power speed in the top two versions was a screaming 6000 rpm—quite high for a pushrod mill—while the 250- and 300-bhp ran out of puff at 4400 and 5000 rpm respectively. The latter two were the only engines available with optional Powerglide, which was treated to a weight-saving aluminum case like the one given to the four-speed manual the previous year.

The deeper-breathing 327 block necessitated a small

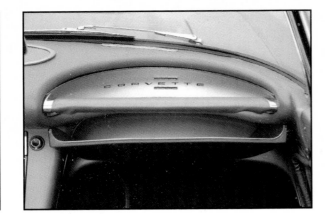

but important change in the Rochester injection system that benefited fuelie driveability. *Car and Driver* magazine, as *Sports Cars Illustrated* now called itself, explained it this way: "Instead of the old, relatively complicated cold-start arrangement, the new injector has a simple choke valve in a port in the center of the intake venturi plug. When this 'strangler' valve is open, the total area made available is adequate to the engine's needs; when it's closed, it has a definite choking effect, although the venturi itself—necessary for metering reasons—remains open. Control of the choke is fully automatic."

Foreshadowing what would happen to its Sting Ray successors a few years later, the '62 'Vette was even

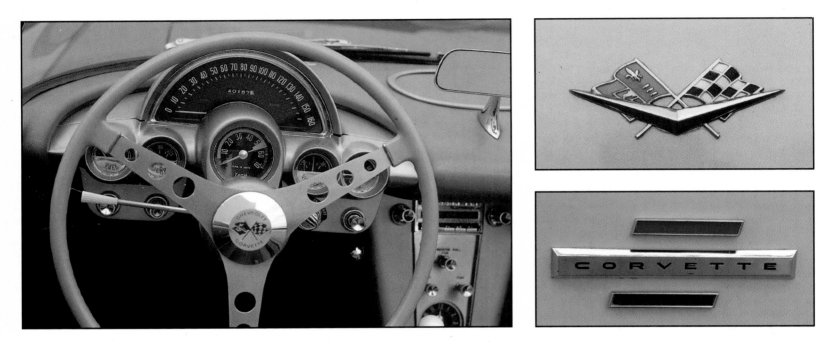

cleaner than the '61. Though the basic '58 styling was beginning to look a bit dated, the last of its worst excesses disappeared on this final variation. The most obvious deletion was the chrome outline around the bodyside coves, which also shed their triple chrome accent spears in favor of more conservative ribbed-aluminum appliques, finished in black for subtlety. Omitting the coves' optional two-toning only enhanced this more cohesive look.

Other elements were similarly refined. The previous chrome mesh grille and its flanking cutouts were finished in black, as was the background of the trunklid medallion. Narrow-band whitewalls were in vogue and looked great on the 'Vette. The only place where decoration was added was the rocker panels, newly adorned with ribbed anodized-aluminum moldings.

The new *Car and Driver* took pains to report that "there are no Limited Production Options (LPOs) for the ['62] Corvette; everything...falls in the RPO ...category. In gearboxes, for example, the Powerglide is RPO 313, and for 1962 there's a new RPO 685 four-speed box that's sold only with the two milder hydraulic-lifter engines. Its ratios are [IV-I] 1.00, 1.51, 1.92 and 2.54, with 2.61 reverse. A specially recommended axle ratio for use with this is the new 3.08:1 cog (RPO 203)...which gives an overall low gear of 7.83:1 for blasting dramatically out of drive-ins and away from lights, yet offers a high highway top gear."

Opposite page: In place of the circular medallion riding up front, the '61 Corvette nose wore a crossed-flags emblem and separate letters spelling out the car's name. The crossed flags seen on the side cove's air extractor on the '60 were replaced on the '61 by a rectangular nameplate with a red hash mark above and a blue one below. This page: The trunk had 20 percent more space. And while the dash and interior went virtually unchanged, the '61 'Vette apparently differed enough— it went on to set another production record: 10,939 units.

Still speaking technically, *C/D* mentioned RPO 687, which for 1962 denoted sintered-metallic brake linings and a quick-steering kit. "You can buy the brake linings alone as RPO 686 and, according to *Corvette News*, you can buy over-the-counter the parts needed to convert to quick steering for about $25. You need one adapter plate...two studs...and one U-bolt. That price would include installation and wheel alignment, according to *Corvette News*. The latter, by the way, is one real bonus to buying a Corvette. It's a top-notch publication with all the factory dope on tuning, specifications and Corvette club activities." *CN* had started back in 1957 as a product of Chevy's Photographic Division and was sent free to Corvette

Evolution of the 283 Small-Block V-8

Bhp @ rpm	Years Offered	Induction	Compression Ratio
230 @ 4800	1958-61	one 4-barrel	9.5:1
245 @ 5000	1958-61	one 4-barrel	9.5:1
250 @ 5000	1958-59	fuel injection	9.5:1
270 @ 6000	1958-61	two 4-barrels	9.5:1
275 @ 5200	1960-61	fuel injection	11.0:1
290 @ 6200	1958-59	fuel injection	10.5:1
315 @ 6200	1960-61	fuel injection	11.0:1

Corvette used the 327-cid V-8 exclusively for 1962.

This page: *Design work on future Corvettes in early 1959 showed the ducktail rear end of 1961, but the front end looked different than anything that actually went on sale. Featured were sunken headlights on a nose that was edging in the direction of the Sting Ray look, but was much bluffer. Opposite page: The '62 Corvette wasn't much changed visually, but it looked more sophisticated by virtue of its single-tone body paint and the lack of chrome surrounds for the side coves, whose scoops sported new trim. Note the exhaust outlet on the prototype (top right).*

owners. It was an instant success and remains quite popular today.

Though more mature in appearance for '62, the Corvette was still a performance fantasy for most every adolescent in the land—and many of their parents. The extra power and torque of the larger 327 V-8 translated into truly ferocious 0-60-mph and quarter-mile acceleration; the four-speed/fuelie routinely reeled off quarters of 15 seconds or less at trap speeds of 100 mph or more in magazine tests.

And with the appropriate options, the 'Vette was still a winning production-class racer. Again in '62, The Sports Car Club of America's A-Production champion was Dr. Dick Thompson. The Corvette was a serious competitor even with only minor modifications. Don Yenko, for example, took the SCCA's B-Production title that season.

Let's briefly return to that *Car and Driver* test, which is interesting in that it contrasts a pair of '62s: a four-speed fuelie with the 3.70:1 final drive but no

Corvette Performance Comparisons 1958-62

Year	Disp.	Bhp	Axle	0-30 (sec)	0-50 (sec)	0-60 (sec)	0-100 (sec)	¼-mi. @ mph (sec)	Max. mph
1958	283	230	4.11	—	—	9.2	—	17.4 @ 83	103
1958	283	250	3.70	3.3	5.8	7.6	21.4	15.7 @ 90	120
1959	283	250	3.70	—	—	7.8	—	15.7 @ 90	120
1959	283	290*	4.11	3.1	5.1	6.8	15.5	14.9 @ 96	124
1960	283	270	—	—	—	8.4	—	16.1 @ 89	—
1961	283	230	3.70	3.8	—	8.3	—	—	—
1961	283	315*	3.70	2.6	4.6	6.0	14.2	15.5 @ 106	Est. 140
1962	327	360*	3.70	2.5	4.5	5.9	13.5	14.5 @ 104	Est. 150

* fuel injection

Positraction, and a 300-bhp Powerglide car with the 3.36:1 axle. "As always," *C/D* began, "the fuel-injected Corvette is a sweetheart to drive. Power is excellent, but even more impressive is the torque curve, which is as close to being flat as any we've seen. From its 4000-rpm peak it falls off only 20 pounds-feet at the extremes of peak power (6000) and 2000 rpm. In action this engine delivers such constant thrust without surges or flat spots that the feel of acceleration is deceptively docile....Performance is much like last year's f.i. Corvette...up to 80, above which the new one just continues to soar. Though the time to 80 is unchanged, time to 100 is cut from 18.0 to 16.6 seconds. Quarter-mile time is improved from 15.6 to 15.0 seconds, though the terminal speed is up only one mph—not bad for a stocker!"

Switching to the Powerglide car, *C/D*'s editors "expected quite a comedown in performance; we were amazed at how little difference there was. Sixty in 8.8 seconds and the quarter-mile in 16.8 is, after all, not waiting around. Doing this by merely stepping down and holding on offers its own peculiar pleasure, as the solid V-8 bites into higher and higher speeds with its distinctive hard, metallic wail. As a comfortable cross-country tourer, the Powerglide Corvette offers a high pleasure quotient." So much for the oft-alleged performance "penalties" of early automatic 'Vettes.

The '62 Corvette marked the end of an era for America's sports car, a changing of the guard. Its design was finalized long before the car actually appeared because Chevy stylists and engineers were already hard at work on the completely reengineered body and suspension ordained for '63. Yet the '62 did introduce the first of the new engines—the versatile 327—and thus bridged the gap between the old and new guards. Both its fiberglass body and X-braced frame harked back to the first '53s. Yet thanks to Duntov, the car had long since shed its pedestrian origins. The '62 was faster, handled better, looked neater, and was more civilized than any previous Corvette, but retained much of the charm of the original roadster concept. Reflecting its transitional nature, the '62 was the first Corvette with a standard-equipment heater and optional factory air conditioning and power brakes—which partly explains why it was also the first Corvette with a base price above $4000.

Far more important to its future than the many evolutionary improvements of 1961-62 was the Corvette's coming of age as a serious money-maker. It happened in 1962 with 14,531 model-year sales, up some 40 percent over 1961. The 'Vette had been making a profit since '58, but only barely. Now, America's only surviving sports car was showing a really healthy return on investment, one that even its staunchest proponents wouldn't have expected a few years before.

This was a sizable relief to the likes of Duntov, Cole, and Mitchell, who'd kept faith with the 'Vette in its darkest days by using all their influence to keep it alive.

And they weren't resting on their laurels, as *Sports Cars Illustrated* had suspected the previous year: "Now that Chevrolet has completed its family of Corvairs, we expect the next project will be a new Corvette. With the experience they've gained with this car, and in view of the trend toward sensible styling and sensational engineering, the next Corvette should be a humdinger. All they have to do is put the same emphasis on *doing* things that they have in the past on *seeming* to do things. Since [the '61] already does more than most drivers can handle, that's an exciting prospect."

How true. Duntov, Cole, and Mitchell were "doing things," all right—big things that would once and for all elevate a sports-car survivor to the status of sports-car legend. A brilliant new Corvette was at hand, and Sting Ray was its name.

The '62 Corvette marked the end of an era—the Sting Ray generation was on the horizon. Nonetheless, the '62 served as an admirable transitional car, still with the old body but the first with the larger 327 engine. And it had been the most popular 'Vette yet, with production up 33 percent to 14,531 units.

1958-62 Serial Spans, Production Figures, and Base Prices

Year	Serial Prefix	Serial Span	Prod.	Price
1958	J58S	100001-109168	9,168	$3,631
1959	J59S	100001-109670	9,670	$3,875
1960	00867S	100001-110261	10,261	$3,872
1961	10867S	100001-110939	10,939	$3,934
1962	20867S	100001-114531	14,531	$4,038

'Vettes on Video: *Route 66* and Other Adventures

Nowadays, major corporations employ armies of publicists to get their products on television—not as commercials but as on-camera props that amount to millions of dollars in free advertising. That's why characters on the tube may conspicuously serve a particular brand of coffee, say, or drive a certain make of car week after week.

This practice was far less prevalent in 1960, when the Corvette, like TV, was just growing out of its infancy. But Chevy's sports car would play a big role in advancing the cause of brand-name plugs and, in the process, its own fortunes. The vehicle was an hour-long CBS series called *Route 66*.

Chevrolet sponsored it, of course—as part of the division's "saturation" spending on prime-time TV advertising that in those days also encompassed NBC's *Bonanza* and ABC's *My Three Sons*. The premise of *Route 66* was as natural as America's long-time lust for the open road: Two all-American guys travel around the country in their all-American sports car, search for adventure, and with help from the scriptwriters, find it.

Martin Milner and George Maharis (later replaced by Glenn Corbett) co-starred each week with a shiny new Corvette. This was initially a 1960 model, as the show premiered in the fall of that year, but with each new season the boys got a new model just like the ones at local Chevy dealerships. After all, it wouldn't do much good for Chevy's TV stars to drive last year's car when the salesmen were trying to sell this year's models.

Regarded at the time as a superior dramatic show, *Route 66* never said much about the backgrounds of its two main characters, though you had some suggestion of a troubled past in Maharis's case. Also left unanswered was how two wanderers with no obvious means of support could manage the upkeep on a new Corvette. (The car itself was revealed to have been a bequest from Milner's late father.) Perhaps the pair's more lucrative adventures took place *off* camera.

However the duo managed it, a lot of viewers must have wanted to learn the trick. Admittedly, many of the stories had our heroes in some job as a situational focal point for the action (and that week's guest stars), but it was usually as an oil rigger, farm hand, stevedore, or similar occupation that would've paid for the car's gas or the insurance, but probably not both. Not that Milner and Maharis stayed in the same job for long; each episode ended with them driving off toward next week's adventure. You had to wonder whether they were on the lam, independently wealthy, unemployable, or just plain footloose.

But that's the magic of television: Nothing is impossible so long as it entertains, and however implausible its premise, *Route 66* did entertain. Alas, like the fabled highway of its title, the show didn't have long to live, lasting only through the 1963-64 season before running out of gas in the ratings. Still, four years of weekly exposure in a successful prime-time TV series was a tremendous boon for the Corvette, not only in introducing it to millions of people who'd likely been unaware of it before but also in enhancing its air of jaunty romanticism. Unquestionably, Chevy got its Corvette sales kicks with *Route 66*.

Corvettes have had other recurring TV roles. One of the first was on the original *Perry Mason* series where the late William Hopper (playing detective Paul Drake) drove a Corvette during the show's first three seasons—but only on alternate weeks, when the Libbey-Owens-Ford glass company, then a GM subsidiary, was the sponsor. The rest of the time Hopper's mount was a Ford Thunderbird.

Lately, a Corvette convertible disguised as a Ferrari Daytona Spyder has been featured on *Miami Vice*, driven by co-star Don Johnson in the role of vice cop Sonny Crockett. Why the camouflage? Cost. With some storylines placing Sonny in high-speed chases and the occasional crash, replacing a Corvette, even a customized one, costs the producers a lot less than replacing that scarce Ferrari model. Amusingly enough, the ersatz *Vice* Daytona has prompted various replicas, and some have sold fairly well—no doubt to the chagrin of both Ferrari and Corvette owners.

CHAPTER 7

1963-67:
STING RAY ALL THE WAY

In its first test of a Sting Ray, *Car and Driver* magazine ended with a telling quote from Zora Arkus-Duntov: "For the first time," said "Mr. Corvette" of the new 1963 model, "I now have a Corvette I can be proud to drive in Europe." For 'Vette fans everywhere, Duntov had said it all. In the Sting Ray, they finally got what they'd been asking for: an all-out, all-American two-seater that could hold its head high next to any other sports car made anywhere in the world.

The 1961-62 Corvette had been a satisfying and successful conclusion to the design generation begun with the '56 model—or maybe even the original '53. But it was time to move on after 10 years, time for the "all-new" Corvette that had been rumored off and on since 1958. Bill Mitchell suggested its surname, here spelled as two words but lifted, along with essential design themes, from his svelte Stingray racer.

The production Sting Ray rocked the sports-car world like an earthquake, recalling the knock-'em-dead debut of Jaguar's slinky, sexy E-Type two years before. Comparisons were inevitable and weren't long to materialize. But perhaps even more important, the Sting Ray was a sell-out success—so much so that the St. Louis factory put on a second shift and *still* couldn't keep up with demand. Inventory, which dealers like to see at around a 60-day supply, went down to a mere 14 days or so, forcing customers to wait up to two months for delivery—at full retail price, of course.

The excitement was not merely over an arrestingly styled new version of the traditional roadster, for there was now an alternative Corvette for the first time: a magnificent *gran turismo* coupe with distinctive styling to match its speed and agility. To say that the Sting Ray was revolutionary would be an overstatement; a good many components were carried over. But to say that it was an instant hit would be to minimize its impact. By St. Louis's standards, it was a blockbuster: 21,513 built for the model year, up 50 percent from record-setting 1962.

Nor was its success to be a passing fad. Except in swan-song '67, the Sting Ray set new Corvette sales records every year. Less than five years after the last one was built, it had become a modern classic. Used-car values turned around quickly and began heading up, making this one of the first postwar cars to surpass its original list price on the collector market. Today the Sting Ray generation stands as perhaps the most desirable Corvette of all—the 1963 split-window coupe in particular.

The Sting Ray was very much Bill Mitchell's car and the first from GM to absolutely rewrite the prevailing design dictums of Harley Earl. Yet like his predecessor, as head of GM Styling, Mitchell always considered the Corvette his private preserve, his personal "pet." The Sting Ray was the first Corvette to bear his stamp alone.

It came together out of three separate projects: the radical Q-Corvette, a Corvair-based model and, of course, Mitchell's racing Stingray. By the fall of 1959, bits and pieces from these efforts had been collected into experimental project XP-720—the start of the production Sting Ray design program.

You'll recall that the Q-model, initiated in 1957, envisioned a smaller, more advanced Corvette boasting a rear transaxle, independent rear suspension, and all-disc brakes, with the rear brakes mounted inboard. Significant for the future Sting Ray, only a coupe was designed; a convertible wasn't even contemplated. Styling, by the same Bob McLean who'd laid out the

original Motorama Corvette, was purposeful, with peaked fenders, a long nose, and a short, bobbed tail.

At the time, GM management had considered offering a full line of large, rear-engine "Q" sedans for 1960, with which the Q-Corvette would share major mechanical components. But when the passenger car was scrapped as too radical, the Q-Corvette went with it. The problem, as usual, was economics: With no high-volume models to borrow components from, the Q-Corvette would have been prohibitively expensive to tool. That, in turn, would have prompted higher retail prices, something GM execs were loath to do given the fact that the Corvette was barely making a profit as it was. But the Q-model would not be forgotten.

Meantime, Zora Arkus-Duntov and other GM engineers had become fascinated with rear-/ and mid/rear-engine design, likely inspired by Porsche but certainly aided and abetted by Chevrolet general manager Ed Cole, who at least managed to get a rear engine for Chevy's first compact, the Corvair. It was during the Corvair's gestation that Duntov took the mid/rear-engine layout to its limits in the CERV I—short for Chevrolet Experimental Research Vehicle—a lightweight, open-wheel single-seat racer in the image of the British Coopers and Lotuses then starting to make their mark in Formula competition.

With this experience, and once the Corvair was

The production 1963 Sting Ray coupe featured a split rear window (opposite). It was very much stylist Bill Mitchell's car, and based in good part on the Stingray racer, particularly in the design of the humped fenders. Mitchell is shown (above) taking time to pose with both the Stingray and the Sting Ray.

This page: GM stylists constantly work on new ideas, and lines similar to what would end up on the Sting Ray were taking form even in early December of 1957. Already prominent are the humped fenders and the general "flavor" of the Sting Ray. The same study showed up in February 1958 (bottom) with an exhaust pipe attached.
Opposite page: Two more photos of the February 1958 study (top and center), along with Bill Mitchell's Stingray racer (bottom).

148

approved for 1960, it made sense to revisit the notion of a new Corvette sharing mechanical and chassis components with a more radically engineered new volume model. This idea was briefly investigated in 1958-60, progressing as far as a full-scale mock-up designed around the Corvair's entire rear-mounted power package—including its complicated air-cooled flat-six as an alternative to the Corvette's usual water-cooled V-8.

First, though, and again with an eye to cost, Chevy considered simple modifications to the existing front-engine Corvette convertible. Changes included peaked front fenders *a la* Q-model; a pointy front surmounting a low rectangular "mouth" with quad headlights under jutting "eyelids"; slab sides relieved by large, sculptured windsplits aft of the front wheel openings, plus a full-perimeter character line; and, interestingly, a "ducktail" almost identical to that of the forth-coming 1961-62 production 'Vette. For all that, it wasn't very inspiring.

But the proposed rear-engine car *was* inspiring— more contemporary and far more graceful. In fact, looking at it now, it has some of the flavor of the pretty second-generation 1965 Corvair. A sharply undercut nose dominated by large, vertical bumper guards led back to crisply beveled bodysides and a long deck terminating in a Corvair-style back panel. The last, plus the large vertical air intakes just aft of the doors, left no doubt that the engine was in the rear ("where an engine belongs," as early Corvair advertising exclaimed). Like the Q-model, this was a technically appealing concept much liked by Duntov and Cole, but GM managers just couldn't see the expense.

While all this was going on, Bill Mitchell had managed to spirit away the Sebring SS development "mule," tested back in 1957 by Juan Manuel Fangio and Stirling Moss. It had been consigned to the corporate attic in the wake of the AMA's "anti-racing" edict. Using his own money and without GM's blessing, Mitchell decided to make the mule into the thorough-

bred racer it started out to be—and to campaign it under his own banner.

There wasn't anything wrong with the chassis that Duntov couldn't fix—he'd learned a lot from the abortive SS project and even more with CERV I—but that old, partly finished body had to go. Mitchell was hardly short on ideas for what to replace it with, and he came up with one of his dandiest: adapt lines from the stillborn Q-coupe to create a dazzling new open body. Stylist Larry Shinoda did the rest, and the Stingray Special was born.

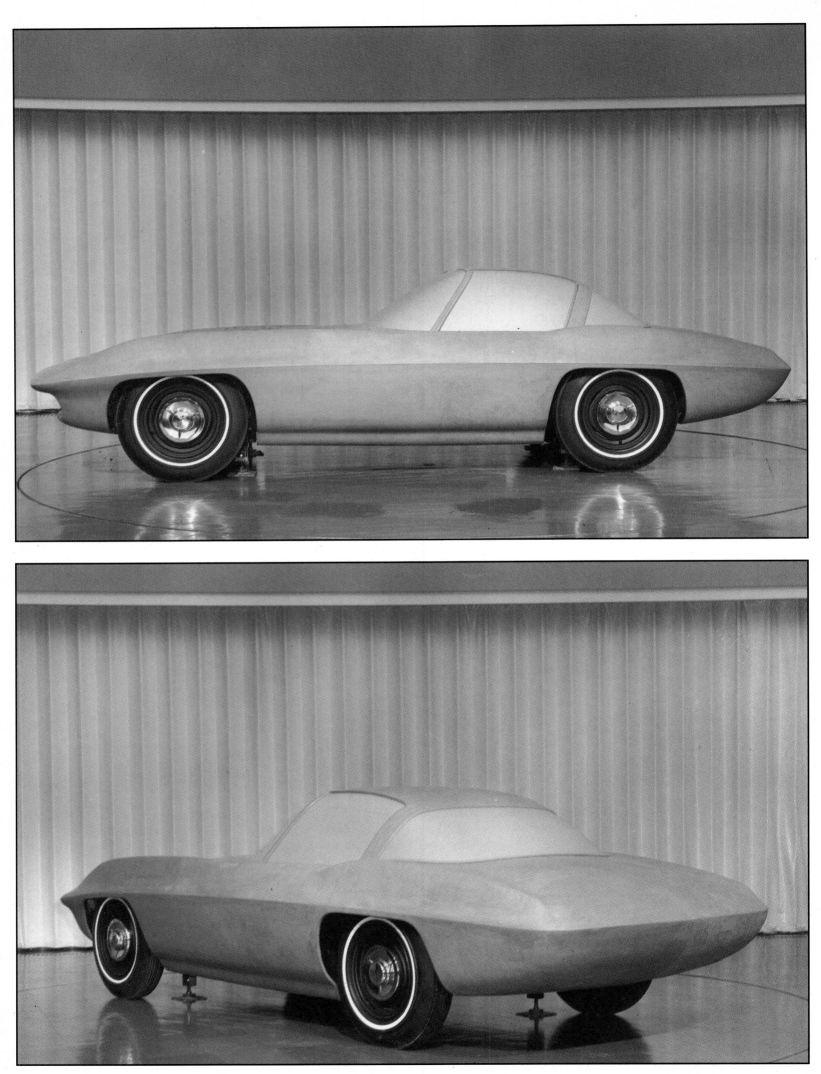

As one of Mitchell's "bootleg" projects, the Stingray Special (also "SS," perhaps a coy reference to that earlier effort) took shape at his "Studio X" special projects area at the GM Tech Center in Warren, Michigan. Dr. Dick Thompson, one of SCCA's winningest Corvette competitors, dropped by, took one look, and promptly promised to drive it in C-Modified events. His showing in that hotly contested class, then dominated by European machines of noble pedigree, stunned even the loquacious Mitchell. Thompson just walked away with the championship in 1959, and again in 1960.

The Stingray Special would later be refurbished and given "Corvette" name script for show-car duty, but in its racing days it was never officially identified as a Corvette—or even a Chevrolet. That just wouldn't do for the image of good-citizen General Motors, which was officially "out of racing" per the AMA decision. Still, a lot of people who saw it race thought the Stingray was a preview of the next Corvette—not exactly a shot in the dark. Thompson's relationship with Chevrolet was well known, and Mitchell and Duntov were conspicuous by their presence in the pits.

Because Mitchell's racer had made such an impression on the public, it figured heavily in the development

of XP-720, the design program leading directly to the production 1963 Corvette Sting Ray. Begun in late autumn 1959, the XP-720 sought to deliver improved passenger accommodation, more luggage space, and superior ride and handling over previous Corvettes, plus high performance, of course. Duntov made sure those last two goals got the greatest emphasis.

The starting point was a ground-up chassis design reflecting lessons learned from the Sebring SS, the Q-model, CERV I, and the Stingray Special. Despite Corvair's arrival, a conventional drivetrain layout was never in doubt. Passengers were placed relatively far to the rear so that the engine/transmission package could sit somewhat behind the front-wheel centerline (in so-called "front mid-engine" position) for optimum weight distribution—the same reasoning that had guided McLean on the original 1953 Corvette. Center of gravity was kept low in the interest of both handling and ride quality, ending up at 16.5 inches above the road, versus the previous 19 inches. Ground clearance was only five inches.

Further enhancing roadability, passengers were placed within the frame, rather than on top of it, and wheelbase was trimmed four inches to 98. For greater torsional rigidity, as well as to allow the driveline

The planning for what eventually appeared as the 1963 Sting Ray initially involved four projects. One of them was the XP-720, the one that did become the '63 Corvette. Although the XP-720 project didn't get underway until autumn 1959, this styling study from February 1958 already has much of the flavor of the XP-720, particularly the humped fenders, the wide, low, mouthy front end, and the general shape of the coupe's top.

151

to ride low and fairly close to the car's longitudinal center, the old Fifties-fashion X-brace was abandoned for a new ladder-type design with five crossmembers. The extra rigidity was deemed necessary not only because of the more potent engines being planned for the future but because the fully independent suspension that Duntov wanted would generate higher lateral stresses than previous 'Vettes had ever known. At one point, the XP-720 chassis proved a little *too* stiff, producing an unacceptably harsh ride. And it cost too much—also unacceptable. The eventual production frame was less rigid but still stronger than it needed to be. With all this, XP-720 emerged a bit tail-heavy, with 53 percent of its total weight resting on the rear wheels. Those larger, heavier engines would correct that soon enough.

Duntov may have gone along with some penny-pinching in chassis construction, but he was adamant about chassis components: The new Corvette would have independent rear suspension (irs), and that was that. Don't misjudge the people who buy the cars, he argued. The new Corvette needs to be more than a pretty face. After all, it will be going head-to-head with the vaunted Jaguar E-Type. Independent rear suspension will help sell 30,000 Corvettes a year. Management

liked the sound of that last remark, and Duntov carried the day.

His Sting Ray irs was simple yet ingenious: basically a frame-mounted differential with U-jointed halfshafts tied together by a transverse leaf spring, a modification of the CERV I arrangement. Rubber-cushioned struts carried the differential, reducing ride harshness while improving tire adhesion, especially on rougher roads. The transverse spring bolted to the rear of the differential case. A control arm extended laterally and slightly forward from each side of the case to a hub carrier, with a trailing radius rod behind. The halfshafts functioned like upper control arms. The lower arms controlled vertical wheel motion, while the trailing rods took care of fore/aft wheel motion and transferred braking torque to the frame. Shock absorbers were conventional twin-tube affairs.

Considerably lighter than the old solid axle, the new irs brought a significant reduction in unsprung weight—important, as the '63 would retain outboard rear brakes. The design originally contemplated splayed coil springs as on CERV I, but they were deemed too bulky. A semi-independent de Dion setup was just as quickly abandoned, its geometry being judged inferior to a true independent arrangement.

Opposite page: *This XP-720 project study (top), dated August 29, 1959, differs from the earlier one on the preceding page mainly from the back end. Corvette shapes can be seen on the wall of this designer's office (bottom left). Zora Arkus-Duntov fought hard for an independent rear suspension for the Sting Ray, and he got it (bottom right). This page: Another design study from August 1961 (top). Clay scale models of the '63 Sting Ray underwent aerodynamic testing in Cal Tech's wind tunnel (bottom).*

Front suspension was much as before, with unequal-length upper and lower A-arms on coil springs concentric with the shocks, plus a standard anti-roll bar. Steering was conventional recirculating-ball, but geared at a higher 19.6:1 overall ratio (previously 21.0:1). Even better, you could change to a still-quicker 17.1:1 by disconnecting the tie rods and moving them to secondary mounting holes in the steering arm, reducing turns lock-to-lock from 3.4 to just 2.9. Bolted to the frame rail at one end and to the relay rod at the other was a new hydraulic steering damper (essentially a shock absorber), which helped soak up bumps before they reached the steering wheel. Optional hydraulically assisted steering was offered for the first time on a Corvette—except on cars with the two most powerful engines—and came with the faster ratio.

While Duntov was earnestly developing an innovative and ultimately producible new chassis, designers had only to refine the basic shape of the racing Stingray, a shape that would seem no less exciting in 1963 than when the public had first glimpsed it in 1959. Styling Staff had been thinking mainly of coupes ever since the Q-Corvette, and early XP-720 mock-ups looked like nothing so much as Mitchell's racer with a fastback roof.

Having this as a starting point made the rest of the

design job easy—and fast. A fully functional space buck (a wooden mock-up created to work out interior dimensions) was completed by early 1960; production coupe styling was locked up in all but details by April; and the interior—instrument panel included—was in place by November. Only in the fall of 1960 did the designers turn to a new version of the traditional Corvette convertible and, still later, its detachable hardtop.

For one of the few times in automotive history and for the first time in Corvette's, wind tunnel testing helped refine the final shape, as did practical matters like interior space, windshield curvatures, and tooling limitations. Both body styles were extensively evaluated as production-ready ⅜-scale models at the Cal Tech wind tunnel.

Inner structure received as much attention as aerodynamics, again for reasons of refinement, though also for greater longevity. Fiberglass outer panels were retained, but the Sting Ray emerged with nearly twice as much steel support in its central structure as the 1958-62 Corvette. The resulting extra weight was balanced by a reduction in fiberglass thickness, so the finished product actually weighed a bit less than the old roadster. Duntov, of course, had hoped for

something even lighter but seemed content with what he got, acknowledging the fact that the 'Vette had long since ceased having any pretentions of being a spartan sports car. Passenger room was as good as before despite the tighter wheelbase, and the reinforcing steel girder made the cockpit both stronger and safer.

The Sting Ray was more than just a beautiful body. Granted, powerteams were completely carried over from 1962, and the new convertible was quite similar to its 1961-62 predecessor from the doorjambs back. But in nearly every other respect, the Sting Ray was entirely and dramatically new.

Symbolizing this transformation was the first-ever production Corvette coupe—a futuristic fastback that attracted even larger crowds than the roadster, thanks partly to its unique, divided rear window. This feature, which dated from the Olds Golden Rocket show car of 1956, had once been considered for an all-new '58 Corvette, and Mitchell thought enough of the backlight backbone to resurrect it for the new '63. The daylight opening's basic shape, a compound-curve "saddleback," had been laid down by Bob McLean on the Q-model.

The split window proved quite controversial. Duntov, for one, was opposed because it hindered driver vision astern. But purely practical arguments were never enough for Mitchell, who insisted, "If you take that off, you might as well forget the whole thing." He was referring to the full-length dorsal "spine" that began as a bulge in the center of the hood (necessary to clear the plenum chamber on engines with fuel injection) and continued as a creaseline over the roof (which itself was imitative of the classic "boattail"), through the window and on down the deck. Mitchell was the boss, so he got his way, and most Corvette fans agree he was right. The Sting Ray split-window coupe remains one of the most stunning automobiles of all time. It certainly met one of Mitchell's prime criteria: It wouldn't be mistaken for anything else.

But the split backlight took a beating in the press. *Road & Track* called it "that silly bar," and *Car and Driver* sided with Duntov, saying the "central window partition ruins our rear view." But if the motoring press sometimes couldn't see the styling forest for the trees, many customers did. They loved the coupe because it looked like it was speeding even when parked. Mitchell relented after one year of production, thus creating a car for future collectors. However, many split-

The Corvette for 1963 not only was all new—including the first use of the Sting Ray name on a production model—but it also debuted the marque's first coupe. It was a fastback whose top tapered to a point; seen from the rear it had a distinct "V" shape (below). A notable feature was the split rear window, a design that stylist Bill Mitchell had insisted upon even though it did nothing for rear visibility. The '63 was also the first 'Vette that lacked a decklid, access to the trunk being from inside the car.

This page: *The '63 Sting Ray coupe listed at $4252, the convertible roadster at $4037 (top). Chevy proudly emphasized the Corvette's heritage—even though the car was but a decade old—by posing the new '63s with the XP-720 and Sting Ray racer (bottom). Opposite page: Chevy did so again in July 1963 with a large gathering of 'Vettes, old and new (top). The '63 dashboard dated back to November 1960 (bottom).*

156

window coupes were lost to customizers, some of whom "updated" the cars with one-piece windows (of Plexiglas) once that change appeared for '64. Chevy itself didn't help by offering replacement one-piecers through dealers. Thus have a good many '63 coupes lost value as collectibles.

The rest of the Sting Ray design was equally stunning. Quad headlamps were retained but newly hidden—the first American car so equipped since the 1942 DeSoto (not exactly a styling landmark, which must have given GM pause). The lamps were mounted in rotating sections that matched the pointy front end with the "eyes" closed. Recalling the '55 Chevrolet was an attractive beltline dip at the door's trailing upper edge, a result of cinching up the racing Stingray at the "midriff." Coupe doors were cut into the roof, which recalled the unlamented Tucker, though the idea was just as practical here, easing entry/exit in a low-slung closed car. Today, of course, you see this everywhere. The dummy vents in the hood and on the coupe's rear pillars were chided, though they wouldn't last long. Functional ones had been intended but were nixed by high cost and, in the case of the hood vents, a little problem caused by aerodynamics: It was found that warm engine air exiting from the top of the hood flowed right back into the cowl intake for the new windows-up interior ventilation system—not what you needed on a warm day.

The Sting Ray's interior carried a new interpretation of the "twin-cowl" Corvette dash motif used since '58, with the scooped-out semicircles now standing upright instead of lying down—something like DeSoto's 1955-56 "gullwing" design. Author Karl Ludvigsen almost gleefully observed that the panel "related not at all in its contours to the lines of the hood ahead of it." And indeed, "The dual cockpit was widely criticized at the time," according to one Corvette designer, though

he also termed it "a very fresh approach to two-passenger styling." It was more practical, too, bringing a roomy glovebox with a proper door, plus an improved heater, the aforementioned cowl-ventilation system, and a full set of easily read round gauges that included a huge speedometer and tachometer set dead ahead of the driver. The "control tower" center console returned, somewhat slimmer but now containing the clock and—another unusual touch—a vertically situated radio with a dial oriented to suit.

Luggage space was improved as well, though the lack of an external trunklid was as criticized as the coupe's divided backlight. This, too, was precluded by cost concerns, which in retrospect seems pretty silly. Of course, any cargo you might carry had to

be stuffed behind the seats; on the convertible you also had to disconnect the folded top from its flip-up tonneau panel, as *Road & Track* noted, "before access is gained. In the coupe, there's room for a couple of young children and lots of baggage....One of those Aston Martin-type rear-window doors would have been an ideal solution. Perhaps Chevrolet could offer one as an option." (Alas, Chevy wouldn't pick up on that suggestion for almost 20 years.) The spare lived at the rear in a drop-down fiberglass housing beneath a gas tank holding 20 gallons instead of 16. The big, round deck emblem was newly hinged to double as a fuel-filler flap, replacing the previous left-flank door.

Besides the new fastback and traditional two-seat convertible, Chevrolet also toyed with a four-place Sting Ray coupe. This idea was suggested by Ed Cole, who felt a back-seat model would provide broader market coverage, enabling Corvette to compete directly with a number of upscale European 2+2s while appealing to those 'Vette fans who occasionally needed to carry more than one passenger.

The four-seat Sting Ray got as far as a full-size mock-up, photographed in the Design Staff auditorium in 1962 alongside a contemporary Ford Thunderbird, which would have been its main domestic rival. It looked much like the production-approved split-window coupe, but with some 10 extra inches in wheelbase, a higher roofline (for some semblance of rear headroom), and revised rear fender contours, plus a pair of fully engineered rear seats with fold-down backrests. Unhappily, it also looked rather awkward, which probably convinced some executives that it might dilute the styling impact of the two-seaters. More to the point, Mitchell, Duntov, and Chevy's sales chief were all against it, so the idea, though basically a good one, was abandoned. But Jaguar, at least, must have liked the notion, because a few years later it released a stretched-wheelbase 2+2 E-Type coupe with similarly awkward lines.

Though not as obvious, the new chassis was just as important to the Sting Ray's success as the new styling. Maneuverability was improved thanks to the faster steering and shorter wheelbase. The latter might ordinarily imply a choppier ride, but the altered weight distribution partly compensated. Less weight on the front wheels also meant easier steering at a time when power steering wasn't commonly ordered on Corvettes. And with some 80 additional pounds on the rear wheels, the Sting Ray offered improved traction.

Stopping power improved, too. Four-wheel cast-iron drum brakes of 11-inch diameter were still standard but were now wider, for an increase in effective braking area, and sintered-metallic linings, segmented for cooling, were again optional. So were finned aluminum

Opposite page, from top: *A January 1962 comparison of the '62 Thunderbird versus the upcoming Sting Ray; an April 1961 Sting Ray clay model, close to the final design; three photos of a January 1962 prototype for an extended-wheelbase four-seater Sting Ray. This page: At the St. Louis assembly line, an overhead conveyor lowers the body onto the chassis (top) and, as Chevy said, a "careful and final inspection prepares the new Corvette for its first meeting with a proud owner."*

("Al-Fin") drums, which not only provided faster heat dissipation and thus better fade resistance but less unsprung weight. Power assist was available with both brake packages, like power steering another first-time Corvette option. Evolutionary engineering changes included positive crankcase ventilation, a smaller flywheel, an aluminum clutch housing and, as elsewhere in Detroit, adoption of the more efficient electrical alternator in place of the old-fashioned generator.

As mentioned, the Sting Ray arrived with the same drivetrains as those available on its '62 predecessor. These comprised four 327 V-8s, a trio of transmissions, and six axle ratios. Carbureted engines comprised

250-, 300- and 340-horsepower versions. As before, the base and step-up units employed hydraulic lifters, a mild cam, forged-steel crankshaft, 10.5:1 compression, single-point distributor, and dual exhausts. The 300 produced its extra power via a larger four-barrel carburetor (Carter AFB instead of the 250's Carter WCFB), plus larger intake valves and exhaust manifold. Again topping the heap was a 360-bhp fuel-injected powerhouse, priced at $430.40 additional. With base prices up to $4252 for the coupe and $4037

continued on page 162

159

The '63 Sting Ray rode a 98-inch wheelbase, four inches shorter than in 1962. It measured 175.2 inches overall, a decrease of two. The convertible (often called a roadster) weighed in at 2881 pounds, a reduction of 44. As in the past, a removable hardtop (left) was offered as an option; it cost $236.75. For 1963, the X-braced frame gave way to a new ladder-type design with five cross members.

for the convertible, adding injection now seemed a more questionable use of funds.

Repeating as standard transmission was the familiar three-speed manual, though neither it nor the optional Powerglide automatic was very popular. As ever, the preferred gearbox was the Borg-Warner manual four-speed, delivered with wide-ratio gears when teamed with the base and 300-bhp engines, and close-ratio gearing with the top two options. Standard axle ratio for the three-speed or Powerglide was 3.36:1. The four-speeders came with a 3.70:1 final drive, but 3.08:1, 3.55:1, 4.11:1, and 4.56:1 gearsets were available. The last was quite rare in production.

Although GM was still nominally adhering to the AMA's 1957 "racing ban," Duntov was determined that anyone who wanted to race his sophisticated new Sting Ray—which was, after all, the best-handling Corvette yet—should have the best possible chance for victory. This was the rationale behind RPO Z06, a new competition-oriented package. To get it, you had to specify a fuelie coupe equipped with four-speed and Positraction limited-slip differential—then pay a formidable $1818.45 over *that*. In exchange you received the top-line Al-Fin power brakes with sintered-metallic linings, plus H-D front stabilizer bar, stronger shocks, much stiffer-than-stock springs, dual master cylinder, and a long-distance 36.5-gallon fuel tank. The package was also listed for the convertible, but production records show no such cars were built.

Chevy had intended to offer beautiful cast-aluminum wheels with tri-spinner knock-off hubs as part of the Z06 package and as a separate option. But though often shown in ads and press photos, these weren't strict "factory equipment" for '63. Chevy withdrew them after announcement due to casting problems that made the wheels so porous that they wouldn't hold air in the tires. The problem was solved for 1964 and later models, and some dealers installed the "working" wheels on '63s post-purchase, but all Z06-equipped '63s left St. Louis on conventional steel rims. By the way, the Sting Ray's initial wheel cover was a rather ornate six-spoke design with dummy knock-off hubs that didn't look nearly as good, one reason so many

'63s have been retrofitted with the finely vaned aluminum wheels.

Looking back, it's remarkable how refined and well developed the Sting Ray was right out of the box. Whether you called it a sports car or a *gran turismo* was almost irrelevant. It had all the right stuff, and to no one's great surprise it was as much a sensation on the street, strip, and speedway as it was in the showroom.

It also made a strong impression on hard-boiled automotive journalists. *Road & Track*, which had lauded past Corvettes for high performance-per-dollar, was nearly ecstatic: "In a word, the new Sting Ray sticks [with] great gripping gobs of traction....The S-bend was even more fun: Every time through it we discovered we could have gone a little faster. We never did find the limit....As a purely sporting car, the new Corvette will know few peers on road or track....It ought to be nearly unbeatable."

That verdict was unanimously echoed. Jim Wright in the May 1963 *Motor Trend* said the Sting Ray was "far in advance, both in ride and handling, of anything now being built in the United States. It's completely comfortable without being mushy and it takes a large chuckhole to induce any degree of harshness into the ride. Sudden dips, when taken at speed, don't produce any unpleasant oscillations, and the front and rear suspension is very hard to bottom. There's very little pitch noticeable in the ride, even though the 'Vette is built on a fairly short wheelbase. At high cruising speeds—and even at maximum speeds—nothing but an all-out competition car will equal it in stability. We drove it under some pretty windy conditions and didn't notice any adverse effects from crosswind loading. We thought the old model corners darn well, but there's no comparing it to this new one. It does take a little different technique, but once the driver gets into it, it's beautiful."

Because of its 49/51 percent front/rear weight distribution, the Sting Ray oversteered in classic sports-car fashion. This was also true of its stablemate, the Corvair, whose handling would eventually force GM to go to court. But the few buyers who appreciated oversteer were happy as the proverbial clam. "The ride and handling are great," said *Sports Car Graphic*. "We won't elaborate on how great: You've got to drive one

continued on page 165

This page: The Sting Ray sport coupe proved to be a popular offering from the very beginning. In its first year, production reached 10,594 units, only 325 less than the roadster. Opposite page: Fuel injection continued as an option for 1963 via the L-84 package, which gave the 327 V-8 a horsepower rating of 360. It cost $430.40; note the fuel injection badges on the front fenders.

to believe it." *Car and Driver* opined that the Corvette was "now second to no other production sports car in roadholding and is still the most powerful."

Car Life bestowed its annual Award for Engineering Excellence on the Sting Ray. "Tricky, twisting roads are this Corvette's meat," waxed the editors. "With its new suspension it seems to lock onto them, going precisely where directed and sticking to the tightest corners without the shadow of a doubt. Where the old Corvette had an annoying penchant for swapping ends when cornered vigorously, the new one just sticks and storms. This suspension is the best thing since gumdrops!"

Despite its carryover status, Chevy's small-block V-8—the most consistent component of past Corvette performance—seemed even better in the Sting Ray. In acceleration, the '63s were virtually identical with the 1962 models, engine for engine, but had an edge in both traction and handling because their new independent rear suspension reduced wheelspin compared to the live-axle cars. Testing a four-speed fuelie with 3.70:1 axle, *MT*'s Wright reported 0-30/45/60 mph in 2.9/4.2/5.8 seconds and a 14.5-second standing quarter-mile at 102 mph. "A course longer than the Riverside Raceway backstretch would've produced something very close to the Sting Ray's theoretical top speed of 140-142 mph," he concluded, "because the engine was still winding when we had to back off."

All things considered, fuel consumption was remarkably good, especially with fuel injection, which, as before, adjusted the air/fuel mixture to compensate for changes in humidity, altitude, and temperature. *Motor Trend* recorded better than 18 miles per gallon at legal highway speeds. Drivers mostly kept the pedal to the metal otherwise, but didn't average less than 13.6 mpg even around town. Overall, *MT*'s test Sting Ray returned 14.1 mpg—not bad for 360 horsepower.

Such glowing reports might be expected from magazines whose income depends partly on GM advertising. Not so the British, harder to please and ever skeptical of Yankee iron, but perhaps more objective. *Motor* ladled out more praise than sister

Autocar, reporting its Sting Ray to be the fastest car it had ever tested yet capable of "not unreasonable" fuel consumption. The gearbox was judged "one of the best we have ever encountered in such a high-performance car.

"In most respects," *Motor* concluded, "the Chevrolet Corvette Sting Ray is the equal of any GT car to be found on either side of the Atlantic. It falls down on refinement (which is surprising in a model from a country where the most unpretentious cars are notably refined) and wet-road behaviour, a shortcoming for which the cure might be found in the choice of tyres....The car is not free of gimmicks, but the performance needs no flattery, the handling is good and the brakes superb."

Autocar, which noted with apparent amazement that its 'Vette used no oil during its test, had a somewhat

The new Sting Ray brought an enthusiastic response from the motoring press. Car Life, for example, gave it its annual Award for Engineering Excellence. The independent rear suspension was praised and so was the performance. When equipped with fuel injection (like the car pictured), four-speed, and 3.70:1 gearing, Motor Trend's Sting Ray covered the 0-60 sprint in 5.8 seconds, the quarter-mile in 14.5 seconds at 102 miles per hour.

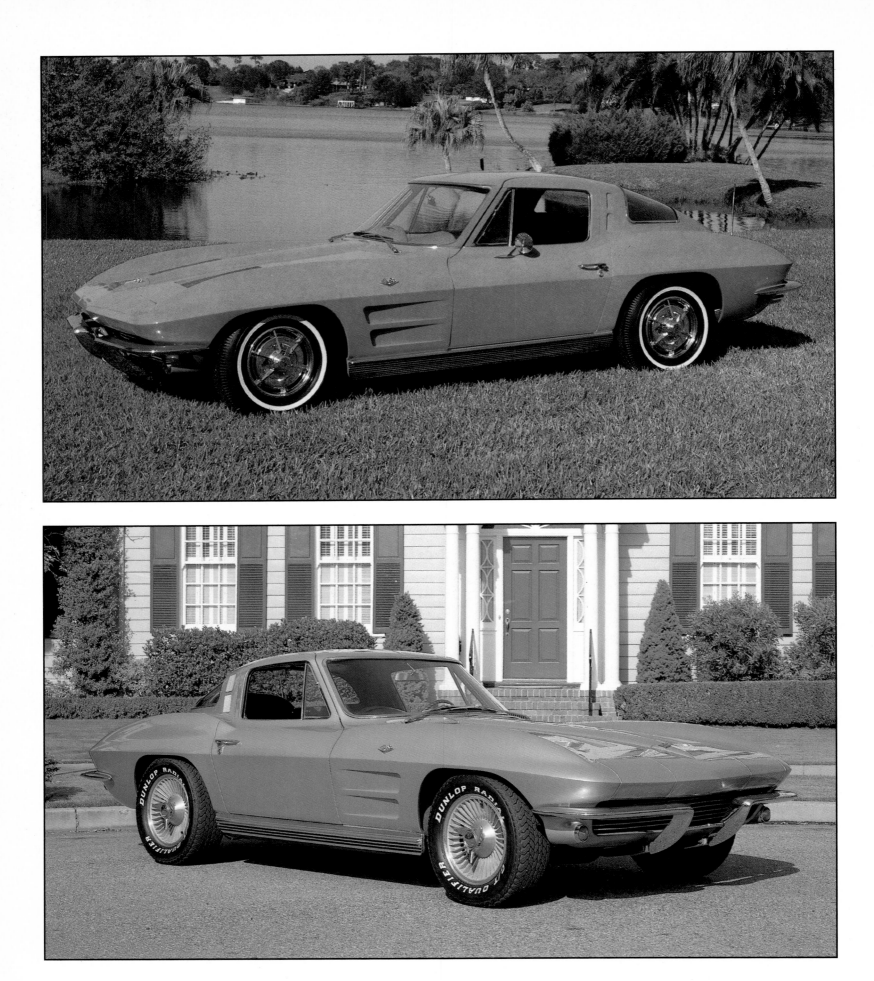

more critical assessment: "Judging by the Sting Ray, American manufacturers are still behind those of Europe when endeavouring to build a car combining real performance and refinement—rather surprising when their more normal road cars are so good in the latter respect. No doubt the less highly tuned versions would be preferred by the majority of owners and give enough performance for them." And so it was. Most Sting Ray buyers opted for one of the smoother and quieter hydraulic-lifter engines, though the fuelie's high cost probably had something to do with that.

American criticisms mainly involved vision through the coupe's split rear window and access to the luggage compartment — or rather the lack of it. Creature

Although initial reaction to the '63 Sting Ray sports coupe (both pages) was quite favorable, two major criticisms surfaced: poor rearward vision due to the split-window design and the difficult access to the luggage compartment due to the lack of a decklid. The first would be dealt with for 1964, the second wouldn't. A racing-style gas cap (above) was located on the rear deck.

comforts met with wide approval. The days of Plexiglas side curtains, doors without handles, and wheezing heaters were gone. Even British two-seaters were getting roll-up windows and two-minute tops.

But the Sting Ray was a notch above even the best European sports cars with its contoured bucket seats, telescopic steering wheel adjustment, functional instrumentation, and a heating/ventilation system fully able to cope with the greater extremes of North American climate. True, the steering column adjustment demanded a little wrench work. And yes, the seats were a little low for some, though that was because Duntov wanted them that way for a low center of gravity. But overall, the Sting Ray was the

most civilized Corvette ever and one of the most refined sporting cars built anywhere on the planet. Why, buyers even had the new options of leather upholstery and air conditioning.

Racers, of course, went for the aforementioned Z06 package, a reflection of Duntov's determination that the Sting Ray coupe at least should be a GT-class and SCCA contender (as if we didn't know already). Sure enough, a quartet of Z06-equipped fastbacks was dispatched to the Los Angeles *Times* Three-Hour Invitational Race at Riverside on October 13, 1962 for

the Sting Ray's competition coming-out party. Dave MacDonald, Bob Bondurant, Jerry Grant, and Doug Hooper did the driving honors. As fate would have it, that was also the debut for Carroll Shelby's awesome Ford-powered Cobra, but the Sting Ray was well up to the challenge of that Anglo-American hybrid. Though three of the four Chevys failed to finish, Hooper took the checkered flag in a car owned by Mickey Thompson, who reportedly exclaimed, "I don't think it's ever been done before...a new production car winning the first time out!"

The Sting Ray would go on to other victories, but it was the Cobra that would come to dominate production-class racing in the Sixties. Street manners were so good, however, that the Corvette didn't really need a racing image to support sales anymore. Duntov still hoped for a full-blown competition version, and his dream would be realized, if briefly, in the spectacular Corvette Grand Sport (see Chapter 8).

Despite its new design, the Sting Ray maintained tradition by offering remarkable sports-car value for

Opposite page: *The Grand Sport (top) was Duntov's reply to Carroll Shelby's Ford-powered Cobra. Dave McDonald drove car 00 at Riverside in October 1962, but another Corvette won (center). Speedometer and tach were right in front of the driver (bottom). Many thought the fake hood vents a bit much (below).*

All engines for the '63 Corvette displaced 327 cubic inches. The fuel-injected version put out 360 horsepower. The base version, as on the red car, used a four-barrel carb and ran a compression ratio of 10.5:1, good for 250 horses. The silver car's engine is stickered 350, but that horsepower rating with the 327 was actually for 1965-68. Intermediate ratings in 1963 were 300 and 340 bhp. All important gauges were in the dash's left cove; the clock resided in the console.

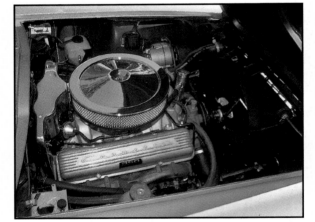

the money—arguably even more than previous 'Vettes. A split-window coupe with the fuelie engine and a few other goodies delivered for around $5300; factored for inflation, that's $14,000-$15,000 in today's money—by any measure a sensational deal. (You can pay that much or more for a tame Japanese family sedan.) It's a lot different now, of course: A prime-condition '63 coupe fetches about the same price as a brand-new Corvette.

It's interesting to note that the 21,513 Sting Rays built for model year '63 divided almost evenly between the convertible and the new coupe—10,919 and 10,594, respectively—and that more than half the convertibles were ordered with the optional lift-off hardtop. Obviously, the greater comfort and convenience of closed body styles were becoming just as important to sports-minded types as to family-car buyers, making the advent of the coupe quite timely in retrospect. Nevertheless, it wouldn't sell as well again in the Sting Ray years. If fact, not until 1969, when the two models had become relatively indistinguishable, did the closed Corvette sell better than the open one.

Equipment installations for 1963 began reflecting the market's demand for more civility in sporting cars. For example, the power brake option went into 15 percent of production, power steering into 12 percent.

On the other hand, only 278 buyers specified the $421 air conditioning; leather upholstery—a mere $81—was ordered on only about 400 cars. The beautiful cast-aluminum knock-off wheels, manufactured for Chevy by Kelsey-Hayes, cost $323 a set, but few were sold owing to the aforementioned porosity problems. However, almost 18,000 Sting Rays left St. Louis with the four-speed manual gearbox—better than four out of every five.

The Sting Ray represented something of a "golden

continued on page 172

mean" for America's sports car, a happy balance it would retain through 1967. Today it's the ultimate Corvette for millions of enthusiasts, many of whom were not yet born when the car was new. And though no one could foresee this in the Sixties, the Sting Ray would have historic significance as the only all-new Corvette between the 1953 Motorama original and the sixth-generation design introduced for 1984. In between came the so-called "shark" Corvette, which looked considerably different but retained the basic Sting Ray chassis all the way to its end in 1982—eloquent testimony to the sophistication and foresight of the chassis designers—and Zora Arkus-Duntov.

With Corvette sales up by some 50 percent for 1963, it seemed prudent to make only evolutionary changes for the follow-up 1964 Sting Ray. Styling modifications were mostly for the better, as Chevrolet

continued on page 174

Major Specifications: 1963 Corvette Sting Ray

Body/Chassis

Frame:	Box-section steel, ladder-type with five crossmembers
Body:	Fiberglass; 2-seat convertible and fastback coupe
Front suspension:	Independent; upper and lower A-arms, coil springs, tubular hydraulic shock absorbers, anti-roll bar
Rear suspension:	Independent; fixed differential, U-jointed halfshafts, lateral struts, radius rods, transverse leaf spring, tubular hydraulic shock absorbers (anti-roll bar with big-block engines; see text)
Wheels:	15-inch bolt-on steel
Tires:	6.70 × 15 4-ply

Dimensions

Wheelbase (in.):	98.0
Overall length (in.):	175.3
Overall height (in.):	49.8
Overall width (in.):	69.6
Track front/rear (in.):	56.3/57.0
Ground clearance (in.):	5.0
Curb weight (lbs):	3150

Engines

Type:	ohv V-8, water-cooled, cast-iron block and heads
Main bearings:	5
Bore × stroke (in.):	4.00 × 3.25
Displacement (ci):	327
Compression ratio:	11.25:1
Induction system:	Ramjet fuel injection
Exhaust system:	Split cast-iron manifolds, dual exhaust
Brake horsepower @ rpm:	360 @ 6000
Torque @ rpm (lbs/ft):	352 @ 4000
Electrical system:	12-volt Delco-Remy

Drivetrain

Transmission:	Close-ratio 4-speed manual with floorshift
Gear ratios:	First—2.20:1
	Second—1.64:1
	Third—1.30:1
	Fourth—1.00:1
Rear axle type:	Hypoid semi-floating; optional Positraction limited-slip differential
Rear axle ratio:	3.70:1
Steering:	Saginaw recirculating-ball; 17:1 overall ratio; 3.4 turns lock-to-lock
Turning circle (ft):	35.0
Brakes:	Self-adjusting 11-inch diameter 4-wheel cast-iron drums with hydraulic actuation; 135 sq in. effective lining area; sintered-metallic linings optional

Performance*

0-30 mph (sec):	2.9
0-45 mph (sec):	4.2
0-60 mph (sec):	5.8
0-1/4 mile (sec @ mph):	14.2 @ 105

* *Motor Trend*, May 1963

Opposite page: Harley Earl, former chief honcho of GM's Art and Colour Studio, indulged himself in a '63 Sting Ray sports coupe (top two rows). As one might expect, it wasn't totally stock. Note, for example, the altered fake extractor vent in the front fender on the passenger's side and the macho exhaust exiting the same spot on the driver's side. A '63 show car (bottom) sported the same exhaust, but added a flashy white hood accent. This page: The '63 ragtop enjoyed a production run of 10,919 units.

began a clean-up campaign that would continue through the design's 1967 finale (similar to the way the busy '58 generation had been progressively tidied). Besides the coupe's backbone window, the two fake hood air intakes were eliminated—though not their indentations—and the simulated air-exhaust vents on the coupe's left rear pillar were made functional. Rocker-panel trim lost some of its ribs and gained black paint between the ribs that remained; wheel covers were simplified (via nine slim radial slots); and the fuel filler/deck emblem gained concentric circles around its crossed-flags insignia. Inside, the original color-keyed steering wheel rim was now done in simulated walnut,

and complaints about glare from the bright instrument bezels were answered with a flat-black finish.

An improved ride was among Duntov's original goals for the Sting Ray, and most reviewers judged him successful, especially compared to previous Corvettes. But shock absorbers weakened as the miles rolled by, and owners began complaining of a deterioration in ride quality. Chevrolet attacked this problem with a few suspension refinements for '64. The front coil springs were changed from constant-rate to progressive or variable-rate and were more tightly wound at the top, while leaf thickness of the rear transverse spring was varied from within. With their wider damping

range, the revised springs could better absorb both large and small disturbances, thus providing a more comfortable ride with no sacrifice in handling.

Shock absorbers were reworked toward the same end. When subjected to frequent oscillation at near full vertical wheel travel, such as on very rough roads, the standard '63 shocks tended to overheat. This caused their hydraulic fluid to "cavitate" or bubble, with a consequent loss in damping efficiency. The 1964 Corvette arrived with a new standard shock containing within its fluid reservoir a small bag of freon gas that absorbed heat to keep the fluid from bubbling.

The European press had faulted the '63 for relatively

high interior noise levels. Accordingly, Chevy added more sound insulation and revised body and transmission mounts. It also fitted additional bushings to quiet the shift linkage and placed a new boot around the lever. The result was a more livable car for regular and long-distance transportation.

Drivetrain choices were basically as before: four 327 V-8s, as many transmissions, and six axle ratios. The two least powerful engines returned with 250 and 300 bhp on 10.5:1 compression, but the high-performance pair received several noteworthy improvements. The solid-lifter unit was massaged with a high-lift, long-duration camshaft to produce 365 bhp and breathed through a big four-barrel Holley carb instead of the base engine's Carter instrument. This was an advantage, since the Holley was more easily tailored to specific needs because a larger assortment of performance pieces were available for it. The fuelie also gained 15 horsepower, bringing its total to 375. But at a hefty $538, it was too rich for most buyers. For the next decade or so, the route to 'Vette power would be through the time-honored expedient of adding cubic inches and not through sophisticated means like injection.

Although transmission options remained ostensibly the same for '64, the two Borg-Warner T-10 four-speeds gave way to a similar pair of gearboxes built at GM's Muncie, Indiana, transmission facility. The "Muncie" was already being used in other GM models, so its adoption for the Corvette made sense for reasons of both manufacturing and cost. Originally a Chevy design, it had an aluminum case like the B-W box but stronger synchronizers and wider ratios for better durability and driveability. The wide-ratio version could be teamed only with the 250- and 300-bhp power-plants; gear spacings were 2.56:1, 1.91:1, 1.40:1, and

Changes to the '64 Corvette Sting Ray were evolutionary in nature and biased toward cleaning up the design a bit. The backlight became one piece, the two fake air intakes on the hood lost their glitter, and the simulated air exhaust vents on the coupe's rear pillars became functional (driver's side only). Also, the rocker panel trim had fewer ribs, the fuel filler door gained concentric circles, and the wheel covers were simpler. Inside, the color-keyed steering wheel was replaced by one with simulated walnut trim and the instrument bezels were painted flat black, rather than chromed.

1.00:1. The close-ratio unit was for the more potent mills; its internals were 2.20:1, 1.64:1, 1.28:1, and 1.00:1. Like the B-W boxes, the Muncies had a reverse lockout trigger, but with a thicker shifter.

Positraction was still a bargain option in 1964 at only $43.05, and it went into more than 80 percent of that year's production. The clutch-type differential was designed to send engine torque to the wheel with greater traction, as opposed to a standard open differential that transfers power to the wheel with lesser traction. Positraction naturally enhanced off-the-line dig as well as getting out of mud or snow. On ice or really hard-packed snow, however, the torque transfer from one wheel to the other could induce fishtailing— unnerving in such a high-powered car. Control on slippery surfaces required a deft foot.

The J56 sintered-metallic brakes were a much costlier option—a whopping $629.50—though you also got the Al-Fin drums from the previous Z06 package. Of course, the J56 brakes were also for competition, and while not as easily modulated as the disc brakes to come, they provided plenty of fade-free stopping power. In fact, Duntov felt that the proprietary disc brakes then available weren't as good as the J56 drums. Magazine testers agreed. As *Car Life* noted: "The harder these brakes have to work, the better they are." But discs were coming into vogue at the time, and the Corvette would have them.

If motor-noters liked the first Sting Ray, they loved the '64. *Motor Trend*'s report of September 1963 covered a fuel-injected four-speed coupe with the super-twist 4.11:1 rear axle, aluminum knock-off wheels

Although the sport coupe had sold head to head with the convertible in 1963, the ratio was more like seven-to-four in favor of the ragtop in 1964.
The hubcap design theme showed up in modified form on the 1966 Mustang, while the driver's side air vent helped keep interior air fresh. Overall, the cleaner styling, along with the numerous engineering improvements, contributed to a more refined edition of "America's sports car."

(perfected at last and available from the factory), the sintered-metallic brakes, and Positraction, which with AM/FM radio and tinted glass pushed the $4394 base price to $6367. With all that and 375 horses, *MT*'s tester screamed through the quarter-mile in 14.2 seconds at 100 mph and streaked from 0 to 60 mph in just 5.6 seconds. "Acceleration in all speed ranges was, to say the least, fierce—of the 'smash-you-into-your-seat' variety. The engine proved willing, and pulled strongly right up to 6700 rpm and beyond in every gear."

At the opposite end of the spectrum, ever-sensible *Road & Track* elected to test the tame 300-bhp Powerglide setup in a '64 coupe and had many good things to say about it. With a 0-60-mph time of 8.0 seconds, a standing-quarter in 15.2 seconds at 85

mph, and average fuel consumption of 14.8 mpg, it was, *R&T* decided, "definitely not for the purists, but...it has decided advantages for anyone who does the majority of his driving in heavy traffic. With a price tag closer to $5000 than $4000, it is by no means cheap but, on the other hand, it represents remarkably good value for money when one considers the performance combined with comfort, and the generally high standard of quality throughout the car."

That assessment was telling: Although not perfect—and what car is, after all?—the Sting Ray was a lot more reliable and better-built than some people thought. Supporting this view was a February 1967 *R&T* report by editor Ron Wakefield, who covered 36,000 miles in a '63 Sting Ray convertible with the base 300-bhp engine, four-speed, Positraction, and

Chevy took pride in the Corvette's "twin-cowl" dashboard, which featured the full instrumentation that sports-car purists insisted upon. Although one didn't particularly notice from the driver's seat, cars equipped with the four-speed manual now used gearboxes made in GM's Muncie, Indiana plant rather than Borg-Warner T10s. Both close- and wide-ratio units were offered, the latter only for 250- and 300-bhp cars.

little else. Repair costs came to just under $400, total operating costs to less than eight cents a mile. Even better for one who'd owned a succession of British sports cars, nothing of consequence went wrong, though a loud "pop," which Wakefield attributed to the Positraction unit, surfaced at around the 20,000-mile mark. "I have not doted on this car," he wrote, "but I have maintained it well. At the end of the 36,000 miles it was performing almost as new. Obviously, it is a long-life car, and one requiring relatively little attention."

However, Wakefield decried the convertible body's "great propensity for rattles, squeaks and general structural shake on rough roads," but judged the folding top to be "one of the best. It goes up and down very easily, seals well and wears well, too. From the looks of it...I'd say it will last the life of the car."

"Even with its smallest engine," Wakefield concluded, "the Corvette can be quite exhilarating to drive; there's always a great reserve of torque and roadholding on tap, so this is no dullard in any sense. It does serve to show that the car can be owned and operated for a very reasonable outlay." Insurance, incidentally, was Wakefield's greatest single expense. It has ever been thus with high-powered sports cars and especially Corvettes—as most any owner will attest.

Insurance costs probably didn't deter too many buyers of the '64 Sting Rays, which numbered 22,229—another new Corvette record, if up only a little from banner 1963. Coupe volume dropped to 8304 units, but convertible sales more than compensated, rising to 13,925.

continued on page 182

The '64 Corvette sport coupe (bottom) and convertible (right) were priced exactly as in 1963: $4252 and $4037, respectively. Production totaled 22,229 units, 8304 of them coupes. Work was well underway on the '66 Sting Ray in September of 1964. The prototype shown here (opposite top) sports the eggcrate grille that was adopted for the '66, but the side vent design never made it to production.

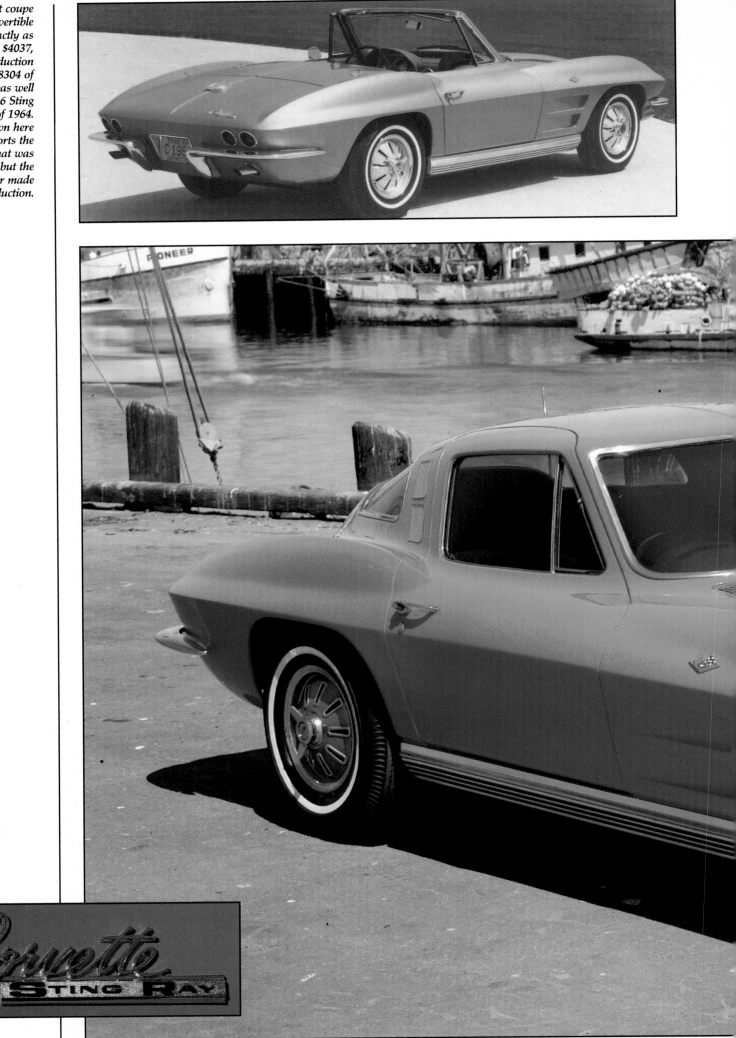

For its third season, model year 1965, the Sting Ray was not only further cleaned up but muscled up in a big way. Styling alterations were subtle, confined to a smoothed-out hood *sans* indentations; a trio of working vertical exhaust vents in the front fenders replacing the previous nonfunctional horizontal "speedlines;" restyled wheel covers and rocker-panel moldings; and detail interior trim revisions.

Two big mechanical surprises emerged for '65. One was the advent of optional four-wheel disc brakes, accompanied by special wheel covers. The brakes had a four-piston design with two-piece calipers and cooling fins for the rotors. Pads were in constant contact with the rotors, but the resulting drag was negligible and didn't affect fuel economy. Further, the light touching kept the rotors clean and didn't diminish pad life, which was, in fact, quite high: a projected 57,000 miles for the front brakes (which because of forward weight transfer supplied most of the braking effort in all-out stops) and about twice that distance for the rears. Total swept area for the new system was 461 square inches, a notable advance on the 328 square inches of the previous all-drum system. Per pending federal regulation, there was also a dual master cylinder with separate fluid reservoirs for the front and rear lines.

Road testers applauded the all-disc binders. Said *Sports Car Graphic* in October 1964: "After experience with the drum-sintered-lining setup—a previous HD option—we found this brake a distinct pleasure to operate, especially as the stopping potential is even greater. Repeated stops from 100 mph produced no deterioration in braking efficiency and over 20-foot decels could be made with hands off the wheel." The old drum brakes were still available for '65 as a $64.50 credit option, but only 316 of the 23,562 Corvettes built that year went without the full disc setup.

The Sting Ray hardly lacked for horsepower, but it seemed that some customers were always craving as much as they could get. Chevrolet obliged them at mid-model year with a new optional V-8: the big-block Mark IV. Originating in early 1963 with the so-called "mystery" 427 racing engine that showed up for the Daytona 500, this husky powerplant was notable for its "porcupine" valvegear, an idea of engine designer Robert P. Benzinger. The nickname referred to the way the pushrods poked through at the oddest angles, the result of working "backward" by starting with the ports and manifolds rather than the combustion chambers. Intake valves were set at an angle of 26 degrees to the cylinder axis, exhaust valves at 17 degrees. Moreover, both sets of valve stems were tilted in side view, one forward and the other backward, by nine degrees; this lined them up with the pushrods to avoid setting up rotation in the rocker arms. The basic head configuration was then tested, fiddled with, and honed until it provided optimal breathing. Then it was frozen, and all other components were designed around it.

Officially called Mark IV but marketed as the Turbo

The '65 Corvette Sting Ray (both pages) could be told from the 1964 model by its black-out horizontal bar grille, still-cleaner rocker panel moldings, and—most obviously—by the triple vertical front fender slots in place of the twin horizontal ones from 1964. Fuel injection was still available—note the front fender badge (right). The big news, however, was the 396-cubic-inch Turbo Jet V-8, part of the "Porcupine" family of engines officially titled Mark IV. It cranked out a thundering 425 horsepower.

Jet, the "Porcupine" arrived in four versions: two high-performance car engines of 396 cubic inches, a 427, and a heavy-duty 427 for marine use. The 396s were scheduled to replace Chevy's hallowed 409 in all its applications for 1965, even though the latter was still fairly young.

In fact, the 409 or "Type W" V-8 was scrapped after only five years because of basic design limitations and the fact that it had been tooled for relatively low production. Future demand for performance cars suggested that Chevy's Tonawanda, New York, engine plant would have to be retooled anyway, and Semon E. "Bunkie" Knudsen, then division general manager, decided that only the most modern engine could justify such a major investment. The Porcupine was selected, with no thought of carrying anything over from the Type W. Production commenced in mid-1965.

Like the head, the Mark IV block was all-new, with 4.84 inches between bore centers, a bore of 4.094 inches, and a stroke of 3.75 inches. The 409 had a deck angled at 33 degrees from horizontal to allow for wedge-shaped combustion chambers with flat head faces. By contrast, the Mark IV had the usual deck angle of 45 degrees to the cylinder axis. Main bearings were 2.75 inches in diameter, a quarter-inch larger than those of the Type W. Main-bearing width was also increased, adding two full inches to the cap-clamping surface. The forged-steel crankshaft was cross-drilled to deliver oil to the rod bearings through a full 360 degrees of rotation (a feature lacking in the 409). Crankpin journals were kept at a 2.20-inch diameter.

With hydraulic lifters, a four-barrel carburetor, and 10.25:1 compression, the 396 Mark IV arrived in two states of tune: 325 and 360 bhp. These were for the intermediate Chevelle and full-size Chevys. For the Corvette, 11:1 compression was specified, lifting output to 425 bhp, aided by impact-extruded alloy pistons with chrome rings, plus solid lifters, bigger carburetors with a double-snorkel air cleaner, and an oversized sump.

Although in short supply, the top Mark IV Corvette wasn't short on performance. Pulling even the moderate 3.70:1 rear axle, it could do standing quarter-miles of around 14 seconds at terminal speeds of 102-104 mph. With enough space to see maximum allowable rpm in top gear, it would show a top speed of nearly 140 mph. Numerically higher or lower axle ratios

would respectively deliver even faster acceleration or higher top speeds (160 mph was not inconceivable).

To handle such brute force, stiff front springs and sway bar, a special rear sway bar, super-heavy-duty clutch, and a larger radiator and fan were included with the Mark IV option. For instant recognition of the monster at rest, there was an aggressive-looking hood bulge and (as an option) side-mounted exhaust pipes. Though the big-block weighed over 650 pounds, it didn't leave the Sting Ray overly nose-heavy. In fact, weight distribution was a near-perfect 51/49 percent front/rear, a tribute to the foresight of the chassis planners.

GM management had decreed that no car line smaller than intermediate should carry an engine larger than 400 cubic inches. Since the 396 squeaked in under that limit, it replaced the fuel-injected small-block. But rules are meant to be broken, and this one was no exception. Reason? The competitive urges of Ford in Dearborn. Ford had no car like the Corvette, but it did have a very impressive 427 V-8 that one Carroll Shelby was installing in his sparse two-seater Cobras. Obviously,

Chevrolet would need a 427, too. It materialized for 1966—basically a 396 with a larger 4.25-inch bore.

For the Corvette, this bigger big-block came in two forms: 390 bhp on 10.25:1 compression, and 425 bhp via 11:1 compression, larger intake valves, a bigger Holley four-barrel carb on an aluminum manifold, mechanical lifters, and four- instead of two-hole main bearing caps. Though it had no more horsepower than the previous high-compression 396, the 427 packed a lot more torque—460 pounds/feet at 4000 rpm. The hydraulic-lifter 390 pumped out 465 lbs/ft at 3600. Of course, engine outputs were sometimes deliberately understated in the Sixties so as not to arouse the ire of insurance companies. Here, 420 and 450 bhp would be closer to the truth.

Ordering a 427 Corvette meant you had to take it with Positraction and the close-ratio Muncie four-speed; there was no other choice. You also got an upgraded suspension, basically the same as the 396 package, as well as stouter, shot-peened halfshafts and U-joints and a higher-capacity radiator and sump.

Regardless of axle ratio, the 427 Sting Ray was an incredible performer. With the short 4.11:1 gearset, *Sports Car Graphic*'s example did 0-60 mph in a nearly unbelievable 4.8 seconds, 0-100 mph in 11.2 seconds, and sailed on to 140 mph. The modest 3.36:1 ratio made things only a bit less sensational: *Car and Driver* reported 0-60 in 5.4 seconds and a standing quarter of 12.8 seconds at 112 mph.

The only thing that could touch a 427 Corvette—and stay ahead of it—was the Ford-powered 427 Cobra. But Chevy needn't have been embarrassed, for the difference was between a spartan, semi-competition car and a comfortable, street-legal *gran turismo*. And with the aforementioned performance figures, who could be unhappy with the big-block 'Vette? As *C/D* said, "It's the power more than the engine that overwhelms every other sensation. There's power literally everywhere—great gobs of steam-locomotive, earth-moving torque."

With big-blocks at hand there was less need for the 327, so small-block offerings were cut from five to two for '66—down to the basic 300- and 350-bhp versions. Arguably, these were still the best all-around engines. Both required premium fuel on compression ratios well over 10.0:1, and they didn't have the rocket-like

thrust of the 427s, but their performance was still mighty impressive all the same. As before, both could be teamed with Powerglide automatic, the standard three-speed manual, or either four-speed option.

Engine choices aside, 1966 was basically a stand-pat year for the Sting Ray. Frontal appearance was mildly altered with an eggcrate grille insert to replace the previous horizontal bars, and the coupe lost its roof-mounted extractor vents, which had proven inefficient. This relative lack of change reflected plans to bring out an all-new Corvette for 1967.

It certainly did *not* reflect a fall-off of Sting Ray

The interior of the '66 Corvette (below) was familiar fare to Sting Ray fans. Who cares if there wasn't a decklid (right) when the monster 427 under the bulged hood could hurl the car from 0-60 mph in five seconds and top 140 mph, depending on gearing.

popularity. In fact, 1966 would prove another record-busting year, volume rising to 27,720 units, up some 4200 over '65. As *Car and Driver* observed: "Many people thought that the Corvette would wither and die when it was no longer the car to beat in the races. To the contrary, they're selling better than ever—and going better than ever as well....If they keep building them this good and this fast, they may *never* have to go racing again."

But initial plans to the contrary, the '67 turned out to be another Sting Ray, because its erstwhile successor was found to have some undesirable aerodynamic traits. Duntov demanded more time in the wind tunnel to devise fixes before it went into production. Even in the Sixties, big car companies could still be made to answer to the wishes of a few gifted individuals.

Mind you, the delay was hardly bad, for the '67 Corvette was a Sting Ray refined to the limit—the very

continued on page 191

This page: GM designers were pondering updates for the '66 Sting Ray in April 1964 (top and center). One clay featured a split-grille front end, a look adopted much later by the Pontiac Firebird. Note the two taillight designs being considered. The production '66 (bottom) didn't adopt any of these features. Opposite page: Two '66 roadsters, one with the 427 V-8 and optional side-mounted exhaust (top), the other in more basic trim (bottom).

best of the five-year run and quite possibly the best Corvette *ever*. Take styling. "It finally looks the way we thought it should have in the first place," enthused *Road & Track*. "All the funny business—the fake vents, extraneous emblems and simulated-something-or-other wheel covers—is gone, and though some consider the

basic shape overstyled, it looks more like a finished product now."

The '67 was certainly the cleanest Sting Ray ever, though changes were again modest. Five smaller front fender vents replaced the three larger ones, and flat-finish rockers *sans* ribbing conferred a lower, less

191

chunky appearance. New, and thus unique, was a single backup light, mounted above the license plate. Sad to say, the lovely cast-aluminum knock-offs were no longer catalogued, but the old-fashioned wheel covers gave way to slotted six-inch Rally wheels with chrome beauty rings and lug nuts concealed behind small chrome caps. Inside were slightly changed upholstery and a handbrake moved from beneath the dash to between the seats. The convertible's optional hardtop was offered with a faddish black vinyl cover, a mixed blessing.

Powerteams changed hardly at all. The two small-blocks returned, as did the 390-bhp big-block (hulking beneath a redesigned hood scoop). But the top two 427s now developed 400 and 435 bhp with a switch to triple two-barrel carburetors. As before, they differed in respective compression ratios—10.25:1 and

11.0:1—and the solid lifters and transistorized ignition that went on the 425-bhp unit. The latter, RPO L71, was also available with special aluminum heads (instead of cast iron) and larger-diameter exhaust valves as RPO L89, though with the same grossly understated horsepower.

The ultimate 'Vette engine for '67 was coded L88, an even wilder L89 that was as close to a pure racing engine as Chevy had ever offered in "regular production." It was the sort of thing you'd expect from an engineer like Duntov, given an open checkbook and a clean drawing board. Besides the lightweight heads and bigger ports, it came with an even hotter cam, aluminum radiator, small-diameter flywheel, stratospheric 12.5:1 compression, and a single huge Holley that gulped in 850 cubic-feet of air per minute. The result was no less than 560 bhp, again

Corvette Performance Comparisons 1963-67

Year	CID	Bhp	Axle	0-30 (sec)	0-50 (sec)	0-60 (sec)	0-100 (sec)	¼-mi. @ mph (sec)	Max. mph
1963	327	300	3.36	2.2	4.2	6.1	14.5	14.5 @ 100	118
1964	327	300[1]	3.36	3.2	6.1	8.0	20.2	15.2 @ 85	130
1965	327	375[2]	3.70	2.9	5.2	6.3	14.7	14.4 @ 99	138
1965	396	425	3.70	3.1	4.8	5.7	13.4	14.1 @ 103	136
1966	427	425	4.11	2.5	4.2	5.6	—	13.4 @ 105	135
1967	327	300	3.36	3.4	5.9	7.8	23.1	16.0 @ 87	121

[1] automatic transmission [2] fuel injection

The '67 Corvette (above and right) was the cleanest of the 1963-67 generation. Five smaller fender vents replaced the three and less distracting flat-black and aluminum rocker panel trim resulted in a lower, less chunky look. Slotted six-inch Rally wheels replaced the ornate, old-fashioned wheel covers. Far right: The L-36 four-barrel, 390-bhp 427 (top) cost $200.15 extra; the interior saw the parking brake relocated between the seats (bottom).

at 6400 rpm. Only one problem: You had to use 103-octane fuel.

Chevy's *Corvette News* owners' magazine immodestly described the L88 as "not an engine for ordinary everyday driving. It gives a rough idle, it is not the easiest engine to start, and was not designed with high fuel economy in mind. As a matter of fact, the L88 requires higher octane gas than most [service] stations carry. It is strictly a high-performance engine for competition use." As if to back that up, Chevy made several individual options mandatory, including Positraction, transistorized ignition, H-D suspension, and power brakes—and RPO C48, which deleted the normal radio and heater "to cut down on weight and discourage the car's use on the street," according to

continued on page 199

1963-67 Serial Spans, Production Figures, and Base Prices

Year	Serial Prefix	Serial Span	Prod.	Price
1963	30837S	100001-121513	10,594 coupe	$4252
	30867S		10,919 roadster	$4037
1964	40837S	100001-122229	8,304 coupe	$4252
	40867S		13,925 roadster	$4037
1965	194375S	100001-123562	8,186 coupe	$4321
	194675S		15,376 roadster	$4106
1966	194376S	100001-127720	9,958 coupe	$4295
	194676S		17,762 roadster	$4084
1967	194377S	100001-122940	8,504 coupe	$4353
	194677S		14,436 roadster	$4141

The '67 Corvette's Rally wheels were supplied with chrome beauty rings; the lug nuts were concealed behind small chrome hubcaps (below). New, and unique to the 1963-67 generation, was a single backup light, centrally mounted above the license plate (left). The 400-bhp Turbo Jet 427 (far left) was listed as option L-68; it ran with three carbs and added $305 to the sticker. The interior (left center), still dominated by the twin-cowl theme, saw the upholstery patterns changed slightly.

Corvette News. Duntov knew how power-mad 'Vette buyers could be.

Powerful it was—and so costly to build that the L88 engine wasn't really a serious offering as far as the general public was concerned. A stiff $1500 price guaranteed few orders, and they numbered only 20, of which just three cars are known to survive today. One might wish for more given the L88's alleged 13-second quarter-mile times.

But the times, as the song said, were a-changin' and Chevy was readying a new Corvette, delayed at least in part because it was a different breed entirely. Perhaps in deference to that, the '68 would arrive without the Sting Ray name.

A buyer had to shell out $4353 to buy a '67 Corvette sport coupe (both pages), but that was only the beginning. Aside from the various engine options, power steering and brakes and air conditioning added about $550. Other extra-cost goodies: side-mounted exhaust, $131.65; aluminum cylinder heads for the L-71 engine, $368; heavy-duty suspension, $36.90; heavy-duty brakes, $342.30; transistorized ignition, $74.75; cast aluminum wheels, $263.30.

But though a bright new chapter in Corvette history was at hand—a long one, too, as it would transpire—it couldn't have happened without the Sting Ray and its unremitting quest for excellence. America's sports car had traveled a long way down the road of progress in the Sting Ray's five short years, and though many great Corvettes were yet to come, they'd never be quite the same. As a mirror of its very special time, as the foundation for Corvette's future success, as a unique and exciting automobile, the Sting Ray deserves a place in our memories—which is why it will always have one.

The '67 Corvette marked the end of an exciting era. The times were changing—government regulations were fast becoming a sobering reality. Thus, with the last of the '67 Sting Rays, the curtain fell on an age of unremitting requests for power and performance by the makers of America's only sports car. The Corvette represented the ultimate in performance and sex appeal to an entire generation of young Americans; today the 1963-67 Sting Rays are among the most prized Corvettes ever built.

200

Profile: William L. Mitchell

As vice president for design at General Motors in the Sixties and Seventies, William L. "Bill" Mitchell influenced the shape of American production cars more than any other single person. He had a great deal to do with contemporary Ford, Chrysler, and AMC products—more, perhaps, than those companies were willing to admit. Many of their efforts were replies—attempts to keep up with GM Design and the gospel according to Mitchell. Some succeeded; others did not.

It is undeniable that they mostly followed. As Theodore MacManus said in his seminal "Penalty of Leadership" ad for Cadillac back in 1912: "If the leader leads, he remains the leader." With the sole exception of Chrysler's 1955-58 "Forward Look" cars, GM led Detroit styling for a full half-century—from Harley Earl's very first LaSalle in 1927 to Mitchell's valedictory Cadillac Seville of 1980.

MacManus also said that leaders have their detractors, and Mitchell had more than his share. A few were also-rans—spear-carriers from the profession that Mitchell dominated for two decades and influenced for four. Some were mere second-guessers who, with myopic misunderstanding, took the chrome-bedecked machinery of late-Fifties Detroit as proof that no stylist in that period was worth discussing. (To draw that conclusion betrays ignorance of a person's career as a whole, not to mention the enormous influence—little of it for the good—exerted by sales personnel and top management.)

Still others simply didn't like Mitchell's dress and manner. Among them was automotive journalist Leonard Setright, who wrote of Mitchell: "His round body clad in bright scarlet or mylar chrome-coated leathers, astride one of his adolescent fantasy motorcycles, was enough to force a guffaw from Samuel Beckett." But then, how Mitchell dressed or what he drove had no bearing on his professional competence. And the evidence is considerable that he was competent in the extreme.

When Harley Earl retired as head of GM Styling in 1958, he picked Bill Mitchell to succeed him. Mitchell found himself with legen-

dary shoes to fill—shoes that some said were too big for anyone. But fill them he did—so well that he might be said to have invented a new shoe style. Admittedly, he got the job at a good time. Earl, who hadn't been on the cutting edge of car design for several years, had surrendered the styling initiative to resurgent Chrysler and Virgil M. Exner. Mitchell reclaimed it in a hurry, bringing General Motors back to the styling pinnacle for a generation. How? Simply by giving upper management—and usually the customers themselves—exactly what they wanted, and sometimes a lot more.

"If vulgarity was called for," Setright noted, "supreme vulgarity was forthcoming." What the English writer didn't say—and discounting European prejudices—was that when elegance and strength of line were called for, Mitchell meted them out generously. General Motors, like any other car company, has had its ugly periods. But by and large, the cars of the Mitchell years were fresh, exciting, and widely imitated. Rarely were they so radical as to turn people off. Never were they dull. Chuck Jordan, who took over Mitchell's job from Irwin Rybicki in 1987, said that Mitchell "had an intuitive feel for beauty and clean, elegant lines. To [him] it was immoral to make an ugly car."

Candor was one of Mitchell's most admirable characteristics, unusual in a field built on ego. In interviews he rarely failed to mention the numerous people at GM Design who'd made his accomplishments possible. He was equally frank—and often colorful—about his likes and dislikes. For example, he once compared designing a small economy car to "tailoring a dwarf," which has since become one of his most quoted phrases. What he liked working on most, he said, were luxury and sports models—preferably a combination of both.

Mitchell's first great design was the 1938 Cadillac Sixty Special sedan, recognized today as one of the most significant styling achievements of the prewar era. Later, Mitchell would be the creative force behind such memorable production cars as the 1963 Buick Riviera and stunning show models

like the Corvair Monza GT and SS.

But his greatest achievement—certainly his greatest love—was the Corvette, which owed its glamour and allure to Mitchell from 1960 through the mid-Seventies. He devoted a good deal of his time to Corvette, which was by far his favorite work of the many projects he supervised at GM. His penchant for the 'Vette is hardly surprising given the personality of the man, who has been described by many of the same adjectives applied to the car itself: brash, flamboyant, even beefy. For Mitchell, like Harley Earl before him, the Corvette was an opportunity not only to have fun as a designer but also to make a personal statement about what a high-performance American automobile should be.

Like most pioneers in a burgeoning field, Mitchell came to his career quite by accident. He grew up in Pennsylvania, where he fell in love with cars on regular visits to his father's Buick dealership. In the Thirties, he secured a job as an

illustrator for the Barron Collier advertising agency in New York City. He spent his spare time drawing cars and, in the evenings, attending classes at the Art Students League. The Collier family also liked cars, especially the racing variety, and spent many weekends in upstate New York at the Sleepy Hollow race track, which they owned. Mitchell went with them, and one weekend his sketches came to the attention of one of Harley Earl's friends.

Earl then contacted Mitchell, asking for more sketches and wanting to know what the young man thought cars "ought to look like in the future." Six months later, Mitchell was at work at the GM Art and Colour Studio under Earl's watchful eye. Six months after that, he was chief designer at Cadillac. Twenty years later, Mitchell replaced his boss and mentor as head of what was by then known as GM Styling Staff. He soon changed the name again, to GM Design Staff, while establish-

ing what's been called the "Mitchell Style."

Controversial, highly visible, and never given to halfway measures, Mitchell pulled few punches in his work, in his arguments over policy with GM managers or, as we see in the following excerpts from various interviews he's given us over the years, in his public pronouncements. Sadly, that voice was stilled forever in late 1988, and we enthusiasts are much poorer for it.

Editor: That must have been something—from nowhere to styling head of Cadillac in 12 months.

William L. Mitchell: It sounds great now, but there were only a hundred of us then at the whole place [Art and Colour]. When I left General Motors [in 1977], I had 1600 people.

Ed: How long were you with Cadillac?

Mitchell: Until I went into the Navy in the war. I came back in '49. After that, I was taken out of General Motors. Earl wanted me to run a business for his sons; he wanted to put them in design. So I took over Harley Earl Design. I did that for four years and got big accounts like Clark Equipment, General Electric, Westinghouse, Parker Pen. Oh, I really went. I didn't like the products, but the newness of it was good for me.

Ed: How did you return to GM?

Mitchell: Earl brought me back as director. I didn't love [Harley Earl Design], but it was good background for me, because when I came back . . . I didn't have to take any lip from any general manager. [Earl] told me four years ahead I was going to take his job. He talked to [then GM board chairman Alfred] Sloan and [then president Harlow] Curtice. I guess you can't do that any more; committees have to put you in.

Ed: How did you first get involved with the Corvette?

Mitchell: Harley Earl—this was his idea. After the war, he was a good friend of [General Curtis] LeMay. They had these activities at the bases to keep the uniformed men happy. They started sports-car racing. They got GM and a lot of different companies to put a lot of money into it to give them some fun. We built a Jeep with a Cadillac engine in it for LeMay, I remember. He said, "Harley, why don't you build an American sports car?"

We showed the first Corvette to a group at the proving grounds, and Earl told Sloan he'd like to put it in the [Motorama] show at the Waldorf. This was a prototype—no engine, nothing. It went over so good, Chevrolet said they'd build it.

Ed: What were some of the problems with the early Corvettes?

Mitchell: It didn't have a good engine. There wasn't a good V-8 then.

Ed: How did the decision to use the V-8 come about?

Mitchell: [Former chief engineer Edward N.] Cole became the head of Chevrolet, and he was a young fireball. He liked to race. He shoved that ahead. Prior to that, people started to try to race [Corvettes] and they weren't any good. But when you got the V-8 in it—boy, she started to go. When we beat the Jaguars—that was something. And then we beat the Mercedes. . . . From then on it was all hell to pay. It was like a Ferrari: It looks good, but it's got to go. Performance is part of the act.

Ed: What was the closest that the Corvette project came to being halted?

Mitchell: There were times when [James M.] Roche [distribution vice president 1960-62, later GM president and chairman] wanted to discontinue the Corvette. I raised hell. I knew Roche well, but he was a Cadillac man. I said, "The Corvette's got far greater owner loyalty than any damn Cadillac made." And the sales manager backed me up. That was before the Sting Ray got going.

Ed: What was your involvement with racing?

Mitchell: I did a lot of bootlegging at GM. I had a studio right down underneath my office. I called it Studio X. [It was] where I'd bootleg all kinds of cars I wanted to do. Chevrolet was racing on a [significant] scale, and then that stopped. I knew they had three chassis they didn't use [after the 1957 Sebring race]. So I went to Cole, and he gave [one] to me for 500 bucks. I did [the racing Stingray] down in Studio X; nobody knew about it.

Ed: Tell us how you liked it.

Mitchell: I always liked its looks. It's my favorite Corvette. That strong shadow underneath makes it very photogenic. The early Corvettes were too rounded, too soft. The Sting Ray has that sharp body edge, and that makes it work.

Ed: When did you have to take the Corvette SS chassis out of GM?

Mitchell: I raced it first in Washington with [Dr.] Dick Thompson [in early 1959]. At the engineering policy committee, [then president John F.] Gordon made a statement: "I thought everybody realized we're not going to do any racing." After the meeting I said, "Were you talking to me?" and he said, "I sure as hell was." He was tough. Instead of taking it lying down, I got a couple good friends of mine who could write better than I could, and we wrote a letter to him saying, "I got my job racing with the Collier boys; racing is in my blood."

In those days, they'd come out in those big limousines. He came out one day and I said, "Jack, did you get my letter?" And he said, "You're a pretty damn good salesman. Go ahead." But he said, "Keep it off [GM Tech Center] property and spend your own money." So I did, and I raced for two years until he said, "Stop it, they're getting back after me for racing." So I had a little bit of my own way, and on my income tax I got away pretty good.

Ed: Where did you keep the race car outside of the Tech Center?

Mitchell: [I had] a shop on Twelve Mile Road that's just five minutes from my office, and I did the work out there. But I got GM engineers and I had a lot of talent at GM helping me. I got good mechanics to go to the races with me. I got a lot of things I wanted.

Ed: Did it cost you?

Mitchell: Plenty. I financed it all out of my own pocket. I couldn't afford to build and race the Stingray today. But back then, it pleased me no end to go up against Cunningham and those boys with the faster cars, and take any of them.

Ed: Did the body design help its performance?

Mitchell: Oh, yes. It was very slippery. It would take a D-Jag, which had a very smooth body and about the same horsepower. The Stingray would do 0-to-60 in four seconds. It had a beautiful engine—first fuel injection, then we tried four Webers with different cams. Tear your head off! The only weakness that car had was the brakes. They never did work right.

Ed: How did the shape translate to production cars?

Mitchell: It was the same, wasn't it? I just took all those lines and turned the Stingray racer into the production 1963 Sting Ray. That made the Corvette. And overnight, the sales just boomed. So I knew I had something.

I went to the races in Europe and saw the cars there. I didn't want a car that looked like everything out of Europe. All their cars looked like Ferraris or Maseratis. They didn't have any sharp identifying features. I wanted a car that—by God, you'd know it a mile away. That was my whole theme. And it did have identity.

Ed: How did the Stingray (Sting Ray) get its name?

Mitchell: I just did it. Jack Gordon never liked those names of mine, the fish names. They wanted everything to start with a "C." But we'd get them anyway. I don't know how the Stingray got to be two words, though.

Ed: The Mako Shark was another of your names, then?

Mitchell: Yes. I love sharks because, in the water, they're exciting. They twist and turn. I caught a mako off Bimini, and it's in my studio in Palm Beach. I've got pictures of my Corvettes below it. That's where I got the impetus to do the experimental Manta Ray. I'd do a lead car on my own. Then we built things off of it.

Ed: Why did you object to

removing the split window on the '64 coupe?

Mitchell: I had to admit it was a hazard. Duntov won that one. By the way, I stole that back line from Porsche. I wasn't above stealing things from European cars. Not American cars—there was nothing over here to steal! There isn't anything today, unless you want a cake of soap. Then you get a Ford. You need identity on a car. If you took the antlers off a deer, you'd have a big rabbit!

Ed: What was your relationship like with Zora Duntov?

Mitchell: Anyone with a foreign accent can get away with arguments because they're hard to understand. He'd mumble around. But he was a good guy.

Ed: Did the Corvette have much influence on other cars?

Mitchell: Remember the early Pontiac Grand Prix and the 1963 Buick Riviera? When they were built, the sales people still thought that the more chrome, the better. The Corvette didn't have much chrome and it sold! So I did those two like the Corvette, and eliminated the chrome. They sold fantastically. That changed a lot of old-fashioned thinking. The European designers recognized it. They had never liked our cars before, but they liked the Corvette—and the Riviera, too. It was the same idea—trim, stylish, classic.

Ed: How close did the Corvair Monza GT come to being a 'Vette?

Mitchell: The Corvair was a great car—very unusual. The Monza GT and SS were the cars that might have replaced the Corvette. The GT was first. It was a rush job, done over several times, in less than 10 weeks. Engineering did a box-section chassis for it, and tested it at different tracks. It outperformed the fuel-injection Corvette and was very aerodynamic. It only weighed 1500 pounds.

Ed: Why wasn't it mid-engine?

Mitchell: I wanted that, but Chevrolet said they could make the car handle the same way with the engine hanging out the back. I got Roger Penske, who was then a great Porsche racer, to drive the

Monza GT. He liked it better than the Porsche. Right at that time the whole Corvair program started to wane, and I couldn't interest management in doing anything with that car. It was just no go.

Ed: The Monza seems like the cleanest design of that era.

Mitchell: Well, you can see where it relates to the Sting Ray shape in many ways. It could have been sold as a small Corvette and done wonderfully. It's one of the classic designs. If you've got a good design, it's timeless. If you drive a Monza GT down the street today, you'll draw a crowd.

Ed: The Monza GT reminds us of the Opel GT.

Mitchell: Oh, yes, of course. The Opel GT was derived from this. It relates to the Sting Ray, too [*the '68 model—Ed.*] and could have been a small Corvette. It was a pretty car, with that same classic Sting Ray look. It could have sold alongside the big Corvette as a cheaper model with no problem at all. But nobody was interested.

Ed: It seems like a big car such as the Corvette would be easier to style than a small car like the Monza GT or Opel GT, even though the body is similar.

Mitchell: That's why today, with all the small cars on the road, it would be hard for me.

I'm glad I retired when I did [*in 1977—Ed.*]. After all my years of designing cars, I was being asked to make them shorter, narrower, and higher instead of longer, lower, and wider. And you know what I used to say: "Designing a small car is like tailoring a dwarf." That's true. It's really tough to do a good small car.

Ed: How did the Mako Shark fit into all this?

Mitchell: That car's a real favorite of mine. We used a dark top and light underbody, and nobody had ever done that. It works very well. It's even got nice lines from the top. On so many cars, the tops just fall away. But the Mako Shark looks good from the top.

Ed: That car is a real goer, isn't it?

Mitchell: The Mako has the old chassis, and it's heavy. But it's got a 650 horsepower Can-Am engine. It goes like hell. And it holds the road.

Ed: A lot of racing cars are painted like the Mako, with a dark top and light underbody.

Mitchell: They got that from me. You know why they do it? The car shows up better for photographers without a dark shadow underneath, so they get more publicity than if they had a dark car with a light top. It's true. That's why they do that. It's the same reason we painted the Mako Shark that

way. That car got fantastic coverage.

Ed: Rumor has it that there was some thought of discontinuing the Corvette and treating the Camaro as the General Motors sports car.

Mitchell: That's very true. The first-series Camaro was done too fast. We didn't get a chance to do much. But the second-series cars [were] in production for a decade, and selling. . . . That [was] really a hell of a package. Stirling Moss saw the first Camaro, and he said to me, "Bill, you've really got a classic. The detail . . . it's not all carved up. It's got a nice swoop to it." He was right. That car's been very popular in Europe, too. Much more than the [1968-82] Corvette[s], which they consider overstyled. No matter what we do to it, [the second-series Camaro] body always works. The Camaro Berlinetta was a show car, you remember, with brass trim. I drove it here for a few months, and everybody liked it. So I said to myself, maybe I've got something here.

Ed: Our favorite Stingray is the Mulsanne [show car]. That's really a nice-looking Corvette.

Mitchell: It's the greatest Stingray ever. We used it as the pace car for all the Can-Am races, way back. It has a powerful LT1 engine. The car's been around a lot, though. It's been red, silver, blue, and now it's back to silver again. The nicest thing about it is that you can take the whole roof off in one piece and the flagman can stand up and see the start of the race, and everybody can see him. It's a terrific pace car.

Ed: There's a lot going on in the Mulsanne.

Mitchell: Yes. The big engines have to breathe in a small car like the Stingray, so you have to cut holes in the body. This car has scoops and spoilers and fins, but a lot of surface tension, too.

Ed: Is everything functional on it?

Mitchell: Sure. The periscope really works as a rearview mirror, for example. I took the flip-flop out and exposed the headlights like the racers do. People don't really want gadgets; they want flexible things. They don't really want headlights that flop up and down—they don't need them. So you can put the lights up on the hood, and create more attention.

Ed: The car is pretty old now.

Mitchell: But it's still a great show car, because it has so much animation in the styling. So many things are happening

in it. If you make a show car too simple, it doesn't hold people's interest; it's just another smooth car. If it's too simple, it's just Simple Simon.

Ed: There must be a pretty fine line between a classic design and a dull design.

Mitchell: Well, like they say, a designer's got to know when to lift his brush.

Ed: Let's talk about the Aerovette. Originally, it was thought to be the 1980 Corvette design, but that never came about.

Mitchell: What's to tell? They took the most beautiful car ever styled and let it hang around. And now, without me to sit on 'em, it's not going anywhere. It's a shame, but that car has had problems from the beginning. Originally, they were going to hire that Italian—Giorgetto Giugiaro—to do it. The Aerovette is my answer to Giugiaro. Giugiaro's cars are all full of angles. He can't draw a simple perspective, you know. He makes a side view and a top view. All his cars look like they've been cut out of cardboard.

Ed: Isn't that deliberate?

Mitchell: I hope not. It's horrible. Now take my Aerovette

by comparison. The Aerovette has nice contours, soft curves, and still a certain sharpness. It has really good balance. It's a design you can look at from any angle. A car is like a girl, you know. You wouldn't want to see a girl from only one angle. You want to get more views.

Ed: You must have spent most of your time with the Corvette.

Mitchell: Well, it was my pet. Nobody bothered me. No high power in Chevrolet was interested—the volume and profit wasn't there. You could do what you wanted without anybody monkeying around. In the other divisions, when you'd have a showing, you'd have the chief engineer and six assistants plus an audience in the studio that would drive you nuts. Committees, committees, committees. The first Camaro and Firebird were so "committeed" that I don't remember what they look like. They were just nothing. The other ones we got done so damn fast that they never saw 'em! But with the Corvette, they would always leave you alone.

Ed: They never tried to make you build it out of steel?

Mitchell: With fiberglass, you can only make, say, 70,000 [units] at most [from a mold]. But you can change it. You can't do that so easily with metal. Every Corvette was different because you can do that. That's where DeLorean screwed up. That thing he had— half metal, half plastic—you couldn't do anything with it. The Pontiac Fiero, that's [a new] beginning. Half of it's plastic. You can make a whole different car—and they ought to, because the one they have looks like a soap box. [*Ed. note: After a strong start for 1984, Fiero sales waned steadily due to mechanical woes, indifferent workmanship, a well-publicized recall, and other problems, leading to the demise of Pontiac's mid-engine two-seater after the '88 model.*]

Ed: How important were show cars to production plans?

Mitchell: That's how you'd find out what people wanted. That's how the Eldorados were born and the Toronados and all that—at the Motorama. Now they don't make those anymore. Show cars were more fun to work on [because] you didn't have a bunch of committeemen telling us, "You can't do this, you can't do that." We did

it, and if people liked it they'd say, "Go make it." It would do more for us in the studio to see one come out of the shop. People want to see something new.

Ed: Where do you think design is going now?

Mitchell: I think fins are going to come back. Even down at Daytona, at the races, your Porsches have fins on them. In that sports-car class just about every car has fins. Now I don't think they'll be high. You need wings; you need that stuff on there or you've got a pickle. A Porsche to me was always—there was a word they used in Germany—like a loaf of bread. If it spun out, you didn't know which end was coming. There's a lot of stuff going on now that's called functional. But you've got to have aesthetics. You can't sell a guy a car that looks like

hell and tell him it looks that way because it's aerodynamic.

Ed: What do you think of the 1984-generation Corvette?

Mitchell: I think [it] looks like a grouper—a blunt look. I think the Camaro and Firebird are sharper. Although—I'll eat my own words—on the highway it looks pretty damn good from the front. But I don't like this lack of whip in the side view—it isn't exciting. And the big taillights look like it was done for A.J. Foyt. I think it should have been done for women as well as men. I like more interest in the car. You look at watches—there's millions of them and they look different all the time. You don't want cars all looking alike.

Ed: What would you have done differently with today's Corvette?

Mitchell: I'd have put more accents on it. But my day is over. . . . [Harley] Earl never bothered me when he left. Earl was a dynamic man, more Hollywood. He looked so out of place in Detroit it was unbelievable. He had power politically and physically. And he was a salesman like you never heard of. He could win. Styling ran

the world, not design, not engineering. . . . He made it his way. I tried to follow him, and I did a pretty good job.

Ed: Things have changed a lot now, haven't they?

Mitchell: The boys that followed me are getting pushed off the map. I love 'em, but they haven't got it. Engineering is running it. The new Corvette is engineering perfect, but design? No. The engineers ran the whole damn show. They wouldn't have done that with me.

You need two things in a car: You need road value and showroom value. You need a little sparkle in a car. On a little misty day they all look dull. You don't want to put chrome on with a trowel like we did in '58, but you need some. There isn't showroom value in these cars today. If I had one, I'd touch it up. You have to have enough interest to keep looking at it. That goes for all the cars.

Ed: What are some specific changes you'd make?

Mitchell: I'd put more flow in the line. I wouldn't have the sideline straight through. I know it wouldn't be as aerodynamic, but I'd put some curve in that. Like a shark is so

much more interesting than a grouper because there's so many little things happening to it. This ['84 Corvette] is a big potato. On the road, yes; but you walk up to it—blah. Black rubber around everything. It needs detail. I think the new little Pontiac [Fiero] is a dead duck; it's just a little box. I think that Fiat [X1/9] . . . is much better. I shouldn't be talking about my company like that; they're still good to me.

Ed: What are some of the cars that you own now?

Mitchell: I've got some pets of mine I love. I've got a Jaguar roadster—the old Jaguar V-12. Everything is copper on it—the body and all the chrome is copper. I've got a Firebird I did over with a Ferrari engine, and all the metal on that is gold, and it's striped in gold. My Corvette is pearl white with two fins on the back, like a race car, with a blade going through it. The Corvette has a 600-horsepower Can-Am aluminum-block motor in it. I like to have a car that when I pull up, somebody says, "Whose car is that?" I want a car that, when it's stopped, people walk around it for an hour. Exciting automobiles.

Profile:
Larry Shinoda

Few designers have had more varied or successful careers than Larry Shinoda. Fewer still have worked on so many high-performance cars. Shinoda not only teamed with GM design chief Bill Mitchell on a variety of Corvette show cars and production models, but also left his mark on the memorable Boss 302 and Mach 1 Mustangs during a short stint at Ford, where he landed with patron Semon E. "Bunkie" Knudsen in one of the most startling executive defections in automotive history.

But then, the unusual has been a Shinoda forte ever since he emerged with his family from a World War II Nisei internment camp in California. Besides studies at the famous Art Center College in Pasadena and service in the Air National Guard in Korea, he spent part of his youth hot-rodding with the Shinoda-Powers "Chopsticks Special," a classic B-roadster. His first major design job came at Ford in January 1955. According to Japan's Car Styling magazine, young Larry showed up to interview in Levi's, a T-shirt, and a

Hawaiian shirt, with an armload of race and road car renderings, some of which he'd doodled that very day. "You guys need me a lot more than I need you," he told Ford design domo Gene Bordinat. Despite that brashness—or maybe because of it—Shinoda was hired on the spot.

After a year at Ford, Shinoda spent seven months "in the bunker" with Dick Teague at teetering Studebaker-Packard, where he toiled on the all-new Packard Clipper that was left stillborn for 1957. Teague later ended up at American Motors, while Shinoda went to GM after a long wait in the personnel office for an audience with Harley Earl. Following brief tours in the Chevy, Pontiac, and Advanced Studios, Shinoda found himself working almost exclusively on Corvettes as Bill Mitchell's chief "pencil" (designer/renderer). He'd continue as such through early 1968, by which time he'd been named chief designer-coordinator. Then Shinoda's friend Bunkie Knudsen, who'd since become GM president, was spirited away to Ford; Shinoda followed within three months. The talents of the audacious designer were soon evi-

dent in cars like the Boss 302, Torino Cobra, and the 1971 Mustang.

Fired by Henry Ford II after less than two years, Knudsen and Shinoda decided to work for themselves by founding Rectrans, a motorhome manufacturing business, in 1970. Rectrans was absorbed by White Motor Corporation the following year, when Shinoda was made vice-president of design. Five years later, when White closed its design and research center, Shinoda formed his own consulting firm, Shinoda Design Associates, which prospers to this day in the Detroit suburb of Livonia. Shinoda also worked on trucks for Chicago-based International Harvester (now Navistar) in 1981-82.

Always outspoken and often outrageous, Shinoda remains a true car enthusiast with more than a little bit of the racing bug still coursing his veins. His sense of humor is a delight, as we discovered when we talked to him in March 1989 about his various Corvette involvements. What follows are excerpts from that interview:

Editor: When did you first start working on Corvettes? Were you involved at all with the Q-Corvette?

Larry Shinoda: The Q-Corvette program was done by Bob McLean. I didn't have any direct involvement on that, but I did on the Stingray race car.

Ed: How did that come about?

Shinoda: [Bill] Mitchell wanted to race his own car, and he had the opportunity to get the mule chassis from the SS Corvette, because when they [the Automobile Manufacturers Association] put the ban on racing, everything pretty much stopped. That was late '57. So he finally got the running chassis and wanted to put a body on it. There were a few people working in the basement studio where that was done.

Ed: That was "Studio X?"

Shinoda: It was before they called it Studio X. When I came [to GM], they were basically trying to do the Q-Corvette, and a lot of things didn't make sense. In fact, they wouldn't work—they didn't quite work with the SS Corvette chassis. So finally Mitchell said, "Let's quit fooling around," and he came up with the basic shape of the car—the original Stingray sports/racing car. Now on

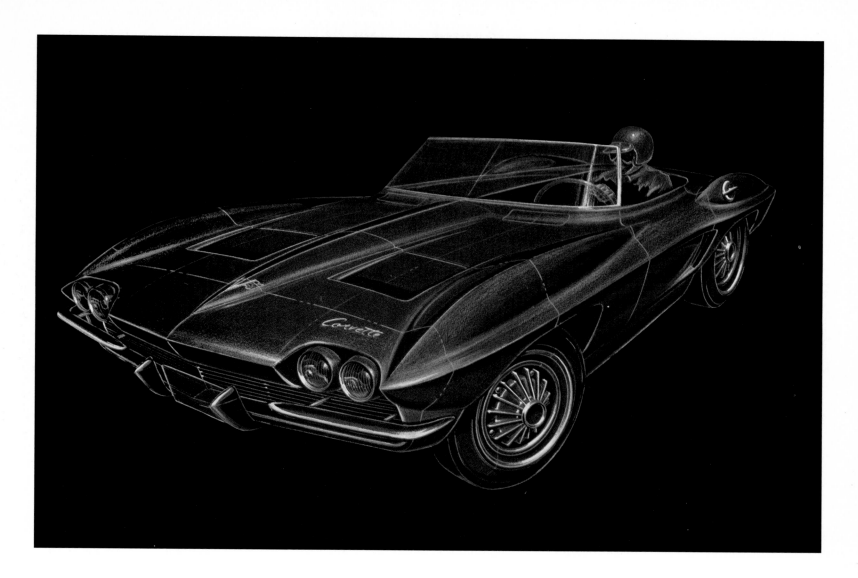

that design, the nose was lower than it was on the '63 [production car] because the nose of the SS Corvette was lower. The research guys kept pushing this inverted-airfoil thing, which was the right idea but many years ahead of its time. In fact, they were never able to prove that it worked, other than in theory. [The Stingray] really didn't work because they didn't have the ideal conditions of the clean shape underneath the body.

Ed: Is that why Zora Arkus-Duntov always insisted that the Stingray was prone to lift?

Shinoda: It did have a lot of lift. But when we dropped the nose down, and we ended up with a much lighter body, the car did run and it ran fairly quick. What it needed at that point was some sort of an airdam in front, which Mitchell didn't really understand at the time. He thought they were kind of ugly, so we never did that. We also needed a rear spoiler. He was bound and determined not to run those pieces on the car, so they never happened.

Ed: Did you try them at all?

Shinoda: I did some sketches, but that's as far as it went.

Ed: The Stingray must have been a handful at speed on some of the longer straights.

Shinoda: Yes. Like at Elkhart [Lake, Wisconsin], where you'd come up to the front straightaway as you crested the hill toward the start/finish line, the nose would really be carrying up high. But the car was actually quite stable. That's a real stable condition for a race car. It may not sound like it, but it is. The other car that was probably as bad or even worse than the Stingray was the first Chaparral, the front-engine Chaparral. I saw that car with its wheels a foot off the ground on the back straightaway at Daytona. The only way you got control going into a corner was when you slowed and the nose and the wheels dropped back down and the g-forces took over. The Stingray wasn't quite that bad, but it had quite a bit of lift.

Ed: When you began working with Mitchell, did you have responsibilities for any other production styling, or was it strictly Corvettes?

Shinoda: Pretty much Mitchell and Corvette. Previous to that, I'd met [then Pontiac Division general manager "Bunkie"] Knudsen at Daytona Beach in 1956. It was the week before the 500. I went to Daytona and worked on the Pontiacs. Knudsen asked me how come one particular Pontiac was so fast. It was running with a real nose-down attitude. That was before the NASCAR rules said you had to clear this box that they'd slide under your car; if it didn't clear, the car was illegal. We had this one car lowered down just about to that point, and we had a right-angle piece of bedframe bolted on that ducted air up into the radiator, because we had blocked off the front radiator intake. What we didn't realize was that we had actually built an airdam. And that car was a good seven miles an hour faster than the factory cars.

Ed: This was a private entry?

Shinoda: It was a partial Pontiac factory deal. But all the factory cars were hardtops, and this was a two-door sedan. Of

A May 1960 design study by Larry Shinoda of what would become the production Sting Ray.

207

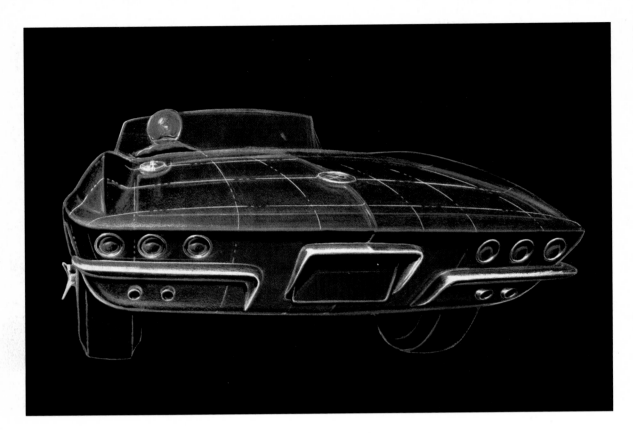

course, the two-door was much lighter than the hardtop to start with, and its roof shape—it had more frontal area, but the shape was rounder. And with the nose-down attitude, the drag I'm sure was quite a bit less. The next day they were jacking all the factory cars up at the rear, and they picked up four mph.

I asked [Knudsen] about a job, and he said I ought to talk to Harley Earl. But there was no way I could get to him, so I submitted a portfolio to Jules Agramonte, who was Harley Earl's assistant. For three days in a row they let me sit out in the lobby—the first day, 8½ hours. The next day I took my lunch and a whole bunch of magazines. The third day I sat there for about six hours. Then they finally came out and told me the answer was no, that my portfolio wasn't strong enough. So I asked them who looked at it, and they said Mr. Agramonte. I asked where was it weak. "Well, we don't know." Then I asked, where's my portfolio? They said, "We'll send it to you." And I said, no, I want it now. So they got it for me. Actually, I saw it sitting right there in this personnel office; it probably never left there. So I wrote Mr. Agramonte a letter; he'd never seen the portfolio. He asked me back, and I went.

When you opened the portfolio, the first shots were of the '56 winning car at Indy, the crew shots. And then there were some sketches of the body shape, and then some pictures where I was actually working on a wood buck for that, and then other pictures of the car and the final configuration. And that's all he looked at. He brought Harley Earl back, and that's about as far as *he* went. He turned to the Indy thing and said, "Jules, how come you didn't tell me this was a famous race-car designer we've got here?" And he offered me the job right on the spot. It was good, because he asked me how much I needed, and I quickly conjured up a figure of about $200 a month more than I was making at Packard. He [Earl] rounded it off to the next higher figure, which was almost 350 bucks more.

Ed: Where did you work first at GM?

Shinoda: I was in an orientation studio for about three weeks. There was a big push to change the design of all the cars, the '59 cars. There was a sketch I'd done of a Chevy that must have caught [Harley Earl's] eye, because it was gone from the orientation studio, and on the following Monday I was kicked into the Chevrolet studio where they were doing a clay model from this sketch. So I was in the Chevy studio through that '59 program. And then Knudsen saw me there one day

and wanted to know why I wasn't in the Pontiac studio. The next day I went to the Pontiac studio.

Ed: Grabbed you for himself, did he?

Shinoda: Right. We worked on the '60 model and the '61 model [Pontiacs]. In the meantime, I was working in Mitchell's special studio. Then there was kind of a little dry spell, and I ended up in the Advanced Studio, a body development studio. They had me doing limousines, and I was doing some pretty racy limousines. I would draw them kind of tilted up a little bit, and I'd put NASCAR numbers on the roof and racing numbers on the doors, and decals, mag wheels.

But one of the reasons I got run out of that studio was that I'd done an airbrush rendering showing [then GM president] Harlow Curtice sitting in the back seat holding a shotgun, and along the doors I'd rendered a bunch of ducks with an "x" through them, because he'd been on a duck-hunting thing. When my boss saw that, we had to quickly clean it up. Next thing I knew, no more limos. I was full-time in Mitchell's studio.

Ed: What was it like to work for Mitchell?

Shinoda: He was probably one of the best bosses I ever had. I was the only designer in the studio. He'd come in and ask for certain things. One thing you learned real quickly: He'd say do something like this and like this, but if you didn't do *more* than he asked, he'd get mad. So you'd always do what he asked, and then you'd take it a couple of steps further. If he liked it, it would go right on the model. He was very supportive. On Corvettes, he finally got to a point where he more or less kept people out of the studio, [people] he felt would screw things up.

Ed: You're talking about development of the racing Stingray?

Shinoda: Yes. He finally told most of the research guys it was kind of hands-off.

Ed: But that was his private project. He couldn't do that with the production '63 Sting Ray, could he?

Shinoda: Oh, yes. The whole theme model was done down in the basement, in Studio X. The first models shown to the board of directors had the scoops in the rear fenders. On the production car, the scoops went up where they should have been, on the front fenders. Originally, the fuel cap was on the left rear fender. In fact, there was a complete hatch for it, but that never happened in production.

Ed: It sounds as though the '63 Sting Ray went together pretty quickly because you'd already done so much of the work with the race car.

Shinoda: It went together fairly fast, but there were a lot of problems. On the race car, there was never any thought of doing a roof. And you had to have doors that opened. And then, the front-end shape: To have the concealed headlights and make it all work, that whole wing section got much thicker in the production car versus the race car, which had a real fast section.

Ed: We've heard that the dummy hood vents on the '63 were supposed to be functional, as on the race car, but that the reason they weren't was that they blew hot air into the cockpit.

Shinoda: It wasn't quite that bad. On the open car, perhaps yes, but on the coupes it didn't seem to be that much of a problem. The real reason is that functional vents would have caused all kinds of leak problems. As it was, they finally had to drill drain holes so the water wouldn't puddle in the engine compartment.

Ed: How did the fastback coupe come about, particularly the roof shape and the divided rear window?

Shinoda: That was pretty much Bill Mitchell. That was kind of his pet thing, to have that boattail shape. And the whole idea of that "ironing board" on the hood was kind of his phallic symbol.

Ed: We know you worked on the original Shark show car and then the Mako Shark II. What kinds of things happened there?

Shinoda: The Shark was done after the fact. Originally we'd had the XP-700 Corvette, with all the different mouths on it. That's something that Mitchell had done before I came in. Now they had to do something that would kind of herald the '63 shape, and they didn't quite know what to do. So we took [a

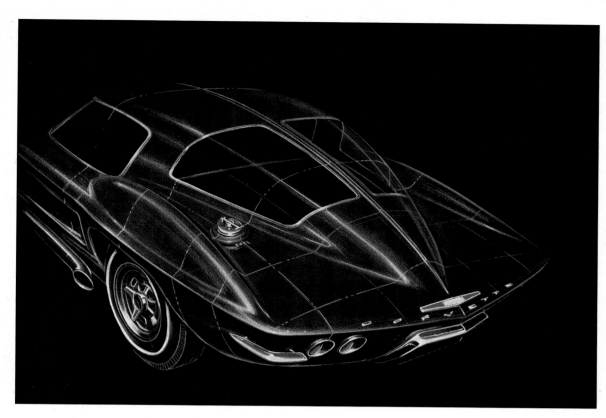

production] Corvette and redid all the shapes, although that double-bubble roof had to stay the same. But we redid the whole front, the bodysides, and most of the rear, and changed the plan forms.

All along it was going to be called the Shark. At one point we mocked up some grille teeth that actually *looked* like shark's teeth. They were basically straight bars, but interlaced with one another; the way the shadows were cast, they curved just like a shark's teeth. And we had these sort of "shark's eyeball" side marker lights right on the peak. When Mitchell saw that, he said, "What are trying to do? Get me fired?" So we backed off. And then, of course, he had to put three little louvers on each side, for the side marker lights—turn indicators and two cornering lights. He liked louvers, so there were louvers on the rear corners, where the bumper sort of went into the louvers. In this car, the more things you'd draw, the more he'd say keep doing it.

Ed: It sounds like Mitchell challenged you a lot.

Shinoda: Oh, yes. He'd always say, "What if? Suppose you do it this way?" He was one of these very inquisitive guys. He wasn't scared to try something. My drawings were very mechanical, and I guess he kind of liked that, because there was never a question of

what I was trying to show them. They'd always understand. He liked flashy renderings, but one day he told me, "When I look at one of your sketches, I know that when we model it, it's going to look [even] better. And that's what I want to see." Which was a real flattering thing for him to tell me.

Ed: He appreciated your literal approach, then?

Shinoda: Yes. If you look at my old sketches, I always put section lines on everything. Most of my old drawings are a series of sections.

Ed: Let's jump ahead to the '68 program, which you were also involved with. That design had cooling and aerodynamic problems. What was the story there?

Shinoda: I don't think it was so much cooling problems. There may have been some, but they were definitely having problems with the body structure. In fact, it was never really satisfactory. The cockpit was awful tight. That's what Mitchell wanted. He wanted the wheels very pronounced and the body shape as narrow as he could get it—that coke-bottle shape. Zora [Arkus-Duntov] fought that part of it. But I think there were more body structure problems than there were cooling problems.

Ed: Did that have anything to do with the T-top on the coupe?

Shinoda: Yes. There were

some structural problems there that they didn't experience on the earlier models, because those coupes pretty much had the steel cage. The steel cage was still in the '68. In fact, I think there was more steel in the '68 than there had been in the '67.

Ed: But there was something about cutting that big hole in the roof. We understand that the longitudinal bar was a late addition because the intention was to have just a single removable panel.

Shinoda: That was the idea. But there was so much shake in it. So it was probably more body problems than anything else. But they still built a roadster model of it also.

Ed: But neither was trouble-free when they first came out, and there were some assembly problems.

Shinoda: The thing is, we did a car called the XP-819. It had a lot of the cues that went on the '68. It had the rear roof, that kind of Ferrari-like cutout. That was a pickup from the Porsche 904, and one earlier Ferrari model had a similar arrangement. But the XP-819 had all these things that Mitchell was talking about for the '68, only it was done on a much shorter wheelbase and the engine was overhanging the rear axle. That was a car that everybody said was impossible, you couldn't build it. The reason it got built was Frank Winchell at Chevy R&D; when everybody told him he couldn't do it, he went ahead and built it.

I was in a meeting where they had all the layouts [for XP-819] in the one studio, and they asked everybody around the room what their thoughts were. Everybody was bad-mouthing it, including Zora. Then they got to Frank Winchell. He said he wouldn't comment until he checked with his styling expert —which happened to be me. I told them, "I think we can make a very nice-looking car out of it, and I'd like to show it to you after lunch." And they just couldn't believe that I wasn't kidding them. What they didn't know is, I had the thing all designed in the warehouse.

So I didn't eat lunch. John Schinella [chief exterior designer for Pontiac in the mid-Seventies and now director of GM's Advanced Concepts Center in Newbury Park, California]

was working for me at the time, and a fellow named Allen Young. We worked right through lunch and finished the tape drawing. When the meeting reconvened, nobody could believe what they were looking at. Zora actually got out a yardstick and started measuring things. He thought we had cheated the hell out of it, which we hadn't. But that car had a lot of the feel of what came out on the '68, a good many of the styling cues.

Ed: When did you do XP-819?

Shinoda: That was built in '64.

Ed: Was the Mako II evolved from that?

Shinoda: No, the Mako show car was done afterwards, but it has a lot of things that are somewhat similar.

Ed: When you did the XP-819 and Mako II, was there any thought that they were what the next production Corvette was going to look like, or had that already been determined?

Shinoda: No, that hadn't been determined yet. In fact, there was a big contest on what shape was going to win. Hank Haga had done a car that was quite nice, but it was "nice" like the '84 Corvette. It was a rounder, softer shape—kind of a soap-dish design with the body wideline, and the upper shape and the bottom shape were about the same. It had a little bit of a flying-saucer look to it. And Mitchell hated it.

Ed: Was that a mid-engine or front-engine car?

Shinoda: Front engine. So we did a car in the warehouse, and Haga did his car in the production studio. And then we viewed those at a little styling display area up at the north end of the Tech Center, a road that sort of emulates driving in a park. The longer Mitchell looked at Haga's car, the madder he got. And finally he kicked it.

Ed: Kicked it?

Shinoda: He said, "Have you ever seen such a fat pig?" Then he kicked it, and almost the whole back end fell off! It was already cracked. Haga thought he'd be kind of cute. He had the paint shop keep adding blue to the silver, thinking he's going to blow us away with this silvery-blue car, but it ended up looking kind of powdery blue. The car we did was just straight silver. But what Hank didn't know was that the area below the wideline was

painted a little bit darker shade of silver, so that our car looked a whole lot lighter and whole lot meaner. And we won the contest. We went back, made a few changes, and our model was picked as the theme model. Then it was sent over to the production studio and I was off that job; I was off doing the Mako II show car.

Ed: As another "herald" for the next production Corvette?

Shinoda: Yes.

Ed: That car had all kinds of opening panels that caused a lot of trouble when they put them on the production car, right?

Shinoda: Yeah, like the windshield wiper panel that kicked up. That was about the only thing that really gave them a problem. Of course, the Mako Shark II didn't have the center beam running forward for the roof. Neither did the XP-819, which had a whole lot of torsional stiffness. It had a center backbone, spine-type chassis like some other cars.

Ed: A Lotus-type chassis?

Shinoda: Yes. All the fuel was carried right down the center.

Ed: We remember seeing in an ad someplace a few years ago that the XP-819 was for sale.

Shinoda: It's been for sale. Knudsen sent the car down to Daytona, gave it to [race-car builder/mechanic] Smokey Yunick. He cut it in half, cut the center section out of it, and then sold all the pieces to this guy from down south. I forget his name. He fabricated a tubular center section and put it all back together. Then, when he was going to show it, the car come out the back of the trailer and pretty much demolished itself. So he rebuilt it again. I guess it's still in pretty good shape.

Ed: Still faithful to what you did originally?

Shinoda: Yes. In fact, I think it has my name and some of the patent papers he got with the car.

Ed: Did you have much contact with Zora Arkus-Duntov?

Shinoda: Oh, yes. I've had a lot of contact with Zora.

Ed: Are you still in touch with him?

Shinoda: I talk to him usually about every other week or so.

Ed: Are you involved in any

projects together?

Shinoda: No, but we do attend a lot of different Corvette functions, and [the Duntovs] are personally good friends of ours, he and his wife, so we see them socially. Plus, I did a little bit of work with him when he was doing all that consulting with Yugo, which I think has become sort of a fiasco.

Ed: We've heard that you're working on a conversion for the current Corvette convertible that emulates the Stingray racer. True?

Shinoda: Right now I'm just putting a few things together. That's something I hope to do. I don't know just how soon, but I think there's a need for something like that. I think there'd be a market for a car of that nature, done properly.

Ed: So you've done the design work?

Shinoda: I've done a few sketches. I haven't done anything that I'm ready to show.

Ed: It seems there should be a market for it, because there's only one Stingray racer and there have to be a lot of people who'd like to own it.

Shinoda: Yes, but nobody'll be able to buy that one. They [GM] aren't going to let that one get away.

Ed: What do you think of the production Corvette that's been with us since the '84 model year? And how do you view what looks to be its successor, which will be something along the lines of the Corvette Indy?

Shinoda: The '84 Corvette is a very nice design. The only problem was that it came out after the [third-generation 1982] Camaro and Firebird, which kind of hurt because they're all so much alike. I think the new Corvette could have been a little more gutsy. And it's been so slow in evolving. The next change won't be until 1992. Then they'll do a little front-end facelift, and with the new rear-end facelift like the ZR-1—a little bit here and there. I think you're pretty far off before it becomes a Corvette Indy—if it ever will. You know, all this talk that the mid-engine car is the way, I don't really believe that.

Ed: Because?

Shinoda: Because there's so many problems in doing a decent mid-engine car.

Ed: That's certainly been a

From April 1960, Shinoda's study of the CERV-1 racer.

recurring theme in Corvette history. Have you driven a ZR-1 yet?

Shinoda: No. I had a short ride in one back in late fall of '87, at the proving grounds. But that was an early prototype. I guess the ZR-1 is pretty awesome—really a good package.

Ed: Do you own a Corvette, and what's your favorite model over the years?

Shinoda: I don't have a Corvette. I never owned a '63. I did own a '64, which was a real bucket of worms—just a bad car—and we owned a '76. I'm now considering getting one. In fact, I've been looking at a '63 split-window at some point in time.

Ed: That one must hold particularly strong memories for you.

Shinoda: Yeah, it does. I probably wouldn't have a purist's car, though. I might have that look, but I think I'd want to have the later-model brakes and stuff. That's what's prompted me to do something with the latest chassis and the old style, the old sports/racing-car look.

Ed: What kinds of cars do you own?

Shinoda: My wife drives a Saab 9000 Turbo, and presently I'm driving an old rusted-out

Honda.

Ed: What kinds of cars do you favor from the driving and design standpoints?

Shinoda: From the driving standpoint, one of the most pleasant cars I've driven recently is the [1989] Mitsubishi Galant GS. And from a styling standpoint of four-door sedans, probably the nicest is the [1986-89] Honda Accord. I don't own one because they're like navels: Everybody has one. But it is very nicely proportioned, quite a nice car to drive.

Ed: Your company, Shinoda Design Associates, is still very active in a number of fields.

Shinoda: We've done motorhomes. Recently we designed the '89 Newell Coach—one of your high-buck motor coaches. I guess they start at around $300,000.

Ed: That's got to be very different from your work on cars at GM and Ford. Vehicles like that must pose very different challenges for you.

Shinoda: It's the same as doing trucks, sport/utilities. In fact, most recently I did some lawn mower work for Honda. Now I'm getting involved in color design, doing some work with PPG and a Japanese paint company. But it's all a challenge.

CHAPTER 8

CORVETTE GRAND SPORT: PROMISE UNFULFILLED

Even before the Sting Ray began wowing crowds in Chevy showrooms, there was the Grand Sport, a very special Sting Ray created expressly for racing. But wait: Hadn't General Motors been *out* of racing since the Automobile Manufacturers Association June 1957 "ban"? Officially, yes; actually, no. With people like Zora Arkus-Duntov and Bunkie Knudsen around, and with Ford and Chrysler beginning to defy the ban by 1961, there was no way "the General"—or at least certain factions within the GM ranks—would be denied.

The impetus for the Grand Sport came from at least three directions. One was Duntov's ever-burning desire that Corvettes win races, openly and convincingly, regardless of the AMA decision and GM's stated adherence to it. That "gentleman's agreement," he knew, had kept his swoopy Sebring Super Sport (see Chapter 5) from realizing its full potential. With the new production Sting Ray in the works, Duntov felt he had the makings for a sure-fire winner in GT competition.

A second factor in the birth of the Grand Sport was Knudsen's arrival as Chevy general manager in 1961 following his great success in the same post at Pontiac Division, which zoomed from number six to the industry's number-three seller in just four years. Like so many at GM in those days, Knudsen was afflicted with that chronic illness called racing fever, and he was solidly behind Duntov's quiet, competition-oriented projects like the exotic mid-engine CERV II. He also backed the Chevy "mystery" engine that would startle the NASCAR world when it briefly appeared at Daytona in 1963.

But the chief spur to the GS was the same change in racing rules that prompted Ford to support Carroll Shelby's Cobra. For the 1963 season, the *Federation Internationale de l'Automobile* (FIA), the world's chief auto-racing governing body, announced that the World Manufacturers Championship would be open to Grand Touring cars as well as prototypes and approved sports-racing models. All that was required was that at least 100 such cars be built to an approved ("homologated") specification within one year of certification. No limit was set on engine displacement, which was just fine as far as Chevrolet was concerned, because the Sting Ray was shaping up to be a little portly and not as aerodynamically clean as might be desired for high-speed enduros.

Duntov, however, had already been working on an answer: a lightweight "Grand Sport" version of the forthcoming Sting Ray coupe powered by a much modified, 327-cubic-inch Corvette V-8. With Knudsen's enthusiastic, if necessarily muted, backing, Duntov's special engineering team got down to work in earnest—and great secrecy—in the summer of '62.

As might be expected, they started from the ground up, resulting in a car that, while fundamentally based on the new Sting Ray engineering, differed from it in most every respect. The chassis, for example, retained the new ladder-type design but featured large tubular-steel side rails that ran utterly straight front to rear as viewed from above, rather than tapering inward. Three equally large crossmembers tied things together at the back; up front was a hefty single crossmember

measuring a half-foot in diameter.

Suspension geometry also followed that of the new production Corvette, but components were specially fabricated and calculated to save weight. The main changes were the use of thin sheet steel instead of thicker cast metal for the front A-arms, larger-diameter coil springs all-round, the lack of flexible rubber bushings for the rear suspension (no need for concern about noise and vibration here), and special rear trailing arms with lightening holes. Less weight than the stock Sting Ray made disc brakes feasible, and these were duly bolted on at each corner: big 11.75-inch-diameter British-made Girling units with two-piston aluminum calipers and solid rotors. The brakes' deeply offset "hat-section" design allowed small rear drums to be incorporated at the rear as an emergency brake, operated from the cockpit by a British-traditional fly-off lever. Steering was by the usual recirculating-ball mechanism within a special weight-saving aluminum case, with modified gearing giving an ultra-quick two turns lock-to-lock.

Bodywork was closely cloned from Bill Mitchell's newly designed Sting Ray fastback and also made of fiberglass, but was of thicker section (0.040-inch) and specially hand-laid. Dimensions were kept close to stock, though front/rear tracks were slightly wider at 56.8/57.8 inches. Duntov summarily removed Mitchell's pet rear-window divider bar, added a small opening panel in the rear deck for access to the spare tire, substituted fixed headlights (behind Plexiglas covers) for the production car's hidden lamps, and placed a racing-style quick-fill fuel outlet in the right rear roof quarter. A sheet-aluminum framework around the doors and windows bolstered the Sting Ray's new steel "birdcage" underbody structure. Fender wells were carefully shaped to accept the largest possible wheels and tires. Duntov chose 6.0 × 15.0 Halibrand magnesium knock-off rims able to mount 7.10-7.60-

The Corvette Grand Sport (opposite) arose not only because engineer Zora Arkus-Duntov and Chevy general manager Bunkie Knudsen loved racing, but also as a response to Carroll Shelby's fabulous Ford-powered Cobra. Of the five Grand Sports built, two were later converted into roadsters (above) to compete at Daytona.

section rubber up front and 8.00-8.20 tires in back.

Inside, the GS was quite civilized for a racer, with full carpeting and the same instrument cluster and steering wheel found in the new Sting Ray. An oil-pressure dial was substituted for the fuel gauge, however, and there was a special speedometer calibrated to 200 mph. Seats were deep one-piece molded bucket affairs bolstered onto tubular tracks, which allowed fore/aft adjustment with a little wrenchwork.

Recalling the SS effort of five years earlier, Duntov and company envisioned GS power as coming from a more exotic version of the versatile Chevy small-block. Starting with the basic 327 production block, they devised new big-valve aluminum cylinder heads with more efficient hemispherical combustion chambers instead of the normal wedge-type and—the tricky part—two sparkplugs per cylinder, activated from a single distributor by twin coils. Rochester constant-flow mechanical fuel injection was specified, basically the familiar "Ramjet" system but modified to feed individual, vertically situated ram pipes. The 327's normal 4.00-inch bore was retained, but stroke lengths of up to 4.00 inches were possible for displacements of up to 402 cubic inches. Ultimately, the team settled on an intermediate 3.75-inch stroke for greater simplicity and reliability, producing a 377-cid powerhouse that could rev happily to 6500 rpm.

Grand Sport power ratings have long been subject to confusion, since compression ratios of 10.0:1, 11.0:1, and even 12.0:1 were contemplated for the 16-plug V-8. Author Karl Ludvigsen states that Duntov's engineers had been hoping for up to 600 horsepower, but had to settle for 550 bhp at 6400 rpm for the 377-cid engine. That output stood to be more than

competitive, however—certainly for the quoted 1900-2100-pound curb weight and enough to overcome the Sting Ray body's relatively high aerodynamic drag. Torque was a massive 500 pounds-feet at 5200 rpm, though, like horsepower, the actual figure was undoubtedly higher. As the peak power and torque speeds suggest, the GS engine gave its best at the top end, which is just where you want it in a racing machine. Completing the drivetrain were a fortified four-speed manual gearbox linked to an aluminum-case limited-slip differential supplied by Dana.

By mid-December, the first Grand Sport was complete and ready for initial testing. The test was conducted at Sebring, with drivers Masten Gregory and Corvette veteran Dick Thompson doing the honors. Excessive heat retention within the brakes proved the biggest problem. Slightly wider ventilated Girling discs were the solution, and were included in the Grand Sport's specification as submitted for FIA approval.

FIA policy at the time was to homologate a car even before the minimum 100 examples had been built, and so it was with the GS. After all, Chevy was hardly a fly-by-night concern. An additional four Grand Sports were built, and Duntov obtained authorization for an additional 20 cars and 40 of the 16-plug engines, all of which were deemed adequate to satisfy customer demand for the '63 season. Production of the remaining 60-plus cars would be handled by an outside firm under contract to Chevy. Sales would be on a first-come, first-served basis.

As with the Super Sport, however, Duntov was about to be thwarted by GM's staunch adherence to the 1957 AMA anti-racing edict. Rumors had been growing louder in the press and even within GM itself that some

Duntov had been plotting a lightweight "Grand Sport" version of the forthcoming Sting Ray as early as 1961, but his engineering team didn't get down to work in earnest until the summer of 1962. The Grand Sport (both pages), Chevy's last "openly" supported factory competition car for many years, had a specially built woven fiberglass body with lines very close to those of the just-released Sting Ray coupe. The instrument panel (opposite bottom) boasted a 200-mph speedometer and all of the gauges/switches necessary for serious competition.

divisions were defying this corporate policy. As a result, chairman Frederic Donner and president John Gordon circulated an internal memo on January 21, 1963, stating that GM was still abiding by the AMA agreement and that the various divisions would thus, in Ludvigsen's words, "comport themselves accordingly." At a news conference less than a month later, Donner went public with this crackdown on internal *sub rosa* racing efforts. With that, the Grand Sport was officially and forever dead. Only five cars had been completed by that point, and the 16-plug engine was still largely undeveloped. In Ludvigsen's words, another "golden age in the history of the Corvette seemed over before it had even begun."

But it *wasn't* over. The GS was about to rise phoenix-like from the ashes of corporate intransigence and would triumph over adversity to write a stirring new chapter in the annals of Corvette history.

It all began with Grady Davis, a Union Oil official, and Dick Doane, a Chevrolet dealer, both with close ties to division higher-ups. Davis and Doane each managed to obtain a GS, allegedly delivered in

unmarked Chevy Division trucks. The Davis car was given minor body modifications and fitted with a stock 360-bhp 327 fuelie for Dick Thompson to drive through the 1963 season in SCCA's C-Modified class. Under the circumstances, it did well. The highlight was an outright win at Watkins Glen in late August, as Thompson staved off a front-engine Chaparral to take the checkered flag with an average speed of 90.82 mph. The "flying dentist" did well elsewhere: third in class and fifth overall at Cumberland, Maryland, in May; third overall at Elkhart Lake, Wisconsin, and fourth overall at Bridgehampton, both in June. Ed Lowther also drove the Davis car, coming home third in class and fourth overall in the 90-minute Governor's Cup at Danville, Virginia, in April. The Doane GS saw less action in '63, but the owner drove it to a sixth-place finish at Meadowdale, Illinois, in August.

Meantime, the remaining three Grand Sports had been sold to millionaire Texas oilman John Mecom, Jr. Mecom had lately become a major force in motorsports by backing the best machinery money could buy, and hiring stellar drivers like Roger Penske, Augie Pabst,

Zora Arkus-Duntov had hoped to build 125 Grand Sports (left), but only five were run off before GM axed it in early 1963. All five somehow fell into private hands, and the Grand Sport did in fact go racing. One drove to victory in 1963 at Watkins Glen, while three competed at the 1963 Nassau Speed Weeks and came in first and third. Note the roof lights on this number 2 car and the inside wires to the roof lights (below center), the roll bar, and the huge filler pipe. Unlike the production Sting Ray, the Grand Sport had a small decklid (below).

This page: *The chassis beneath the body of the Sting Ray-like Grand Sport (top) was a special tube-ladder affair with stock suspension mounting points. The drivetrain consisted of a four-speed gearbox designed to hook up to a special 377-cid racing version of the Chevy V-8, which was to have an aluminum head and block, two spark plugs per cylinder, and 550 bhp. In fact, engine development hadn't been completed, and none of the five Grand Sports that "got away" had an engine (bottom). Opposite page: Detail shots show coolers and air scoops, hood tie-down, aluminum door handle, gas filler cap for the 36-gallon tank, Grand Sport badge, and taillights.*

218

and A.J. Foyt. Carroll Shelby's Cobras had been running wild on the tracks, and despite GM's reaffirmed adherence to the AMA racing ban, Chevy officials from Bunkie Knudsen on down were just itching to get even. As Karl Ludvigsen recorded: "Blocked...from building the 100 Grand Sports, Chevrolet...felt an overpowering urge to use the cars it did have to show Ford what it would be up against if Chevy were seriously in racing. It chose to do so through the Mecom Racing Team, the first target being the Nassau Speed Week events early in December [1963]." The scene was set for the Grand Sport's greatest triumph.

Three Grand Sports were prepared: the Davis and Doane cars, plus another GS that had been languishing at the GM Tech Center in Warren, Michigan. Again in great secrecy, Duntov's team focused on the 377 V-8, giving it a new aluminum block and discarding the original fuel injection for four big-bore Weber carburetors on a special light-alloy manifold with cross-over intake pipes. A raft of body alterations occurred: a new hood with a pair of tall, front-facing scoops to feed the carbs; eight holes cut in between the taillamps to aid brake cooling; functional engine-compartment air vents in the front fenders (replacing the previous dummy outlets); opaque shrouds for the headlights; and, most noticeable, wheel openings radically flared to accommodate huge 11-inch-wide Halibrand wheels wearing the latest low-profile Goodyear racing tires. "These Sting Rays with hormones" Ludvigsen records, "were magnificent-looking cars with an air of forbidding malevolence. Now they *looked* like competition cars, and Chevy engineers were in Nassau *en masse* to see that they had the performance to match their appearance." Officially, the Chevy folks were there "on vacation." As one of them remarked to writer Leo Levine, "You realize, of course, you're talking to a man who isn't here."

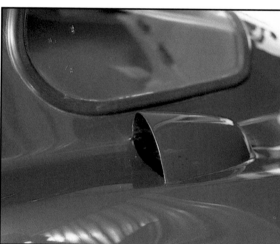

But the Grand Sports *were* there, and became the talk of Nassau '63. In qualifying for the December 1 Tourist Trophy race, Dick Thompson and Jim Hall (of Chaparral fame) blasted away from a pack of Cobras and a Ferrari GTO to capture the front-row grid positions, only to retire from the actual race with differential trouble. Insufficient cooling was the culprit, but it was rectified in time for the Governor's Cup Trophy on December 6, a 25-lap, 112-mile dash with 58 entries. To Carroll Shelby's dismay, Roger Penske led all the way, finishing third overall and first in the prototype class. All three Grand Sports contested the week's longest and most important event, the 56-lap, 252-mile Nassau Trophy race on December 8. Although one GS dropped out, Thompson flew home fourth overall and first in class, while newly recruited teammate John Cannon drove to eighth overall and third in class.

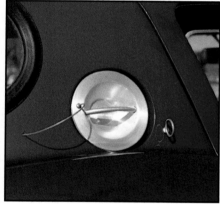

Elated by this showing, and having learned some valuable lessons at Nassau, the Duntov team immediately set to work on improvements. Among these were a new timed fuel-injection system with cross-ram manifolding, a suitably redesigned hood with stronger fasteners (excessive underhood pressure had caused hoods to pop open at Nassau), and a pneumatic jacking system to speed pit-side servicing and tire changes. All this was intended for Sebring in March 1964, but the GS proved disappointing there. Delmo Johnson and co-driver Dave Morgan endured numerous mechanical breakdowns to finish only 32nd overall, while Penske and Jim Hall put their white car across the line in 18th.

Meantime, the two remaining Grand Sport coupes that had been sitting around in Warren were prepped for the 2000-kilometer Daytona Continental in February 1964, run on the combined infield/tri-oval

course used for long-distance road races at the Florida speedway. Reasoning that the coupe body's high drag would limit maximum speed on the high-banked sections, Duntov decided to reduce frontal area by converting this pair to roadster configuration. The result was a mean-looking open GS with a low racing windscreen and stylishly integrated roll-over bar surmounting a faired-in driver's headrest. These cars were also given the pneumatic jacking system and even a left-side fuel filler for quickest accessibility at that particular track (versus the right-hand access required at most other venues, including Le Mans and Sebring).

But once more, the Grand Sport was about to be stopped cold. Irked by press reports that Chevy was racing again, management told Knudsen to cease and desist or risk losing an annual bonus equal to his entire yearly salary, which was substantial. Knudsen was wealthy, but he wasn't foolish, and he withdrew all his previous support. The roadsters were unceremoniously moved to a warehouse, where they would remain for three years.

The GS saga still wasn't finished, but what little was left to come would be anticlimactic. Further rules changes and advancing age conspired to limit the competitiveness of the five Grand Sports, and some of the private parties who'd been involved with them in 1963 were being pulled off in other directions. This led to a rather confusing series of ownership changes among the hardy quintet. The three coupes, which Chevy had repurchased in preparation for Nassau, were sold— one to Jim Hall, the others to John Mecom, Jr. —unchanged save substitution of iron-block engines for the all-aluminum powerplants. Mecom then sold one his coupes, the original Grady Davis car, to Delmo Johnson of Dallas. Johnson entered it in the late-1964 revival of the legendary Mexican Road Race, then fitted a big-block Mark IV engine for Sebring in '65, but the car fared poorly on both occasions.

The Jim Hall car, chassis 005, soon wound up in the hands of Roger Penske, who'd retired from driving after Nassau to build his own racing team. Penske decided to overhaul this car, intending to enter it at the Bahamas speed weeks in late 1964. "We tore the gearbox apart," he recalled, "completely disassembled

the rear end and installed a new ring gear pinion, rebuilt the brake calipers, and took the suspension off and Magnafluxed it to make sure there weren't any cracks. We Magnafluxed the wheels, put on new wheel bearings and new spinner knock-off nuts....To reduce weight, we took off the automatic jacking system. The Grand Sport weighs in at about 2000 pounds, but ours was a lot lighter." Penske's modifications paid off: With engine preparation by Traco Engineering, the Penske GS won the Tourist Trophy, beating back a prototype 427 Cobra and John Mecom's other GS (driven by Jack Saunders).

Penske then sold this winningest of Grand Sports to friend and fellow Philadelphian George Wintersteen, who had it prepped for Sebring '65. The one major engineering change was a stroke shortened an eighth of an inch, an adjustment that scaled displacement back to 365 cid on an engine again massaged by Traco. Driven by Wintersteen, Peter Goetz, and Ed Diehl, the car weathered 12 rain-soaked hours to finish 14th overall and second in the prototype category despite completing two fewer laps than the year previous. Wintersteen then sold the car, less engine, to a New York collector.

Early in 1966, the two roadsters were taken out of storage and sold to Penske, who engaged Californian Dick Guldstrand to prepare one of them, chassis 002, for Sebring. Guldstrand, who's still renowned for the racing magic he works on Corvettes, fitted a 427 Mark IV engine, tried aluminum heads (iron ones were substituted for the actual race), and made minor suspension changes. He then agreed to a co-drive with

the redoubtable Dick Thompson, but the car retired due to engine trouble after five hours.

Soon afterward, Wintersteen purchased Penske's other newly acquired roadster. With big-block power and other modifications, this car, chassis 001, appeared in several East Coast events during 1966, but never finished high enough to leave Wintersteen in contention for points. Wintersteen sold this car the following year, much to his later regret. Roadster 002 was subsequently acquired by none other than John Mecom, Jr.

With that, the Corvette Grand Sport passed into history, another promising hope of new competition glory for America's sports car cut short by corporate image-consciousness. But in the end, part of the Grand Sport's promise *was* fulfilled—at Sebring and especially Nassau—thanks to the efforts of true believers like Duntov and his associates, who persisted against all odds and ultimately triumphed. Come to think of it, they still do, for Grand Sports still show up at important Corvette meets and vintage-car events, where they generate the same excitement they did in the Sixties.

This level of attention amounts to a moral victory that overshadows any actual victories the Grand Sport might have earned in the major international events for which it was designed. As Karl Ludvigsen observed: "Running under wraps, the GS Corvette was a reminder to Ford, then on the way up in its historic assault on the racing world, that the way would not always be easy. It was also a marvelous morale-builder for the engineers of Chevrolet and others in GM who felt that racing was not among the seven deadly sins." You can't ask much more from any car than that.

Two Grand Sport coupes were converted into roadsters for the 1964 2000-kilometer Daytona Continental run because it was feared that the coupe's high drag would limit maximum speed on the high-banked sections of the track. Alas, GM management intervened, and the cars didn't compete there. This car, chassis 001 (both pages), wound up in the hands of George Wintersteen, who modified it and gave it big-block power, and ran it in several East Coast events in 1966.

221

CHAPTER 9

1968-77: ENTER THE SHARK

t's uncanny how often automotive history repeats itself, sometimes with ironic twists. The Corvette has had more than its share of both irony and *déjà vu*. Take the fifth generation that arrived for 1968. Like the new Corvette of 10 years before, it was greeted in many quarters as a step backward—fatter and flashier than its well-loved predecessor, and thus something of a disappointment. It certainly was not the mighty leap forward 'Vette fans I ad been led to expect. In fact, cynics said it was just another example of that old Detroit maxim, "nothing succeeds like excess."

Then again, the Sting Ray was a very tough act to follow, even for a big outfit like General Motors, with all its redoubtable resources. The fourth generation had literally remade Corvette's image, so it was logical that the fifth would be expected to be another swoopy trend-setter. Perhaps a mid-engine car, thus confirming all those rumors that had circulated since 1958. Or maybe a rear-engine slingshot based on Corvair technology—something like Bill Mitchell's exciting Monza GT and SS show cars. But even GM has its limits, and for a variety of reasons, none of this came to pass.

What did was a Corvette given to more compromise than any previous one. In concept, the new "Shark" design was a very different sort of sports car: less dual-purpose race-and-ride machine than lush and powerful boulevard cruiser. This domestication gained

momentum once the federal government got involved in car design and many would-be Corvette buyers went to Southeast Asia for military duty, though a good many other Detroit hot rods suffered the same fate.

But let's not be too hasty. Though initially flawed, the '68, like the '58 (and even the first Sting Ray), would improve and mature into a car precisely right for its time. Moreover, the fifth generation would prove the longest lived in Corvette history, running all the way through 1982—a full 15 model years--which naturally makes it the most popular in Corvette history (so far). As it's highly unlikely that any future generation will run that long, this staying power attests as much to the adaptability of the basic Shark design as to GM's talents in adapting it to changing times.

And make no mistake: The times demanded changes, even if they weren't the sort Detroit was used to making—let alone *wanted* to make. Consider the momentous events that occurred during the Shark's 15 years: the advent of government-imposed safety regulations (1968, and still with us); soaring insurance premiums that for a time severely reduced the demand for high-performance cars (1969-72); an unprecedented global energy crisis, which almost killed the performance market entirely (1973-74); federally mandated fuel-economy standards, a result of said crisis (1978); yet another fuel shock, followed by an economic downturn so sharp as to recall the Depression (1979-82).

Opposite page: The Mako Shark II, built in 1964 on a Sting Ray chassis, traveled the auto show circuit in 1965 to test public reaction to what would become the 1968 Corvette. This page: Zora Arkus-Duntov had a hand in engineering the 1964 XP-819, a prototype running a rear-mounted 327 V-8.

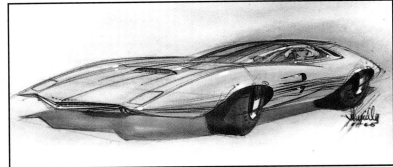

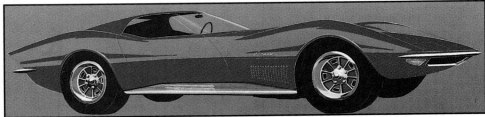

Remember, too, that although the Corvette was highly profitable in the Sting Ray years, it remained a fringe product by the standards of Chevrolet Motor Division—in some corporate minds, more a public relations gimmick than a serious business venture. This view and the historic events noted above explain why the Shark was allowed to hang on year after year with only enough change to keep it saleable and/or legal. In those days, GM and all Detroit were like the man who was sent in to drain the swamp and forgot the task once alligators started nipping at his posterior. Yet even with most everything conspiring against it, the Corvette remained anything but dull.

Traditionally, Detroit begins working on new designs even before the old ones go on sale, and so it was with the '68 Corvette—initiated almost from the moment the Sting Ray went into production. Over the ensuing five years it would be shaped by at least three market developments and a rivalry within GM itself, which in retrospect made the finished product more or less inevitable.

The Sting Ray's second year, 1964, was pivotal to fifth-generation development in that it ushered in two new kinds of American performance: the big-engine mid-size "muscle car" exemplified by Pontiac's GTO, and the winsome "ponycar" as defined and pioneered by Ford's Mustang. Both concepts proved enormously popular in that "go-go" age, and they inspired a host of imitators. By 1967, the market was awash in muscle machines like the Olds 4-4-2, Dodge Charger, and Mercury Cyclone, as well as such Mustang clones as the Plymouth Barracuda and Mercury Cougar.

Chevrolet could be expected to play tough in these fields, and it did, offering hot ones like the intermediate Chevelle SS 396, turbocharged versions of the compact Corvair, and a bow-tie ponycar, the new Camaro. Even full-size Chevys of the day could be equipped for 0-60-mph times on a par with those of recent Corvettes. Impressive performers all, these new Chevys offered a variety of answers to the same performance question. Significantly, they were also priced well below Chevy's usual answer, the Corvette.

Europe, meantime—Italy in particular—was starting to produce sports and GT cars a lot more sophisticated than the Corvette. Granted, they also cost a lot more, but the leading-edge mechanicals and exotic style of cars like the mid-engine Lamborghini Miura made the Corvette and its traditional formula seem dated. GM may be a giant, but its pride is easily wounded. To Bill Mitchell, Zora Arkus-Duntov, and the Chevrolet Engineering Center under Frank Winchell, the Miura and its ilk represented a challenge that could not go unanswered—or at least not unexplored.

Which brings us to the intramural rivalry we mentioned—actually a friendly competition among several GM departments, all envisioning a far more radical new Corvette than the one that would ultimately come to pass. Introduction was targeted for 1967, and there were at least two separate lines of development. Significantly, both of these assumed the mid/rear-engine format that had fascinated Corvette planners since before the stillborn Corvair-based proposals of the early Sixties.

The styling of the Mako Shark II (top row)—one of the most famous show cars of all time—set it apart from anything else on four wheels. It had presence, pizzazz, and the looks of a born runner. The Mako II that toured the auto shows was non-functional. A second car was built, this time a running prototype, the one seen here. Bill Mitchell wanted a different look for the new Corvette, so he put his designers to work to come up with as many fresh new ideas as possible (bottom three rows). A couple of the renderings seen here, all from early 1965, point the way to the '68 Corvette.

By 1965, when work toward a fifth-generation 'Vette was well underway, the Corvair had matured into a unique, well-rounded little car, its original swing-axle rear suspension and quirky handling having given way to a more capable independent rear suspension and equally competent handling. Corvair's design similarity with the honored Porsche 356 and 911 was obvious, and its technology intrigued Corvette stylists and engineers alike. But the market was demanding high power, which virtually demanded a V-8.

There was no shortage of ideas for a mid-V-8 'Vette. Winchell's group conjured up an advanced, very compact design with a Lotus-type backbone frame, all-independent suspension, and a 327-cubic-inch Corvette engine in the tail, driving a modified version of the Pontiac Tempest rear transaxle. But with an aft weight bias of no less than 70 percent, the concept was simply unworkable. Author Karl Ludvigsen quotes

journalist Paul Van Valkenburgh, then a Chevy Research and Development engineer, as saying that "the car could be set up to handle properly on a skidpad in steady-state cornering, but [its] transient or dynamic response was nearly uncontrollable at the limit." One test driver actually lost control of a cobbled-up prototype in a series of high-speed lane changes at the GM Proving Grounds. "[It] was even more uncontrollable traveling sideways," Van

Valkenburgh chuckled.

A separate team under Zora Arkus-Duntov took a slightly different approach: a true mid-engine design with a big-block Mark IV riding just ahead of the rear wheels in a platform-type chassis with a 99-inch wheelbase. Rear suspension was similar to the production Sting Ray's save substitution of twin parallel trailing links for the single radius arm on each side. The radiator was placed in the extreme rear behind the

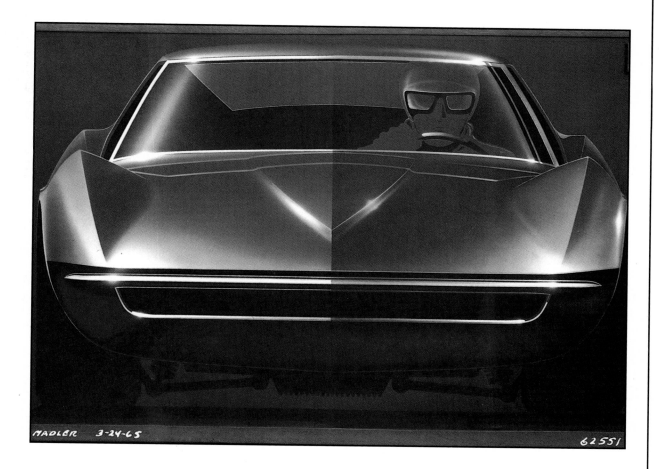

More renderings from early 1965 show the next-generation Corvette taking shape. Prominent early on was the low, pointed nose, as on the Mako Shark II. Bulges over the wheels figured prominently, too, as they had on the 1963 Sting Ray, but the bodyside character line was softened and moved down to mid-body height. The ducktail rear was also predictive of the '68, but the roofline would not be used.

227

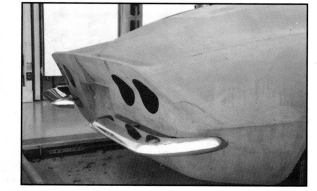

By October 1964, the designers were well along toward the final front-end shape of the '68 Corvette (opposite top). Further refinement can be seen on a clay mock-up from June 1965 (above). The shape of the rear end was also well along at that time, although the bumper design was still undecided (this page, bottom). The major hurdle seemed to be what sort of roofline would best fit the Corvette "spirit" (opposite bottom).

engine; a pair of fans driven by the transaxle provided low-speed cooling via a "forced draft" forward.

Duntov's group also devised a shape for their car's separate fiberglass body, preparing a couple of small scale models in 1965. These married the basic front-end theme of that year's experimental Mako Shark II to a curvy midsection and a long, squarish tail. Beltlines swept sharply upward to a "flying buttress" or "sugar scoop" rear roofline of the sort seen on Porsche's mid-engine 904 sports-racer, with a shallow, vertically set backlight flanked by long, gracefully tapered C-pillars.

Bill Mitchell's crew had their own ideas, producing a powerful-looking full-size mock-up dominated by a very pointy front, a severe "ducktail," a tapered "boattail" roofline á la the Sting Ray fastback, and bulging, fully skirted rear fenders with vertical air slots in their leading edges. The bulky mid-mounted V-8 made a rear window useless, so a rear-facing periscope was devised, faired into the forward portion of the roof.

Ultimately, however, these and other efforts were just so much wishful thinking and for one rather obvious reason. A rear- or mid-engine Corvette demanded mechanical components that just didn't exist at GM. The company had yet to produce a transaxle able to withstand the torque of a high-power V-8, and the design and tooling expense for a transaxle that would be used only in a low-volume model would have sent Corvette prices out of sight. So why not adapt the front-drive transaxle from Oldsmobile's new-for-'66 Toronado? A different animal entirely.

But Mitchell and company had just the thing to make their baby considerably more exotic at the relatively low price of a new fiberglass body. It was the aforementioned Mako Shark II, one of the most famous show cars of all time. The Motoramas were a thing of the past by the mid-Sixties, but GM was still gauging public reaction to its near-term models by displaying them as slightly exaggerated "concept cars." The Mako II was quickly recognized for what it was: a trial balloon for the next-generation Corvette. As if to support that view, the original nonrunning Mako II mock-up first shown in April was retired during 1965 and replaced on the show circuit by a fully operational version. Completed in October of that year, this

This page: A clay model from December 1965 shows how close the designers had finally come to settling on a roofline for the '68 Corvette (center). The other side of the clay (top) is not quite as close to the eventual shape, nor is an earlier study (bottom). Note the unusual rear treatment (center). Opposite page: A trimmed clay model from November 1965 looks close to production, but note the grille, taillights, and the vents both ahead of and behind the front wheel.

second Mako II was less radical than the first and thus—tantalizingly—more producible. The ever-busy Corvette rumor mill went into overdrive.

Executed under Mitchell's direction by young Larry Shinoda, the Mako II had been initiated in early 1964, more than a year before the first show model appeared. Although adaptable to either front- or rear-engine positioning, its basic design became the take-off point for a new front-engine "theme car" as an alternative to the more radical mid-engine shapes proposed by Duntov and the Advanced Design studios. Once the midships format was abandoned for good, the Shinoda/Mitchell car was sent to Chevrolet Styling under David Holls, where Henry Haga's studio adapted it for production on the existing Sting Ray chassis. Underneath, then, the next new 'Vette wouldn't be all

that different from the Sting Ray, but Chevy was betting that a sexy new shell and higher-performance engines would be enough to keep America's sports car on its upward sales course.

The result was much like the Mako II from the beltline down except for softer, less extreme contours. The one major change on the way to production involved the show car's "boattail" roof. Although retained for the first production prototype, this quickly gave way to the "sugar scoop" treatment of the mid-

engine models designed by the Duntov group. Chevy may simply have been seeking a different look or perhaps better rearward vision than in the Sting Ray fastback. In any case, it was intended from the beginning that the vertical backlight—as well as that portion of the roof above the seats—be removable. Though the traditional Corvette convertible would continue, Chevy felt this new coupe configuration—really a semi-convertible—would appeal just as much to the open-air crowd while offering the better weather protection

and structural rigidity associated with closed body types. Porsche's 911/912 Targa convertible reflected similar thinking.

Unfortunately for Holls, Haga, and Duntov, the Mako II's basic shape proved problematic, and the production styling job didn't go as smoothly or as quickly as expected. For one thing, the new design turned out to have excessive front-end lift at high speed, which seriously compromised stability. A rear spoiler was added to help keep the tail down, but this

only lifted the nose more. Duntov had experienced something similar with the Sting Ray, and he was determined to lick the problem here before production began. Additional wind tunnel work produced functional front-fender louvers that relieved pressure buildup within the engine compartment at speed, and also yielded a small "chin" or "lip" spoiler below the grille to direct air around the car instead of beneath it.

The Targa-style roof also proved thorny. Its removable section had been conceived as a single piece of fiberglass all along, but production engineers found that the resulting body/frame combination wasn't stiff enough in torsion to prevent creaks and groans. Accordingly, they added a longitudinal support bar between the windshield header and the roof's fixed rear "hoop" section, thus creating the first T-roof. This solution came so late that it didn't appear in some early publicity photos of the new coupe. The Sting Ray name *did* appear on those pictures, though not on the car itself, another last-minute change.

The most serious deficit of the Mako-inspired styling was poor engine cooling, especially with the big-block mills carried over from the Sting Ray. With the new design's narrow engine bay and shallow grille, radiator air flow was found to be marginal in hot weather, especially with the air conditioning on. That didn't bode well for the annual long-lead press meeting in July 1967, so Duntov hastily cut two oblong slots into

This page: *A view of the design studio in November 1964 (top), when work on the '68 Corvette was underway. Even seemingly minor design aspects of a car, such as the vents on the 'Vette's front fenders, underwent considerable scrutiny year after year. Opposite page: At last, the design of the '68 Corvette is finalized! The license plate (top) calls this model a fastback coupe, and while it may appear so from the sides, note the almost vertical rear window.*

the body just above the front spoiler and made the spoiler deeper so as to force cooling air through them (the original one had actually impeded flow). That did the trick: The Mark IV-equipped prototype kept its cool on the 85-degree press day, so the slots were ordered for production and the grille blanked off, since it contributed little or nothing. Marginal cooling, however, would dog the fifth generation right to the end, especially in big-block form.

One Mako II feature that survived to production virtually intact was a vacuum-operated flip-up panel concealing the windshield wipers. It was a great idea for a show car, flashy and futuristic, but something less than wonderful for a real-world car that had to contend with ice and snow. A good deal of development time was spent making it work, but the final product was none too reliable. Hidden headlamps were continued but were now simple flip-up jobs rather than the Sting

Ray's rotating assemblies; they also operated via engine vacuum, versus the previous electric motors. An external trunklid was still conspicuously absent from both body styles, but the convertible retained Corvette's traditional rear-hinged top cover, and an accessory hardtop was designed to match the new Shark styling.

Obviously, the fifth-generation 'Vette had its fair share of development bugs (like any new car), which explains why introduction was postponed from 1967 to 1968. It was probably just as well. Although the government's first safety and emissions standards took effect nationwide with the '68 model year, Chevy would doubtless have seen to it that the engineering of an all-new '67 reflected the new standards. As it was, the delay took some of the pressure off of "federalizing" the new design, to the undoubted relief of harried engineers who had to worry about government scrutiny of the five other model lines in the 1967-68 Chevy fleet.

The Mako II may have been a great show car, but its styling proved controversial in the showroom. "If there's such a thing as a psychedelic car, the 1968 Corvette is

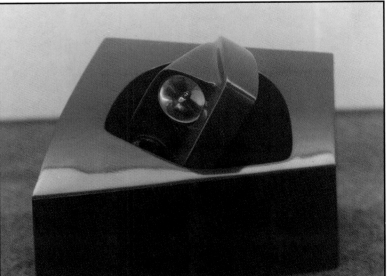

it," sneered *Road & Track* magazine in its initial test. Of course, it doesn't seem all that radical now, but it was definitely distinctive for 1968—exotic, really—compared to most other road cars.

The new-design 'Vette garnered decidedly mixed reviews. To many, its styling was wretchedly excessive. "We wish we could express more enthusiasm for the new model," *R&T* continued, "but we feel that the general direction of the changes is away from Sports Car and toward Image and Gadget Car. And since the Corvette is America's only sports car, this direction is a disappointment to us." In particular, the magazine decried the new model's seven-inch gain in overall length, "nearly all of [it in] front overhang. It is 0.4 in. narrower, but the stylists have had such control over its layout that no attempt has been made to maximize interior dimensions relative to exterior ones." There was less luggage space, too, and weight was up by some 150 pounds.

R&T went on to praise driving position and major control relationships, but deplored the difficulty of getting in and out and griped about the secondary gauges being in the center of the dash, away from the driver's direct line of sight. The editors also groused about inadequate interior ventilation despite the arrival of Chevy's new flow-through "Astro Ventilation" system with dash-mounted vents, exterior air extractors on the rear deck—and no door ventwings. Of course, factory air was available and ordered by more than 5000 customers, who must have agreed with *R&T*.

As with the first Sting Ray, '68 powerteams were essentially those of the previous year. The one significant exception was substitution of GM's fine new three-speed Turbo Hydra-Matic transmission for the old two-speed Powerglide automatic. Drum brakes were also consigned to history as the previous all-disc option became standard equipment.

Another sign of Duntov's still-considerable corporate clout was a change to higher spring rates to reduce fore/aft pitching, especially under hard acceleration. This also served to lower the rear roll center and was nicely complemented by newly standard seven-inch-wide wheels, an inch broader than before, wearing low-profile F70 × 15 tires.

Opposite page: The hidden headlights on the 1963-66 Sting Ray had presented engineering difficulties, and the completely revamped front end of the '68 Corvette called for another redesign of the headlight mechanism. But Chevy also wanted to incorporate better headlights (which were not legal when these photos were taken in November 1967) and found that their use would require yet another round of changes. This page: The '68 Corvette received a completely new dashboard (top) with a huge tach and speedometer in front of the driver, but with the other gauges moved to the center. As on the Sting Ray, there was no trunklid (bottom).

237

Styling work did not progress smoothly on the '68 Corvette because of excessive front-end lift, but additional time in the wind tunnel led to a front spoiler and functional front-fender louvers. These and other problems caused a one-year delay in reaching production. The 1968 coupe (right), still on a 98-inch wheelbase, stickered at $4663, a jump of $310, but the T-top came as standard equipment.

With these modifications and the resulting wider track dimensions (now 58.7/59.4 inches front/rear), the '68 clawed the road even better than the Sting Ray—to the tune of 0.84g according to Ludvigsen, "a substantial improvement on the previous Corvette peak figure of 0.75g. Wet-road performance was also markedly better." The penalty was a perceptibly harsher ride. Duntov admitted as much, but said "stability is increased, so it's well worth it." Interestingly, Ludvigsen records that "tests had been run with radial-ply tires, even though they weren't then widely available in the United States, but they showed no increase in cornering power and were less predictable at the limit in a turn."

As ever, Corvette's straightline performance earned plenty of kudos from "buff book" scribes. Some thought the big 435-horsepower 427 too brutish, but the 300- and 350-bhp small-blocks impressed as much as ever. Ditto the Muncie four-speed manual transmission and the new Turbo Hydra-Matic. As for handling, the press seemed to like the skidpad and slalom numbers they got, but not the way the car felt generating them. Several complaints were made about the harder ride, and nobody much liked the power steering and brakes. *Road & Track* labeled them imprecise and suggested that potential customers skip them entirely.

Negative though it was, *R&T*'s review was downright benign next to Steve Smith's attack in *Car and Driver*, which slammed everything from the ashtray to the new windshield wipers. Smith's biggest complaint was fit-and-finish—or rather the lack of it. "Few of the body panels butted against each other in the alignment that was intended," he wrote. "Sometimes the pieces chafed against each other, sometimes they left wide gaps, sometimes they were just plain crooked." He also complained about a chronic water leak from the T-top and claimed that one of the door locks was so stiff it bent the key. For Smith, it all added up to "a shocking lack of quality control" in a car "unfit to road test."

Unhappily, such problems weren't confined to *C/D*'s example. Today, the '68 is generally regarded as the low point for Corvette workmanship, with bad paint, knobs that fell off, cooling bothers, and other problems. Many feel that Chevrolet simply put too big a rush on too many new ideas.

On the other hand, the Corvette had undeniably become more complicated than the pre-Sting Ray models of just six years before. For example, power steering, power brakes, and air conditioning weren't available in '62 but were by '68. In addition, there were items like electric rear-window defroster, speed warning indicator, AM/FM stereo radio, and a futuristic fiber-optic light monitoring system, not to mention the disappearing headlights and that gimmicky, "peak-a-boo" wiper panel. With more gadgets, more was likely to go wrong.

But when everything was working right, a '68 Corvette was mighty satisfying. It had plenty of power even in small-block form; its all-independent suspension, if not exactly state-of-the-art, was certainly more than adequate; and cooling bothers aside, the problems noted in early road tests had nothing to do with basic design or mechanicals. The gadget glitches were irritating, but not major flaws in the overall package.

And, of course, they hardly affected performance, which remained brilliant. Testing a 350-bhp 327 roadster with four-speed and 3.70:1 final drive, *R&T*'s

continued on page 242

The styling of the '68 Corvette (left) was quite distinctive—exotic, in fact, compared to most other contemporary road cars. It was also highly controversial, at least to sports car purists. Road & Track commented that "If there's such a thing as a psychedelic car, the 1968 Corvette is it." The traditional crossed flags emblems were found on the exterior (top left), and inside on the steering wheel (top right).

The rear end design of the '68 Corvette embraced the familiar four-taillight theme (below). The cabin's bucket seats were narrower and the seatbacks more steeply raked (far right, top). Road & Track complained about the location of the secondary gauges in the center of the dash (bottom right).

Ron Wakefield reported a top speed of 128 mph, a standing quarter-mile of 15.6 seconds at 92 mph, and 0-60-mph acceleration of 7.7 seconds. Mileage was pegged at 11-15 mpg for a cruising range of only 220-300 miles from the 20-gallon tank. Even in relatively mild-mannered guise, the new Corvette could be a thirsty beast indeed.

Big-block cars were even thirstier—but faster, of course. *Car and Driver*, running a 400-bhp 427 coupe with the same tranny and axle ratio as *R&T*, hit 60 mph in 5.7 seconds and posted a 14.1-second quarter-

mile at a flashing 102 mph. "How fast would our test Corvette go [all out]?" *C/D* asked aloud. "Who knows? With the 3.70 axle, top speed runs and wounded engines may come in matched pairs, because when we hit an indicated 125 mph the tach needle had already used up half the red zone and was obviously headed back for zero the hard way....LSD makes a great trip, but our choice is a few seconds of wide open throttle in a 427 Corvette."

Incidentally, that quote comes from *C/D*'s second test of a '68 Corvette. That car must have been screwed

together a lot better than the one Smith drove, for construction quality was judged mostly "good" and "very good."

Again, though, some aspects of the new body design didn't appeal. "The lower roofline and pinched waist have resulted in a more intimate-feeling cockpit," said *C/D*'s follow-up test. "The interior width dimension is definitely reduced. Sitting in a...Sting Ray was like sitting in a room compared to an E-type Jaguar, but that feeling is gone now—the new Corvette feels much more like the intimate two-passenger sports car that

it's intended to be. Intimacy is perfectly fine with us, but we'll choose the time and place, and a '68 Corvette is neither. The one-piece molded inner door panels are particularly thick at the window sills, just where men are the widest."

Even the innovative T-top wasn't unequivocally endorsed. "We can't decide whether to like it or not," *Car and Driver* mused. "With the pieces all assembled there were no extra rattles, shakes or water leaks.... Assuming you like an occasional patch of daylight on top of your head, the only real problem is what to do with the pieces after the disassembly operation. Two latches hold each panel and, in typical Corvette fashion, the panels come out with ease. They're meant to go into the trunk, but if you've already got anything more than a bag of popcorn there, forget it. A pair of giganto vinyl envelopes has been provided to protect the roof panels [when strapped] to the side walls of the trunk

compartment....The back window clamps to a false roof that drops down from the top of the trunk compartment [but] the latch that holds [it] up is feeble...and the whole business drops down whenever it feels a mind. Still, nobody says you have to take it apart and it didn't cost extra, but it would be nice if it *worked*. Driving the open-air coupe is pleasant enough—with the side windows up there is almost no draft, even at speed, but...you're thinking about putting everything back together when you get where you're going."

Your destinations probably weren't far away, what with that high fuel thirst and only 6.7 cubic feet of cargo space available. The slimmer cabin was matched by slimmer seats with fixed backrests raked much farther back than in the Sting Ray to accommodate the Shark's two-inch lower roofline. The resulting laid-back stance conspired with a high cowl to give the

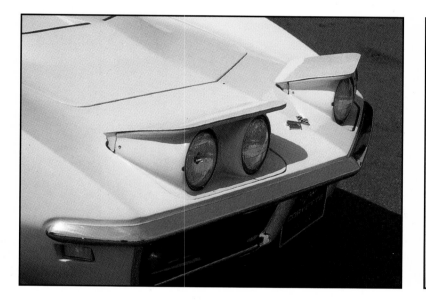

Opposite page: *The hood of this '68 Corvette announces that there is a 427 V-8 lurking beneath.* This page: *The hidden headlights (top left) were vacuum powered. The space they—and the centrally mounted license plate— occupied restricted air flow, which made it tough for engineers to provide for proper engine cooling (a problem with the '68s). The Turbo Jet 427 V-8 (bottom) was available in three horsepower ratings for 1968— 390, 400, and 435.*

impression of being in a cave. A long, low nose disappearing somewhere near the horizon hardly helped, especially in close-quarters jockeying.

To a great degree, the mixed press reviews reflected the compromise nature of the car itself. They certainly weren't as laudatory as those given the Sting Ray, and Chevy was particularly stung by *Car and Driver*'s initial pasting. *R&T*'s Wakefield, who owned a Sting Ray at the time, had a more evenhanded assessment: "The Corvette 327 remains a comfortable, fast, safe, and reliable automobile. For those who like their cars big, flashy, and full of blinking lights and trap doors, it's a winner. The connoisseur who values finesse, efficiency, and the latest chassis design will have to look, unfortunately, to Europe."

Yet for all the problems and press carping, more people than ever looked to the 'Vette. Model-year sales set a new record at 28,566 units, some 5000 up on the final Sting Ray, though only fractionally ahead of 1966, the previous all-time best year.

Except for the rocker panel moldings, the sides of the '68 Corvette were devoid of chrome trim (above). The dashboard (top right) featured high-level fresh-air inlets. Stale air was exhausted through vents on the rear deck. The '68 Corvette's lines looked a bit cleaner, especially with the top down, due to the lack of vent windows this year (right). The convertible listed at $4320. Output hit 18,630, compared to 9936 coupes.

Reflecting its popularity, the new Corvette was chosen Best All-Around Car in *Car and Driver*'s annual reader's poll (the '67 Sting Ray had been likewise honored) as well as Best Sports/GT Car Over 3000cc. "In its own category," said the editors, "the super strong, super trick new Corvette had a hell of a battle against the epitome of automotive exotics, the Lamborghini Miura. But when it got down to...Best All-Around Car, where price plays more of a part, Ferruccio Lamborghini's $25,000 dohc V-12 sex symbol was no match for the latest from Chevrolet. We've always been Corvette fans, feeling that it has led the way in American automotive engineering. And the new Corvette...is, in our opinion, the best yet. It's not perfect, but it's the only fiberglass-bodied, independently suspended, V-8-powered, 4-wheel disc braked production car in the world....When you consider that it can be had for less than $6000, we can't think of a better deal—and evidently neither can you."

As 1968 was the Year of the Big Switch, 1969 was the Year of Little Fixes, Duntov and company making as many detail changes as they could to remedy problems noted by owners and the press. They began with the cockpit. Steering-wheel diameter was trimmed an inch for more under-rim thigh clearance, and Duntov pushed through a $120,000 tooling change for the inner door panels to open up a half-inch per side in extra shoulder width. Thanks in part to Ralph Nader's safety lobbying, interior door handles were revamped to be less lethal; control knobs were rubberized for the same reason. The previous dash-mounted ignition switch moved to the steering column, where it combined with the newly mandated column lock for additional security. A warning light was added to advise the driver that the pop-up headlights hadn't popped up completely. Attempts were also made to increase Astro Ventilation flow volume, but *Road & Track* judged the '69 no better in this regard than the '68. Finally, a flexible three-section map pocket was slapped onto the dash ahead of the passenger—a poor substitute for a glovebox but more convenient than the pair of covered stowage wells behind the seats (where a third well held the battery).

Exterior alterations were minimal—not that any were really expected in the second year of this way-out new design. The most obvious was the return of the Stingray designation—as one word—in script over the front-fender louvers. Another change involved the

door handles. Engineering problems had prompted conventional chrome handgrips and thumb-operated pushbuttons for '68, but the '69s got the intended design: slots with spring-loaded covers for releasing the latches. A new headlight washer system was added, and the already overengineered wiper arrangement, which *Road & Track* had termed "amusing," became even more complex. Not only were the washer jets put on the wiper arms, but an override switch was added so that the vacuum-operated panel could be left up in freezing weather and the wipers stopped for blade-changing. At the rear, the previously separate backup lights were incorporated with the inboard taillamps.

Engine alterations were more telling, seeing as how carmakers were in the second year of federally mandated, and still relatively straightforward, emission controls. The famed Chevy small-block was stroked about a quarter-inch to 3.48 inches, which boosted displacement from 327 to 350 cubic inches on the same 4.00-inch bore. Corvette offered 300- and 350-bhp versions, the same ratings as their 1968 equivalents but with compression dropped a quarter-

continued on page 251

This page: *The big-block 427 powerhouse for '68 was RPO L88, good for 435 bhp.* Opposite page: *The roof treatment of the '68 Corvette featured flying-buttress sail panels flanking an upright flat rear window. From the beginning, it had been intended that the Sting Ray coupe's successor would feature both a removable backlight and Targa-style roof panel. The latter ended up as a two-panel T-top to reduce body flex.*

248

point in each case—to 10.25:1 and 11.0:1, respectively. Significantly, peak power engine speed was also lower by 200 rpm, to 4800 and 5600 rpm, respectively. The big-block 427 trio returned unchanged, along with a fourth version rated at 430 bhp at 5200 rpm on high 12.5:1 compression, although few were built. Axle ratios ranged from a super-low 4.56:1 to a long-striding 2.75:1. The frame was stiffened to reduce body shake, and standard rim width went up another inch—to eight—for improved handling.

Although Chevrolet was supposedly tightening up Corvette quality control, the '69s showed only partial success. *Road & Track*, reporting on a 435-bhp big-block car, remarked that fit-and-finish was actually worse than on its '68 test car. Again, the complaints involved mostly minor maladies like squeaks and rattles rather than major mechanical ills, but *R&T* staffers evidently expected more from Chevy's costliest car: "The Corvette 427 is an entertainment machine," they said, "and compared to some of the more exotic entertainment machines we drive from time to time, it's a rather crude one. But it's cheap when you compare it to other sports cars that offer performance anywhere near its own, so we shouldn't expect a great deal of refinement."

Appearing in *R&T*'s June 1969 issue was an interesting GT comparison test pitting a base 350 'Vette with Turbo Hydra-Matic against a self-shift Mercedes-Benz 280SL, a manual Jaguar E-Type, and a Porsche 911T. When it was all over, the Corvette still plainly bothered the folks in Newport Beach: "In purely objective terms, the Stingray was the biggest, heaviest, most powerful, fastest, thirstiest, and cheapest of the four GTs included in this test." To Chevy's likely consternation, none of the four testers chose the 'Vette as his personal favorite. One picked the SL and the other three chose the Porsche with its rear-mounted flat six. The SL was the most expensive of the four at $7833. Next came the E-Type at $6495, followed closely by the Porsche at $6418. The 'Vette cost $6392 as tested—including the automatic, stereo, and air conditioning. The clear implication was that Corvette no longer led the sporting-car parade in performance-per-dollar.

R&T attempted to sum up the style and character of each car, and its description of the 'Vette was telling:

Opposite page: After an all-new Corvette in 1968, it was hardly expected that the '69 would differ much. Even so, the styling studio was busy tinkering on the '69, here in September '67. Note the lack of a T-bar in the roof. This page: The most obvious change for 1969 was the Stingray badge on the front fenders—spelled as one word now.

"The word that comes to mind is 'Plastic.' The image, like the styling, is flashy, with lots of deliberately eye-catching angles and gimmicks that aren't strictly necessary. Lacks finesse; like using a five-pound axe when a rapier, properly designed, could do as well. And with more grace. The personality we associate with the Stingray is the Animal, one who prefers to attain the goal with brute strength and bared chest rather than art and fast footwork." Hardly complimentary, especially next to the Porsche: "The word is serious. The driver will take himself and his driving seriously. Damned serious in fact. Almost certain to have no more than a limited sense of humor, especially concerning Porsches....A car for the technician rather than the engineer, if you get the distinction."

Even if you didn't, the latest Corvette was obviously far from satisfactory overall. *Car and Driver* thought it knew why: "It being a mass-class sports car, the Corvette's excellent engineering tends to be obscured by some rather garish styling gimmicks....This confusing identity is the result of a confrontation on the part of Chevy engineer Zora Arkus-Duntov...and the Chevrolet styling department....Duntov on the one hand [views] his automobile as a purposeful well-balanced sports car, while his rivals see it as a Flash Gordon Thunderbird for the Hugh Hefner school of mass-cult glamour."

Nevertheless, Corvette sales took a vertical leap for '69, rising by over 10,000 units to 38,762—a record that wouldn't be broken until 1976. Evidently, at least a few sports-car buyers disagreed with the press pundits and their conclusions about the 'Vette's true value.

Before leaving 1969, we should mention two new performance options announced that year: One was extremely rare—only two installed—the other was ostensibly available but put back a year. The former was RPO ZL1, essentially the mighty big-block L88 with all-aluminum construction plus numerous other modifications including dry-sump lubrication. Devised for the British-built McLarens that would dominate the

SCCA's Canadian-American Challenge Cup series for some five years, this engine had the same compression and carburetion as the L88 but turned out a colossal 585 bhp. It, too, lurked beneath a special domed hood (RPO ZL2) with an air intake at the high-pressure area near the base of the windshield. The L88 itself, which also came with the special hood, was still around, rated at a nominal 435 bhp and priced at a towering $1032. L88 installations remained few and far between, running to just 116 for the model year.

Of course, Duntov hadn't dismissed the potential of small-block power, as shown by the special solid-lifter version of the new 350 that was listed for '69 but not available until 1970, owing to development and manufacturing problems. Coded LT1, it was right in line with "Mr. Corvette's" longtime goal of minimizing

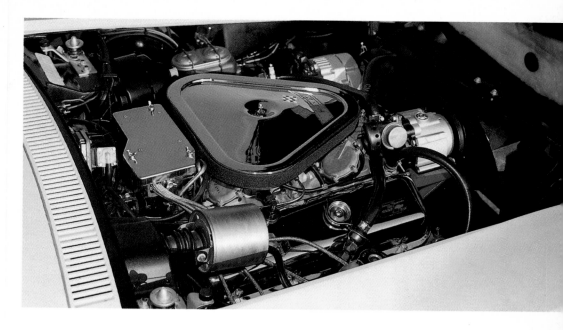

continued on page 256

The T-top of the '69 coupe (left and far left) offered most of the fun-in-the-sun feeling of a convertible, but was vastly superior in terms of weather protection and security. Retooled door panels (top) expanded interior width by one precious inch, while one lap-saving inch was carved from the diameter of the steering wheel.

This page: Top dog among Corvette engines for '69 was the L88, the 427-cid unit with aluminum heads; it was still rated at 435 bhp and cost a whopping $1032 extra. Opposite page: An L88 Corvette looked meaner than a junkyard dog in black, and it could deliver neck-snapping acceleration. Like other '69s, it rode on a stiffer frame and one-inch-wider wheels to better handle all that power. The new door handles (bottom right) were an improvement.

weight in a performance car growing ever heavier with the addition of more and more creature comforts. Unlike tamer small-blocks, the LT1 had more radical cam timing with more generous valve overlap, used the big-block mills' fat 2.5-inch-diameter exhaust system, breathed through the same 850-cfm Holley carb fitted to the L88/ZL1, and came with transistorized ignition.

With hot-car insurance premiums soaring, Chevy downplayed LT1 output, listing horsepower as 330 at 6000 rpm and torque at 380 lbs/ft at 4000 rpm. The actual figures were no doubt higher, because the typical example could streak through the standing quarter-mile in 14.2 seconds at 102 mph, comparable to big-block performance of just a few years before. Visual identification was subtle—just the special domed hood with perimeter striping and discreet "LT1" lettering—but there was no mistaking the rap-rap exhaust or the distinct tapping of those mechanical lifters.

None of this exotica stemmed speculation that the Shark's days were already numbered in 1969. Said *Car and Driver* that September: "The present Corvette will doubtlessly be the last front-engine model. It remains uncertain if the new rear-engine version will be introduced in 1971 or 1972 (a great deal depends on Ford and its rumored rear-engine sports car).... Although a number of prototypes have been tested, a certain amount of turmoil exists within Chevrolet as to exactly what form the new car will take. The present general manager, John DeLorean, is as much an automotive purist as ever reached the top ranks at General Motors, and it is known that he is unhappy with the present Corvette. Rumors from deep inside the company indicate that DeLorean has pronounced that the mid-engine version must be a functional sports/GT car weighing in the neighborhood of 2600 lbs. and containing an engine of about 400 cu. in. This places a giant challenge before Duntov and his engineers....[Whether] this can be accomplished with a fiberglass or steel body remains to be seen, but it can be assumed that DeLorean, an engineer himself, will drive hard to make the new Corvette lean and tough. If he succeeds, it could mean goodbye to the [present] jet-

plane gimmickry. And for that we'd all be thankful."

But churning rumor mills don't design cars—or sell them. For all the talk of an imminent mid-engine successor (some of it quite well founded), forces were gathering that would preclude anything really new for some time—even a new front-engine design. (Ford took some of the pressure off by cancelling its domestic midships sports car and selling the Italian DeTomaso Pantera instead.)

Chevrolet, therefore, issued another evolutionary Stingray for 1970. A UAW strike forced a two-month extension of '69 production, which gave Chevy the time it needed to make the '70 a better-built Corvette, and was doubtless a factor in 1969's record volume. But the strike also delayed the '70s from reaching dealer showrooms until February, which pushed Corvette output to its lowest point since 1962—just 17,316 units.

Cosmetic changes were slight. The extreme bodyside tuck-under was found to be susceptible to stone damage, so Chevy flared the aft portions of each wheel opening, which helped somewhat. The grille went from horizontal bars to a fine eggcrate pattern. (The real radiator air intakes, Duntov's original slots, were on the car's underside.) The eggcrate also appeared on the front fenders in place of the previous four "gills." Front parking lamps switched from small, round units to rectangular fixtures with clear lenses and amber bulbs. The dual exhaust outlets also shifted from round to rectangular.

Inside, seats were reshaped for better lateral support, more headroom, and easier access to the trunk. Shoulder belts, still separate from the lap belts, got inertia storage reels, thus ending some cockpit clutter. A Deluxe Interior package was added to the options list, comprising full cut-pile carpeting and ersatz wood trim on console and doors. Some people liked it, but purists sneered that the fake wood made the Corvette seem too much like a Monte Carlo.

Engines were again the main Corvette news for 1970. The LT1 was now genuinely available, though

continued on page 260

257

This page: More details of the '69 L88 Corvette. Note the air cleaner in the L88's special hood (bottom right). Opposite page: The license plate on this red coupe tells what's underhood. With all that power on tap, a buyer would have been wise to invest an extra $42.15 for the Custom Deluxe shoulder belts and $11.60 for a speed warning indicator. Front-fender louver trim was a popular dress-up option at $21.10.

258

at a hefty $447.50. Lesser 350s returned unchanged. The mighty L88 and ZL1 weren't even theoretically offered, though Chevy continued to sell Can-Am engines to *bona fide* teams. Instead, big-block buyers got a 427 stroked out to a full 4.00 inches and 454 cid. Two versions were listed, one real, the other not. The former, RPO LS5, offered hydraulic lifters, 10.25:1 compression, single four-barrel carb, a fairly modest 390 bhp at 4800 rpm, and a massive 500 lbs/ft torque. Listed but never officially sold was RPO LS7, with aluminum heads, mechanical lifters, 11.25:1 compression, higher-lift cam, and transistorized ignition. Depending on your source, output was either 460 or 465 bhp.

Like the previous year's enlarged small-block, the bigger big-block for 1970 was a response to the increasing stranglehold of emissions tuning. Also like the 350, the 454 produced less power per cubic inch than its predecessor, but a lower peak power speed made it somewhat torquier and thus more flexible at low rpm.

The only test report of an LS7 'Vette seems to be that of Paul Van Valkenburgh, who drove the first one built from Los Angeles to Detroit in December 1969 for *Sports Car Graphic*. Reporting a standing quarter-mile of 13.8 seconds at 108 mph, he enthused that "this car gives the impression that it could do *anything* you demanded....Never have we tested a car with such a secure speed potential." It was hardly refined—"like taxiing a DC3 at full throttle up and down a freshly plowed runway."

Maybe it was just as well that Chevy didn't run off many copies, because the LS5 version was smoother yet almost as thrilling. *Road & Track* tried one with automatic and obtained 7.0 seconds for the 0-60-mph run, a 15.0-second quarter-mile at 93 mph, and a top speed of 144 mph. Although the editors described this car as "one of the better Corvettes we've driven lately," they found the ride suffered from "lack of suspension travel [that] decrees too much damping in the up direction and too little in the down; the result is considerable harshness over sharp bumps but a distinct 'floatiness' over gentle undulations at speed. On bad roads the Corvette simply loses its cool, rattling, shaking and squeaking in a scandalous manner." The brakes got only "fair" marks as they "faded more than in any recent Corvette we've tried; the extreme weight of the car [4070 pounds as tested] with the heavy engine and air conditioning, etc., are responsible."

Not that these criticisms mattered much, because 1970 would be the beginning of the end for big-inch,

big-power Corvettes in the traditional mold. Besides skyrocketing insurance premiums and fast-falling demand for hot cars generally, they were doomed by GM president Ed Cole's desire to eliminate low-volume options and to retune all his company's engines for 91-octane fuel, correctly anticipating the catalytic converter that he knew would be needed to meet ever-tightening emissions limits. Cole also ordered that beginning in 1971, all GM divisions would quote engine outputs in SAE net measure rather than the usual gross figures, which did not reflect power losses to engine accessories, mufflers, and other components.

The results were steadily decreasing compression and lower outputs for engines with more realistic power ratings that only made them seem punier still.

But there would be a positive side to these mandates. As the Seventies wore on, America's sports car legend would become a more balanced performer of the sort people like *R&T* could endorse—not that it really had anywhere else to go, you understand. Drag racers naturally weren't thrilled, but a tamer Corvette was better than no Corvette at all.

Emasculation was evident the very next year: 1971's base small-block (RPO L48) ran on mild 8.5:1

compression and was down to 270 bhp at 4800 rpm; the LT1 sighed to 9.0:1 and 330 bhp. These respective compression numbers also applied to a brace of 454s. The LS5 came in with 365 bhp at 4800 rpm, and a new aluminum-head big-block called LS6 boasted 425 bhp at 5600 rpm. Clearly, '71 Corvette engines weren't weak. If they seemed so at the time, it was only in relation to the prodigious power outputs we'd grown used to in the heyday of less fettered muscle cars.

Regardless of engine, the Corvette was still a speedway star. Consider these figures from a 1971 *Car and Driver* comparison test:

	L48	LT1	LS5	LS6
cid	350	350	454	454
bhp (SAE gross)	270	330	365	425
trans tested	4 man.	4 man.	3 auto.	4 man.
axle ratio (:1)	3.08	3.70	3.08	3.36
0-60 mph (sec)	7.1	6.0	5.7	5.3
0-100 mph (sec)	19.8	14.5	14.1	12.7
0-1/4 mi (sec)	15.55	14.57	14.20	13.80
mph @ 1/4 mi	90.4	100.6	100.3	104.7
est top speed (mph)	132	137	141	152
est economy (mpg)	12-15	11-16	8-11	9-14

The LT1 is the obvious standout here, offering big-block punch with small-block economy. It did demand premium fuel, however, like the LS6; the other two ran on low-calorie regular.

The ZR1 option available exclusively with the solid-lifter small-block is significant for engineering, if not production. It was another racing package, of course, comprising the LT1 engine, heavy-duty four-speed transmission, power brakes, aluminum radiator, and a revised suspension with special springs, shocks, stabilizer bar, and spindle/strut shafts. Since it was competition equipment, the ZR1 could not be ordered with power windows, power steering, air conditioning, rear-window defogger, wheel covers, or radio—which helps explain why this "regular" production option saw only eight installations for '71. We mention it here only because the ZR1 designation was destined to take on vast new significance in the late Eighties. A similar ZR2 package was listed for the big LS6 and was just as rare.

Otherwise, Corvette again marked time for '71. Styling and equipment changes were virtually nil for at least three reasons: The 1970 run had started late; engineers were scurrying to meet emissions limits and upcoming safety regs; and the car still looked fine the way it was. And no real tampering was called for.

A strike delayed the introduction of the 1970 Corvette (both pages) until February 1970. One very useful change was made in response to complaints of paint damage from stones kicked up by the tires. This happened because of the extreme tuck-under of the body sides. Chevy responded by flaring the aft portions of each wheel opening, which helped somewhat.

This page: *Due in part to the short 1970 model year and to engineering efforts to meet the Fed's emissions rules, the '71 Corvette was hardly changed on the exterior (below). The interior, however was treated to a freshening up (right). Opposite page: Although eclipsed by the ZR1 racing package, the hottest "regular" Corvettes for '71 ran the LS6 option: 454-cubic-inch Turbo Jet V-8, four-barrel carb, 425 eager horses. It set the buyer back an extra $1221 and is much sought after by collectors today.*

With supplies healthy again after the UAW strike, sales made a satisfying recovery for model year '71, moving up to 21,801 units. The coupe had taken a slight lead over the convertible in 1969, perhaps reflecting the T-top model's greater all-weather versatility. Now the gap had widened to a ratio of about five to three.

It was another sign of the times. Convertible demand was on the wane generally, and the government accelerated the trend by threatening to enact safety standards for rollover protection that would have effectively banned fully open cars in the United States after 1975. Ironically, the legislation never materialized, but it gave domestic producers the excuse they'd been waiting for to drop slow-selling ragtops, and the romantic 'Vette roadster would disappear with the lot—though fortunately not forever.

Nineteen seventy-two was yet another stand-pat

year, except that performance was further deemphasized as engines bore the full brunt of emissions tuning. Worse, there were fewer engines now with cancellation of the LS6. The LT1 eased from 275 to 255 bhp net in this, its final year. At least it could finally be ordered with air conditioning. Chevy engineers had been reluctant to offer this combination, fearing the LT1's high revving ability would pull the A/C belts off their pulleys; tachometers on cars so equipped were redlined at 5600 rpm rather than 6500 rpm.

· Some detail refinements made for '72 were quite welcome. For example, the useful but distracting fiberoptic light monitors were deleted, thus cleaning up the center console considerably, and a previously optional anti-theft alarm system was made standard in belated

continued on page 268

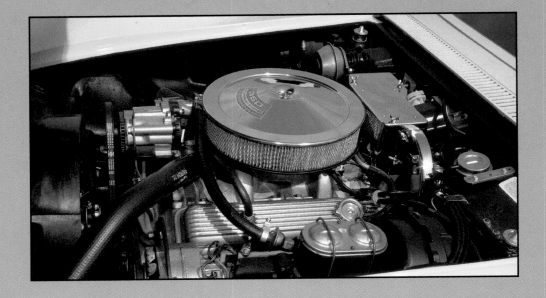

Those who insisted on the ultimate small-block Corvette in 1970-71 checked off LT-1 on the dealer's order form. This option bought a 300-cubic-inch V-8 breathing through a four-barrel carburetor. It was rated at 370 horsepower in 1970, but the tightening emissions regulations, the general cutting back of compression ratios, and the onset of lower-octane unleaded gas reduced the horsepower rating to 330 bhp for 1971 (275 net, the rating system that would come into industry-wide use beginning in 1972).

recognition of the 'Vette's high desirability among car thieves. Sales continued crawling back toward the '69 record, tacking on nearly 5200 units for a model year total of 26,994.

For 1973, the coupe exchanged its removable backlight for fixed glass, but a new nose treatment, shared with the convertible, was more obvious—the first major appearance change in the fifth generation's checkered history. In styling at least, technology was beginning to find answers to federal mandates, and the Corvette had a most effective solution for the new five-mile-per-hour front-impact protection rule applied to all automobiles this year. It was quite ingenious: a steel bumper covered by deformable urethane plastic matched to body color. It added only about two inches to overall length and 35 pounds to curb weight. Even

better, it would bounce back to its intended shape after most any kind of parking-lot bump. Better still, it looked terrific, which was more than could be said for the ungainly battering rams devised by less clever sportscar builders. "I'm sick of these great, ugly, dirty black bumpers," moaned Bill Mitchell, who once again got his wish—to the benefit of the product. Another piece of mandated safety equipment appeared on cue:

a longitudinal steel beam in each door to ward off side impacts.

Standard radial-ply tires weren't federally mandated for '73, but the Corvette had long needed them, though you might not think so. As Duntov had discovered back in '67, radials delivered poorer performance than bias-belted covers. Road tests confirmed it, the '73 showing longer stopping distances despite unchanged brakes,

Opposite page: Stylewise, Corvette coasted again for 1972. Emissions tuning knocked the big-block LS-6 out of the lineup, leaving the 365-bhp LS-5 as the most potent '72 offering. The small block LT-1 was now in its last year, but for the first time it could be combined with air conditioning. This page: The first major restyling of the 1968 Corvette came for 1973. Chevy's answer to the federally mandated five-mph bumpers was ingenious—and attractive: a urethane plastic soft nose that bounced back to its original shape after a parking lot bump.

269

Although the Corvette got a new nose for '73 (above), it still retained the old chrome bumper in the rear. Right and far right: The five-mph bumper regulations included the rear bumpers for 1974, so the logical move for Chevy was to give the Corvette a plastic tail to match the front. This was done, resulting in a Corvette that looked "new," even though only the front, rear, side scoops, and trim differed.

and lower lateral-G figures on the skidpad. Moreover, the Goodyear and Firestone radials supplied to Chevy had a maximum speed rating of "only" 120 mph, versus 140 mph for the bias-belteds, though that wouldn't matter much once the national speed limit went to 55 mph in the winter of 1973-74.

So why switch tires at all? Because radials had some real advantages for the Corvette. As *Road & Track* noted: "Tire life will be better, the car is more stable at speed, and wet-weather grip is improved. One could wish that the radials used were the best grade, like the Michelin XWX, but Zora Arkus-Duntov says such high-speed radials are noisy (true) and much more expensive (also true)."

Detuning and new anti-speed measures from Washington were affecting performance cars everywhere, import and domestic. If the Corvette seemed to fare worse than most, it was only because it had been such a sizzling performer for so long. Less sizzle was listed on the powerteam chart for '73, which excluded a mechanical-lifter engine for the first time since 1956. This left a choice of the three hydraulic-lifter units: the base 350, RPO L48, at a rated 190 bhp net; an uprated 250-bhp small-block, the L82; and a solitary 454 called LS4, advertised at 270 bhp.

On a happier note, Chevrolet began concentrating more on driveability, passenger comfort, and practicality, all of which deserved attention. Engine roar was lessened by adding extra body sound deadener at strategic points and a new underhood insulating pad. Body mounts were changed to a rubber/steel type whose increased flexibility and strength helped eliminate all but good vibrations. Nobody was sorry to see the problem-prone pop-up wiper panel replaced by a simple rear hood extension. The coupe's fixed rear window added a couple of inches to trunk space, since the old removable pane's stowage receptacle also went away. Handsome aluminum wheels were a new option that served both form and function, though structural problems forced a recall of the first 800 sets (some of which weren't replaced, as rumor had it). A later aluminum wheel used very similar styling.

After testing a four-speed L82 coupe with 3.70:1

continued on page 272

final drive, *Road & Track* generally approved of the latest changes. If the '73 wasn't as fast and didn't handle quite as well as previous Corvettes, it was notably more civilized. "For all its age, size and compromises, if the Corvette is equipped with the right options, it is a pleasant and rewarding car to drive... [this] example was one of the best Corvettes we've ever driven."

Even with the faults that remained, the Corvette was still an extremely good value against all but the really low-buck sports cars of the time. Though down on power compared to previous models, the '73 could run the quarter-mile in the mid-15-second range, virtually the same as a Porsche 911E or DeTomaso Pantera. Yet Corvette prices started at only $5635, versus some $10,000 for the German and Italian cars. With a

17.7-second quarter-mile, the Datsun 240Z, fresh from Japan three years earlier, wasn't even in the same ballpark, though it did carry a very tempting $4600 price tag.

Once more, a relatively static Corvette design fueled rumors that a far-reaching new one just had to be around the corner. As ever, those rumors made good copy. Witness that *R&T* test: "The '73 Corvette is not

the exciting new Corvette, not the mid-engine car promised to us (and by us to you) for this year. That is still most definitely on the way, however." As we know now, it wasn't, though it would come closer than most could guess. Actually, the next new Corvette was still a decade away in 1973, and even that one wouldn't be a "middie." Yet despite styling and body engineering that were six years old in '73, the Shark continued to enjoy steadily increasing sales. Chevrolet retailed a healthy 34,464, some 8000 more than in '72.

Car enthusiasts don't remember 1974 with much fondness. It was, after all, the year the Organization of Petroleum Exporting Countries (OPEC) turned off its pipelines and touched off a global energy crisis. Gas prices soared as dwindling supplies had motorists waiting in long lines at the pumps; some areas even had to resort to rationing. Suddenly, the big, heavy, thirsty ol' Shark looked woefully anachronistic, though the '74 version had been locked up well before OPEC's dirty deed. There was nothing Chevy could do anyway but carry on and hope. Fortunately, the crisis didn't last long, though its effects sure did.

Providing instant identification for the '74 was a new body-color rear-end treatment to complement the previous year's reworked front. Another federal dictate

GM Styling had some ideas for the '74 Corvette (opposite, top), but what actually emerged (below) looked somewhat different. This would be the year that marked the end of genuine dual exhausts, and the last of the breed still able to burn leaded gas. Engine choices were three (as since 1972). The 350 V-8 came as a 195-bhp Turbo-Fire or 250-bhp Turbo-Fire Special (shown), the 454 as a 270-bhp Turbo-Jet.

was behind it—a five-mph *rear*-impact standard. Also sheathed in urethane, the new ensemble conferred a smoother, more integrated look, and though it tapered downward instead of upward like the previous Kamm-type tail, it didn't seem to harm aerodynamics. The bumper was a two-piece affair with a visible seam in the middle of its plastic cover; a seamless one-piece unit would be substituted from 1975 on.

Symbolic of the changing times, 1974 marked several Corvette "lasts." Engines, for example, would henceforth be tuned to run only on unleaded gas—aided by the industry's wholesale switch to catalytic converters for 1975. Genuine dual exhausts would give way to separate manifolds routed to a single catalytic converter, then on to separate pipes and mufflers. This was also the last year for big-block power. The base and extra-cost small-block V-8s were still available and unaltered from '73 specs.

Elsewhere, it was the same old story: detail changes, most for the better. The market's growing preference for performance automatic transmissions yielded a sturdier Turbo-Hydra-Matic designated M40. Shoulder belts, a fixture since '71, were combined with the lap belts into a single three-point harness, and the inertia-reel setup was changed somewhat. The rearview mirror became wider; radiator efficiency improved; the burglar alarm switch was moved from the rear of the car to the left front fender; and the power steering pump was made more durable.

New for '74 was one of the all-time bargains in Corvette performance packages: the RPO FE7 Gymkhana Suspension—a mere seven bucks. FE7 was little more than higher-rate springs and firmer, specially calibrated shocks—the tried-and-true formula used since the mid-Sixties in Chevy's popular F41 package—but it improved handling all out of proportion to its paltry price. The F41 itself, which had begun with the Z06 racing option back in 1963, was still around in RPO Z07 and included heavy-duty brakes.

Here was another mirror of the times. Mammoth engines and pavement-peeling acceleration had been rendered obsolete by inflation, rising insurance rates, and the much higher cost of gasoline in the wake of the OPEC embargo. Buyers were becoming more sophisticated, demanding more balanced cars that combined straightline go with handling, sizzle with civility. Chevy didn't get to be "USA-1" by ignoring its buyers, and changing public tastes were as important a factor as new economic realities in the steady transformation of the Corvette's character during the Seventies. Of course, marketing efforts changed right along, too.

The results were dramatic. The Shark never seemed as nimble as the Sting Ray, and the mid-Seventies small-block cars were nowhere near as brutal as the big-block 'Vettes of old, but the '74 was satisfyingly quick all the same. The 250-bhp L82 could take you from 0 to 60 mph in about 7.5 seconds and on to 125 mph while averaging about 14-15 mpg—not bad, all things considered. The '74 also marked a new high for 'Vette luxury, which by that point was no longer the contradiction in terms it once was. If still a bit noisy, the Corvette had evolved into a very refined grand tourer with plenty of creature comforts and far greater reliability than most of its high-buck competition.

For all that, the '74 prompted some enthusiasts to wonder whether Corvette development hadn't been frozen. It hadn't, of course, and rumors continued that an all-new mid-engine 'Vette was imminent. But what most observers failed to notice was that the fifth generation defied industry sales trends by selling at or near its best-ever levels at a time when it should have done anything but. The total was up again for '74, hitting 37,502 units, quite close to record 1969, a year when the U.S. economy and the world energy picture had been considerably brighter. No wonder Chevy was content to stay with the basic Shark package. Buyers certainly were.

They stayed with it again for 1975, when the only physical change was a pair of small extrusions with black pads for each bumper as additional parking-lot protection. Convertible volume continued to sink,

falling to 4629 units for the model year. The body style would not return for bicentennial 1976 or for another decade.

At least the convertible hung around the entire 1975 model year. The big-block V-8 ostensibly returned, only to be dropped early in the season, leaving the small-block L82 as the only power option. And its power was down, to 205 bhp. The base 350 also withered, detuned to a measly 165 bhp. Those ratings might have been even lower had it not been for the catalytic converter, that new and more efficient emissions cleanup device adopted for most 1975 American cars. A happier development was the advent of breakerless electronic ignition, accompanied by an electronic (instead of mechanical) tachometer

continued on page 279

Despite a rapidly changing environment, the lack of a big-block V-8, and steadily rising prices (now starting at $6537 for the roadster and $6797 for the coupe), 1975 Corvette output came to a satisfying 38,465 units. Of those, 4629 were ragtops—the remaining 33,836 were coupes.

277

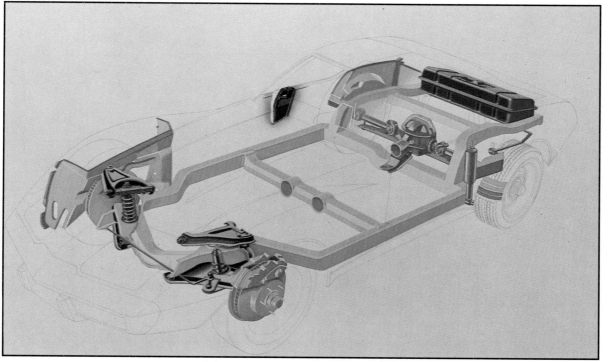

One of the few exterior clues to the '76 Corvette (both pages) was a new rectangular Corvette badge centered between the taillights. Underneath, a partial steel underbody replaced the fiberglass due to the greater heat generated by the catalytic converter. The base L48 350 V-8 (shown) had apparently taken a few vitamins as horsepower jumped by 15 to 180; the optional L82 went to 210. The cutaway shows frame and suspension components.

drive. A headlights-on warning buzzer was added per federal dictates.

Against all odds, Corvette sales continued to climb. The '75 total rose to within 300 units of the '69 peak—precisely 38,465. The car's hold on the public was such that the old record was decisively smashed the following year, despite the convertible's demise

and few changes to the T-roof coupe. Dealers moved 46,558 Corvettes before closing the books on model year 1976, a reflection of the recovering market and diminishing competition in the Corvette's price/performance class.

To the delight of speed freaks, horsepower began climbing again on slightly higher compression, one benefit of the "cat con." The L48 gained 15 horses for a total of 180; the L82 went up to 210 bhp. Modified induction helped. Both engines inhaled through an intake that was now in front of and above the radiator, instead of at the cowl near the windshield. The change was made to remedy the noise of air being gulped in so close to the passenger compartment.

Stylewise, the veteran Shark was nicer than ever for '76. The bogus air-extractor vents vanished from the rear deck; rear bumper trim was slightly altered; and a new four-spoke sport steering wheel arrived, though the last irritated some 'Vette fans because it was borrowed from the subcompact Vega GT. To increase rigidity and reduce heat seepage from the hotter-running engines, a steel subsection was added to the forward body structure.

As a sort of wake for the end of old-fashioned Detroit performance, *Car and Driver* staged a five-way "Bicentennial Civil-Disobedience Test" in 1976. This exercise pitted an L82 automatic 'Vette against a Super-Duty 455 Pontiac Trans Am, a 302 Ford Mustang II Cobra II, a Dodge Dart Sport 340, and a Chevy C-10 pickup packing the big-block 454 that less stringent emissions standards still allowed in trucks. Of course, *C/D* was woefully premature in reporting the demise of American muscle, but the results here are interesting all the same. The 'Vette was the most expensive of the quintet but the hands-down speed champ at 7.1 seconds 0-60 mph, 15.3 seconds and

91.9 mph in the standing quarter, and 124.5 mph flat out. The little Dart Sport was a surprising second for top speed, but the Trans-Am was slightly quicker off-the-line and turned in the shortest 70-mph stopping distances (the 'Vette wasn't far behind, though).

"Chevy's Stingray may seem an obvious overdog," *C/D* observed, "but it is down on displacement and horsepower compared to the competition....The factory's strongest 'Corvette offering is the optional L82 engine at a cost of $481. This fat chunk of money buys only 30 hp over the base L48, but besides the hotter cam timing, bigger valves, and higher compression to make the power, you get the durability insurance of forged pistons, a four-bolt main-bearing block and a forged crankshaft.

"The four-speed manual transmission would probably be your next check on the order blank...but due to a strange combination of circumstances, the Turbo-Hydramatic has a good four-mph edge in top speed. The old rules of performance unfortunately don't always apply when your exhaust pipes come plugged with catalysts. Today's horsepower curves peak early in the midrange and fall off precipitously long before the redline. So...you need a tall gear to keep engine revs down where the power lies. Once you've specified the L82 engine, the best you can do is a 3.36 rear axle that comes *only* with the automatic transmission."

Such curiosities were typical of the Seventies, but they'd pass soon enough. Detroit was learning how to

The 1976 Corvette (both pages) listed at $7605, a jump of more than $800. Its weight had been sneaking upward, too, now coming in at 3445 pounds. Production slipped slightly to 46,558 units. The bucket seats (left) sported a textured-vinyl material and deep-pleated saddle-stitched seat panels. Interior color choices consisted of black, dark firethorn, light buckskin, or white. The center console came standard; it housed the ashtray and lighter. The smaller-diameter steering wheel was borrowed from the Vega. Three carpeted storage bins were behind the seats.

make performance compatible with lower emissions and higher fuel efficiency, which boded especially well for Corvette.

Unfortunately, the industry had no answer for the sharp inflation that had plagued consumers since the 1973-74 energy crisis—except to pass it along. Though the base price of *C/D*'s test '76er was about $7800, options and the usual ancillary charges put it just over 10-grand as delivered. "Chevrolet has raised the dues [this year] a fat 12 percent," the editors lamented, "a

continued on page 284

move you should look upon as profit-taking in aid of keeping the corporate decision-makers interested in perpetuating the car's existence. This has brought a stay of execution for our only sports car; it will live on in much the same trim for at least three more years. Beyond that is anybody's guess. Right now, it's overweight, bulky on the outside, cramped on the inside and underpowered. But there's a lot of consolation in the fact that 120 mph off the imported rack will cost you a cool five grand more."

Once again we see those three constants of Corvette press commentary: high interest in the next new model coupled with growing criticism of the existing one, tempered by praise for high performance-per-dollar. Of course, perspective invariably changes with time, and the 'Vette has always inspired dreams of more exciting tomorrows. The Shark may have been aging,

but there was still nothing else quite like the Corvette—there were certainly far fewer Detroit performance cars of any kind by 1976--a definite factor in the car's renewed sales strength.

The fifth generation returned for '77 with only a few new wrinkles. Mechanicals were left alone, as the year's tweaks generally aimed for more refined cruising. The most visible changes were inside. The console was redesigned to accept a larger array of Delco music-makers (including an AM/FM stereo radio with integral cassette tape deck as a first-time option); its instruments were restyled for greater legibility; and climate controls were simplified. A leather-rim sport steering wheel was adopted (tilt/telescope adjustment remained

continued on page 286

Fifth-Generation Corvette Major Specifications

	1968	1970	1974	1977
Body/Chassis				
Frame:*	Box-section welded			
Body:	Glass-reinforced plastic, 2-seat coupe and convertible (except 1977)			
Front suspension:	Independent; upper and lower A-arms, coil springs, tubular hydraulic shock absorbers, anti-roll bar			
Rear suspension:	Independent; lateral leaf spring, struts, U-joint halfshafts, trailing arms, tubular hydraulic shock absorbers			
Wheels:	15×7JK steel disc	15×8.5 cast alloy	15×8.5 cast alloy	15×8 cast alloy
Tires:	F70-15	205-15	GR70-15	GR70-15
Dimensions				
Wheelbase (in.):	98.0			
Overall length (in.):	182.1	182.5	185.5	185.2
Overall height (in.):	47.8	47.4	47.8	48.0
Overall width (in.):	69.2	69.0	69.0	70.0
Track front/rear (in.):	58.3/59.0	58.7/59.4	58.7/59.5	58.7/59.5
Ground clearance (in.):	4.9	4.5	4.2	5.0
Curb weight (lbs)	3260	na	na	3450
Engines				
Type:	ohv V-8, water-cooled, cast-iron block and heads			
Designation:	L46	LS5	L82	L82
Main bearings:	5			
Bore × stroke (in.):	4.00×3.48	4.25×4.00	4.00×3.48	4.00×3.48
Displacement (ci):	350	454	350	350
Compression ratio:	11.0:1	10.25:1	9.0:1	9.0:1
Induction:	Rochester 4-bbl carburetor			
Exhaust system:	Split cast-iron manifolds, dual exhausts			
Brake horsepower @ rpm:	350 @ 5800	390 @ 4800	250 @ 5200	210 @ 5200
Torque @ rpm (lbs/ft):	360 @ 3600	500 @ 3400	285 @ 4000	255 @ 3600
Electrical system:	12-volt Delco-Remy			
Drivetrain				
Transmission:	4 man.	3 auto.	4 man.	4 man.
Gear ratios:				
First	2.20:1	2.48:1	2.64:1	2.64:1
Second	1.64:1	1.48:1	1.75:1	1.75:1
Third	1.27:1	1.00:1	1.34:1	1.34:1
Fourth	1.00:1	—	1.00:1	1.00:1
Rear axle:	Hypoid semi-floating			
Rear axle ratio:	3.70:1	3.08:1	3.70:1	3.70:1
Steering:	Saginaw recirculating-ball (power assist std. exc. 1968)			
Steering ratio:	17.6:1	17.6:1	17.0:1	17.0:1
Turning circle (ft):	40	37	38	38
Brakes:	Vented 4-wheel discs, 11.75-in. diameter, single caliper; 461 sq. in effective lining area			
Performance				
0-50 mph (sec):	6.0	5.5	6.3	5.5
0-60 mph (sec):	7.5	7.0	7.5	7.0
0-90 mph (sec):	15.0	na	na	na
0-100 mph (sec):	na	14.0	18.5	19.0
0-¼ mi (sec):	15.5	15.0	16.0	15.5
Mph at ¼ mi:	90-94	92-95	90-93	90-92
Top speed (mph):	130	145	124	na
Fuel consumption (mpg):	11-15	8-12	12-15	13-16

* one entry indicates same data for all versions

For its 1977 edition, the Corvette lost its Stingray badges, so the car was now simply called a Corvette. Power steering and brakes became standard equipment, part of the reason the base price jumped by over $1000 to $8648. The optional luggage rack (bottom) was reworked so that the twin lift-off roof panels could be carried there instead of in the luggage compartment, where they were less convenient to stow. The crossed-flag emblems, mounted front and rear, were new this year.

optional), along with a new "Smart Switch" steering-column stalk combining headlight dimmer and wipe/wash functions with the turn indicators. The steering column itself was shortened to permit a more "arms-out" driving posture; the change also eased entry/exit a little. A related modification lengthened the manual transmission lever for easier use of the handbrake. The alarm switch moved again, now incorporated with the left door-lock button. The rearview mirror also shifted a tad, and sunvisors were revamped. Leather upholstery was now standard, and cloth seats with hide bolsters became an extra-cost item. Power steering and brakes were newly standardized, too.

Outside, the optional rear-deck luggage carrier that had been offered all along was reworked so that the

1968-77 Serial Spans, Production Figures, and Base Prices

Year	Serial Prefix	Serial Span	Prod.	Price
1968	194378S	400001-428566	9,936 coupe	$4663
	194678S		18,630 roadster	$4230
1969	194379S	700001-738762	22,154 coupe	$4781
	194679S		16,608 roadster	$4438
1970	194370S	400001-417316	10,668 coupe	$5192
	194670S		6,648 roadster	$4849
1971	194371S	100001-121801	14,680 coupe	$5536
	194671S		7,121 roadster	$5299
1972	1Z37K2S	500001-520486*	20,486 coupe	$5472
	1Z67K2S	500001-506508*	6,508 roadster	$5246
1973	1Z37K2S	400001-424372	24,372 coupe	$5921
	1Z67K2S	400001-406093	6,093 roadster	$5685
1974	1Z37J4S	400001-432028	32,028 coupe	$6372
	1Z67J4S	400001-404629	4,629 roadster	$6156
1975	1Z37J5S	400001-433836	33,836 coupe	$7117
	1Z67J5S	400001-404629	4,629 roadster	$6857
1976	1Z67J6S	400001-446558	46,558	$7605
1977	1Z67J7S	100001-149213	49,213	$8648

* proportional figures

A new numbering system took effect in 1972. Using the prefix 1Z37K2S as an example, the numerals and letters designate the following:

1 = Chevrolet Division	K = Base engine 1972-73
Z = Model	J = Base engine from 1974
37 = Convertible	2 = Model year, where 2 is 1972
67 = Coupe	S = St. Louis plant

Most of the changes on the '77 Corvette (both pages) were hidden, such as a steel hood reinforcement. The interior, however, came in for some modifications, and the four-spoke steering wheel with a leather-wrapped rim (opposite, bottom) was new. So was the console, which now housed the power window switches. The ammeter was replaced this year by a voltmeter, and the heater/air conditioning controls were newly configured.

T-tops could be carried there instead of in the lidless trunk, where they were less convenient to stow. Glass roof panels were shown as a new option at the start of the model year, but GM canceled them in a reputed dispute with the supplier over sales rights. The vendor eventually marketed them itself—and Chevy promptly went to another source for 1978. One final exterior change for 1977 would be noted instantly by car spotters: The Stingray nameplate came off the front fenders, replaced by the traditional crossed-flags insignia. The car was again simply Corvette.

Sales set another new record at 49,213 for the '77 model year—amazing for a decade-old design and eloquent testimony to its enduring, near-universal

continued on page 291

Despite the higher prices, Corvette production set another record in 1977: 49,213 units. As in 1976, the 350 V-8 came in two horsepower ratings: 180 and 210. Only 6148 cars were equipped with the optional L82 engine, and just 5043 'Vettes came out of the factory with the M20 four-speed gearbox; 2060 had the M26 close-ratio unit.

1968-74 Corvette Powerteams

The engine, transmission, and axle ratio combinations available to Corvette buyers skyrocketed in the late Sixties. The chart below will help you sort them out. It was compiled from factory records but runs only through 1974 because the permutations shrank to manageable size afterwards. The listings do not account for mid-year changes, such as the advent of the 350-cid V-8 in January 1968. Engine data are for cars without air conditioning, which sometimes altered availability.

Engine	cid	bhp @ rpm	Transmission	Axle Ratio Standard	Optional

Model Year 1968

Engine	cid	bhp @ rpm	Transmission	Standard	Optional
Turbo-Fire V-8	327	300 @ 5000	3-speed manual (2.54:1 low)	3.36:1	3.08:1
			4-speed manual (2.52:1 low)	3.36:1	3.08:1
			Turbo Hydra-Matic	3.08:1	—
Turbo-Fire V-8	327	350 @ 5800	4-speed manual (2.52:1 low)	3.36:1	3.55:1
			4-speed manual (2.20:1 low)	3.70:1	4.11:1
Turbo-Jet V-8	427	390 @ 5400	4-speed manual (2.52:1 low)	3.08:1	3.36:1
			4-speed manual (2.20:1 low)	3.36:1	3.08:1 3.55:1 3.70:1
			Turbo Hydra-Matic	3.08:1	2.73:1
Turbo-Jet V-8	427	400 @ 5400	4-speed manual (2.52:1 low)	3.08:1	3.36:1
			4-speed manual (2.20:1 low)	3.36:1	3.08:1 3.55:1 3.70:1
			Turbo Hydra-Matic	3.08:1	2.73:1
Turbo-Jet V-8	427	435 @ 5800	4-speed manual (2.20:1 low)	3.55:1	3.36:1 3.70:1 4.11:1

Model Year 1969

Engine	cid	bhp @ rpm	Transmission	Standard	Optional
Turbo-Fire 350	350	300 @ 4800	3-speed manual (2.54:1 low)	3.36:1	3.08:1
			4-speed manual (2.52:1 low)	3.36:1	3.08:1
			Turbo Hydra-Matic	3.08:1	—
Turbo-Fire 350	350	350 @ 5600	4-speed manual (2.52:1 low)	3.36:1	3.55:1
			4-speed manual (2.20:1 low)	3.70:1	4.11:1
Turbo-Jet 427	427	390 @ 5400	4-speed manual (2.52:1 low)	3.08:1	3.36:1
			4-speed manual (2.20:1 low)	3.36:1	3.08:1 3.55:1 3.70:1
			Turbo Hydra-Matic	3.08:1	2.73:1
Turbo-Jet 427	427	400 @ 5400	4-speed manual (2.52:1 low)	3.08:1	3.36:1
			4-speed manual (2.20:1 low)	3.36:1	3.08:1 3.55:1 3.70:1
			Turbo Hydra-Matic	3.08:1	2.73:1
Turbo-Jet 427	427	435 @ 5800	4-speed manual (2.20:1 low)	3.55:1	3.36:1 3.70:1 4.11:1
			Turbo Hydra-Matic	3.08:1	2.73:1 3.36:1

continued on next page

Model Year 1969 (continued)

Turbo-Jet 427 (L88)	427	430 @ 5800	4-speed manual (2.20:1 low)	3.36:1	3.08:1 3.55:1 3.70:1 4.11:1 4.56:1
			Turbo Hydra-Matic	3.08:1	2.73:1 3.36:1

Model Year 1970

Turbo-Fire 350	350	300 @ 4800	4-speed manual (2.52:1 low)	3.36:1	3.08:1
			Turbo Hydra-Matic	3.08:1	3.36:1
Turbo-Fire 350	350	350 @ 5600	4-speed manual (2.20:1 low)	3.70:1	4.11:1
			4-speed manual (2.52:1 low)	3.36:1	
Turbo-Fire 350	350	370 @ 6000	4-speed manual (2.20:1 low)	3.70:1	3.55:1 4.11:1
			4-speed manual (2.52:1 low)	3.55:1	3.36:1 3.70:1
Turbo-Jet 454	454	390 @ 4800	4-speed manual (2.20:1 low)	3.36:1	3.08:1 3.55:1 3.70:1
			4-speed manual (2.52:1 low)	3.08:1	3.36:1
			Turbo Hydra-Matic	3.08:1	2.73:1
Turbo-Jet 454	454	460 @ 5200	4-speed manual (2.20:1 low)	3.36:1	3.08:1 3.55:1
			Turbo Hydra-Matic	3.08:1	3.36:1

Model Year 1971

Turbo-Fire 350	350	270/210* @ 4800	4-speed manual (2.52:1 low)	3.36:1	3.08:1
			Turbo Hydra-Matic	3.08:1	3.36:1
Turbo-Fire 350	350	330/275* @ 5600	4-speed manual (2.20:1 low)	3.70:1	3.55:1 4.11:1
			4-speed manual (2.52:1 low)	3.55:1	3.36:1 3.70:1
Turbo-Jet 454	454	365/285* @ 4800	4-speed manual (2.20:1 low)	3.36:1	3.08:1 3.55:1 3.70:1
			4-speed manual (2.52:1 low)	3.08:1	3.36:1
			Turbo Hydra-Matic	3.08:1	3.36:1
Turbo-Jet 454	454	425/325* @ 5600	4-speed manual (2.20:1 low)	3.36:1	3.08:1 3.55:1
			Special 4-speed (2.20:1 low)	3.36:1	3.08:1 3.55:1 3.70:1 4.11:1
			Turbo Hydra-Matic	3.08:1	3.36:1

Model Year 1972**

Turbo-Fire 350	350	200 @ 4800	4-speed manual (2.52:1 low)	3.36:1	3.08:1
			Turbo Hydra-Matic	3.36:1	3.08:1
Turbo-Fire Special	350	255 @ 5600	4-speed manual (2.52:1 low)	3.36:1	3.55:1
			4-speed manual (2.20:1 low)	3.70:1	—
			Turbo Hydra-Matic	3.36:1	—

* Gross/net   ** All bhp figures net after 1972

continued on next page

Turbo-Jet	454	270 @ 4800	4-speed manual (2.52:1 low)	3.08:1	3.36:1
			4-speed manual (2.20:1 low)	3.36:1	3.55:1
			Turbo Hydra-Matic	3.08:1	3.36:1

Model Year 1973

Turbo-Fire 350	350	190 @ 4400	4-speed manual (2.52:1 low)	3.36:1	3.08:1
			Turbo Hydra-Matic	3.08:1	3.36:1
Turbo-Fire Special	350	250 @ 5200	4-speed manual (2.52:1 low)	3.55:1	3.36:1 3.70:1
			4-speed manual (2.20:1 low)	3.70:1	3.55:1
			Turbo Hydra-Matic	3.55:1	3.36:1 3.70:1
Turbo-Jet	454	275 @ 4400	4-speed manual (2.52:1 low)	3.08:1	3.36:1
			4-speed manual (2.20:1 low)	3.36:1	3.55:1

Model Year 1974

Turbo-Fire	350	195 @ 4400	4-speed manual (2.52:1 low)	3.36:1	3.08:1
			Turbo Hydra-Matic	3.08:1	3.36:1
Turbo-Fire Special	350	250 @ 5200	4-speed manual (2.52:1 low)	3.55:1	3.70:1
			4-speed manual (2.20:1 low)	3.70:1	3.36:1 3.55:1 4.11:1
			Turbo Hydra-Matic	3.55:1	3.70:1
Turbo-Jet	454	270 @ 4400	4-speed manual (2.52:1 low)	3.08:1	3.36:1
			4-speed manual (2.20:1 low)	3.36:1	3.08:1 3.55:1
			Turbo Hydra-Matic	3.08:1	3.36:1

appeal. The figures also said a lot about GM's knack for successfully updating a design to meet changing conditions without making major alterations and, more importantly, without detracting from aesthetics or performance. (This was as much a factor in the resurgence of the Chevrolet Camaro and Pontiac Firebird ponycars as it was for Corvette's.)

The Shark had become such a familiar quantity by now that "buff books" hardly bothered with it anymore. An exception was *Road & Track*, which tested two '77s, a 4-speed L82 and an automatic L48. Excerpts from that report bear repeating, if only to show that the more things change, the more they stay the same. For example, "[Drivetrains,] in the tradition of Chevrolet [are] so unobtrusive they're easy to forget. Each engine ran flawlessly....The Corvette is still one sports car in which you needn't apologize for having an automatic transmission and that applies to surprisingly few such cars."

As for those who wondered whether the 'Vette was still a real sports car in 1977, *R&T* offered "more

proof: [This] L82 had the fastest time we've ever recorded through our slalom test, 63.6 mph. As a comparison, the Porsche [911] Turbo Carrera managed 62.8." Skidpad performance wasn't the best, "hampered at stock tire pressures by throttle understeer most likely designed in to keep the less astute Corvette drivers out of the weeds should they overcook it on the on-ramp." But straightline go was trending upward again, *R&T* clocking 6.8 seconds 0-60 mph, 0.4-seconds quicker than its test L82 of four years before.

"Probably even more important," *R&T* concluded, "is the quality of assembly of both Corvettes we tried. This pair felt quite solid. We have to say it again, this is still the best all-around value in the sports car market."

By any measure, the fifth generation had fared exceptionally well, prospering through some of the most difficult years in American automotive history. And though elderly, the Shark was far from finished. It was, in fact, about to be rejuvenated with some special revisions for a very special year. America's sports car was about to celebrate its Silver Anniversary.

CHAPTER 10

1978-82:
OLDIE BUT GOODIE

America's sports car reached a significant milestone in 1977. On March 15 at precisely 2:01 p.m., Chevrolet general manager Robert D. Lund drove the 500,000th production Corvette off the St. Louis assembly line. It was an historic occasion to rival that day in late June nearly a quarter-century before when Job 1 had rolled out the door of the small plant in Flint.

Nineteen seventy-seven was a time for looking back, and looking ahead. Indeed, even as the half-million milestone was being documented for posterity, the Corvette's future was being decided. That wasn't immediately apparent, however, and the fifth-generation design would carry on for another five successful years.

The wonder of the Silver-Anniversary 1978 model was not that it was so much like the 10 Corvettes before it but that it was changed as much as it was. Despite everything that Washington, the safety lobby, and OPEC had thrown the Corvette's way, annual sales were approaching 50,000—the height of acceptance for a car that General Motors once thought would never sell half as well. The Corvette was now indispensable as a high-profit personal car as well as a showroom traffic-builder. And though long removed from its original "dual-purpose" concept, owner loyalty was as fierce as ever. GM understandably saw no need to replace the old warrior any time soon.

Yet Chevrolet would soon need all the traffic-building Corvette could provide. Reason: the events triggered by the 1973-74 energy crisis had already had enormous impact on the entire U.S. auto industry—and on planning for the next new Corvette.

One immediate effect of the Middle East oil embargo had been to stunt big-car sales, while making compacts and subcompacts premium-price items. As Lee Iacocca later noted: "The market flip-flopped by 40 percent literally overnight. That had never happened before, not even in the Depression." Equally unprecedented, the embargo forced millions of American motorists to wait in ever-longer lines at gas stations, prompting some states to enact rationing laws.

But the crisis would also have a positive effect, one with vital, long-term consequences: It made the nation energy-conscious in a way it never had been before. In particular, the energy shortages highlighted the need for the sort of cars the "buff" magazines had been advocating for years: smaller, more fuel-efficient, better-built.

For a time, buyers flocked in record numbers to domestic compacts and the smaller, high-mileage imports. The big sales winners were the various Japanese makes, which heretofore had made only a modest dent in the U.S. market. Toyota and Datsun did especially well—much as the Beetle had established Volkswagen as a major competitor during the sharp recession of the late Fifties. Most buyers ended up in Japanese cars not to be chic but because thriftier, less expensive transportation had become a practical necessity for them. The Japanese models also impressed consumers as being more reliable than comparably priced Detroit products, which only added to their appeal.

Within a few months, the oil started flowing again and gas supplies improved. Predictably, perhaps, many

The Corvette celebrated its 25th Anniversary in 1978, but since Chevy didn't have an all-new model ready, it modified the existing car with a fastback roofline (below), created by a wide wraparound rear backlight. Emblems front and rear commemorated the Silver Anniversary (opposite).

buyers forgot all about the shortages and went back to their beloved big cars, even though gas cost a lot more than it had before. But the damage had been done. Japanese models continued to sell well, though not so much for fuel efficiency as for their Americanized styling and creature comforts. These factors, along with superior value per U.S. dollar and high reliability, made the Japanese automakers major players in the American market.

How did all this affect the Corvette? The fuel scare was really not an issue, because 40,000 or more buyers a year were still quite willing to pay any price to drive a large, V-8-powered sports car. Quality was another matter, though, and testers, buyers, and even ardent fans complained that the Corvette had been below par for too long. Ergonomics was becoming a familiar term, and the Corvette ranked low in that area as well. Last but not least, the 'Vette's "ride comfort" was a contradiction in terms, especially with the optional Gymkhana Suspension, which gave the car the suppleness of a tank.

Despite these drawbacks, Corvette sales continued strong through the end of the decade. Though the '78 tally eased by about 2500 cars from the previous year (to 47,887), 1979 brought another record: 53,807—the first 50,000-unit year in Corvette history. This was really quite remarkable—and in more ways than one. As Zora Arkus-Duntov told *Road & Track*'s John Lamm in 1977: "In 1970, production in the St. Louis Corvette plant reached 32,000 and they said no more, that is the utmost capacity. But the Corvette was not affected by the oil crisis...and with the same facility and the same floor space we ended up eventually producing 44,000 Corvettes."

Still, this was only a drop in the bucket for mighty GM, which was understandably more concerned about its volume-car business in the wake of the energy crisis. The grim new realities after the winter of 1973-74 were that natural resources were finite and that in an increasingly interdependent world, the U.S. economy—indeed, the American way of life—could be easily and severely disrupted by the actions of other countries. Other fuel shortages could occur just as suddenly as this one, said the experts. And indeed, some pundits were predicting more.

Meanwhile, the much stiffer energy prices created by the embargo started an inflationary spiral that soon pushed interest rates and the prices of all consumer goods to new highs. Cars were no exception. By the late Seventies, aggravated by the added costs of additionally mandated safety equipment, prices were heading toward the stratosphere, making new-car ownership increasingly difficult for a growing number of Americans who found they could no longer indulge their traditional habit of trading cars every two or three years.

Yet even before OPEC shut down the pipelines, GM had decided that the old "bigger is better" approach to car design had outlived its usefulness. If times were changing—as they definitely were by 1970—cars must too. Thus, while Ford and Chrysler returned to business as usual after the energy crunch, GM embarked on a massive, long-term program to revamp its entire fleet. Its future cars would be smaller, lighter, and more economical. Some would exploit the space-saving potential of front-wheel drive to provide about as much interior room as older models, but within smaller exterior packages.

Thus arrived the 1975 Cadillac Seville successfully breaking ground as a compact luxury car, followed by the equally popular downsized B- and C-body standards of 1977—hundreds of pounds and many inches trimmer than their behemoth predecessors, yet every bit as spacious and comfortable. The big shrink continued with the A-body intermediates for 1978, new front-drive X-body compacts for 1980, and J-body subcompacts two years after that.

Despite GM's preoccupation with downsizing, the Corvette was not forgotten. It was still an important car, the line-leader for GM's largest-volume division. It

just didn't have the highest priority at the time. As John Lamm observed in 1977, there was "little point in spending the money on a new car when the old one is selling out year after year." In other words, Chevrolet had precious little incentive to change the old one very much.

"Yet there has always been an alternative waiting for a quieting of Corvette sales," Lamm went on, "a mid-engine alternative. It was first meant, according to Duntov, as a possible counter for the mid-engine Ford Mach I program, but when that died, so did the new Corvette. On two other occasions, the car was so close to production that actual production techniques had been developed—once with 350 and 427 engine choices, once as a rotary—but the folks just kept buying the old ones."

Lamm refers to XP-882, the experimental program begun in the late Sixties that fueled persistent, widespread speculation that the next Corvette would be a midships design. As chronicled in the last chapter, the original full-scale running prototype was a low-slung coupe with an Olds Toronado-style "split" drivetrain specially engineered by Duntov for a production midships installation. By mid-1970 the car was major news in "buff books" everywhere. "We'll stake our reputation on this being the Corvette of the future," *Road & Track* predicted in July 1970, "but don't expect it until 1972 at the earliest." A January 1971 story forecasting a 1973 announcement

would prove equally premature, though the car had since been given Corvette badges and looked near production-ready.

But then came a second XP-882, one of two experiments powered by the Wankel-type rotary engine then under development at the insistence of GM president Ed Cole. Unveiled at the Paris Salon in late 1973, this car employed Duntov's original chassis and drivetrain configuration, but the conventional V-8 had given way to a pair of two-rotor engines bolted together.

With an arresting new gullwing-coupe body by Bill Mitchell, this "Four-Rotor Car" made a mid-engine 'Vette seem closer than ever. *Car and Driver* termed it "the betting man's choice to replace the Stingray." But the energy crisis was just beginning to hit, exposing the Wankel's comparatively poor fuel economy. GM soon stopped work on its rotary—and on the new Corvette designed around it.

Yet even that wasn't the end. At Mitchell's request, a 400-cubic-inch Chevy V-8 was slipped into the four-rotor coupe, which was renamed Aerovette. The car again went on tour and, as before, everyone assumed it was the next Corvette.

Mitchell, meantime, began lobbying GM management for a production version. As usual, if he wanted something badly enough, he got it, and GM chairman Thomas Murphy actually approved a productionized Aerovette for 1980. Ironically, Murphy's approval

came about at least partly due to the threat posed by the rear-engine DMC-12, the soon-to-be-announced brainchild of none other than former Chevy general manager John Z. DeLorean.

For a time, then, the Aerovette was not only the long-awaited, long-rumored "next Corvette" but the mid-engine design that partisans of America's sports car had so hungered for. By the end of 1976, clay models were complete and tooling orders ready to be placed. Recalling 1953, the finished product retained the Aerovette's lines virtually intact, as well as XP-882's basic steel platform chassis design, complete with Duntov's clever, transverse drivetrain. The production Corvette V-8 was a 350 by then, so that engine would have been used (though there was plenty of room for the 305-cid small-block then coming on-line at Chevy). Four-speed manual and Turbo-Hydra-Matic transmissions were planned, and suspension was pulled right off the Shark as per Duntov's original, cost-cutting goal.

But the Aerovette-as-1980-Corvette was not to be. For one thing, the project lost its two most influential

supporters when Duntov retired in 1974 and Mitchell followed suit three years later. Ed Cole was gone by then, too. A further blow came from Duntov's successor, David R. McLellan, who preferred the "front/mid-engine" concept, inaugurated with the '63 Sting Ray, over a rear/mid layout for reasons of packaging, manufacturing ease, and performance.

In the end, though, it was sales—or rather the anticipated lack of them—that proved the decisive factor. Back in the Sixties, mid-engine design had seemed the wave of the future for roadgoing sports cars; by the mid-Seventies, disappointing sales had rendered that promise mere wishful thinking. Although Porsche, Fiat, and others had offered mid-engine sports cars for several years, none had sold very well. Datsun, meantime, couldn't build enough of its (admittedly less expensive) front-engine 240Z. As if to sound the death-knell, Porsche replaced its mid-engine 914 with a front-engine design, the 924, in 1976.

It bears mentioning that one other line of thinking was explored while the "production Aerovette" was being developed. This was a midships *V-6* design with

running gear adapted from the forthcoming new X-body compacts. It was the same basic idea later applied to Pontiac's Fiero: a transverse front-drive power package plunked behind a two-seat cockpit to drive the rear wheels. The proposed engine was the now-familiar 60-degree 2.8-liter V-6 then in the works at Chevrolet. The Chevy Three Production Studio under Jerry Palmer sculpted clean, somewhat angular styling with Aerovette overtones.

The general concept was hardly new. Porsche, Lotus, and Fiat had all used high-volume, off-the-shelf components to create their roadgoing middies of the late Sixties and early Seventies—the "corporate kit car" approach that promised similar savings in tooling costs for GM. Although definitely more attractive to the bean-counters, the mid/V-6 was doomed by the same considerations that killed the Aerovette-based

proposal. And it had one additional drawback, as recounted by *Car and Driver* in March 1983: "A new front-engine/rear-drive [F-body] Camaro had just been approved with 5.7-liter [350-cid] V-8 capacity; there was no way a V-6 Corvette could continue as the flagship of the Chevy fleet without turbocharging and intercooling, and it would be tough to sell such a costly, high-tech alternative to management. At the same time, the corporation had yet to develop a transaxle that could withstand the torque such an engine would produce [sound familiar?]. In addition, GM had big plans for widespread use of its X-car components in future high-volume car lines (A- and F-cars), limiting the availability of parts [for Corvette]. Engineering shelved the [V-6] mule car in late 1977, and the mid-engine body designs were sent to the Advanced Design studio for future reference."

Because the new "glassback" on the '78 Corvette left the luggage area visible, a security shade was mounted at the rear of the cargo compartment. Chevy was quick to provide graphic evidence of the enlarged luggage area (opposite top). Silver Anniversary 'Vettes came in coupe form only. Since they were a favorite with car thieves, the standard anti-theft system was wired into the lift-out roof panels, which had an unfortunate habit of disappearing on dark nights. The panels were available in glass as well as steel, and both were modified to provide more headroom and simpler locking procedures.

Thus, 1978 was another historic Corvette year—and in more ways than one. With the rear/mid-engine idea again totally abandoned—seemingly for good this time—work toward a new front-engine design got underway even as the press and Corvette fans celebrated 25 years of America's sports car. Apparently, there was no timetable attached to the new model. The sixth generation would not appear until it was completely "right"—all the better for quality control. Of course, there was hardly any need to rush things what with the Shark still selling so well.

Because the Shark would continue to fill the gap, a problem arose regarding the silver-anniversary 1978 edition. Chevrolet wanted something dramatically new to celebrate that milestone birthday, but how new could you make a 10-year-old design without spending tons of money?

The answer proved as simple as trimming away the old "flying buttress" sail panels and substituting a large, compound-curve rear window. *Voila!* The Corvette fastback was back. Not only was this a relatively inexpensive alteration that freshened appearance but, said a bubbly Chevrolet press release, it also improved "rear-quarter visibility while contributing to a greater feeling of interior roominess." Even better, it made for a slightly larger and more accessible luggage area. A *tilt-up* backlight would have

made it even more accessible, but GM didn't want to spend *too* much money.

Not that there weren't other changes for '78. Predictably, Silver Anniversary badges appeared outside. Inside were squared-up housings for the speedometer and tachometer to match the previous year's revamped console gauges; redesigned door panels with new armrests and integral door pulls; and, at last, a proper dashboard glovebox with a real door. A fuel-tank capacity increase from 17 to 24 gallons was another positive change, but moving the windshield wiper/washer control from the steering column stalk back to the dash was not.

Corvette had long been one of America's most frequently stolen cars—the sort of "popularity" no automaker really wants—so the standard anti-theft system was rewired on the '78 to encompass the T-tops, which had an unfortunate habit of disappearing on dark streets even when the rest of the car didn't. Likewise, a new roller-blind security shade was added to keep would-be thieves from peering into the cargo area through the big new backlight. The glass T-tops promised for 1977 were now genuinely available from the factory, and both they and the normal fiberglass panels were modified to provide more

continued on page 301

headroom and easier locking. The three-point seat belts were given a single inertia reel, and belt guides were eliminated.

Power ratings for 1978 shifted a little in deference to emissions standards, as well as to the government's new Corporate Average Fuel Economy (CAFE) mandates that took effect for '78. As before, there were two basic versions of the veteran 350 small-block. The base L48 produced 185 bhp in "49-state" trim and was the only choice for customers in California and high-altitude areas, where horses numbered 175. For an extra $525, the L82 gave you 220 bhp via a dual-snorkel air intake and a revamped exhaust system designed to reduce back pressure aft of the catalytic converter.

More heartening was the return of a close-ratio four-speed manual gearbox as an exclusive option for the L82; a 3.70:1 rear axle made this the best-performing drivetrain. The same gearset was also offered for the L82 with the wide-ratio four-speed, while the L48 came with a 3.36:1 axle (also available for the L82/wide-ratio setup). Also offered for the L82 was a revised Turbo-Hydra-Matic of the new, so-called "CBC" type, with a low-inertia high-stall-speed (2400-rpm) torque converter. It and the regular THM pulled a 3.55:1 final drive except with the L48 at low altitudes, where it was 3.08:1. Such juggling reflected the relative difficulty of balancing performance against low emissions and decent fuel economy, but technology would soon ease the task and restore some of the 'Vette's old *brio*.

The main chassis change for '78 was first-time availability of 60-series tires—raised-white-letter Goodyear GTs in HR60 size (225/60R-15 metric). As

an optional alternative to the standard GR70s, they necessitated some shearing of the fender liners, but Chevy Public Relations extolled the engineers for "putting the most aggressive tire on the car as possible"; Aramid-belt construction contributed to a claimed improvement in ride smoothness. The FE7 Gymkhana Suspension package was still around, though at $41 it was quite a bit costlier than the original $7. As before, it included heavy-duty shocks and higher-rate springs all-round, plus a rear anti-roll bar and a thicker front stabilizer.

Cashing in on the birthday cachet, Chevy offered the '78 Corvette with "25th Anniversary paint." This stemmed from the division's desire to change appearance via a relatively inexpensive striping package that would be viewed as a desirable option and could thus be considerably marked up. Before he retired, Bill Mitchell had suggested a Silver Anniversary model in his favorite color—silver—and it appeared as this B2Z option package. The first factory two-toning offered since 1961 (save the removable hardtops for the now-discontinued roadster), it presented silver over a gray lower body with a separating pinstripe, plus nice-looking alloy wheels and dual "sport" door mirrors as "mandatory options." Otherwise, the Silver Anniversary Corvette was depressingly stock for a celebration car.

The same might be said for another bit of anniversary schmaltz. Chevrolet had negotiated with the Indianapolis Motor Speedway to have a modified Corvette chosen as pace car for 1978's Memorial Day 500, a decision announced in October 1977. Ad types always like the publicity such cars generate. When Chevy got the Camaro named as Indy pacer back in

Opposite page: The Limited Edition Pace Car Replica sported a front spoiler similar to a contemporary Firebird Trans Am (top) and a rear spoiler (bottom) that wrapped down to mid-body height. This page: The L-82 350-cid V-8 option put out 220 horsepower, 35 more than the base version. The Limited Edition badges rode on the front fenders. The Pace Car decal package, which included the Indianapolis Motor Speedway logo, was not factory installed—its use was at the owner's option.

'69, it had built a spate of replica orange-and-white Camaro convertibles. The plan was repeated here.

Initially, 2500 replica Corvette pacers—100 for each year of production—were scheduled for sale on a first-come, first-serve basis. Only trouble was, Chevrolet had 6200 dealers at the time, and with General Motors being very sensitive to charges of favoritism, any such Corvette special would have to be built to a minimum order of 6200 units in order for each dealer to have at least one. And so it was. At

This page: The Pace Car Replica (top) was actually an option package—RPO Z78. The Replica listed at $13,653, fully $4008 more than the base coupe. Chevy built 6200 of them, and most buyers paid way over sticker to get one. The thin-shell silver leather seats (bottom) previewed the seating that would be standard in the '79 'Vette. Opposite: The 1979 Corvette (the Stingray label had disappeared the year previous) soldiered on with few changes, but it hardly mattered as output expanded to another record: 53,807 units.

year's end, what was officially called the Limited Edition Indy Pace Car Replica Corvette made up some 15 percent of total production—not really all that "limited".

Like the Silver Anniversary model, the Pace Car Replica was actually an option package—RPO Z78—with two-tone paint as its main distinction. Here it was black over silver metallic with a bright red pinstripe in between, but a spoiler was tacked on at each end to alter appearance more dramatically. The front spoiler was similar to the one on the contemporary Firebird Trans Am, wrapped under and around to blend into the wheel wells. Also recalling the '69 Aero Coupe show car, the prominent rear spoiler curved down at its outboard ends to meet the bodysides.

Pace Car interior trimmings reflected Bill Mitchell's influence, with full silver leather or silver leather/gray cloth upholstery and gray carpeting. Chevrolet had scheduled new Corvette seats for '79; the program was rushed forward so that the '78 Pace Car could have them first—a new thin-shell design with more prominent (some said *too* prominent) lumbar support. Rumor had it that Goodyear would supply special tires for the Replicas, with C-O-R-V-E-T-T-E in raised white letters, but it didn't happen. Also, Turbo-Hydra-Matic was supposedly the only transmission available, but four-speed manual showed up on quite a few Pacers.

All Replicas were equipped with the new glass T-tops, alloy wheels, power windows, rear defogger, air conditioning, sport mirrors, tilt/telescope steering wheel, heavy-duty battery, power door locks, and an AM/FM stereo with either an eight-track tape player or CB radio. The final touch was a set of regalia decals for owner installation. These included "winged wheel" Indy Speedway logos for the rear fenders, and legends for the doors reading "Official Pace Car, 62nd Annual Indianapolis 500 Mile Race, May 28, 1978."

Base-priced at $13,653, the Pace Car Replica was quite a jump over the $9351 standard model. But

because it looked like an "instant collectible," not one Pace Car sold at list price. Recalling the hysteria that bid Cadillac's "last convertible" Eldorado to absurd heights two years before, most Replicas sold for at least $15,000, with many dealers asking $22,000-$28,000. Some poor souls actually parted with as much as $75,000 for one.

This rabid interest tempted some owners of standard '78s to try to pass them off as factory PCRs—at the same high prices, of course. It was easy enough. All you needed were a spray gun, a black or silver car with the right options, and a friend in your dealer's parts department willing to sell you the two spoilers and special silver cabin trim. What most of the counterfeiters forgot was the special new seats. All this created a lot of unexpected publicity for Chevrolet—and a lot of anguish for dealers, buyers, and would-be collectors. In fact, it still does. Fortunately, the division would remember this experience when creating another limited-edition Corvette a few years later.

If the Shark was now a very old fish, its '78 changes seemed to rejuvenate it all out of proportion to their magnitude. "We can happily report," beamed *Car and Driver*, "[that] the twenty-fifth example of the Corvette is much improved across the board. Not only will it run faster now—the L82 version with four-speed is certainly the fastest American production car, while the base L48 automatic (0-60: 7.8 seconds, top speed: 123 mph) is no slouch—but general driveability and

road manners are of a high order as well....

"...It is obviously a taut, tough automobile that steers straighter, stops stronger and accelerates with more passion than any Corvette since the explosive days of the L88, ZL1 and LT1. To be sure, this latest Corvette...isn't going to rupture anybody's spleen through the quarter-mile, but it presents a balance of overall performance that has been lacking in Corvettes for some time. Riding on the [optional] Goodyear GT radials and utilizing the nicely articulated Muncie four-speed gearbox, the driver can run quickly in a Corvette under almost any conditions. Of course, the old weaknesses persist; the rather high prow [and] submerged seating position [tend] to restrict close-up visibility, and the rear suspension produces the distinct impression during quick directional changes that

the back wheels have no interest whatsoever of coordinating their movements with the front pair. Nevertheless, the Corvette is a genuine pleasure to drive again."

Inevitably, people still wondered when the next-generation Corvette would appear. C/D had its own answer in late '77. "...For better or worse, the headlines for the next few years should read: 'Secret New Corvette? Forget it!'...Because it would be impractical for GM to build a new facility to manufacture the uniquely fabricated Corvette, there is no question that customers will far exceed automobiles for the foreseeable future."

Events would prove C/D's crystal ball a bit off in later years, but not in banner 1979. Product changes were the same old boring, evolutionary kind. The base

L48 gained 10 horsepower—20 in the California and high-altitude versions—by adopting the L82's more efficient twin-snorkel air cleaner; the optional engine itself tacked on five horses. Shock rates were standardized instead of varied with transmission. On cars with automatic, final drive ratio was lowered from 3.08:1 to 3.55:1.

The lightweight seats previewed in the '78 Pace Car Replica appeared as planned, bringing more rearward travel and different inertia seatback locks. Still missing, though, even at extra cost, were the seatback recliners found on the cheapest Japanese cars. Pace-Car-style front and rear spoilers became optional, and tungsten-halogen high-beam headlamps were phased in. The basic AM/FM radio option became standard, and crossed-flags insignia returned to replace the now

obsolete silver anniversary emblems. The added features, combined with a strong inflationary spiral, pushed base price beyond $10,000 for the first time—all the way up to $12,313, in fact—a depressing sign of the times.

A much happier development was the five-speed manual transmission devised for the booming Corvette aftermarket by drag-racer Doug Nash. It featured a light magnesium-alloy case that was split like a clamshell to facilitate servicing and changing gear-wheels, which had straight-cut spur teeth for higher strength and lower friction than conventional helical-

continued on page 308

The '79 Corvette (opposite page) debuted on September 25, 1978. It boasted 195 bhp in base form, up 10, and 225 with the L-82 option, up five. Regular crossed-flags insignia (front and rear) replaced the Silver Anniversary badges from the year before. Pace car spoilers were optional on the '79s (this page). Base price skyrocketed to $12,313, caused mainly by the inflationary times.

The Duntov Turbo (both pages) was actually a product of American Custom Industries of Sylvania, Ohio. It started with a 1980 Corvette coupe equipped with the L-48 engine and automatic. After tearing off the factory body, ACI added special Bilstein shocks and extra wide wheels and massive tires. Steering was tightened and a Turbo International blower bolted on to the engine. A fiberglass convertible body took its basic styling from the Corvette, but sported wider fenders, a modest rear spoiler, and fixed rectangular headlights.

cut gears. Called the "4+1 Quick Change" and available with a choice of 17 different final gearsets, it retailed at $995 as a street gearbox and $1000 in dragstrip-ready guise. Its fifth gear was not an overdrive ratio of the sort then coming into vogue but rather a direct 1.00:1. "The combination of a low numerical axle ratio and high numerical transmission gearing will live longer than the reverse combination," observed *Road & Track*'s John Dinkel, "because as the final drive ratio increases numerically, the size of the pinion gear decreases and the number of pinion teeth increases ....And because most of today's cars are being built with low numerical axle ratios for reasons of improved fuel economy and lower emissions, it means no change in final drive ratio is necessary to take advantage of the Nash five-speed."

R&T found that the Nash gearbox raised the 'Vette's top end from 116 to 130 miles per hour compared with the factory four-speed. It made no difference in quarter-mile performance but did improve fuel economy by about 1.5 miles per gallon, and also reduced noise levels. The interesting thing about the Nash transmission is that it forecast a radically new manual gearbox being developed for the still-distant sixth-generation Corvette.

Also in 1979, *R&T* conducted a comparison test of four sports and GT cars equipped with automatic transmission: a 'Vette, a Mazda RX-7, a Datsun 280ZX, and a Porsche 924. The American sports car came in last overall, the editors jumping all over its harsh ride, vintage "bathtub" driving position, minimal cargo space, and indifferent workmanship. But listen to their summary: "Much loved and still very desirable, [the Corvette is] quick, has excellent brakes, a superb automatic transmission, and is filled with many appreciated amenities...all of which make it an excellent value." Some things never change.

Well, almost never. *Car and Driver* changed its tune a bit after driving the '79 edition with the L82, four-speed, and 3.70:1 axle. After noting that women were now accounting for a solid 15 percent of Corvette sales, the editors weren't "quite sure what to make of the hordes outbidding each other for an obsolete sports car. On the one hand, we'd love to be at the head of the

line with a fistful of money....On the other, we'd feel guilty about casting another vote of approval for the Corvette in its present, out-of-date form. About all we can do is...appeal to all the true friends of the Corvette *not* to buy, in the hope that GM will get the message and invest in a redesign."

That was not a unanimous opinion, however. *C/D*'s Rich Ceppos dissented when he praised the '79 as the "most refined" Corvette ever, with "sophisticated" road manners and controls "evolved into useful instruments that not only direct forward progress but respond reassuringly....And though the Corvette's personality has been honed and polished, it's still full of character—in much the same way as the latest Porsche 911s. There's still a rumble in the exhaust, a hint of twitchiness in the suspension, and a subdued orneriness that demands your attention when you hurry. An undercurrent of excitement tingles through the whole car; the beast has been tamed, but its soul is still wild....So while everyone else looks ahead to the new high-technology, fuel-efficient Corvette looming on the horizon, I advise you to buy now or forever hold your peace."

For some folks, then, this oldie was still a goodie. No wonder. *C/D*'s test L82 ran 0-60 mph in 6.6 seconds, 127 mph flat out, and the standing quarter-mile in 15.3 seconds at 95 mph. Who said Detroit performance was dead?

Weighty gas guzzlers were a dying breed, however, victims of the new CAFE standards that meant the Corvette would have to be put on a diet sooner or later. *Car and Driver*, among others, had been urging *sooner*. They got their wish with some first-stage measures that slimmed the 1980 'Vette by some 250 pounds. The differential housing and front-frame crossmember were switched from steel to aluminum, and greater use was made of plastics throughout the car. The aluminum intake manifold previously used on the L82 engine was extended to the base L48, which in federal trim lost five bhp to emissions tuning—back to 190 bhp at 4400 rpm and 280 lbs/ft torque at 2400 rpm. However, the L82 actually *gained* another five horses—up to 230 in all. California's increasingly stringent emissions standards forced buyers there to

settle for a detoxed 180-bhp 305 small-block, available only with automatic transmission.

Also in the interest of better mileage, the previously optional front and rear spoilers were slightly reshaped and made integral with the bodywork, and the grille was raked back slightly. As a result, the coefficient of drag (Cd) fell from 0.503 to a more respectable 0.443—still not great, but a welcome improvement. Confusingly, the 1980 brochure also boasted of "functional air exhaust vents...added to the front air vents. They're black in keeping with the many other styling accents"—ad-speak for less exterior chrome. Removing the crossed-flags emblems from the front fenders may have been taking things a little *too* far, though.

Other 1980 changes included newly standardized air conditioning and tilt/telescope steering wheel, relocated power door lock buttons, and a speedometer calibrated to only 85 mph—yet another government mandate. Finally, the two behind-the-seats storage compartments were combined, though the battery remained in its separate cubbyhole directly aft of the driver.

The weight-saving measures came none too soon, for early 1979 brought another fuel crunch in fulfillment of earlier prophesies. OPEC had less to do with this energy crisis than the overthrow of the Shah of Iran, but its effects on Americans were much the same: increasingly tight supplies of ever-more expensive fuel that sent the car market and the national economy as whole into a tailspin. Once again, the future of America's sports car looked dubious. Yet the Corvette continued to ride high. Although model-year volume was down some 20 percent from '79, the 1980 tally of 40,614 units was still quite respectable for a heavy, thirsty, specialty car that had become almost too expensive—now $13,140 base—for many of those most likely to buy it.

As had been true since the very beginning of the Shark generation, press opinion of the 1980 Corvette

The big news regarding the 1980 Corvette (above) was that it had shed 250 pounds as part of GM's quest to meet CAFE standards. This was accomplished by using more aluminum and plastic in place of steel. A subtle restyling also helped fuel economy a bit. Featured were a more laid-back grille and smoothly integrated front and rear spoilers. Cd improved from a miserable 0.503 to a more respectable 0.443. The interior (left) saw a few subtle changes: the power door-lock button was relocated and the two storage compartments behind the seats were combined, with the battery remaining in a separate cubbyhole behind the driver.

Chevrolet claimed that the 1980 Corvette (both pages) had "a recognizably new, aerodynamic appearance," and certainly it did look smoother. The hood, in particular, showed a lower profile. The Rally wheels, sporting trim rings and center caps, rode on P225/70R15 SBR tires. The line drawings (opposite center) show details of the Corvette front end with the headlights up (left), the hidden compartment behind the passenger seat (center), and the T-top roof panels mounted on the rear deck.

was mixed. First, though, it's worth recording the key performance stats obtained by the three major "buff" monthlies, all of which somehow ended up testing four-speed L82s:

	Car and Driver	Motor Trend	Road & Track
0-60 mph (sec)	7.6	7.1	7.7
0-1/4 mi. (sec)	15.9	16.2	16.0
mph @ 1/4 mi	88	86	87
top speed (mph)	123	NA	124

Such close results are about what you'd expect. Yet none of the three seemed that enthusiastic anymore. *Motor Trend*, for example, had "misgivings" about the slenderizing measures—especially the "lighter-duty" rear axle—and the greater overall emphasis on fuel efficiency. But they did concede the obvious by breathlessly observing that "the 1980 Corvette is in fact a Corvette, standing proud, the final survivor of the visionary philosophy of a bygone time. Though there are other cars that now represent a challenge to the Corvette's traditional performance supremacy, none of them look like it, make you feel the same when you drive them, or have the same effect on bystanders. People treat you differently when you arrive in a Corvette. The car's appeal has completely transcended its mechanical capabilities, which are still considerable, and acts directly on the psyche of the buyer. It is still a symbol of...status and is for many the shining goal of a misty dream."

As ever, *Road & Track* was more precise and evenhanded: "The engine, its transmission and tall 3.07:1 final drive aren't the great whomping powertrain of yore, but the assemblage certainly will propel the Corvette along in fine ticket-gathering style, if this happens to be your thing. You will need a good credit rating with OPEC, though, because the Corvette's

14.5 mpg in ordinary driving [is] hardly what we'd call fuel-efficient. The... suspension continues to thrive on nice smooth roads and on such, it'll keep up with the best of them....On rough roads or transitional surfaces, however, the car can get skittery and become quite a handful. The four-wheel ventilated disc brakes do a fine job of hauling the car down from any speed, although again, it's wise not to ask too much of them when the suspension is otherwise occupied."

R&T found little to like about Corvette workmanship in 1980, but now they also found fault with "the spirit of the car, which just doesn't appeal to us. Perhaps it simply isn't exotic enough (too common?) to excuse its shortcomings."

The general media malaise over Corvette's unchanging nature was also evident at *Car and Driver*, which groused about the sloppy execution of some details but concluded that the 1980 model was "exactly the same thing as always: America's only sports car. Since this alone seems to be enough to guarantee commercial success, there is probably little point in belaboring the Corvette's shortcomings. Suffice it to say that this is a different kind of American car. While the differences aren't always in the direction we think they should be, we're nonetheless convinced that the new-car market is a brighter place because of the Corvette. You can take that as an endorsement. Sort of."

All this damning with faint praise did little to sway Chevrolet, which knew exactly where the 'Vette should be heading. Further evidence came with a 1981 model lightened even further via more materials substitutions. Heading the list was a new monoleaf transverse rear spring made of reinforced plastic instead of steel, eliminating 33 pounds from cars with standard suspension and automatic transmission. (Cars with manual and/or the Gymkhana Suspension retained the familiar metal spring.) Other weight-saving

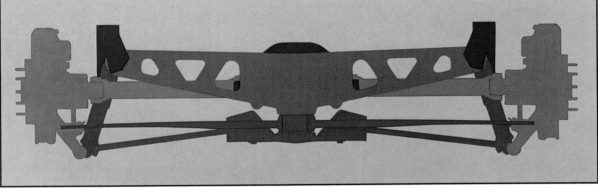

measures included thinner glass for door windows and the optional see-through T-tops, plus a stainless-steel exhaust manifold and magnesium rocker covers.

Progressively rising CAFE standards dictated that the Corvette do its bit to help GM's compliance as a whole, so the previous pair of 350 V-8s were retired in favor of a single, reworked version designated L81. With 190 bhp @ 4000 rpm and 280 lbs/ft peak torque at just 1600 rpm, it had almost exactly the same outputs as the superseded L48. Besides the aforementioned lighter components, it featured an auxiliary electric

cooling fan that allowed for a smaller, engine-driven fan, thereby reducing noise. But the big newsmaker was Computer Command Control (CCC). Also adopted for other '81 GM engines, CCC used electronics to integrate the emissions and fuel systems in order to reduce smog and fuel consumption. Toward the same ends, it tied in with the automatic transmission's new lockup torque-converter clutch. This provided a direct mechanical link between flywheel and propshaft in second and third gears at steady-state speeds, thus eliminating gas-eating frictional losses through the converter.

Changes evident in the showroom included a spiffed-up interior with a standard quartz clock and optional six-way power driver's seat, plus electronic instead of mechanical tuning for all factory radios. Prices were more eye-catching in a different way: up again, thanks to inflation, the window sticker now reading a bit over $15,000 minimum.

For some reason, buff-book editors didn't bother to test the '81 Corvette, but CONSUMER GUIDE® did— two of them, in fact. Our manual car hit 60 mph from standstill in 8.1 seconds, a mere 0.1-second slower than our previous L48 manual; the automatic '81 needed 8.9 seconds for the same sprint. None of this was surprising, as weight and engine output were little changed from the 1980 base car. However, a peak power speed lowered by 200 rpm made for "easier low-speed lugging and quicker midrange acceleration." It did little for economy, of course. As we lamented: "EPA mileage has crawled up by 1 mpg to 15. We averaged a grim 16.5 mpg overall."

Workmanship was still pretty grim as well, leading us to wonder why "Chevy can't seem to [improve things] even after all these years." Otherwise, we listed much the same pluses and minuses as the enthusiast magazines: a ride "sub-par...even by sports-car stan-

continued on page 315

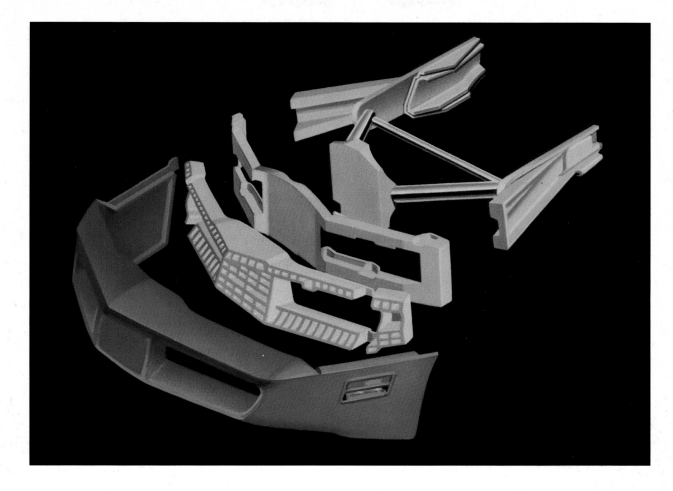

Although the price of the '81 Corvette (both pages) had crossed the $15,000 mark, 45,631 were built. Weight reduction continued as a top priority. For example, a reinforced plastic monoleaf transverse spring (opposite center) saved 33 pounds on automatic transmission models. The interior (top) was spiffed up with an optional six-way power driver's seat ($173) and a standard quartz clock. The front-end assembly (left) was both strong and light.

1978-83 Serial Spans, Production Figures, and Base Prices

Year	Serial Prefix	Serial Span	Prod.	Price
1978	1Z67J8S	100001-147667	47,667	$9,645
1979	1Z87A	400001-453807	53,807	$12,313
1980	1Z87A	100001-140614	40,614	$13,956
1981	1G1Y87L	100001-145631	45,631	$16,259
1982	1G1Y87*	100001-125407	25,407	$18,290
	1G1Y07**			$22,538

1983 No model year production

* = coupe   ** = hatchback

dards"; good handling marred by "twitchy transient responses...ready to catch the unwary in sudden direction changes"; and the aging design that made certain options almost mandatory—like the electric rear window defroster, "practically a necessity for best [wintertime] vision...."

Yet even we couldn't escape a certain conflict of emotions: "One of our testers summed it all up nicely by saying that people who want a Corvette buy one regardless of its faults, numerous though they are. It's a desirable car because of its...performance, good-to-excellent handling...and that sexy styling, of course. But it's becoming increasingly difficult to rationalize a big, heavy gas-guzzling car like this, especially one with a cramped two-seat interior and so-so quality control. In short, the Corvette appeals on an emotional, not a rational, basis."

A good many folks evidently followed their hearts. Despite a generally dismal year for the industry as a whole, Corvette again showed well in 1981, as sales recovered smartly to 45,631 units.

By far the biggest Corvette news of 1981 was the announced transfer of production from the old St. Louis plant to a brand-new high-tech facility in Bowling Green, Kentucky. Many of the loyal Missouri workers were relocated to the sleepy college community that would be the 'Vette's new home. An interesting historical footnote is that for two months during the summer of 1981, the cars were built simultaneously in both places.

A fully up-to-date paint shop was a big plus for the new factory. St. Louis had used lacquer exclusively, but Bowling Green used more automated means to apply more durable enamels as well as the new "clearcoat" final finishes, emulating European and Japanese practice. The Kentucky plant was also planned around much more automated manufacturing hardware than St. Louis could accommodate, reflecting the quest for tighter quality control. It was an expensive proposition, but Chevy evidently felt the Corvette was worth it. How things had changed!

With the opening of the Bowling Green facility, some observers concluded that Chevy was preparing for the arrival of an all-new Corvette. And they were right, of course. The existence of a new front-engine design was more or less an open secret by then. Said *Road & Track* in November 1982: "...After all these years of rumors, conjecture, glimpses of exotic mid-engine project cars, hearsay, and slightly blurred photos shot through knotholes in the Milford Proving Ground fence, we can swear with confidence...that there really is an all-new 1983 Corvette in the wings."

But testing new machinery and working out

Opposite page: Weight-saving tricks used on the '81 Corvette included the use of thinner glass and the adoption of a stainless-steel exhaust manifold. Weight now came in at 3179 pounds, down from 3448 pounds in 1977. Of the 40,606 'Vettes built for '81, some 8995 were built in the new Bowling Green, Kentucky factory. This page: Chevy called the '82 model "An enthusiast's kind of Corvette" because of its new drivetrain.

assembly procedures made more sense with a familiar design than with a new one, so the fifth generation would put in one final appearance. Using the existing platform to gain field experience with the future model's drivetrain also made sense, so the '82 Corvette was, as *R&T* put it, "truly the last of its series...a transition car [with the] new drivetrain in the old body."

That engine was still the time-proven 350 V-8, but with a newly developed twin throttle-body fuel injection system instead of a carburetor—the first production Corvette "fuelie" since 1965. Called "Cross-Fire Injection," it was very different from the old Ramjet mechanical setup. An injector unit within a carb-like throttle body was used for each cylinder bank, with a cross-over intake manifold feeding the air/fuel mixture to the bank on its opposite side. This speeded up mixture velocity for more complete combustion and hence greater thermal efficiency and power, plus reduced emissions. Computer Command Control electronics governed the duration of injector opening in response to signals from various engine-mounted sensors. Intriguingly designated L83, the Cross-Fire 350 came in with 200 bhp at 4200 rpm and peak torque of 285 lbs/ft at 2800 rpm—modest but satisfying gains over the L81.

Unfortunately, the '82 was the first Corvette since 1955 without a manual gearbox available, but the newly standard automatic had four speeds anyway— basically the previous three-speed Turbo-Hydra-Matic with a long-striding overdrive fourth gear tacked on. As before, there was a torque converter lockup effective on all forward gears save first, governed by the engine's electronic control unit.

Detail mechanical changes for '82 began with an in-tank electric fuel pump and a new solenoid-operated trap door in the hood that opened at full throttle for better breathing. The air filter, which had previously contained charcoal, reverted to plain paper. The exhaust system was extensively redesigned around a significantly smaller and lighter catalytic converter.

Cosmetic alterations were slight. Small "Cross-Fire Injection" labels appeared above the front-fender vents, and 1982's two-tone paint option recalled the '78 Silver Anniversary treatment: silver over a deep burgundy, separated by a red pinstripe.

There was reason for looking back that way, because the Shark was in its last year. To leave no doubt that

continued on page 320

Corvette Performance Comparisons 1978-82

	1978	1979	1982
Engine (cid):	350	350	350
Induction system:	Carb	Carb	Fuel injection
Bhp:	220	220	200
Axle ratio:	3.70:1	3.55:1	2.87:1
Transmission:	4-speed manual	3-speed automatic	4-speed automatic
Weight (lbs):	3490	3655	3425
Acceleration (sec)			
0-30 mph:	2.3	2.5	2.7
0-60 mph:	6.5	6.6	7.9
0-100 mph:	17.9	18.5	24.8
0-1/4-mi.:	15.2	15.6	16.1
Mph @ ¼-mi.:	95	91	85
Top speed (mph):	132	130	125
Av. mpg:	15	12	21

The front fenders of the 1982 Corvette carried "cross-fire injection" badges to announce the arrival of its new twin throttle-body fuel injection system. The revised 350 V-8—dubbed L-83—was rated at 200 bhp at 4200 rpm and 285 lbs/ft torque at 2800 rpm. For the first time since 1955, no manual gearbox was available—a four-speed automatic with lockup torque converter did the shifting.

At $22,538, the '82 Collector Edition earned the distinction of being the first Corvette to break the $20,000 barrier. It featured cloisonné emblems, special paint, and a lift-up hatch. To discourage the building of bogus Collector Edition cars out of regular Corvettes, Chevrolet wisely fitted special vehicle ID plates. Perhaps because of the faltering economy, and perhaps because a new model was known to be close, the last of the "big 'Vettes" saw output of 25,407 units, the lowest since 1967. Of these, only 6759 were Collector Edition models.

319

The 1982 Collector Edition (both pages) was built only as needed to fill customer orders, not as a fixed proportion of production. It featured a unique silver-beige metallic paint scheme; graduated shadow-like contrasting paint stripes on hood and body sides; bronze-tint glass roof panels; and finned, cast-aluminum wheels styled like those first seen on the '63 Sting Ray. The exterior cloisonné emblem also graced the steering wheel (above right). The revised 350 V-8 (above) utilized Command Control electronics to run the fuel injection system.

the end of an era was at hand—the last of the "big" 'Vettes—Chevrolet issued another commemorative special for '82, tellingly titled "Collector Edition." However, recalling its experience with the bogus '78 Pace Car Replicas, the division handled the '82 series differently, building the Collector only "as needed" to satisfy customer orders and not as a fixed proportion of scheduled production. Unique vehicle identification number plates were affixed to further deter someone's turning a standard car into the Collector model.

In many ways, the Collector Edition was the best fifth-generation 'Vette of all. Setting it apart were cloisonné emblems on hood, rear deck, and steering wheel; silver-beige metallic paint with graduated shadow-like contrast striping on hood and bodysides; bronze-tint glass T-tops; and finned, "Turbine alloy" wheels like the ones first seen on the '63 Sting Ray. Inside were matching silver-beige leather upholstery and door trim, leather-wrapped steering wheel, and luxury carpeting. The most obvious external difference was the Collector's frameless lift-up glass hatch, precluded from the '78 restyle because of

cost considerations and, incidentally, *not* included on the base '82, though several aftermarket suppliers had turned to offering this as a conversion for "glassback" models.

Reflecting its name, the Collector Edition carried the dubious distinction of being the first Corvette to break the $20,000 price barrier, listing at $22,538—a far cry from the $4663 it had taken to buy a nicely equipped '68. But the anti-counterfeiting measures had their intended effect. Add in fair scarcity—a mere 6759 built—and it's clear that this Corvette might one day be the "incredible collectible" Chevy advertising said it was—er, would be.

With 10 extra horsepower and again blessed with fuel injection, the latest small-block Corvette showed definite performance gains despite being hobbled by the economy-minded automatic transmission. *Road & Track*, comparing the '82 with its four-speed '81 car, reported that the extra "power shows in quicker dragstrip numbers. The new car ran the quarter-mile in 16.1 seconds at 84.5 mph and accelerated from 0 to 60 in 7.9 seconds. The pre-wundermotor did it in 17.0

at 82 mph and 9.2 seconds. At last, relief from years of backsliding. And throttle response is excellent. In the 1983 Corvette, predicted to be at least 500 pounds lighter than this year's 3425-pound car, it should be a very nice engine." The injection also improved economy a little and deterred most owners from making anything remotely like hot-rod modifications.

The return of "fuelie" power and the Shark's imminent demise moved *Car and Driver* to run a comparison test of two "last-of-their-kind" Corvettes: "Old Red," a restored '62 convertible with manual four-speed and the injected 360-bhp 327, and a "New Blue" '82. It was an entertaining perspective on the march of Corvette progress since the Sting Ray, even if

321

its conclusions were foregone. The '62, *C/D* reported, was wild and woolly, the '82 smooth and sophisticated. Both were fun and exciting but in different ways, each reflecting the very different priorities and technology of its time.

"The answer to the riddle that set this adventure rolling," *C/D* summed up, "is yes. The 1982 Corvette is still a sports car. The Flash Gordon fenders are a bore, the curb weight needs a 10-percent chop, and a five-speed transmission would be a joy. But we've got to hand it to the old girl: New Blue could inhale pavement when its pedal was pushed.

"And we found Old Red more fun than a high-school class reunion. It's not every day we get to work with a 6300-rpm redline and launch ourselves to 60 mph in six seconds [the '82 was two seconds slower] ....What more could you ask for than a chestful of that big 'competition-type' steering wheel, a handful of

Major Specifications: 1982 Corvette

Body/Chassis

Frame:	Box-section steel, ladder type with five crossmembers
Body:	Glass-reinforced plastic, 2-seat coupe
Front suspension:	Independent; upper and lower A-arms, coil springs, tubular hydraulic shock absorbers, anti-roll bar
Rear suspension:	Independent; lower lateral arms, axle halfshafts as upper lateral arms, trailing arms, transverse leaf spring, tubular shock absorbers, anti-roll bar
Wheels:	8 × 15-inch cast alloy
Tires:	P255/60R-15 Goodyear Eagle GT

Dimensions

Wheelbase (in.):	98.0
Overall length (in.):	185.3
Overall height (in.):	48.4
Overall width (in.):	69.0
Track front/rear (in.):	58.7/59.5
Ground clearance (in.):	5.0
Curb weight (lbs):	3425

Engine

Type:	ohv V-8, water-cooled, cast-iron block and heads
Main bearings:	5
Bore × stroke (in.):	4.00 × 3.48
Displacement (ci):	350
Compression ratio:	9.0:1
Induction system:	GM "Cross-Fire" dual throttle-body fuel injection
Brake horsepower @ rpm:	200 @ 4200
Torque @ rpm (lbs/ft):	285 @ 2800

Driveline

Transmission:	4-speed automatic
Gear ratios:	First—3.06:1
	Second—1.63:1
	Third—1.00:1
	Fourth—0.87:1
Rear axle ratio:	2.87:1
Steering:	Saginaw power-assisted recirculating-ball
Turns lock-to-lock:	2.6
Brakes:	11.75-inch ventilated discs front and rear; 461 sq. in. effective lining area

Performance

0-50 mph (sec):	5.8
0-60 mph (sec):	8.0
0-90 mph (sec):	19.0
0-¼ mi. (sec):	16.0
Speed @ ¼ mi. (mph):	83
Top speed (mph):	125
Fuel consumption (mpg):	19-21

close-ratio shifter, and the solid-lifter serenade rattling your eardrums?"

If nothing else, we can hope that the passing years are as kind to us as they were to the fifth-generation Corvette. Besides rising prices in its long 15-year career, it had seen two restyles, the demise of big-block engines, significant performance losses and slight performance gains, and the addition of more and more creature comforts. Yet for all that, it never lost its essential character. As *R&T* noted in 1982: "No matter how much luxury...you pack into a Corvette, the basic honesty of the car rises above its own image. It tells you this is an uncompromised two-seater with a big engine and that it's made to go around corners and come out of them fast. The car has its own particular flavor and appeal, and the automotive world would lose a great deal if the Corvette were to become too much like other automobiles."

Chevy wasn't about to let that happen, of course. Yet perhaps because a new model was known to be near, and aggravated by an ailing national economy, production fell to 25,407 units for '82, the lowest Corvette total since 1967.

It was a disheartening finish for a motorcar as remarkable as the Shark, but one that was tempered by thoughts of new beginnings with an even more remarkable motorcar. The long wait was over: The next Corvette was ready.

The long-running fifth-generation Corvette saw many changes. Besides rising prices, it had seen two restyles, the demise of the big-block engines, significant performance losses and slight gains, and the addition of more and more creature comforts. Yet for all that, the essential character of America's sports car had survived. Road & Track said of the '82 that "No matter how much luxury...you pack into a Corvette, the basic honesty of the car rises above its own image." But now the long-awaited sixth-generation Corvette was ready, and a new era was about to begin.

CHAPTER 11

1984-89:
THE NEXT GENERATION

Winter was definitely on its way. Southern California was being whipped by a fair-sized late-fall storm, and though the skies were clearing as we approached Ontario International Airport that afternoon, the plane's descent was even bumpier than the departure from our home base in Chicago had been. But any airborne queasiness was more than outweighed by anticipation, for CONSUMER GUIDE® had been invited to Riverside Raceway for the formal press introduction of the first new Chevrolet Corvette in 15 years. It was November 30, 1982, and history was in the making.

Few cars have been more eagerly anticipated. This was not just another new model but a new *Corvette*—an automotive institution re-cast for the Eighties and maybe the Nineties. No wonder it had long been the subject of intense speculation by journalists and widespread debate among enthusiasts.

We already knew that this new Corvette would be a 1984 model, not an '83 as widely predicted. The reason, we would later learn, was that the mid-model year introduction made certifying the car as an '84 more convenient (if tougher) in terms of emissions and fuel-economy standards. Still, we couldn't help thinking how cheated Corvette fans—and more than a few historians—would feel at being denied a Corvette of any kind in the car's 30th anniversary year. At least Chevy wouldn't have to bother with another potentially troublesome birthday commemorative.

But who cared what year it was: The new Corvette really *was* here at last. It had been a very long time coming, so great things were expected of it. The automotive world had seen sweeping changes since the last generation 'Vette was born. Fuel economy standards were now a fact of life—and law—and materials, labor, and petroleum products had become much more expensive. Along the way, America's sports car had ceased being the ultimate wheeled possession for many people. The Porsche 928, Ferrari 308, Lotus Esprit, and a raft of machines even cheaper than the 'Vette—Datsun Z, Mazda RX-7, *et.al.*—had considerably raised the standards by which sports cars were being judged. How would the new Corvette fare against such respected rivals? Equally important in the minds of many, how would the sixth generation compare with its illustrious predecessors? Would it be worthy of the hallowed Corvette tradition, and would it be able to preserve that heritage in the demanding, competitive atmosphere of the Eighties?

After several design and manufacturing delays, which only served to heighten interest, the new Corvette was publicly unveiled in the early spring of 1983. As at the Riverside press introduction, the general reaction was a mixture of relief and unrestrained excitement. The '84 was, thank goodness, still a Corvette in appearance and mechanical layout, yet was startlingly and entirely new—completely up to date and oozing high technology from every pore of its fiberglass being. In certain ways, it wasn't exactly the car some had expected, but it was obviously a car to be respected.

The press was quick to give the '84 its due. Said *Car and Driver* in March 1983: "You have waited long enough....The new Corvette is a truly stout automobile.

It is all that the fevered acolytes so desperately wanted their fiberglass fossil to be—a true-born, world-class sports car loaded with technical sophistication....The roadholding on this new machine is so advanced that we recorded the highest skidpad lateral acceleration—0.90 g—ever observed with a conventional automobile by this staff. That figure practically trivializes the previous high-water marks...generated by such exotics as the Porsche 928 and assorted Ferraris....[The new Corvette] is the hands-down fastest American automobile, capable of 140-mph top speeds, 0-60-mph times under seven seconds, and 15.2-second quarter-mile forays...one of the half-dozen fastest production automobiles in the entire world."

Echoed *Motor Trend* that same month: "All the qualities it needed to have, it has in great abundance. Stylish appearance? Obviously. Fresh engineering? Just look. Proper comfort? But of course. Formidable performance? Stand back. There may be no better way to see the USA. Mission accomplished."

Said *Road & Track*: "There's a great deal of thoughtful design evident in this new Corvette, quite enough to bring it to the attention of those who felt the previous versions had become increasingly tacky. Is it

After 15 long years, a new Corvette finally bowed for 1984. The sixth generation 'Vette (both pages) faced stiff competition, but it measured up as a world-class competitor—one of the half-dozen fastest production automobiles in the world.

corvette

1983 CORVETTE

now the best exotic car in the world? The best exotic car value? Its performance levels...stack up very well with those of the Ferrari 308GTSi or Porsche 928. Or should we measure the tremendous market pressure the Corvette puts on less expensive high-performance cars?....Resolution of these questions awaits proper comparative testing, but three things are clear: The new Corvette is abundantly more than an updated clunker to any of us, the questions posed are far from trivial, and the car's enthusiast appeal is immensely broad."

Work toward the sixth generation began in earnest in mid-1978, shortly after General Motors management canceled plans for a production version of the mid-engine Aerovette (see previous chapter). This development program involved the closest collaboration between Engineering and Design yet seen at GM. The chief collaborators were Corvette chief engineer David R. McLellan and designer Jerry Palmer, then head of Chevrolet Production Studio Three. Their close liaison was vital if the new model was to be built with a high level of quality—important, because the new 'Vette

Despite all the labels (both pages), there was not to be a 30th-anniversary 1983 Corvette. And even though it might have been contemplated, a turbo 'Vette was not in the cards either. After a half dozen years of planning and development, the '84 'Vette emerged as the logical successor to the fifth-generation model, but much improved in almost every respect. Jerry Palmer, chief designer, saw to it that the new model still looked like a Corvette, but it was smoother, leaner, and more aerodynamic. If it borrowed a little from the all-new '82 Camaro, nobody really noticed, because the new Corvette had a look all its own.

Major Specifications: 1984 Corvette

Body/Chassis

Frame:	Unitized steel/aluminum "birdcage"
Body:	Glass-reinforced plastic, 2-seat coupe
Front suspension:	Independent; unequal-length upper and lower A-arms, transverse fiberglass leaf spring, tubular hydraulic shock absorbers, anti-roll bar
Rear suspension:	Independent; upper and lower trailing arms, lateral arms, tie rods, halfshafts, transverse fiberglass leaf spring, tubular hydraulic shock absorbers, anti-roll bar
Wheels:	Unidirectional cast-alloy; 8.5 × 16-inch front, 9.5 × 16-inch rear
Tires:	Goodyear Eagle VR50, P255/50VR-16

Dimensions

Wheelbase (in.):	96.2
Overall length (in.):	176.5
Overall height (in.):	46.7
Overall width (in.):	71.0
Track front/rear (in.):	59.6/60.4
Ground clearance (in.):	5.0
Curb weight (lbs):	3200

Engine

Type:	ohv V-8, water-cooled, cast-iron block and heads
Main bearings:	5
Bore × stroke (in.):	4.00 × 3.48
Displacement (ci):	350
Compression ratio:	9.0:1
Induction system:	GM "Cross-Fire" dual throttle-body fuel injection
Brake horsepower @ rpm:	205 @ 4300
Torque @ rpm (lbs/ft)	290 @ 2800

Drivetrain

Transmission:	4-speed automatic
Gear ratios:	First—3.06:1
	Second—1.63:1
	Third—1.00:1
	Fourth—0.70:1
Rear axle ratio:	3.31:1
Steering:	Power-assisted rack-and-pinion
Turns lock-to-lock:	2.0
Turning circle (ft):	40.0
Brakes:	4-wheel ventilated discs, 11.5-inch diameter; 184 sq. in. effective lining area

Performance

0-50 mph (sec):	5.0
0-60 mph (sec):	7.0
0-90 mph (sec):	16.0
0-¼ mi (sec):	15.5
Mph @ ¼ mi:	88
Top speed (mph):	140
Fuel consumption (mpg):	16-20

would sell for considerably more than the last of the fifth-generation cars.

According to Palmer, the keynote for the '84 design was "form follows function." While many automakers had paid only lip service to that well-worn dictum over the years, both Palmer and McLellan deemed following it essential in order for the new Corvette to be competitive with more recently designed sports cars. Specifically, their task was to eliminate the deficiencies for which the fifth generation had been criticized, while at the same time maintaining the traditional Corvette look and driving feel. The new car would have to have superior aerodynamics, more passenger room, and—most important of all for a driver's car—even better handling than earlier models.

The sixth generation was thus engineered almost literally from the ground up. Both design groups began with the so-called "T-point"—the position of the seated-driver's hip joint relative to the interior and the rest of the car. This was raised an inch and moved an inch or so rearward compared to the fifth generation, which opened up more legroom and also made for a higher driving position relative to the road, contributing to better visibility. Further, the change enabled the chassis to sit higher than before for more ground clearance, though the use of 16-inch instead of 15-inch wheels and tires also played a part.

With handling a major consideration, the chassis was engineered around Pirelli's P7, then the state of the tire art, but the tire ultimately used in production was Goodyear's Eagle VR50, specifically designed for the new Corvette and sized at P255/50VR-16. The "V" designated a maximum rated speed of over 130 miles per hour, a hint of the car's performance potential. Mounted on cast-alloy wheels of 8.5-inch width front and 9.5-inch width rear, these tires were notable for their "gatorback" tread design—a deep V-pattern with horizontal slots perpendicular to the sidewalls, all of which suggested the appearance of an alligator's back. Evolved from Goodyear's Formula 1 and Indy-car rain-tire program, the design was said to shed water more effectively to resist hydroplaning, a perpetual problem with wide, low-profile rubber. The tread was designed to be effective in only one direction, so wheels were "unidirectional". The tires' radial fins were shaped to scoop in cooling air to the brakes only when turning forward. This, in turn, necessitated specific left and right wheels front and rear, none of which were interchangeable.

Complementing the new wheel/tire technology was a considerably revised chassis. The old perimeter-type ladder frame was replaced by a steel backbone design not unlike that pioneered by Lotus of England, (later to become a GM subsidiary). In the Corvette, the "spine" took the form of a C-section beam rigidly connected to the differential and carrying the driveshaft. This arrangement reduced weight and opened up more cockpit room by eliminating the transmission and differential crossmembers, and by permitting the exhaust system to be run beneath the driveshaft instead of alongside it.

Welded to the backbone was what Chevy called an "integral perimeter-birdcage unitized structure" or "uniframe," making the sixth generation the first Corvette to employ unit construction instead of body-on-frame. The "birdcage" formed the windshield and door frames, lower A-pillar extensions, rocker panels, rear cockpit wall, and front subframe. It also included a "hoop" above and behind the cockpit for additional rigidity and as a hinge point for the lift-up rear window that would be continued from the '82 Collector Edition. Galvanized inside and out for corrosion resistance,

One of the design goals for the 1984 Corvette was to make it more user-friendly. Despite its sleek shape (opposite), it had more legroom than the Shark and, relative to the road, a slightly higher driving position, which aided visibility. Much thought was given to the instrument panel (this page). The various design approaches all sported a space-age look, but the traditional tall center console was familiar to Corvette fans.

this structure was effectively a "skeleton" to which the fiberglass outer panels would attach. Completing the basic assembly were an aluminized bolt-on front suspension carrier and a bolt-on extension for the back bumper.

This more rigid platform allowed McLellan's staff to rework the suspension for greater handling precision. Front geometry was the familiar unequal-length upper-and-lower A-arm arrangement of previous years, though with a new twist. Instead of a coil spring on

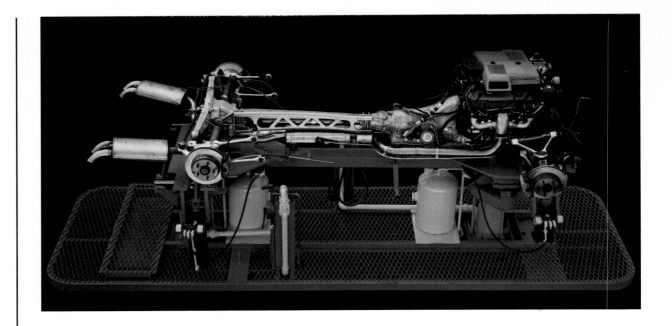

each side, a single reinforced-fiberglass leaf spring was mounted transversely between the two lower arms, as at the rear. A 20-millimeter anti-roll bar was standard, while a 25-mm. bar was included in an optional handling package designated RPO Z51.

Even bigger changes occurred out back, where Zora Arkus-Duntov's old three-link geometry gave way to a more sophisticated five-link design. This comprised upper and lower longitudinal links between the body and hub carriers, twin lateral strut rods tying the differential to the hub carriers, another transverse plastic leaf spring (as used since '81), and the customary U-jointed halfshafts and rear tie rods.

Steering was changed from GM's usual recirculating-ball mechanism to rack-and-pinion, with a forward-mounted rack for greater precision and a standard high-effort booster for better directional control at high speeds. Normal ratio was a constant 15.5:1, quite

fast for an American car; the Z51 package carried even quicker 13.0:1 gearing. A tilt/telescope steering wheel was standard.

As before, stopping power was supplied by large ventilated disc brakes at each wheel, hydraulically assisted. The brakes themselves were a new design created by Girlock, an offshoot of the British Girling company. Making extensive use of aluminum, they had large 11.5-inch-diameter rotors and featured quick-change semi-metallic pads (held by a single bolt) with audible wear indicators.

McLellan declared that "even in base suspension configuration, the new Corvette...is absolutely superior to any production vehicle in its part of the market." An extra margin of superiority was the rationale behind the Z51 option, a $51 bargain comprising heavy-duty shocks (RPO F51) and lower-control-arm bushings, uprated front and rear springs and stabilizer

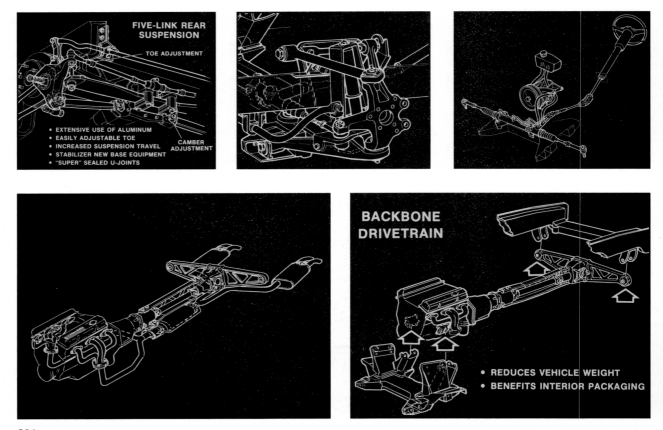

bars, plus the quick-ratio steering.

More evidence of Design and Engineering teamwork was found under a new "clamshell" hood, a part of the design concept from the beginning. Recalling Jaguar's E-Type and various mid-engine Corvette experiments, this integrated the hood with the front fender tops and lifted to a near-vertical position.

Beneath the clamshell was a familiar friend in somewhat different dress: the frusty 5.7-liter/350-cubic-inch small-block V-8 as used for 1982, with twin throttle-body electronic fuel injection and "Cross-Fire" manifolding with dual ram-air intakes. Though still designated L83, it now produced five more horsepower—a total of 205 at 4300 rpm—and five extra pounds-feet of torque—290 at 2800 rpm—via a more efficient radiator fan and accessory drive.

Dominating the underhood area was a flat-top silver-finish air cleaner created by Palmer's crew and made of die-cast magnesium. Separate vacuum-modulated doors molded into the underside of the hood regulated incoming air flow; the ducts mated with the air cleaner assembly when the hood was closed. A single air intake below the front bumper fed outside air to the underhood ducts, making the '84 a "bottom-breather" like its Shark predecessor. The entire engine compartment was color-coordinated in silver and black. Palmer even persuaded GM's AC-Delco Division to develop a suitably styled battery.

To the undoubted delight of performance fans, a four-speed manual gearbox returned after a year's absence as the Corvette's standard transmission, but it was nothing like any seen before. Called "4+3 Overdrive," it was basically an orthodox four-speeder with a second set of three planetary gears attached at the rear. When signaled by the engine's Computer Command Control electronics, the auxiliary gearset engaged through a hydraulic clutch to provide a stepdown or overdrive reduction of 0.67:1 in each of the top three gears. The result: improved part-throttle fuel economy. For best performance, engagement was electronically inhibited at wide throttle openings, but

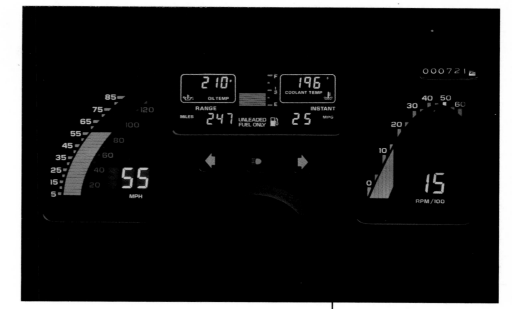

this was quickly supplemented by a console-mounted manual override switch. Standard final drive was 3.07:1, with 3.31:1 gearing available for better standing-start performance. Returning from 1982, but as a no-cost option now, was the GM 700-R4 four-speed overdrive automatic, still with a lockup torque converter clutch effective in all forward ratios save first.

Production delays postponed deliveries of the 4+3 Overdrive until early calendar '84, so the first of the new 'Vettes were equipped only with automatic. Dennis Simanaitis, engineering editor for Road & Track, called the 4+3 "a gearbox smarter than your average driver," and liked the way it worked. But he noted that "even with all [its computerized] wizardry, [fuel economy] is little different from that with the automatic. We recorded 15.0 mpg versus 15.5 for the car with the Turbo-Hydramatic, and that sounds like a wash."

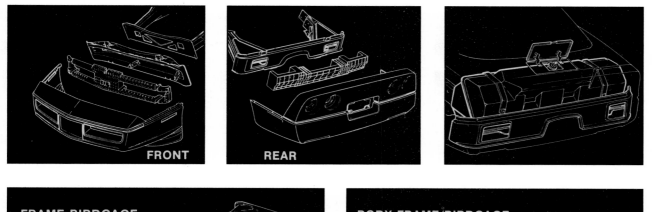

FRONT   **REAR**

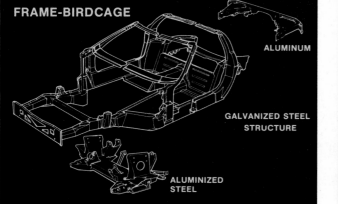

FRAME-BIRDCAGE

ALUMINUM

GALVANIZED STEEL STRUCTURE

ALUMINIZED STEEL

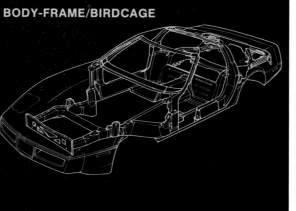

BODY-FRAME/BIRDCAGE

Opposite page: The new Corvette boasted a five-link rear suspension and rack-and-pinion steering (center). The backbone drivetrain (top and bottom) helped reduce weight and provided more interior space. This page: The front and rear bumper systems (center) also cut down on weight while meeting strict federal standards. The 20-gallon fuel tank allowed for long-distance cruising. "Birdcage" construction enhanced safety (bottom). The 1985 dashboard (top) looked just like the '84.

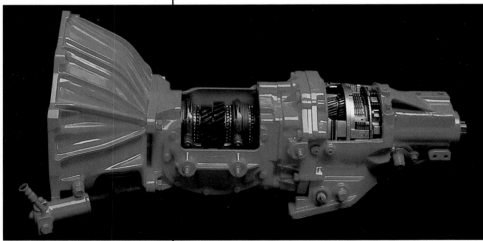

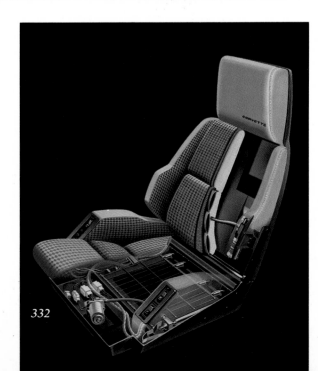

Originally, the overdrive override switch was reserved for a special export version of the new Corvette, owing to the vagaries of EPA fuel economy test procedures. Had the car been tested without the automatic engagement, it might well have qualified for the dreaded "gas guzzler tax" newly mandated by Corporate Average Fuel Economy (CAFE) guidelines. McLellan stated that the override was intended for U.S. sale all along, even though the manual cars first shown to the press didn't have it.

Still, the transmission situation brings up a telling point: Despite Chevy's considerable effort to keep weight as low as possible, the new Corvette emerged heavier than expected—by a good 300 pounds—though it *was* 250 pounds lighter than a comparably equipped '82, a worthwhile improvement.

Numerous subtle tricks contributed to this. We've already mentioned a few, but there were others, some of which marked industry firsts in the use of lightweight materials. One of these was a driveshaft and supporting yokes made of forged aluminum, welded together. Another was a radiator support made of plastic sheet molding compound (SMC). The twin transverse reinforced-fiberglass leaf springs weighed half as much as four steel coil springs of comparable size. (They were also claimed to be more durable, capable of withstanding five million full jounce/rebound cycles, versus about 75,000 for the steel coils.) Plastic was also employed for the cooling system's twin expansion tanks, radiator fan, and shroud.

Aluminum figured extensively elsewhere. Front-suspension control arms and knuckles as well as the rear lateral arms were all aluminum forgings (and beautiful to behold up front). So was the chassis' C-section "spine." The automatic transmission's torque converter housing was formed from aluminum sheet. Brake splash shields were aluminum rather than steel, and calipers were an iron-aluminum alloy that gave greater strength with less weight.

While McLellan's engineers busied themselves with technical intricacies, Palmer's staff was shaping the car in Production Studio Three. The design brief was imposing. First and most obviously, the new generation had to *look* like a Corvette; in other words, it couldn't break with the model's traditional appearance "cues." Drivelines would be carried over, and though the new model could be a bit smaller outside, it had to have more room inside. Improved outward vision and less aerodynamic drag were additional goals.

Despite all the demands, the styling job went quickly. A full-scale "theme" clay model based on a Palmer sketch was completed in September 1978. By mid-November of the following year—a scant 14 months later—the design was more or less final except for taillamps, front-fender trim, and nose contour.

Although wheels and tires were the dominant design element in all the various sketches and clay models, Palmer's team wrestled with overall proportions as much as with surface detailing. "The evolution...was a very slow, methodical one," Palmer told *Car and Driver*. "We made incremental changes—very slight. I'm talking about ⅛-inch movements, just enough to change the accent of a form or the loading of a line." A key development affecting room, drag, and visibility was Engineering's decision to mount the steering linkage farther forward than originally envisioned. By allowing the engine to ride lower in the chassis, a correspondingly lower hoodline was achieved, with better vision forward and reduced frontal area. The latter was a big contributor to reducing *effective* aerodynamic drag, which is not the drag coefficient alone but the product of the Cd times frontal area.

What emerged was distinctively new but every inch a Corvette. "I really believe we've designed a car without compromises," Palmer said, "but we've managed to retain the Corvette identity. The car still, for example, has folding headlamps [modern dual rectangular units now]. It has a Corvette 'face,' even though there are foglamps and turn lamps where air intakes used to be. The front fender vents are still there, as is the large backlight and the functional rear spoiler. The first time people see this car, they're going to know what it is...[Yet] the new car's massive surfaces, such as the hood, are deceiving. On first glance you probably wouldn't believe it is smaller than the previous year's model in every dimension except width."

Though some of those dimensions weren't changed much, proportions definitely were. Overall length was down a significant 8.8 inches despite a mere two-inch cut in wheelbase—from 98.0 to 96.0 inches—and just a 1.7-inch reduction in front overhang. The secret was the 5.2-inch chop in rear overhang, which gave the effect of a longer hood even though it was actually shorter. Another contribution was a 64-degree windshield angle as measured from the vertical—the steepest of any American production car in history. Compared to the fifth generation, the base of the windshield was 1.5 inches lower and a bit farther

forward. This, in turn, allowed the beltline to be dropped, giving the '84 a slimmer, glassier appearance.

As Palmer suggested, the biggest appearance change came from that increase in width. The old pinched-waist midsection was gone, along with the bulged front and rear fenderlines. In their stead was a smoother, more organic contour, especially when viewed from the front or rear three-quarter angle. The car retained its predecessor's flared wheel arches, which combined with the fat tires to accentuate the hunkered-down look. Fenders no longer conflicted with the beltline, which rose uninterrupted from the windshield toward a near-vertical Kamm-style tail (a modified throwback to '68) with the traditional quartet of lights. In profile, the shape was a discernible wedge—pleasing and functional in the GM idiom.

One styling element new to Corvette was a full-perimeter rub strip at roughly mid-body height. This not only tied the front and rear bumpers together visually but concealed the one major seam in the new bodyshell, as well as the shutlines around the clamshell hood.

After 15 years of Corvettes with T-tops, the '84 hardly could have reverted to a fixed roof. But the T-bar was gone, replaced by a one-piece removable panel with four attachment points—two on the

"I really believe we've designed a car without compromises," said designer Jerry Palmer regarding the completely restyled '84 Corvette (below). Features included a 205-bhp 350 V-8 (opposite top), a 4+3 overdrive manual gearbox (center), and the most comfortable seating in Corvette history (bottom). This page: The clamshell hood was a part of the design concept from the beginning (top right), and the coefficient of drag was lowered from a high 0.44 to a much more satisfactory 0.34 (top left).

windshield header, two on the rear roof hoop—the "Targa" treatment originally planned for the fifth generation. As on early Sharks, the panel stowed in special slots built into the top of the luggage bay. For added protection against vandals, the top could be removed only with a special wrench. Buyers had a choice of either a body-colored panel or a tinted transparent top made of scratch-resistant acrylic, the latter an option that was delayed until well after the car's introduction. Either top was far lighter and easier to handle than the awkward glass panes of old.

Chevy boasted that the '84 Corvette was partly

shaped in the wind tunnel. One new wrinkle in that aspect of development was the use of a sensor to compare pressure differences at various points on the car against pressure in other parts of the tunnel as the car sat in a moving airstream. According to Chevrolet, this technique yielded a detailed picture of the "actual pressure variants and vortices created by passage of the vehicle. Such an image is far more useful than is a picture of surface flow only, and Corvette is believed to be the first sports car ever designed with the assistance of such a tool." While the resulting drag coefficient was not exceptional for the day at 0.34, reduced frontal

area made the new Corvette much more slippery than that often-misleading value suggested. And even at that, the Cd number represented a useful 23.7 percent reduction compared with the '82 model's 0.44.

With its striking exterior, the Corvette needed an equally striking cockpit, and it got one. Created by GM's Interior Design group under Pat Furey, it was dominated by a space-age instrument panel and the usual tall center tunnel/console. Despite a seating position that was slightly lower than before, the cabin definitely felt more spacious and open than the fifth generation's.

Appearances were not deceiving. Despite the shorter wheelbase and a 1.1-inch reduction in overall height, the '84 offered fractional gains in head and leg room, plus a whopping 6.5-inch increase in total shoulder room, an area where the old car was decidedly tight. Cargo room was also greater, by a useful eight cubic feet or so, and was more accessible thanks to the lift-up hatch window.

Instrumentation was now directly ahead of the driver; no more secondary dials in the center of the dashboard. In fact, there were now no dials at all in the usual sense, but a jazzy all-electronic display supplied by AC-Delco. Road and engine speeds were monitored by both graphic analog and digital displays; between them was a sub-panel with digital engine-function readouts, including a permanent vertical-bar-graph fuel gauge. A quartet of switches, to the left of a bank of warning lights in the center of the dash, allowed the sub-panel to display up to four additional readouts, including instantaneous and average miles per gallon, trip odometer, fuel range, engine temperature, oil pressure and temperature, and electrical system voltage. Like other recent electronic dashboards, this one could be changed from American-standard to metric values at the flip of yet another switch.

The console also housed the heat/vent/air conditioning and audio system controls. A Delco electronic-tune AM/FM radio was standard, while a similar unit with cassette tape player was optional. But the audiophile's choice was the $895 GM-Delco/Bose system. Similar to systems offered on other recent GM cars, it featured four speakers in special enclosures shaped and placed to match the interior's acoustic properties. Not everyone liked the way the system sounded, but no other sports car had anything like it.

New standard seats were specially designed high-back buckets with prominent bolsters on both cushion and backrest, plus manual fore/aft adjustment and—at long last—reclining backrests. Full cloth trim was standard, with leather upholstery optional. Also offered at extra cost was the latest in "super seats," supplied by Lear-Siegler. These added electric adjustment for backrest angle and cushion bolster in/out, plus a powered three-stage lumbar support adjuster using inflatable bladders that could be individually air-bled to achieve the proper contour.

Several running changes were made shortly after the '84 was announced and sales began. An engine oil cooler was made standard equipment, and the originally standard 15-inch wheel/tire package was deleted, making the 16-inchers the only choice.

Meanwhile, the new Corvette was being subjected to its first full road tests, which cooled the initial enthusiasm of some "buff book" scribes. *Car and Driver* seemed to have the biggest change of heart. While most everyone described the ride as harsh, *C/D* technical editor Don Sherman had special scorn for the Z51 package: "The problem...is that it's a balls-out calibration that ruins the car for day-to-day use.... Really bad pavement sent its wheels bounding, and even minor bumps or irregularities threw the car off on a momentary tangent....In exchange for these hardships you get lightning reflexes...and imperceptible body roll."

Motor Trend's Ron Grable was more charitable, praising the quick acceleration and phenomenal handling of his manual-transmission example. But then he noted: "This level of cornering performance does not come totally without cost....The Corvette can be a harsh environment at times, on certain surfaces. For instance, you definitely want to stay out of the far right lane on freeways that have seen lots of heavy 18-wheeler traffic. The 'Vette will jiggle your eyeballs on any surface the big rigs have roughed up."

CONSUMER GUIDE® also faulted the "tough" ride—and that was with the base suspension, which though softer than the Z51 was still too stiff and jarring on patchy surfaces. CG also found "exhaust and road noise...loud at anything above idle speed, though the exhaust settles down when cruising in OD. The automatic transmission is sensitive to throttle changes in city driving, so it seems to be changing gears almost constantly. It's also slow to come out of high gear unless you really pour on the throttle."

The flashy instrumentation was also roundly criticized. *C/D's* Sherman described it as "purposely too futuristic to be appreciated by anyone mired in the twentieth century." Fellow staffer Patrick Bedard quipped that "everything about the cockpit is so George Lucas, from the glow-winkie dash to the g-couch seats." CONSUMER GUIDE® simply termed the instruments "complete and entertaining, but the bar graphs are just for color...too hard to read to be useful....The test car's panel was dimly lit on one side, and the entire display

Although some of the dimensional changes on the '84 Corvette weren't all that large, the car's proportions were definitely fresh. Overall length was down a significant 8.8 inches despite only a minor cut in wheelbase—from 98.0 to 96.2 inches—and a mere 1.7-inch reduction in front overhang. The secret was a 5.3-inch chop in rear overhang. But the real change that gave the Corvette its striking good looks was the wider, hunkier body.

Contributing to the '84 Corvette's sleekness was a 64-degree windshield angle as measured from the vertical— the steepest of any American production car in history. A perimeter rub strip completely encircled the car (both pages). The '84 still had a Corvette "face" even though the fog and turn lamps were located where the air intakes used to be.

is hard to read in sunlight."

Incidentally, the electronic setup was originally slated as an optional alternative to a beautiful mechanical/analog gauge cluster, the design for which was given—free—to Steve Blake, then the hard-pressed proprietor of Avanti Motor Corporation. Having seen the cluster there, all we can say is that it's too bad Chevy didn't offer this grouping. Marketing types had no doubt dictated the electronic dash as being more in keeping with the "high-tech flagship" image they were trying to create for Corvette—which only shows how easy it is to go *too* far.

By and large, the press had nothing but praise for the '84's performance and roadholding. Most reports showed 60 mph available from standstill in around seven seconds and handling numbers nearly untouch-able by any other series-production automobile. CONSUMER GUIDE® rendered this verdict: "More sophisticated and technically up to date than its predecessor, and a world-class sports car with few rivals in performance. You have to live with a bump-and-grind ride and plenty of noise to enjoy it, but it provides motoring thrills in potent doses."

Motor Trend's Grable mostly agreed: "The '84 Corvette is...taut, responsive, predictable, and desirable. The running changes...have addressed—and improved—a couple weak areas, areas that had been uniformly criticized. Does this mean Chevrolet is listening? We certainly would like to think so, because that bodes well for the future of this outstanding American representative in the GT arena."

That report, published in *MT*'s December 1983

issue, was one of the earliest evaluations of the 4+3 Overdrive manual, and Grable took some pains to explain it—and why the manual override control was hastily reinstated. Without it, as on the first '84s, "driving was quickly reduced to waiting to see which gear the computer wanted, and most of the time it would select OD/direct when you least expected it—or needed it." The reason for this "computer tyranny," as Grable termed it, was that the original EPA certification tests "were all completed in the automatic overdrive mode, and the mileage numbers thus generated were acceptably outside the 'gas-guzzler' classification.... Inasmuch as the vehicle was...not certified otherwise, no 'defeating' of the overdrive system was allowed.

"Since the original certification, Chevrolet has been petitioning the EPA to accept a manual lockout, [reasoning that] under conditions such as mountain driving (or any time the engine is needed to help decelerate the vehicle) the ability to lockout the overdrive would actually be a safety feature. Logic has finally prevailed, and EPA has given its permission for a 'lockout' mode...with no fuel-mileage penalty."

The result, Grable reported, "is a much more driveable car....We find ourselves using the off position for most around-town driving...The gear ratios are well fitted to the torque curve....but it is a shock when overdrive is selected; the engine just falls on its face... To cite just one example, at 60 mph in the 1.0:1 fourth gear, the engine is turning 2500 rpm (3.07:1 axle ratio). Punch the OD switch and it falls all the way to 1700."

It got worse. "In the auto-OD mode," Grable continued, "the transmission schedules are subtly different from the original...[Now] accelerating in first gear, when vehicle speed reaches 10 mph (at 18 percent throttle or less), the computer will interpret and remember the light throttle conditions as a light-load scenario, and when you upshift to second, it will give you second overdrive. If you continue the leisurely pace, the computer will maintain overdrive through the rest of the gears.

"A downshift can be forced by opening the throttle past 60 percent, after which the transmission will stay in direct drive with no further upshifts—until fourth is engaged and the other control parameters are met. In

fourth overdrive, if the car is manually downshifted (still in auto-OD) it will get third overdrive and on down to second OD. The only way out of OD at this point is to load the engine above the parameters the computer needs to give you direct."

Grable admitted that all this was perhaps "intimidating and/or confusing," but opined that the 4+3 "works very well in the real world." CONSUMER GUIDE® thought otherwise. Aside from the difficulty of trying to out-think a computer, a clunky, high-effort linkage made stop-and-go work very tedious indeed—aggravated by an equally unpleasant high-effort clutch. The transmission would also prove less than reliable, so it's no wonder that most Corvettes left Bowling

The 1984 model was the first Corvette to employ unit construction (below), which Chevy called an "integral perimeter-birdcage unitized structure." The '85 (opposite) was virtually identical to the '84. The displacement of Chevy's long-lived small-block V-8 remained unchanged for 1985 (above), but multiport fuel injection increased horsepower from 205 to 230 bhp.

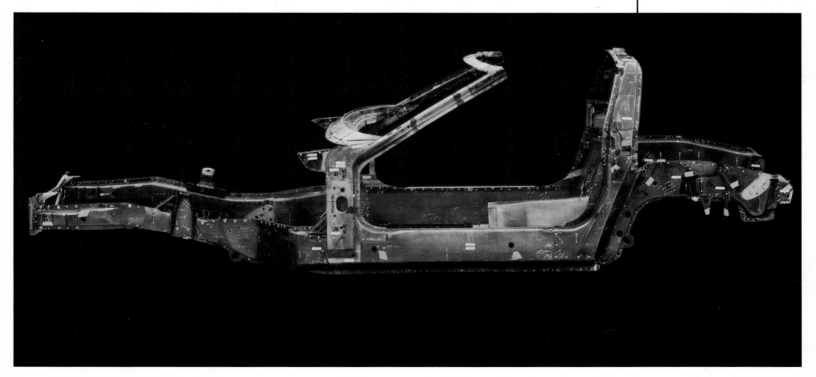

Green with automatic in 1984—and would continue to do so through 1988. Only then was the car finally given an acceptable manual gearbox.

Speaking of reliability, the sixth generation fared pretty well in an early owner's survey published by *Popular Mechanics* in November 1983. To be sure, researcher Mike Lamm found "glitches," but not enough "to dampen the enthusiasm of most 1984 Corvette buyers....Brand-newness turned out to be one of the car's main attractions." Other reasons cited for purchase included styling (nearly 57 percent of those responding), performance (21.5 percent), handling (16.9), and "past experience" with a 'Vette (24.1 percent).

Reported problems generally weren't serious—just the "teething troubles" common to most new-design cars. Engine V-belt pulleys tended to loosen and fall off on about 10 percent of the cars in the *PM* survey, knocking out the smog pump and rendering the engine inoperable. More serious was the tendency of the front brake calipers to shed their restraining bolts, which prompted a recall of the first 10,000 '84s in early July. Other complaints involved unexpectedly loud brake squeal (21.7 percent of those owners responding), body rattles (especially around the lift-off roof section, 13.1 percent), difficult entry/exit (9.1 percent), faulty power window motors (20 percent), miscellaneous trim bits coming adrift, and lack of readily available replacement parts (6.3 percent). "They talked about just [these] little things," Lamm said, "but on these more minor items only 51.8 percent gave workmanship a mark of excellent, while 15.1 percent graded it average to poor."

The *PM* survey also showed that some 20 percent of the early-'84 owners complained about a rough ride, but only 12 percent wanted it changed. Interestingly,

7.5 percent longed for more horsepower. "There weren't many comments about the LCD digital instrumentation," Lamm observed. "A few owners mentioned that the displays wash out in bright sunlight, but no one seemed unduly annoyed." Fuel consumption (all the cars surveyed had automatic) averaged out to 16.6 mpg city and 22.8 mpg highway.

Despite their peeves and problems, the *PM* survey group heartily endorsed the new '84: 79.1 percent said they'd buy another Corvette versus only 7.8 percent who said they wouldn't. Remarkably, this positive response came despite a certain amount of price-gouging reflective of another kind of endorsement: high buyer demand. The median price paid by the buyers in *PM*'s sample—excluding destination, tax, license, etc.—was nearly $3000 above the suggested $21,800 base. "A few early customers spent as much as $30,000," Lamm reported. "On the other hand, several GM employees (who happened to be among the owners we surveyed) got their new 'Vettes for as little as $19,000."

Needless to say, the excitement of being able to buy a really new Corvette for the first time in 15 years made the '84 a fast sellout. Helped by an extra-long model year, volume zoomed back over the 50,000 mark, the total coming to 51,547—the second highest in Corvette history and almost double the disheartening '82 tally. There was even another production milestone, observed in November 1983 with completion of Corvette number 750,000.

By happy coincidence, the sixth-generation Corvette arrived at about the time the U.S. economy began recovering from its early-Eighties doldrums. What had been an oil shortage was unexpectedly replaced by an oil glut that pushed gas prices way down. With

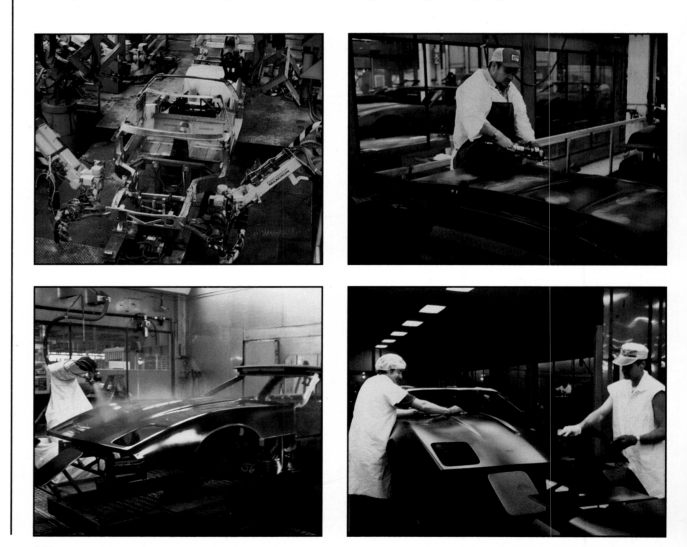

Pavlovian predictability, buyers went scurrying back to big V-8 cars and as much good old Sixties-style performance as Detroit could muster. Motown moved fast and a "hot car" revival was soon underway, another reason the '84 Corvette sold so well despite higher-than-ever prices. The Reagan Administration had also been helping out, convincing Japanese automakers to voluntarily limit their car exports to the U.S. via the Voluntary Restraint Agreement (VRA). In this new, more hospitable climate, American performance was

flourishing anew by mid-decade, and Chevy wasted no time in turning up the Corvette's wick.

In fact, things heated up the very next year, as the sophomore 1985 model arrived with "Tuned Port Injection" written where "Cross-Fire Injection" had been. That minor alteration signaled a major engine change. Although the time-honored Corvette small-block still measured 350 cubes, the substitution of multi-port fuel injection with tuned intake runners, along with a half-point compression increase to 9.5:1,

Although Chevy had begun turning out Corvettes at its new Bowling Green, Kentucky, plant in 1981, the facility was really planned with the sixth-generation Corvette in mind. Many of the loyal workers from the St. Louis plant were relocated to the sleepy college community that would be the 'Vette's next home. A key advantage of the new plant was its more advanced paint shop. And in the quest for tighter quality control, which the Corvette badly needed, the Kentucky factory used more automated manufacturing hardware.

343

lifted output dramatically. Horsepower rose by a healthy 25 to reach 230 bhp at 4000 rpm, and torque improved by no less than 40 lbs/ft, going from 290 at 2800 rpm to a meaty 330 lbs/ft at 3200. So extensive were the changes that Chevy was moved to use a new engine designation: L98.

As *Road & Track* explained it, the new Tuned Port Injection, basically the German Bosch system, employed an intake manifold "designed so that incoming air is collected in a plenum that sits on top of the engine." The name came from the "tuned runners [that] curve out from the plenum, then run under it to the [individual] intake ports. Essentially, each runner stacks a column of air just above each port, and this is rammed into the combustion chamber when the intake valve opens. The Bosch injection system also uses a hot-wire airflow sensor that has better throttle response than last year's vane meter." Because it metered fuel so much more precisely, TPI "should realize an 11-percent increase in fuel economy," *R&T* observed, "though the EPA label may not reflect this because of a more conservative labelling process that starts with the 1985 model year." Sure enough, the label stayed the same, the '85 earning the same 16-mpg city rating as the '84.

Responding to all those complaints about harsh ride, Chevy softened up spring and shocks rates on both the standard and performance Z51 suspensions for '85. The latter now came with larger-diameter fore and aft stabilizer bars to maintain total roll stiffness with the softer calibrations, plus 9.5-inch-wide wheels at the front as well as the rear, Delco-Bilstein shocks of the new gas-pressurized type—available as a separate

option with the base suspension—and a revised heavy-duty cooling system.

Of course, engineers were still interested in handling. The Z51 package was fine-tuned by Corvette development engineer John Heinricy to be "our Showroom Stock GT car," according to McLellan, referring to a hotly contested class in SCCA racing. Intriguingly, the suspension changes lowered ride height on the '85 by an imperceptible ¾-inch—enough to drop the drag coefficient to 0.33 and, with the 3.07:1 axle, raise top speed to a genuine 150 mph. This year's standard axle was an even taller 2.73:1—too tall for the car to pull 150 mph. For better straightline stability at three-figure speeds, steering caster angle was increased one degree (to four). For better stopping ability from high speeds, the brake system was fortified with a larger master cylinder and booster, as well as different pads imparting more braking power and improved feel.

Transmission-wise, the 4+3 Overdrive manual received a heavy-duty 8.5-inch differential ring gear (up from 7.9 inches) for extra longevity, as well as an override button more conveniently placed atop the shift knob. To make the overdrive less busily intrusive, the computer was again reprogrammed. Toward the same end, the electronics governing the automatic transmission's lockup torque converter clutch were also revised.

Cosmetics and convenience weren't overlooked. Instrument graphics were reworked for improved legibility, and leather upholstery became optional for the extra-cost Lear-Siegler seats. Finally, Chevy began eliminating the sources of the rattles and squeaks that

The exterior appearance of the
'85 'Vette remained
unchanged, except that the
"Cross-Fire Injection"
badging gave way to "Tuned
Port Injection." The extra
horsepower improved
acceleration, and top speed
came in at about 150 mph.

had so plagued the '84. Engineer Walt Banacki proposed some 200 small structural changes throughout the car, and Chevy claimed 90 percent of these had already been made for the '85.

"Though the tightly knit Corvette engineering team is always loath to admit their car has *any* failings," said *Car and Driver* in December '84, "the fact is that they've spent the past eighteen months worrying over just about every major system under the Corvette's tight skin." As a result, the '85 was judged a vastly improved Corvette. "...Every change is in the right direction," *C/D* bubbled. "In fact, the new 'Vette is so good it makes your heart soar."

The magazine sampled two cars—an automatic with the base suspension and a Z51 manual—and found both to be "tight and solid indeed." The former ran 0-60 mph in 5.7 seconds and the standing quarter-mile in 14.1 seconds at 97 mph—"a full second quicker in both tests than last year's car. The manual is no slouch, either, with a 60-mph charge of six seconds flat and a quarter-mile of 14.4 seconds at 95 mph... And they just keep on going, all the way to an honest 150 mph.

"In fact," *C/D* went on, "the new Corvette makes great numbers in any direction. Roadholding is up at the 0.84-g mark for both versions....Braking from 70 mph is in the 182-to-185-foot range, some of the shortest stopping distances around....Our test cars even managed respectable gas mileage...the automatic delivering 16 mpg, the manual coming in at 17."

So what wasn't to like? Well, the Z51 suspension was still "shaded toward the race-car end of the performance spectrum," as *C/D* put it. "It strikes most of us as a little too stiff, too quick-steering and too nervous on beat-up two-lane pavement....But the base-suspension model is the Corvette we wished for in the first place...so fast and so sure-footed that [for] minimum expenditures of time and adrenaline, the Corvette may be the absolute top of the heap in America....Best of all, the Corvette now does all this without ever hammering on you.

"Oh, sure, it's got rough spots," *C/D* concluded. "The digital dash is still not as good as a top-flight analog setup. The manual shifter sounds trashy....The brakes still don't seem to have the endless high-speed reserves of Porsche binders. And we doubt whether the long-term quality of the Corvette body structure and trim pieces is up to the level of the German brands. On the other hand, there's a lot to be said for a car that can run with the very best GTs in the world, in any contest or on any road, with the same kind of confidence and poise, and deliver it all for a fraction of [their] cost....The Chevrolet Corvette has finally arrived."

Those sentiments were echoed by *Road & Track*, *Motor Trend*, and most other "buff" publications. Even the normally skeptical British found something to like. *Autocar*, for example, said ride was "at the bottom of the [GT] class, by a long way, and also refinement. [The Corvette] is also not the easiest car to drive really fast over a winding, bumpy road—but it is immense fun. It doesn't shine as a long-distance tourer...but drive it quickly over a give-and-take road for an hour, and you know you are living. We loved it, naughty as it is, and would certainly give it house room in our collection of contemporary classics."

For all that, 1985 model-year sales took a steep plunge, dropping to 39,729, the lowest annual total since grim 1975. This was something of a shock to many at Chevrolet Division. After all, the sixth-generation 'Vette might have to last until the millennium. But the drop was at least partly due to 1985's whopping price increase—up to about $24,400. Alas, prices would go even higher for 1986.

But that year's hike—to just over $27,000—was more than justified by the inclusion of several new standard features. Prime among them was Corvette's first anti-lock braking system (ABS), the latest ABS II setup from Bosch in Germany. Like earlier Bosch systems offered by BMW and Mercedes, as well as GM's own new system designed in collaboration with the German Alfred Teves company, this prevented wheel locking in panic stops by "pumping" the brakes rapidly, but at a rate far quicker than even the best driver could manage—up to 15 times a second.

Briefly, modern computer-activated ABS systems comprise an electronic control unit (ECU), a hydraulic modulator, and sensors to monitor wheel rotation (typically one sensor per wheel, though some installations, including Corvette's, have one sensor keeping tabs on both back wheels). Whenever the ECU detects one or more wheels decelerating more quickly than the others, as signaled by the sensors, it interprets this as a locked-up condition and actuates the modulator, which reduces line pressure to the affected brake until the wheel again starts rotating normally. In practice, pressure modulation during panic stops is accomplished in very rapid on/off cycles. A fast judder or "pulse" action that can be felt through the brake pedal alerts the driver that the system has kicked in.

Because a locked wheel cannot be steered, it's easy to see why ABS has been hailed as one of the greatest "active safety" devices ever invented—one to rival the disc brake itself. "The whole [Corvette] system weighs only about nine pounds," reported *Car and Driver* in October 1985, "and it's worth every ounce....[It's] undetectable in normal driving. But if you apply the brakes on slippery pavement, or if you are forced to brake hard while trying to execute an *in extremis* evasive maneuver, the Corvette will tiptoe to a stop, its four wheels locking and unlocking in an uncanny, computer-controlled syncopation that almost eliminates brake-induced skids. We found that it is indeed possible, despite Chevy's claims, to make the car spin if one is foolish enough to mash the brake pedal while cornering hard, and it is said that ABS is not the hot tip on undulating gravel roads [true—making GM's decision not to fit a defeat switch a little curious], but for the normal driver encountering rain-slicked streets, ice, or sleet, or in emergency straightline stops on dry pavement, it is an answered prayer." Though the brake system was otherwise as before, ABS moved the sixth-generation 'Vette even closer to being the true world-class sports car Chevy said it was.

Making '86 Corvettes safer from thieves was VATS, short for vehicle anti-theft system, a new standard feature designed to augment the existing burglar alarm. The idea was simplicity itself. A small pellet with a specific electrical resistance was imbedded in the ignition key and had to be read by a hidden electronic "decoder" box (Chevy wouldn't say where it was, of course) before the engine could be started. Use the wrong key and the decoder shuts down the starter relay and fuel pump for at least two minutes before allowing another try. "A VATS-equipped 'Vette will have one of 15 resistance values [and 2000 mechanical codes—30,000 possible combinations] in its system," a Chevy press release explained. "A would-be thief will be faced with the prospect...of plugging as many as 15 resistors into the circuit until he finds the right one. The average defeat time by trial-and-error has turned out to be about 15 to 20 minutes—considered enough to deter most thieves."

Indeed, figures later compiled by the Automobile Club of Michigan would show that while the theft rate for 1984 and '85 Corvettes was better than seven percent, the "pass-key" system reduced it to less than one percent for 1986 models—and to near *zero* for 1987-88s. It was enough to prompt the Michigan AAA and other insurers to reduce their comprehensive premium rates for Corvettes so equipped by 20-25 percent—happy news for owners.

Next to ABS and VATS, other changes in the '86 were comparatively minor. A switch from cast-iron to aluminum cylinder heads plus careful weight-paring elsewhere took some 125 pounds off curb weight, making for the first sub-3000-pound 'Vette in about

Although the '85 Corvette (bottom) was a spectacular performer and a terrific handler, testers found the revised suspension still too stiff for day-to-day use. Nonetheless, the slippery shape (opposite) and the potent V-8 (below) provided plenty of excitement. But sticker shock had set in, and with prices at $24,873, many couldn't afford the tab.

20 years. However, Chevy made the new heads a little too thin, and they had to be thickened again when durability testing revealed that cracks could occur around the head attachment bosses under high engine loads. Though delayed until about the middle of the model year, the new heads were worth waiting for, incorporating centrally located copper-core spark plugs for better combustion, plus larger intake ports and sintered-metal valve seats. The exhaust system was also revised, taking on triple catalytic converters.

For all this, though, output of the L98 engine was unchanged.

Other '86 alterations included the addition of a third stoplamp per new federal decree—centrally mounted just above the backlight and rather too prominent—and wheels given raised hub emblems and a bright brushed finish. In a rather silly weight-saving measure, fuel capacity on automatic cars shriveled by two gallons to 18. Instruments were re-angled as an aid to daytime legibility (which

remained difficult all the same), and the cluster now contained an upshift indicator light that helped drivers achieve maximum mileage by signaling when to shift. (Oddly, the indicator light came with the automatic transmission, too.) Standard tires were upgraded to P245/VR50-16s; the Z51 package continued with P255s.

But the happiest event of 1986 occurred at mid-model year with the return of the Corvette convertible—the first in 11 years—announced just in time to

be chosen as pace car for that year's Indy 500. The revival didn't do much for model-year sales, which slipped to 34,937, of which just 7264 were ragtops. Still, it was a heartening sign to all those traditionalists who'd keenly felt the absence of a factory-built Corvette convertible.

Chevrolet stated that the sixth generation had been designed with a topless model in mind, so the transformation from coupe to convertible was straightforward. With an eye to preserving torsional stiffness

Convertible production was underway by January 1986. Since all '86 ragtops were considered Indy Pace Car Replicas, each one came with pace car decals, but the buyer decided whether or not to put them on.

in the absence of a fixed roof, reinforcement was applied to the frame crossmember ahead of the engine; larger K-shape braces were used to connect the under-engine member to the frame rails; and X-braces were added to tie door-hinge pillars to the rear chassis torque boxes. Cowl structure, including the steering column, its mounts, and the dashboard mounting beam, were all strengthened, as was the front torque box. A crossbeam was added atop the rear torque box and the steel riser behind the seats became a sturdier, double-wall affair. A center stoplamp neatly integrated into the top of the back panel did nothing for rigidity, but looked infinitely better than the coupe's roof pod.

All this was engineered with help from American Sunroof Company, with whom GM had collaborated on its recent Cadillac Eldorado, Buick Riviera, Chevy Cavalier, and Pontiac Sunbird convertibles. The result was a new drop-top Corvette that weighed only some 50 pounds more than the coupe and actually proved stiffer. Steve Kimball reported in *Road & Track* that

"when body engineer Bill Weaver was asked if [the convertible's] reinforcements could be added to the coupe, he smiled and said it's being looked into." Sure enough, some coupes got the treatment for '87.

Per tradition—and recalling the days of less costly Corvettes—the convertible's top folded manually beneath a rigid, lift-up cover. It was also quite easy to fold, as we discovered. The convertible also had its own suspension—with no options available—about midway in stiffness between the standard and Z51 setups. However, the Z51's 9.5-inch-wide wheels were standard for the ragtop, along with Delco's new smoother-riding deflected-disc shock absorbers. Recommended tire pressures were slightly lower than the coupe's, and ride height was a nominal 10-mm higher to maintain ground clearance with the new chassis-stiffening members. Kimball reported that the rejiggered suspension "allows some wallowing at high speeds, but this is only in comparison with the Corvette coupe."

Bowling Green turned out the first of the new Corvette convertibles in January 1986. All of those built for that abbreviated model year were considered "Indy Pace Car Replicas" and were supplied with the expected regalia decals for owner installation. Although the full range of standard colors was available to buyers, the actual Indy pacers were bright yellow.

With the convertible selling for about $5000 more than the coupe, Corvette was beginning to encroach on territory occupied by some very exotic sports and GT cars, and many observers felt that America's entry still lacked the refinement this market demanded. But there was scant little else to criticize. Mused John McGovern of Britain's *Motor* in August 1986: "It's nice to know that even after 33 years, the Corvette hasn't become a plain Jane car and can still produce strong feelings in people, even those very close to its development and production. Long may it continue to do so."

United again, the coupe and convertible saw several praiseworthy changes for 1987. Chevy's continuing quest for reduced engine friction in the interest of both performance and economy resulted in roller bearings for the hydraulic lifters and rocker-arm covers with raised rails to forestall oil leaks. Thanks chiefly to the former, horsepower went up by 10, to 240 in all, and torque improved by 15 lbs/ft, for a total of 345. A new six-way power passenger's-seat option appeared (matching the standard driver's item), and major body and mechanical components were given special identification marks to further foil thieves.

Chevy also announced a newly optional electronic monitoring system that warned of low air pressure in any of the four tires. A drop of as little as one psi below the preset limit was detected by a pressure sensor within each wheel. The sensor was combined with a small radio transmitter that in turn activated a dashboard light. Altogether, the sensors/transmitters and other components weighed less than two pounds. Though similar in concept to the system on Porsche's super-

Opposite page: The 1986 pace car replicas (top) were available in the full range of standard colors, but the actual car that paced Indy was painted bright yellow. The coupe (bottom) sold for $27,027. This page: Quality control continued to be a major goal in 1986 (top). Chevy's first Corvette convertible in 11 years (bottom) listed at $32,032. Traditionalists loved it.

Production came in at 7315 units for the '86 Corvette ragtop (both pages). The coupe was far more popular—27,794 were built. Total output was down to 35,109 units, caused largely by the fact that 'Vette prices kept climbing, although it was still cheap by exotic-car standards. The '86 pace car (opposite bottom) was the first street-legal car to lead the pack at the Indy 500 since the '78 Corvette.

high-tech 959, the Corvette's was postponed two full model years by development and manufacturing bugs.

Another development did materialize as planned: a second suspension option for coupes only. Designated Z52 and priced at $470, this was essentially a softer version of the Z51 package, with the wider (9.5-inch) wheels, plus a solid and thicker front anti-roll bar, the new gas-charged shocks, quick-ratio steering, and all but one of the chassis stiffeners developed for the convertible. A thicker-core radiator and a second electric cooling fan were also included. Spring rates and bushings were those of the base chassis. The racing-oriented Z51, listing at $795 for 1987, had all the Z52 hardware but much stiffer springs and front lower-control-arm bushings, plus a solid (instead of link-type) rear stabilizer. "To discourage dilettantes from electing this option," observed *Car and Driver*, "it is not available with either the automatic transmission or the convertible body style."

C/D compared the three suspensions in its June 1987 issue, and its observations are worth mentioning: "On smooth California roads, the base car felt almost plush; its suspension oozed over small bumps and stroked gently over larger ones. The Z52 didn't filter out tiny imperfections quite as well, but [its] stiffer chassis...was definitely a benefit over rougher pavement, practically eliminating the base car's front-end quiver and chassis flex. On most California roads, the two suspensions were about even in comfort, but we know from experience that the Z52 is the better choice for the pockmarked roads of the Midwest." The Z51 was termed "significantly harsher" than the other two but "wasn't terribly uncomfortable on smooth roads." As expected, it made for a "noticeably more direct" connection between the pilot and the pavement.

Intriguingly, *C/D* found handling differences less pronounced. "...The three Corvettes produced nearly identical skidpad numbers. The base car circulated very neutrally at an impressive 0.86 g. The Z52 'Vette felt similar while cornering at 0.87 g. Like the base car, it understeered a touch under power, then very gently swung out its tail as we eased off the throttle. In contrast, the Z51 car worked its front tires much harder, and easing off the gas had little effect. It cornered at 0.86 g with much greater understeer." In short, something for everyone.

Summing up, *C/D* picked the Z52 as the best choice for all-round use. "It provides excellent handling and a good ride, and it works on just about any road surface. On the best roads, the base car rides a bit better than the Z52, without much loss of performance....The Z51 shouldn't be considered for everyday street use, unless you drive only on perfect pavement."

C/D didn't bother with acceleration in that particular test, but *Motor Trend* timed a manual-shift 240-bhp roadster at 6.3 seconds 0-60 mph and clocked the standing quarter-mile at 15.11 seconds and 93.8 mph. *Road & Track* got similar numbers for its like-equipped ragtop, and editor John Dinkel raved about most every aspect of the car—except price. Of course, the sixth generation had never been seen as a performance-for-money bargain like Corvettes of yore, but that was even less true now, with the coupe starting at $30,000 and the convertible at close to $33,200. Then again, Dinkel wrote, "the 'Vette will outhandle, outbrake, outperform and 'out-look' a variety of more expensive European exotics. So if you put that...price into perspective, you'll discover you truly are getting a world-class high-performance sports car at a reasonable price."

Still, those loftier new stickers must have scared off some potential purchasers, because Corvette sales

The '87 Corvette (both pages) saw few changes, and most of them were found under the hood: roller lifters reduced friction losses, rocker arm covers were given raised rails to forestall oil leaks, and the spark plugs were moved closer to the center of the combustion chambers for improved fuel-burning capabilities. Horsepower rose modestly to 240, but torque jumped from 290 lbs/ft to a stump-pulling 345. Pop-up headlights were still part of the Corvette package.

354

continued their downward trend, sliding to 30,632 for model year '87. The one bright spot was the convertible, which gained some 3400 sales despite its higher price, suggesting that the 'Vette had indeed moved up into that rarefied realm of "money-no-object" buyers.

Chevy marketing studies tended to support that conclusion, and it's interesting to note the changes in Corvette buyer demographics with the advent of the sixth generation. Consider these survey results for buyers of the 1982, '84, and '87 models:

Model	1982	1984	1987
Average age	35	40	40
Median income	$44,350	$67,200	$83,000
% male	NA	84	82
% married	NA	59	84
% 4-yr. college degree	NA	46	53
% white-collar jobs	NA	75	59

None of this is really surprising. As car prices go up, buyers tend to be older people with more of the education necessary to hold down a job that pays well enough to afford the car in the first place. Yet the 'Vette was hardly appealing only to the Olds and Buick crowd now. A 1985 Chevy survey showed fully 32 percent of Corvette buyers in the 25-34 age bracket, another 44 percent in the 35-44 group (up 10 percent from the '82-model figure).

As long as we're talking research, the sixth generation was giving fair accounts of itself in various long-term magazine tests and owner surveys, reflecting the yearly "second thoughts" measures. For example, *Popular Mechanics*, in an October 1985 follow-up to its initial 1984-model poll, found that owners of 1985 models had 20 percent fewer complaints about mechanical problems and nine percent fewer gripes about ride comfort. However, opinions on overall workmanship and needed design changes were little different.

By contrast, *Car and Driver*, which lived with an '85 for 30,000 miles, reported in February 1987 that "nagging electrical failures, the frequent need for new brake pads and tires, and the squeaks and rattles that developed over the miles gradually undermined our affections....A car that costs nearly $30,000 shouldn't burden its owner with the problems our test car had. On the other side of the ledger are the sheer g-joy the Corvette delivered to us on a daily basis and the charisma of a torquey engine, a rumbly exhaust, and a pop-top two-seater. There is simply nowhere else where one can buy so much performance and personality for less than $40,000."

Road & Track had somewhat better luck with its manual-shift '86 Z51 coupe, though again the news was mixed: "Compared to other long-term cars, the 'Vette retained a healthy 65-percent resale value....[But even with that] figured into the mix, the car still ended up costing about 38 cents for each mile driven....Further analysis, however, shows [that] high figure to be misleading....Even though it maintains a high resale value, an expensive car—like the Corvette—will [always] cost substantially more per mile after one year than a car that costs less yet has a relatively low resale value....With the...Fun Factor...measured in...the car is all profit."

For its fifth season and the Corvette's 35th anniversary year, the sixth generation was again treated to important engine and chassis upgrades. Freer-breathing cylinder heads and a reprofiled camshaft gave the L98 small-block another five bhp—245 in all. Torque was unchanged. The big news was literally that: an optional

17-inch wheel/tire package, RPO QA1. Also included with the Z51 and Z52 packages, this comprised newly styled 17 x 9.5 "Cuisinart" rims wearing huge, P275/40ZR-17 Goodyear Eagle GTs. Enthusiasts were quick to note the tires' "Z" speed rating—good for sustained running at over 149 mph. The new wheel styling was also applied to the standard 16 x 8.5-inch rims, which were likewise upgraded to Z-rated rubber of 255-mm section.

To make the most of the new super-performance tires and for better directional control in hard stops, front suspension geometry was reworked to incorporate

The '87 Corvette could be ordered with an optional electronic system that monitored tire pressure to within one pound of a preset figure. Anti-lock brakes were standard, a good safety feature for a car that could top 150 mph. An anti-theft system also was standard; it disabled the starter and fuel pump if the car was tampered with.

"zero scrub radius." This means a steering axis that intersects the road at the exact center of the tire's contact patch, rather than outboard (positive scrub radius), as on previous Corvettes or inboard of it (negative scrub radius) as on some European cars. Rear suspension was also revised, with slightly more rebound travel and reduced camber for improved straightline and braking stability. Brakes were fortified, too, gaining two-piston front calipers, thicker rotors all around, and a handbrake integral with the rear discs, (replacing the previous small, separate drum brakes).

Like Porsche's 928, the sixth generation had always had its pull-up handbrake mounted outboard of the driver's seat, with a lever that could be folded down after engagement so as not to interfere with entry/exit. This was retained for '88, but the whole assembly was moved a bit lower and farther back to be even less intrusive. For the coupe only, interior air extractors were modified for increased flow rate to enhance the effectiveness of the climate system, which was now offered with the extra-cost automatic temperature control that was phased in toward the end of 1987 production.

With total Corvette production nearing 900,000 units over 35 years, it was time for another birthday special. Recalling the Waldorf debut of the original '53 Motorama car, the anniversary car bowed at the New York Auto Show on April 1, 1988, with announced production of only 2000 units.

Offered only as a coupe, the 35th Anniversary edition (officially, option package Z01) was quite striking, with a bright white lower body (including color-matched door handles, mirrors, bodyside moldings, and 17-inch wheels) set off by a black roof hoop and transparent black acrylic roof panel. Special commemorative badges appeared above the front-fender "gills," and as embroidery on the seatbacks in an all-white leather-upholstered interior. Other standard features included dual six-way power sports seats, automatic climate control, the GM-Delco/Bose audio system, and heated door mirrors. A pity it wasn't done as a convertible, but you can't have everything.

Or can you? Looking at all that Chevy had done in the first five years of the sixth generation, one could easily agree with *Road & Track* and *Car and Driver*, both of which termed the '88 the best 'Vette yet. "Chevrolet has worked hard to refine this newest Corvette," wrote *R&T*'s Lowell Paddock, "and the result is a fine machine indeed." After five years, the rough-riding, roughly built car of 1984 had been honed and polished to a fine, brilliant edge—a speedy, suave

continued on page 360

357

Corvette International: ASC's Geneve Show Car

Dreamy-eyed car nuts have never been able to keep their hands off of Corvettes, and that's been just as true for the sixth generation as any previous model. ASC's Geneve was a case in point. First shown soon after the mid-1986 revival of the production Corvette convertible—and loosely based on it—the Geneve, like so many other non-GM Corvette specials over the years, represented an alternative vision of America's sports-car legend.

Headquartered in the Detroit suburb of Southgate, Michigan, ASC Incorporated consists of three interrelated operating companies. Its American Sunroof branch, ASC's original core business (hence the initials), supplies sunroofs and other products to the automotive aftermarket. A second division, Automobile Special Company, builds limited-production models, including convertible conversions, for the major Detroit producers and other clients, as well as one-of-a-kind concept vehicles to demonstrate its design and engineering capabilities. A third component, Aeromotive Systems Company, provides the consultant design and engineering services that often lead to limited editions and one-offs.

ASC spearheaded Detroit's early-Eighties ragtop revival by collaborating with Ford and Chrysler as well as GM in the engineering and production of several "factory" convertibles. Besides the E-body Buick Riviera/Cadillac Eldorado convertibles of 1982-85 and the J-body Chevrolet Cavalier/Pontiac Sunbird models offered since 1983, ASC also figured heavily in creating the reborn convertible Corvette.

The Geneve took that effort a step further as "a three-dimensional demonstration of how advanced design elements can be integrated with pure practicality to create a car that surpasses the expectations of either." Specifically, it was "developed as a hybrid of ASC's advanced design concepts and the current production-model Corvette . . . a one-of-a-kind study in engineering possibilities."

ASC's primary focus was interior and exterior design. Outside, the Geneve was reminiscent of the Corvette Indy (see separate sidebar), particularly its low, gently curved nose. The rear blended sixth- and late fifth-generation styling elements, and was notable for a modest, neatly integrated horizontal "winglet" that picked up where the rear deck left off. A third stoplight utilizing high-intensity LEDs was mounted centrally in the thin-section spoiler—one of the most unobtrusive treat-

ments of this federally mandated device yet seen. Equally modest, and also evocative of the Indy, were race-inspired rocker-panel skirts that continued around the nose and tail. Functional front-fender air vents were similar in shape to those of late fifth-generation production 'Vettes. Door handles and LED fore and aft side markers were blended into full-length body moldings color-keyed to the vivid red paint. A black Cambria-cloth top stowed beneath a traditional Corvette-style hard tonneau behind the cockpit.

The cockpit itself was similar to the familiar sixth-generation design but made lavish use of leather. Steering wheel, instrument panel, and console were all covered in black hide. So, too, were the "sculptured" seats —special contoured affairs with charcoal suede inserts, integral "hoop" head restraints, and "Geneve" written in red on the upper backrests. Everything was tied together visually by a console armrest that swept up to a rear cockpit bulkhead trimmed to match the seats.

Mechanically, the Geneve was 1987 Corvette, and thus fully driveable. Power was supplied by the aluminum-head, 230-horsepower version of the 5.7-liter Corvette V-8 with Tuned Port Injection; transmission was the familiar four-speed overdrive automatic. Foreshadowing a 1988 development were 17-inch-diameter aluminum wheels supplied by Kelsey-Hayes and wearing special Z-rated Goodyear Eagle GT radials—big 275/40s in front, massive 315/35s at the rear. Other production features included Bosch anti-lock brakes and the GM "pass-key" anti-theft system.

According to ASC design director D. Mark Trostle, the impetus for creating the Geneve "was to combine the excellent engineering characteristics of the present-day Corvette chassis with a new evolutionary exterior and interior design. With the cooperation of General Motors Design staff, we were able to take creative license in merging our interpretation of the future design trends of Chevrolet with the chassis of a car that has proven to be world class."

Pretty though it is, however, the Geneve is not the shape of the upcoming seventh-generation Corvette, which at this writing is likely to appear around 1993. GM seems to have something more radical in mind—something like the Corvette Indy, in fact. Still, the Geneve stands as a handsome tribute to the 1984 Jerry Palmer design that inspired it, and to the artistry and skill of ASC that created it.

The 1987 Corvette Geneve was built off a production chassis by ASC Incorporated to test "advanced design concepts" on both the exterior and interior of the sixth-generation Corvette. It sported two rear spoilers, one above and one below the tail, and flush-mounted quad taillights (below).

GT that demanded comparison with any other regardless of origin. The reborn convertible was merely the crowning touch for an increasingly lustrous gem.

What's more, the sixth generation was continuing Corvette's winning ways on the track—the undefeated class champion in SCCA Showroom Stock racing for three straight years (see Chapter 13). The only possible thing left for 'Vette fans to wish for was increasing, rather than decreasing, sales. Alas, the downturn continued for 1988, with production slipping to just under 23,000 units, the lowest model-year total since 1972.

By 1989, the Corvette—like many of its longtime devotees—was approaching middle age an enormously successful, thirty-something baby-boomer that had weathered many changes through turbulent times. The 36th edition of America's oldest surviving sports car was the most exciting in years (though that's always

been a relative term when applied to Corvettes). As Chevy chief engineer Fred Schaafsma told the press in the summer of '88: "A lot of Corvette enthusiasts have been awaiting the technological marvel known as ZR-1 ever since word began filtering out three years ago. But even if we didn't have the ZR-1...the 1989 Corvette [would still] go down as heralding a new chapter in the increasing sophistication of the high-performance sports car. Anyone who has the privilege of owning and driving the '89 'Vette can feel confident in knowing they're in the best 'Vette we've ever built."

A significant car in its own right, the ZR-1 makes use of an intriguing new suspension option and a completely different manual transmission with *six* speeds instead of five, both also available for the stan-

continued on page 364

The '88 Corvette (both pages) boasted new wheels and tires. Goodyear Eagle GT P245/ 60VR15 tires came standard, but a buyer could order 275/ 40ZR17 Eagles as part of the $1295 Z-51 handling package. The suspension was modified and the engine was tweaked to 245 horsepower. The ragtop (opposite) listed at $32,085; the coupe (this page) sold for $27,165. Leather sport seats cost $1025; a blue or bronze removable roof panel added $615 to the bottom line.

Major Specifications: 1988 Corvette

Body/Chassis

Frame:	Unitized steel/aluminum "birdcage"
Body:	Glass-reinforced plastic, 2-seat coupe and convertible
Front suspension:	Independent; unequal-length upper and lower A-arms, transverse fiberglass leaf spring, tubular hydraulic shock absorbers, anti-roll bar
Rear suspension:	Independent; upper and lower trailing arms, lateral arms, tie rods, halfshafts, transverse fiberglass leaf spring, tubular hydraulic shock absorbers, anti-roll bar
Wheels:	Unidirectional cast-alloy, 9.5 × 16-inch
Tires:	Goodyear Eagle ZR50, P255/50ZR-16 (P275/40ZR-17 with optional Z51 and Z52 handling packages)

Dimensions

Wheelbase (in.):	96.2
Overall length (in.):	176.5
Overall height (in.):	46.7 coupe, 46.4 convertible
Overall width (in.):	71.0
Track front/rear (in.):	59.6/60.4
Ground clearance (in.):	4.7
Curb weight (lbs):	3333-3298

Engine

Type:	ohv V-8, water-cooled; cast-iron block, aluminum heads
Main bearings:	5
Bore × stroke (in.):	4.00 × 3.48
Displacement (ci):	350
Compression ratio:	9.0:1
Induction system:	Bosch multi-port fuel injection
Brake horsepower @ rpm:	245 @ 4300
Torque @ rpm (lbs/ft):	340 @ 3200

Drivetrain

Transmission:	"4 + 3" overdrive manual	4-speed overdrive automatic
Gear ratios:	First—2.88:1	First—3.06:1
	Second—1.91:1, 1.30:1 OD	Second—1.63:1
	Third—1.34:1, 0.91:1 OD	Third—1.00:1
	Fourth—1.00:1, 0.68:1 OD	Fourth—0.70:1

Rear axle ratio: 2.59:1/2.73:1 std. coupe/convertible; 3.07:1 optional
Steering: Power-assisted rack-and-pinion, 15.5:1 standard ratio (13.0:1 with Z51/Z52 handling packages)
Turns lock-to-lock: 2.4
Turning circle (ft): 40.5
Brakes: 4-wheel ventilated discs, 11.5-inch diameter; Bosch ABS II 3-channel anti-lock braking system; 184 sq. in. effective lining area

Performance*

0-50 mph (sec):	4.2
0-60 mph (sec):	5.6
0-90 mph (sec):	13.0
0-100 mph (sec):	16.3
0-¼ mi (sec):	14.3
Mph @ ¼ mi:	95
Top speed (mph):	154
Fuel consumption (mpg):	14-18

* May 1988 *Car and Driver* test of Z52 coupe with automatic and 3.07:1 axle

*CONSUMER GUIDE®
described the '88 Corvette
(opposite) as "an overt
performance car that appeals
mainly to driving enthusiasts
and Corvette fanatics" and
said it had "neck-snapping
acceleration" and "superb
handling." Chevy dealers
offered a GTO fiberglass kit
(above) in 1988, part number
10051200, to dress up any '84
or newer 'Vette. It had the
"swoopy appearance of the
IMSA-GTO racer that
debuted this past season."*

dard Z98 models. The ZR-1 is thoroughly detailed in Chapter 12, but we shouldn't overlook the other significant developments for the '89 model year.

An important one is the standardization of the previously optional Z52 package. This means that all '89 Corvettes, coupe and convertible alike, have the fast-ratio steering, 17-inch wheels and tires (the 16-inchers were dropped entirely), Delco/Bilstein gas-charged shocks, and fortified front-end structure. We should also note that the Z51's engine oil cooler, heavy-duty radiator, and auxiliary radiator fan are also included on cars with the six-speed gearbox. The optional tire-pressure monitoring system delayed from '87 finally reaches production, and the new Multec fuel injectors from the LT5 ZR-1 powerplant are applied to an otherwise unchanged L98 engine.

Appearance and accoutrements haven't been forgotten. Both the standard cloth seats and the extra-cost leather-covered sport jobs are restyled, the latter restricted to cars with the ZR-1 or Z51 options.

Upholstery materials have also shifted a little.

Last but not least is something that convertible fanciers have been asking for ever since the open Corvette's mid-1986 revival: a bolt-on hardtop. Thoughtfully designed to fit any sixth-generation convertible and boasting a convenient single-bolt attachment, this is a composite affair engineered with help from ASC, Inc., which also supplies it from a new plant near the Corvette factory in Bowling Green. It's made of fiberglass-reinforced polyester resin over rigid urethane, molded around a steel/aluminum "cage" and coated with polyurethane inside and out. A cloth headliner and window weatherstripping are included, as well as an electrically heated rear window (which plugs into the rear-deck socket provided for the soft-top's heated backlight). Because it's being phased in as an "interim option," the hardtop is hard to come by in '89 but should be readily available in future years.

Yes, the future, because the story of America's sports car legend is far from finished.

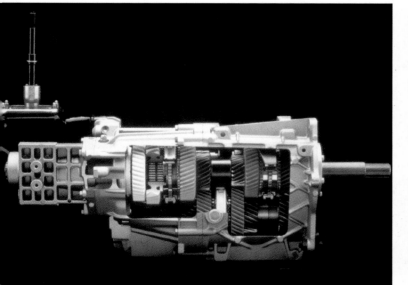

Opposite page: The '89 Corvette convertible (top) sold for $36,785; the coupe (bottom) went for $31,545. This page: A fiberglass removable hardtop with a heated glass rear window (top and bottom right) made its appearance later in the model year. Also new was a ZF six-speed stick shift (bottom left) and an FX-3 Selective Ride Control System (only with manual shift and the Z-51 handling package). It could be adjusted to Touring, Sport, or Competition settings.

Callaway Twin-Turbo Corvette: GM-Authorized Aerobics

Chevrolet's interest in TurboVettes didn't end when the fifth generation did in 1982. If anything, the advent of the slipperier new sixth-generation design intensified turbo development efforts within the Corvette Group, as Dave McClellan's crew still tried to make their car fully competitive with the fastest exotics Europe could muster. The result was a new Regular Production Option for 1987 designated B2K: the Callaway Twin-Turbo Corvette. It wasn't cheap—a formidable $19,000 above the cost of a new Corvette coupe. But by most accounts, this super-performance conversion was cheap at twice the price.

As *Car and Driver* related the story, the Callaway originated in May 1983, when Chevy contracted with Specialized Vehicles Incorporated (SVI), a consultant engineering firm in Troy, Michigan, to develop a turbocharged version of the then-new 4.3-liter Chevy V-6 as a possible Corvette option. Though essentially an extension of the division's own work with the experimental Twin-Turbo V-6 (see previous chapter), the project was plagued by numerous technical troubles. Accordingly, Chevy dropped the idea in October 1984, but asked SVI to proceed with a twin-turbo version of the 350 V-8, which was in hand the following January.

A few months later, *C/D* technical editor Don Sherman was approached by Reeves Callaway, who since 1977 had built his one-man garage in Old Lyme, Connecticut, into a thriving business by developing and marketing turbocharger systems for various Volkswagens and Porsches, as well as the BMW 3-Series. Callaway wanted to know how to win such business from Detroit. Sherman referred him to Chevy chief engineer Don Runkle.

In May 1985, Callaway introduced his turbo conversion for the Alfa Romeo GTV-6. It piqued GM's interest, and he was asked to evaluate SVI's twin-turbo V-8. Callaway judged it good but not particularly practical for production. By August, McLellan had visited Callaway's facilities, and SVI had completed its contract, having built and tested 16 examples of its dual-blower engine. The very next month, Callaway was contracted to develop a prototype of his own, with Chevy targeting 400 horsepower, 450 pounds/feet torque, 0-60-mph capability of five seconds or less, a quarter-mile of 13 seconds, and top speed of at least 170 mph. The car was ready in December and was well received by an inspector from McLellan's team. Within six months the Callaway package was in Chevy's RPO catalog and available through selected dealers—complete with the same factory warranty given other Chevys, from Cavalier to Caprice.

As expected from Callaway Turbosystems, its Corvette conversion was thoroughly thought-out and professionally executed. It began with a stock Corvette—coupe or convertible—delivered from the Bowling Green plant with the "4+3 Overdrive" manual gearbox and top Z51 suspension package. Callaway then installed what amounted to a brand-new engine. For extra reliability under pressure, this was based on the sturdier block of the LF5 truck version of the 350 V-8, with four-bolt main bearings and a crankshaft of forged steel instead of the Corvette's usual cast-iron crank. The main bearings were honed and aligned, and everything else was balanced and blueprinted.

Next, pistons were changed to forged units supplied by Cosworth in England to a Callaway design. Dished piston tops lowered compression to 7.5:1 from the 9.5:1 of the 230-bhp L98—the usual precaution observed with turbocharging to minimize the risk of damaging detonation (knock). The stock camshaft and aluminum cylinder heads were retained in the interest of meeting emission standards; so were the stock electronic ignition and Rochester Tuned Port fuel injection. The latter, however, was supplemented by Callaway's "Micro Fueler II," an auxiliary fuel-enrichment device (mounted under the dash) that compensated for the extra air volume delivered by the turbos.

Of course, Callaway's special-ly designed induction system was the heart of it all. It comprised a pair of Warner-Ishi IHI turbochargers (RHB52Ws) fed by new-design exhaust headers. Twin NACA ducts were cut into the hood to help the engine breathe fresh air. As in Chevy's own twin-turbo experiments, using two smaller blowers instead of a larger single unit had the advantage of less rotational inertia for faster throttle response (less "turbo lag"). In line with the latest turbo technology, each blower had its own integral wastegate, water-cooled center bearing, and air-to-air intercooler, again for reasons of longevity as well as for maximum thermal efficiency. The wastegates were set to pop open at maximum boost pressures of 10-12 psi. Completing the package was a reworked exhaust system with twin "warm-up" catalytic converters fed from a single main converter.

The results of all this were a 50-percent increase in horsepower—to 345 bhp at 4000 rpm—and a near 41-percent gain in torque—from 330 lbs/ft at 3200 rpm to a meaty 465 lbs/ft at 2800. Although the Callaway missed Chevy's horsepower goal by a wide margin, it easily met most of the other stipulations. *Car and Driver*, with an assist from 1986 Indy 500 winner Bobby Rahal, clocked 0-60 mph at 4.7 seconds, 0-100 mph at 11.6 seconds, a standing quarter-mile of 13.2 seconds at 108 mph, and a top speed of . . . only 161 mph. But then, the engine was only running on seven cylinders. As *C/D* explained, a loose spark plug that hadn't been caught in Connecticut created a hot spot intense enough to reshape an intake valve during one of Bobby's all-out runs. *Road & Track* had no such problems, running its car up to 177.94 mph on the 7.5-mile oval at the Transportation Research Center in Ohio.

As for how the Callaway fared against Europe's speediest cars, *R&T* reckoned it faster all-out than a Lamborghini Countach and Ferrari's 3.2 Mondial, 328GTS, and 412, but about two mph shy of a Ferrari GTO and Testarossa. However, as the editors were

The Callaway Twin-Turbo Corvette, RPO B2K, wasn't cheap—it cost $19,000 more than the standard 'Vette coupe. But it could go: 0-60 mph in 4.7 seconds, 0-100 mph in 11.6, and the quarter-mile in 13.2 seconds with a terminal speed of 108 mph.

quick to note, the latter two "cost $175,000 and $102,500, respectively, while the 'Vette costs about $51,000. And there's no question about legality, not to mention driveability, serviceability and durability." As Callaway's chief engineer on the project, Tim Good, told *R&T:* "We want this to be a 50,000-100,000-mile car and we don't want an owner to have to make any concessions because it's turbocharged."

There were certainly no concessions to the "Hey, lookit me!" crowd. Aside from the aforementioned hood ducts,

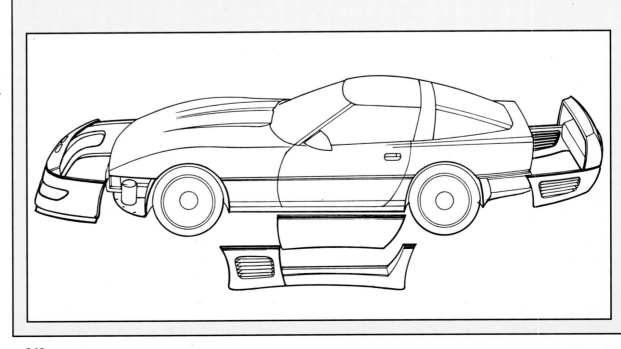

the Callaway's only visual differences were confined to discreet badges on the sides and at the rear, plus a manifold absolute pressure gauge in place of the far-left air vent at the top center of the dash.

Underhood distinctions were more pronounced. *Automobile* magazine's Jamie Kitman was impressed by the "chromed turbo plumbing, black crinkle-finished valve covers and polished aluminum for the intercoolers and the rest of the inlet tract. These complement what must already be one of the most appealing underhood views available. . . . "

Still, the Callaway was "a bit understated," as *Road & Track* observed, but only because "Chevrolet prefers it that way. Research has shown that while the performance buffs want to go as radical as possible, the conservatives among Corvette owners don't like ostentation. So, the Twin-Turbo 'Vette is the

best of both worlds—a radical car that looks essentially stock." Said project engineer Good: "This is not a car for the guy who can't decide between a Testarossa and Countach. Rather, it's a car aimed at those individuals who don't care what it says on the outside. They simply want to have the fastest, best-handling, best-braking car they can buy. We're able to give it to them. We're also proud because it's American-made."

Chevy announced its own mighty potent non-turbo ZR-1 option for 1989, but Callaway continued turning out Twin-Turbos, though at considerably higher prices—up to $26,895 for the basic package. Perhaps underlining Chevy's commitment to RPO B2K, Callaway began offering automatic transmission during 1988 as a $4500 option. This was not the stock THM 700-4R but the older, sturdier three-speed Turbo 400 unit, to which Callaway added

an overdrive fourth gear to maintain comparable fuel economy. As before, fancy wheels, audio equipment, and other accessories could boost the bottom-line cost well beyond $50,000 (still not counting the car); but excellence, like exclusivity, is never cheap. And exclusive it is, too, for Callaway production all but assures "instant collectible" status: By early 1989, a mere 342 had been built, of which 140 were convertibles.

But even if money *is* an object, the Callaway Twin-Turbo is still quite a bargain when you consider how special it is: the fastest, most potent factory-backed 'Vette since the mighty L88—a high-performance exotic with a unique all-American character found nowhere else at any price. It's a happy reminder that Detroit performance was not only alive and well in the Eighties but better than ever in most ways—just like the Corvette itself.

Road & Track *described the Twin-Turbo 'Vette as "a radical car that looks essentially stock." But one could add new front and rear body panels, as well as lower side panels (far left) to create a few subtle distinctions from a run-of-the-mill Corvette.*

CHAPTER 12

1990 ZR-1 AND BEYOND: TOWARD TOMORROW'S LEGEND

Although the sixth generation was still plenty exciting, it was just part of the Corvette story for 1989-90. The major news was another Regular Production Option destined for greatness. Called ZR-1, it denoted the long-rumored, much-discussed "King of the Hill" Corvette conceived as nothing less than the world's fastest production sports car.

The climb to such lofty aspirations was not without obstacles. Although blessed with a world-class chassis, the sixth-generation 'Vette inherited a relatively low-tech overhead-valve V-8 that had literally been left in the dust by the more sophisticated and powerful engines of European GTs like the Porsche 928S, Lamborghini Countach, and Ferrari Testarossa. Chevy chief engineer Fred Schaafsma and Corvette engineering chief Dave McLellan weren't at all happy with this state of affairs, but corporate policies, politics, and finances left them scant hope for a more state-of-the-art powerplant.

Of course, the Corvette staff *had* been working on one, capable folks that they are. In the early Eighties, Chevrolet solicited outside firms for ideas that would take small-block performance a "quantum-leap" ahead. Soon, some very interesting vehicles began appearing on the Corvette Group's test schedules, including V-6s and V-8s with twin turbochargers, and a naturally aspirated V-8 capable of up to 600 horsepower.

These efforts produced a long list of dislikes and a short list of likes. The turbo V-6 was dismissed as too noisy, harsh, and vibratory, convincing McLellan that the V-8, with its inherently greater smoothness and tractability, was the only answer. The twin-turbo V-8 garnered considerable internal support, but though 14 such cars were built and tested (leading Chevy to approve Reeve Callaway's twin-turbo 1987 conversion), the concept was rejected for factory production. After all, it wasn't exactly cutting-edge technology, and emissions and fuel consumption were both unacceptably high.

Still, these aborted efforts led to one requirement that would shape the character of the eventual ZR-1: The final product should be "Bi-Modal"—meaning it had to be quiet, docile, smooth, unobtrusive, and undemanding in routine driving, yet be able to summon race-car speed and handling at a moment's notice. In other words, a performance lion with "a pussycat personality," as Schaafsma put it.

Among the consultants Chevy called in was England's Group Lotus, world-renowned constructor of championship Formula 1 cars and a leader in high-output engine technology. Chevy had, in fact, been talking with Lotus for years. But it wasn't until the spring of 1985, when GM began negotiations to purchase the British firm, that the Corvette Group met with Lotus Managing Director Tony Rudd to discuss adapting Lotus's four-valve head technology to the 'Vette's 350-cubic-inch V-8. Somewhat surprisingly, Rudd proposed an all-new engine that would meet Chevrolet's performance, emissions, and economy targets.

With continued prodding from Chevy Engineering, and with the takeover of Lotus concluded in 1986, GM management approved a new no-holds-barred version of the classic small-block. Thus was born the powerplant Chevy labels LT5, the latest in the long and storied line of L-badged Corvette performance options.

The goals for this singular new engine were exacting:
- acceleration second to none
- superior driveability at all speeds
- fuel economy comparable with that of the existing L98 engine
- external size compatible with the existing body/chassis structure (i.e., no structural modifications required for installation)

Specific engineering objectives were as follows:
- power and torque gains of at least 50 percent over the L98
- four valves per cylinder and twin overhead camshafts per cylinder bank for superior breathing and reduced valvetrain mass
- electronic control of ignition, fuel delivery, and throttle actuation to ensure good driveability
- overall fuel economy of at least 22.5 mpg as installed
- able to meet all U.S. emissions requirements
- pleasing underhood appearance
- all the above with no compromise in reliability or durability

A tall order? Most definitely. But on paper, Lotus and the Chevrolet-Pontiac-GM Canada engineering groups have filled it superbly.

Like the L98, the LT5 is a 5.7-liter/350-cid 90-degree V-8 with 4.4 inches between bore centers. Beyond that, it's significantly different. All-aluminum construction was nothing new for Corvette engines, but here it was more or less mandatory to minimize weight and promote rapid heat dissipation in the interest of operating efficiency and fuel economy. Because the existing front frame rails could not be altered, so as to facilitate production on the normal Corvette assembly line, engineers chose an included valve angle of 22 degrees to make the four-valve V-8 as narrow as possible. At just 26.6 inches across at its widest point, the LT5 takes up no more space in the Corvette engine bay than the L98.

Unlike the Porsche 928's aluminum V-8, where the pistons run in linerless silicone-etched bores, the LT5 employs separate, "wet" cylinder liners, also of aluminum. These reduce bore by 0.1-inch compared to the L98 (3.90 versus 4.00 inches), thereby increasing stroke from 3.48 to 3.66 inches to maintain the 5.7-liter displacement. The liners are specially matched to their bores, into which they lock via a simple slip-fit. Interior surfaces are coated with Nikasil, a nickel-silicon alloy providing an extremely tough wearing surface for the lightweight cast-aluminum Mahle pistons specified.

For strength and durability, forged steel was chosen for connecting rods and crankshaft (the latter also nitrided), and the block was heavily ribbed and gusseted. The usual five main crankshaft bearings are supported by a special one-piece aluminum cradle that attaches to the block by no fewer than 28 bolts. The bearings are oversized at 70 mm, deemed necessary for reliable, sustained operation at 7000 rpm.

Proper lubrication is essential for any high-performance engine, so the LT5 crankshaft is cross-drilled for internal centrifugal oiling from the front of the crank to the conrod pin bearings and main bearing journals. A separate oil cooler with thermostatic control is fitted per usual high-performance practice. The crankcase is a two-piece aluminum assembly, with an integral pickup assuring proper feed and bottom-end oiling during hard cornering, when sloshing might otherwise leave part of the sump momentarily dry. A literally neat touch designed with do-it-yourselfers in mind is an oil filter with a one-way valve that prevents spillage during changes.

One of the most intricate and intriguing aspects of the LT5 is its unique three-stage induction system. This takes advantage of recent advances in integrated electronic engine controls and also the well-known dynamics of "natural supercharging" or pulsed "ram-effect" tuning (much like the Tuned Port Injection used since '85). A large forward-mounted air cleaner feeds a cast-aluminum throttle-body assembly with three throttle blades—a primary blade of 0.87-inch diameter and two larger, secondary blades measuring 2.32 inches across. The throttle body, in turn, connects to an aluminum plenum chamber that branches into no fewer than 16 individual runners, one for each intake port. Eight of these feed the so-called primary ports and function full-time; the remaining eight have individual throttles for supplying the secondary ports under certain conditions. Each runner has its own fuel injector supplied by twin tank-mounted electric fuel pumps and activated in sequence by the engine control module (ECM) "computer."

Air is first drawn into the throttle body and past the primary throttle blade to the plenum, from which it's distributed to the eight primary ports. In this "first-stage" mode, the secondary throttle blades remain closed below roughly 80 degrees of primary blade opening, which corresponds to about 70 miles an hour on the road. Above that, they begin opening to admit air to the eight secondary runners and ports—the full-power "second-stage" mode—provided that certain conditions are met as calculated by the ECM. These relate to throttle position, engine rpm, coolant temperature, and manifold absolute pressure. Only when the "brain" is satisfied that full power is required does it trigger the vacuum actuator that opens the secondary-runner throttles. The actuator can be manually disabled via a key in the center console; this third, "valet" mode inhibits full-power operation for temporary users like parking-lot attendants or a teen intent on "risky business."

Also per modern practice, the lengths and diameters of the 16 runners are individually selected ("tuned") to take maximum advantage of the high-pressure internal air pulses created by the opening and closing of the intake valves. The pulses increase the density of air in the fuel/air charge by forcing more air into the combustion chamber—the "natural supercharging" effect that improves cylinder filling and hence volumetric efficiency.

The LT5 arrived with "Multec" (for Multiple Technology), the latest in fuel injectors from GM's Rochester Products Division. Besides improved fuel atomizing and spray control, this design is claimed to need less operating voltage for improved cold-

From the side view (bottom), the ZR-1 differs from the regular Corvette because of its convex rear end design. Top left and clockwise: A look at the cylinder head line-bore operation; silk screening the cam covers with anaerobic sealant; the ZR-1 engine on the dynamometer; installing a camshaft cover.

weather cranking performance, and is less susceptible to clogging. The eight primary squirters are triggered by the ECM in response to signals from an engine-speed sensor and a camshaft position sensor, with firing sequence and fuel volume calculated from these and other parameters. Of course, the ECM also governs the eight secondary injectors in the full-power mode. A regulator continually adjusts fuel pressure with changes in manifold vacuum in order to maintain a constant 50.7 psi, which helps prevent unwanted fuel heating and vapor-lock problems. An ECM-governed fuel shutoff limits maximum rpm to 7200.

Almost as intricate as the induction system are the LT5's valvetrain, cylinder head, and ignition. There are four camshafts in all: two per cylinder bank, one for each set of intake and exhaust valves. Each bank's pair of camshafts is driven by a steel duplex roller chain with hydraulic tensioner. Valves are actuated directly from the cam lobes, and the intake cams have distinct primary and secondary lobe profiles to match the valve operation of the staged induction system.

Valves are canted at 11 degrees to their respective ports in a classic cross-flow cylinder head, which with four valves per cylinder results in a "cloverleaf" combustion chamber. Essentially a modified pentroof type, it allows spark plugs to be centrally placed for good flame propagation and hence faster, more complete combustion, which enhances both efficiency and emissions control. With this combustion-chamber shape and slightly dished pistons, compression ratio is a high 11.25:1, only a quarter-point below that of the Jaguar XJ-S V-12. Yet the fast-burn design coupled with electronic injection/ignition and staged induction enables the LT5 to run happily on regular unleaded fuel (87 pump octane).

GM has been moving steadily toward distributorless ignition systems in recent years, so the LT5 has one. Termed a "direct fire" type, it employs four coils, each sparking two plugs simultaneously. This, too, is coordinated by the ECM, which computes spark advance based on engine speed, manifold pressure, throttle position, and coolant temperature, plus a signal

loads. The other is CAGS—short for Computer-Aided Gear Selection—like the 4+3 a subtle extreme to eke out maximum mileage. This employs an integral-rail shift linkage with a solenoid actuator that guides the lever from first gear directly to fourth whenever the car is running at 12-19 mph with at least a partly warm engine on a throttle opening of no more than a third. It sounds silly, but it enables the ZR-1 to squeak through the EPA city-mileage test cycle without dropping below the "gas guzzler" threshold in violation of longstanding GM policy (now effectively abolished with the 4.5-liter 1989 Cadillac Allante, which *does* qualify as a guzzler).

CAGS is activated only when all three of the aforementioned conditions are satisfied, something that rarely occurs in normal driving. What's really significant is the ZF unit's vastly improved shift quality compared to the stiff, clunky linkage of the old 4+3. Driving a six-speed Corvette, standard or ZR-1, you'd almost think you were in a Japanese econobox, so light and precise is its shift action. Of course, the base L98 engine, let alone the LT5, has so much torque that you can almost leave the thing in fourth and forget about it. But you won't, because the ZF has that satisfying well-oiled feel that invites running up and down the gears purely for the pleasure of doing so.

Run quickly through those gears with your foot to the floor in a ZR-1 and you'll get phenomenal acceleration: 0-60 mph in less than five seconds, 0-*100* mph in under 11. Those numbers come from Chevrolet, which hadn't released any ZR-1s for testing at this writing. (We tried the ZF gearbox in a prototype '89 L98 convertible.) As in workaday five-speed manuals, fourth is direct drive in the ZF transmission (1.00:1), fifth a modest overdrive (0.75:1). Sixth is something else: an extremely long-striding 0.49:1 ratio giving no less than 42.5 mph/1000 rpm despite a shorter final drive (initially 3.54:1, changed mid-season to 3.33:1). Still, the car reaches maximum velocity in fifth—an estimated 180 mph at 6500 rpm.

Final word on ZR-1 performance awaits formal road tests. However, it's interesting to note that mounting criticism of Detroit's latest "horsepower race" has prompted Chevy insiders to back away from their initial "world's fastest production car" claims, and may even have prompted some doctoring of the engine's computer controls to limit top end.

Yet even if the ZR-1 proves no faster than the likes of the Lamborghini Countach, Ferrari F40, or Porsche 911 Turbo, it should be the most attainable modern supercar around. Assuming Chevy holds to the $50,000-$60,000 base price that has been suggested to the press, the ZR-1 comes in $15,000 under the low-volume Porsche 928S and Mercedes 560SL, and way, way under the even lower-volume Lambo and Ferrari. Obviously, the ZR-1 maintains Corvette tradition by offering high performance-to-dollar value.

Of course, there's more to this new SuperVette than an exotic engine, neck-wrenching acceleration, and light-aircraft terminal speed. For one thing, the ZR-1 package is available only on the coupe. Chevy says it could have been offered as a convertible too, but that Bowling Green had all it could do to turn out the specially modified coupe body. Still, we wouldn't be at all surprised to see an open version within a few years.

"Specially modified" coupe body? Yes, but don't feel badly if you missed the differences. A Chevy engineer we talked to says only dyed-in-the-wool 'Vette fanatics seem to notice. The most visible changes are behind the doors. Like some great shoulder muscles, rear fenders bulge three inches wider than on standard-body L98 models (which retain familiar sixth-

generation flanks), and there are square (instead of round) taillamps in a convex (rather than concave) back panel that Chevy says may benefit aerodynamics. Oh yes: A small "ZR-1" badge (changed at the last minute from the "LT5" shown in early press photos) graces the rear bumper at the extreme right, below the perimeter rub strip.

Of course, the car's haunches are broader to accommodate the wider tires virtually demanded by the LT5's stupendous strength. They're truly massive: 315/35ZR-17s—nearly 12.5 inches wide—which means an extra 1.5 inches of "footprint" compared to

the standard-issue 275/40ZR-17s (still used up front, as on L98 models). Rear wheels are naturally wider too, up from 9.5 to 11 inches, though offset is reduced from 56 to 36 mm (2.2 to 1.4 inches).

The only other alterations are under the skin: a beefier differential, the 13-inch twin-caliper front disc brakes introduced optionally for the '88 Z51 package, and a reinforced front-end structure designed to counter cowl shake on rough roads. The last reflects the demand that the LT5 slot in without heroic chassis bracing or body alterations—for which we can be grateful. One development car seen in published "spy" photos carried a huge hood bulge that not only ruined the basic styling but would surely have compromised forward vision.

As you might expect of a new UltraVette, the ZR-1 package includes the race-oriented Z51 handling option with all the usual features. However, Chevy has added a literal twist for '89 in what it calls "Selective Ride Control" (RPO FX3). Another Delco-Bilstein collaboration, it's also available at extra cost for Z51-equipped L98 coupes with the new six-speed manual.

Basically, SRC is a more sensitive and sophisticated version of the three-stage auto-adjusting shock-absorber setup of the type seen on Nissan's 300ZX and other mid-Eighties Japanese cars. A cockpit switch allows the driver to choose Touring, Sport, or Performance as gross suspension settings. Each mode provides up to six levels of damping, varied directly with vehicle speed.

In line with the "pussycat personality" philosophy, the ZR-1 looks like a sleeper alongside a regular 'Vette (opposite). However, sharp eyes will note a few subtle changes, such as the bulged-out rear end cap and square (instead of round) taillights. The rear fenders also had to be bulged out to accommodate the wider tires (above).

Chevy says the changes between damping levels within each mode "will probably not be noticed by drivers" so much as the differences between the three modes. Touring is described as giving the driver the "smoothness and comfort normally associated with luxury sedans, but not sports cars." Sport is supposedly "not unlike Corvette's standard suspension, offering precise handling and well-controlled ride motion." Claimed for the Performance setting is "a new ultimate level in Corvette handling—the race-proven Z51 package and then some!"

Thanks to modern electronics, there's nothing terribly exotic about Selective Ride Control. Besides the cockpit switch, the system includes its own computer and four special gas-charged shock absorbers with large-diameter pistons capable of generating the high damping forces required by the Performance setting. An electrically operated actuator assembly atop each shock connects to a rod that can rotate through 160 degrees; the rotation adjusts the size of the bypass orifice through which fluid passes between the shock's valve body and compression chamber, thus changing its damping force. The computer monitors road speed and position of the cockpit switch, and sends current to the actuators as needed to adjust the rods for the damping force required by its programming.

"For example," says a Chevy press release, "if the [cockpit] switch is in the 'Sport' mode, the...damping rod will be in the 60-degree position at any speed below 25 mph. If...speed rises to about 25 mph, the computer signals the actuators to rotate the damping rods to the 80-degree position, stiffening the suspension. The...rods stay in the 80-degree position until...speed reaches 50 mph. Then the computer commands the actuators to rotate the damping rod to the 100-degree position, stiffening the suspension even more. This process...happens three more times [in 20-degree increments] until the car reaches top speed." Of course, the process is reversed when speed drops.

For the widest possible damping range, Chevy specifies the softer springs and smaller anti-roll bars of the Z52 package for the new FX3 suspension. A division press release notes that in the "Tour" mode "at low speeds, the ride will be somewhat softer than a Corvette equipped with the standard suspension; at higher speeds, the ride will be almost as stiff as Z51-equipped Corvettes....In the 'Perf' mode, the ride at low speeds will be softer than with the Z51...but at higher speeds will be stiffer...for maximum handling." Interestingly, the Performance mode was originally named "Competition"—a clue to its *real* intent.

Does SRC work as advertised? Yes, according to preliminary evaluations. *Road & Track*, which tried it in a standard-engine coupe, reported that "ride quality using the [Performance] setting is on a par with the Z51 package, stiff and jiggly, whereas the Touring setting—much easier on the collective editorial tush—was our choice for freeway runs. Through the frenetic zig-zag of the slalom [test], we could feel no difference between the modes; this was borne out by near-identical speeds averaging an impressive 64.2 mph. Driving on canyon roads, the [Performance] setting telegraphed an extra sense of sure-footedness and handling crispness." *Car and Driver*'s editor, William ("Never Bill") Jeanes, agreed: "The three-way suspension can take you from a secure 100-mph-plus run on a banked test track to a reasonably comfortable ride around a bumpy road circuit. In between, there seem to be enough damping options that most drivers will be able to find a suitable combination of ride and comfort." *AutoWeek* reported hearing "tales from

Chevy racers of sustained 1.25 g cornering for several seconds on a racetrack. Braking forces also exceed 1 g." Obviously, the ZR-1 gets around as well or better than most any exotic European.

With such developments as the ZR-1 and its accompanying technology, the Corvette would seem to have a vigorous future. It's appropriate, then, to close with a few thoughts on what lies ahead.

At this writing, the sixth-generation Corvette seems likely to last through 1992—a good 10-year run. The ZR-1 and 1989's other developments are clearly rejuvenating measures aimed at keeping the car fresh and exciting—which they certainly do—and it seems safe to say that a few more improvements can be expected before the design is retired.

Meantime, there's the question of whether Chevy can reverse the steady sales slide that has plagued this Corvette since 1985. In our view, the product isn't to blame; it was good to begin with and keeps getting better by leaps and bounds. Rather, the downtrend reflects diminishing demand for two-seaters in general (insurance rates have lately shot up again) plus price pressure that forces the relatively old-fashioned Corvette to compete against more exotic machinery in a market sector where technical innovation is prized as much as performance. And in that regard, it's interesting to observe that with base prices up to nearly $31,600 for the coupe and close to $37,000 for the convertible, the Corvette of 1989 is 10 times more expensive in raw dollars than the Corvette of 1953.

Then again, the Mercedes SL is a front-engine/rear-drive car that continues to sell well despite a $65,000 price tag. So maybe the trouble is that even after all these years, America's sports car lacks a certain cachet because of its status as a Chevrolet—a name that is associated with family transportation.

And that brings up a curious double bind. A few years ago, GM reportedly considered marketing the Corvette separately from the Chevrolet line, but decided against it. The reason is obvious: Over 30-odd years, the Corvette had become so inextricably linked with Chevrolet, so crucial to the division's image and sales, that such a divorce would be the utter height of folly—as foolish as deviating from the front-engine/rear-drive format that's as much a part of Corvette tradition as the Chevy name. That's the other problem. For all the talk of mid-engine designs over the years, GM has been

continued on page 382

The ZR-1 rides the same 96.2-inch wheelbase as the regular Corvette. It measures 176.5 inches overall, is 74.0 inches wide, and stands just 46.7 inches high. Estimates peg its top speed at about 180 mph in fifth gear.

The Mid-Engine Indy: Your Next Corvette

We should have known better. Just when we'd thought Chevy had given up on mid-engine sports cars, up pops what was quickly dubbed "Super-Vette," the "FutureVette"—the wild Corvette Indy. Yes, against all odds, the mid-engine dream is still alive within the vastness of General Motors—only this time it really seems destined for reality and, as some Chevrolet officials hint, a not-too-distant reality at that.

The Indy was unveiled in late '85 as a "work-in-progress" design project under the direction of Donald P. Runkle, then Chevy chief engineer. "Rarely has Chevrolet given the public such an early look at a project under development," Runkle said at the time. "What we've done is raise the shroud of secrecy—just a little—on a concept program that's been underway for over a year. . . . We do these cars as much for inspiration as experiment, because it gives our people a chance to turn their dreams into reality."

Picking up where the Aerovette and XP-895 left off, the Indy was conceived around a mid/rear transverse V-8, a special 2.65-liter derivative of the twincam Chevrolet-Ilmor racing engine that had come to dominate the CART Indy-car series (hence the car's name). Converted from alcohol to normal gasoline operation, it inhaled through a special induction system with twin turbochargers and air-to-air intercoolers. Multiport electronic fuel injection was retained from the racing engine. Output wasn't disclosed, but some estimates put horsepower as high as 600.

Appearance was low-slung and voluptuous in the newer GM idiom established under company design chief Irwin W. Rybicki. A short, rounded, ground-sniffing nose with hidden headlamps led back to a smooth, bubble canopy with a small, removable center section, then on to a reverse-curve rump topped by a low "loop" spoiler. The rear-end design was calculated to provide maximum aerodynamic downforce. Huge, forward-facing air scoops cut deep into the lower bodysides left no doubt where the engine was. Wide 17-inch-diameter "Cuisinart" wheels and equally massive tires put the finishing touch on an aggressively futuristic package.

Although designed to accommodate four-wheel drive, four-wheel steering, and "active" electro-hydraulic suspension among other computer-controlled systems, the Indy wasn't fully driveable at this point. It had no windshield wipers, for instance, and some observers noted that its fenders left scant room for a practical amount of wheel travel. At its unveiling, Runkle described the Indy as being "in mid-development stage. . . . Chevrolet wants to show the public how a car this exciting actually is developed, and this concept vehicle sets the theme of the design from which will evolve the running prototype."

Sure enough, a fully working model was unwrapped less than a year later. Finished in red (the first Indy was white), it looked suspiciously like a production prototype, the original design having gained most normal road-car equipment. For example, there was provision now for windshield wiping (via a single long blade) and vehicle lighting (small, high-powered covered headlamps, a full-width taillamp comprised of multiple LEDs, even side marker lights). Adequate wheel travel had been attended to as well, via higher fenders.

The revised cockpit also looked more "production." Where the design study had a impractically angular dash, sketchy instrumentation, an implausibly tiny steering wheel, and nonadjustable molded-in seats, the working Indy boasted a soft-contour instrument panel, twin cathode-ray-tube displays, a normal-size helm, a realistic ventilation system, and fully adjustable seats. Pushbuttons were everywhere, flanking the steering wheel and slathered on the wide center console typical of Corvettes. Some of those buttons governed the transmission, replacing the first Indy's one conventional cockpit item, a central gearlever.

Retained from the original design were individual left and right audio and climate systems independently operable from door-mounted control panels. Instead of an inside rearview mirror, a small TV screen atop the center of the dash monitored a rear-facing video camera—a new example of an old idea. The second CRT, directly ahead of the wheel, could display a variety of information on engine and suspension conditions as well as trip functions.

Chevy was understandably reluctant to get *too* specific about the Indy's nuts and bolts—what few of those there were. New chief engineer Fred Schaafsma said the car "demonstrates intent, not necessarily solution." Nevertheless, certain broad engineering details were evident.

Start with the engine, which was no longer the small racing V-8 but a new high-output version of the venerable 350 with twincam heads, four valves per cylinder, 16 tuned intake runners (one for each inlet valve), and sequential multi-port fuel injection with a separate injector at each intake valve. Designated "350/32," this was, in fact, a preview of the LT5 powerplant destined for the forthcoming ZR-1 production model Corvette.

Construction was also different. Where the first Indy employed a Kevlar tub, the running model rode a freestanding backbone or "torque-tube" type chassis made of carbon fiber, with the fibers wound at different angles to provide appropriate stiffness for the various parts of the structure. Chevy claimed torsional rigidity of nearly 83 tons per square inch, versus 17.9 tsi for a steel chassis of like design. A sub-chassis fit over the basic "spine" for additional rigidity and as a mounting platform for things like the battery and the planned twin radiators and fuel cells. Topping it all off was an outer shell made of various materials because, as Chevy put it, "performance requirements vary from panel to panel." The materials were actually "sandwiches" of fiberglass, fiberglass/carbon fiber, and fiberglass/CF/Nomex —all rather exotic.

The backbone connected a pair of "suspension modules" comprising conventional upper and lower A-arms at each end, plus the expected rear engine/transaxle pack. But with four-wheel drive contemplated, far more was involved. A pair of halfshafts led out from a differential in front; the rear module included a transfer case with a propshaft running forward to a viscous coupling that acted as a center differential for apportioning torque between the front and rear wheels. As initially set up, the torque split was 35/65 percent front/rear— logical for a tail-heavy car.

But the running Indy's most radical—and secret—feature was its so-called "Active Suspension," an idea pioneered by Lotus in England, which GM was in the process of buying out (partly, one suspects, to gain access to this technology). Basically, the Lotus system is designed around computer-controlled hydraulic "actuators" that provide all the wheel movement and locating functions of conventional springs, shock absorbers, and stabilizer bars. Aside from being lighter and more compact, the Lotus system is advantageous in two respects: The actuators apparently respond more quickly than the old-style components they replace, and the computer's programming can easily be tailored to provide ride/handling characteristics appropriate for a given car's weight, size, and purpose.

Those who have sampled Active Suspension rave about it. *Road & Track's* Joe Rusz, who drove a late-model production 'Vette equipped with a prototype system, reported in June 1987 that "while the normal 'Vette launches itself (and you) at the zenith of a particularly nasty whoop-de-do and then crashes to the ground on the downside of the hump, the active 'Vette merely glides over . . . with the wheels tracking perfectly and the body, supported by the hydraulic actuators, following the profile of the road." In corners, Rusz found, "the active 'Vette's body barely moves and the forces at that corner [of the car] are sent to the opposite corner (just like weight jacking in a NASCAR stocker) to keep handling neutral. And through it all, the car rides very smoothly. Incredible!"

But no more incredible than other features envisioned for the Indy, such as computer-controlled four-wheel steering and, perhaps linked with it, an electronic "drive-by-wire" system. The latter replaces the familiar mechanical throttle linkage with yet another computer that compares accelerator-pedal

position against road conditions and varies engine power delivery to suit. The Indy also marked another test for GM's ETAK in-car navigation system, a James Bond-ish device that continuously spots the car's location on a video map in the right-door control panel.

Performance? It's there in abundance. With some 380 horsepower for a reasonable 3300-pound curb weight, the Indy tops 180 mph, scales 0 to 60 mph in less than five seconds and 0-100 in under 11 seconds, according to Chevrolet.

How soon can you buy it?

Sooner than you think. "Corvette Indy provides us with a single platform to integrate and test advanced vehicle systems," says Schaafsma, "some of which will appear in the near future on production Corvettes." We can reliably report that the future arrives with

model year 1993, when something very much like the Indy in basic design and engineering will be launched as the seventh-generation production Corvette. At that point, and barring any interim disasters, the mid-engine dream will come true at last.

Corvette ushers in the Nineties with the ZR-1 (above), the attainable supercar. Chuck Jordan (right); a Corvette (far right) for the future?

cars, the division is now saying that the "next" Corvette could have many of the Indy's advanced features: mid-rear V-8 (probably the LT5 or an evolution thereof), four-wheel drive, four-wheel steering, active suspension, slinky bubbletop styling. In fact, division officials seem to be *promising* all this (and maybe more) for a near future that's likely to arrive with model year 1993, when the Corvette will reach the big four-oh. What a birthday present *that* would be.

If or when a "productionized" Indy appears, it will mark the end of an era: the end of Corvettes with any tangible link to the original 1953 concept. Some may mourn that day, but we'll always have the cars to remind us of the way it was—grand, glorious Corvettes like the fuelie '57, the '63 Sting Ray split-window coupe, the big-inch Sharks, the super-smooth ZR-1, and all the rest.

But let's not reminisce too much, for there'll be reason to celebrate at the dawn of the mid-engine age. For if there's a constant in Corvette history—from Harley Earl, Ed Cole, and Zora Arkus-Duntov to Jerry Palmer, Fred Schaafsma, and Dave McLellan—it is that this car—perhaps more than any other American automobile—has always been about *change*: change for the better, change that advances the state of the automotive art, change that's exciting, change that enriches everyone who loves to drive and drive well. Somehow, we suspect that this will be no less true for the next Corvette, and the one after that, and the one after that....

understandably reluctant to risk alienating the sturdy, vocal band of 'Vette loyalists who would almost surely reject such a car as heresy.

Nevertheless, it appears that the seventh-generation production model will indeed be a "middie," with the rapidly evolving Indy show car its prototype. We think it significant that instead of denying its intent, as Chevrolet did with all those earlier midships dream

Profile:
Chuck Jordan

Charles M. "Chuck" Jordan is one of the most likeable and enthusiastic design executives in all Detroit. He's also a man in a hurry.

Jordan was 59 years old when he succeeded Irwin W. Rybicki in October 1986 as only the fourth design vice president in GM history. Per company policy, Jordan must retire at age 65, which he will reach in 1992. That means he will have barely six years to chart a new design course for a company much criticized lately for having lost its way in that area. But Jordan has a clear vision of where GM design should be heading, and his influence will be evident in the company's cars well into the Nineties.

He was certainly well prepared to assume the job once held by Harley Earl and Bill Mitchell, having worked for both of his illustrious predecessors. Jordan joined GM in 1949 after earning a degree in mechanical engineering from MIT. He served early on in the Advanced Styling section, where he first became enamored of Corvettes when the original 1953 Motorama show car was being developed under Earl. Jordan's first major assignment came in 1957 as chief designer for Cadillac. Five years later he was put in charge of all GM car and truck exteriors. Then, in 1967, he

was named design director at Opel, GM's German subsidiary, where he spearheaded the lovely little 1970-75 Manta coupe.

Jordan was brought back to Detroit in 1970 to take charge of exteriors for Buick, Olds, and Cadillac, while Rybicki was given the same responsibilities for Chevrolet, Pontiac, and commercial vehicles. The two then switched jobs in 1972. When Rybicki succeeded Mitchell as corporate vice-president for design in 1977, Jordan became his second-in-command as director of design, a position he held until Rybicki's 1986 retirement.

Blessed with a delightful "down home" manner that quickly puts guests at ease, Chuck Jordan is always eager to talk cars—especially high-performance cars—whether it's his latest Ferrari or the latest GM projects on which he will ultimately pass judgment. He's also surprisingly candid for a high-ranking executive of the world's largest automaker, as you'll see in the following excerpts from a February 1989 interview with these editors concerning Corvettes past, present, and future.

Editor: Mr. Jordan, you're a well-known admirer of Ferraris. How does this influence design work on the Corvette, and what can you tell us about the next generation?

Chuck Jordan: As we move forward with the Corvette, which we're doing right now, we're starting from the inside out. We're taking care of all the things that we and our loyal customers—the people who love Corvettes—feel should be improved. Our own feelings are influenced somewhat by our experience with Ferraris. [Chevy designer] Jerry Palmer has a Ferrari. I've got a Ferrari—a Testarossa that, for example, I can get in and out of very easily. I've also got a Corvette convertible that I've driven for about 10,000 miles—and it's a lot more difficult to get in and out of. So there are some things that we learn both from driving our own product and the experience with other cars that we drive and that some of us own, like Porsches, Ferraris, and Lotuses—high-performance cars, which is what the Corvette is. All this influences what we're doing as we move ahead.

Ed: It sounds like a more liveable driver compartment is one of your biggest priorities in the next new Corvette.

Jordan: We're starting with the driver and passenger. We're going to get the beltline down, lower the cowl to open up the feeling inside, get the instruments where you can really see them, and put the controls where you can easily reach them. We're building a seating buck right now to test the geometry. After we get all of that right, *then* we'll talk about what "style" we want inside.

One thing I've experienced in my Corvette is that it feels and looks "plastic" inside. I'm used to the Testarossa. Wherever you touch that car, there's something soft. Whether it's vinyl or leather, is not the point. The point is, it's soft. So I retrimmed my Corvette to show our guys and management what we ought to be doing in a car of this caliber—a world-class sports car.

But to go back to your first question, you know that I love Ferraris, but I sold my Lusso, my Daytona, and my Boxer because I'm not a collector. I just always want to drive the current car, the state of the art, because that's the jumping-off point for us.

Ed: The late Bill Mitchell once told us that the current Corvette lacks the character and excitement of the ones he did.

How do you respond to that?

Jordan: Well, you know I worked with Bill for many, many years. I really admired him. He was our leader—he was almost a god to us. He was a hard taskmaster and raised a lot of hell with us, but we learned well and learned clearly under Mitchell. The Corvette was his preoccupation, it really was. I know, because I was Mitchell's assistant for a long time. I saw all these things happening: the Stingray race car, the split-window Sting Ray, the show cars he did. He really ate and slept Corvettes, and he had a profound influence on the car. Now the last one he designed was after he left GM—his own personal car. He thought that our design was too tame or too conservative. But his car was a throwback to what he was doing 10 years earlier with the show cars, and that wasn't an answer either.

It wouldn't be constructive to go into how we got the car that's on the street today. It's there, it's a good design, and it's going to be at least 10 years old before we replace it. But when we *do* replace it, I can guarantee you that the next Corvette is going to be a *great* design. Its proportions will be striking. Its interior will look like performance and feel like performance. The shape of the car will make you drool. But you're still going to know it's a Corvette—even from a block away.

Ed: As you know, there are now a good many styling kits and conversions available that try to make Corvettes look like Ferrari Testarossas and Daytonas. Does this bother you?

Jordan: Yeah. A lot of them aren't tasteful and don't compliment the car. Just things that are added on to be different. We've done some things ourselves for the present Corvette—things to improve its performance and help the aerodynamics. That, I think, is valid. Wheels are a part of that. But some of these kits and conversions on the aftermarket are like putting a chrome-plated Rolls-Royce radiator on a Cadillac—tasteless.

Ed: What do you think of the new ZR-1?

Jordan: The ZR-1 is fantastic—just a wonderful car! The new 6-speed gearbox is smooth. The engine is unbelievable, and driving the car is a real pleasure. It's very civilized to just tool around in, but underneath your foot you've got all that potential—when you punch it, it really, *really* goes.

Ed: How does it compare to your Ferrari in that respect?

Jordan: Both the ZR-1 and the Testarossa have outstanding performance. The ZR-1 reminds me more of a [Porsche] 928 in sound and feel—very smooth, quiet, and silky—whereas the Ferrari is a Ferrari with all that goes with it—it's a different

deal. But one thing is for sure: the ZR-1 is a world-class sports car—right up there with the "big boys."

Ed: Why isn't the ZR-1 visually different from the regular Corvette other than in the tail? Were there any plans to set it more apart from other 'Vettes?

Jordan: We [Design Staff] had a long discussion about that, and Marketing had something to say about it. We had to change the rear because the rubber is wider, so we had to kick the body out over the rear wheels. That even got into the doors, so there was a change in the door as well as the rear quarter.

We also wanted a different front fascia, but Marketing felt strongly that that wasn't important. And maybe they're right. We, as designers, would always like to do a whole new car. We're always impatient to do more, so they kind of keep a balance. As a matter of fact, there's a facelift coming for the regular Corvette that will be more like the ZR-1.

But really, a Corvette's a Corvette. We don't want a "standard" model and a "deluxe" model. We want to make sure that the image of the Corvette is not diluted, that it's clear. Whether you've got a ZR-1 or not, the image is going to be just *one* image.

Ed: So you wouldn't want to follow Ferrari by having two entirely different Corvettes the

way they have the 328 and the Testarossa?

Jordan: No. To follow Ferrari we'd have to have two separate cars—a Corvette like we have now and something like the Corvette Indy, a mid-engine supercar. Maybe someday that'll happen. But right now, the ZR-1 and the regular Corvette aren't like that. They're different in their performance characteristics, but not in their basic character.

Ed: Out of all the Corvettes built since 1953, what's your personal favorite?

Jordan: There are two that stand out for me. One is the '53, because I was a kid here then, as a designer, and I was working on the floor above where the original Corvette was being designed for the Motorama. When we'd work overtime, which we did almost all the time, we used to sneak down there at night and look at that car. We weren't supposed to, but we did. That was Harley Earl's car, and it had the most profound influence on me. I couldn't believe it. Wow! You know, it was the time of the Jag XK-120 and Austin-Healey, cars like that. It was hard to believe this was really happening.

But the most exciting [Corvette] to me was the split-window Sting Ray [coupe of 1963]. We couldn't believe when we were doing that car that it would actually be on the street. That's how different it seemed in those days, how exciting it was. And it's still an exciting-looking car. We got everything right on that one.

Ed: What's your least favorite?

Jordan: My least favorite is the '58 Corvette with dual headlights and all that chrome. I was chief designer on that one and I guarantee it was the result of the era we were in. Fifty-eight was not a vintage year.

Chuck Jordan (right) and Jerry P. Palmer

Ed: Of the many Corvette-inspired show cars and experimentals built over the years, such as the Two-Rotor car and the Aerovette, are there any you think should have been produced for sale?

Jordan: There's a lot of great Corvette show cars—all interesting cars. Many of them had big pipes, made a lot of noise, and went like a banshee. They were Mitchell's toys. They were wonderful—and we all loved them. But, I suppose I felt strongest about the Aerovette as a candidate for production. Our newest Corvette show car and, I believe, the strongest Corvette statement yet, is the Corvette Indy. Now there's a car I'd really like to see in production!

Ed: What would you have to do to the Corvette Indy to make it a production car?

Jordan: We've already done it. We started with the static show model [silver car], then made a running version [red car]. Now we have a productionized ver-

sion. It's somewhat higher. It meets all the conditions [federal requirements], and it's sensational! But keep in mind, because of its layout and sophistication, if the Corvette Indy were to be produced, it would fall in the supercar category—very expensive. So don't expect a Corvette Indy type of car to replace the front-engine/rear-drive car any time soon.

Ed: Where are you right now with the new Corvette design?

Jordan: We're in the fun part—the search stage where anything goes. It doesn't get better than this—designing a new Corvette with no holds barred. We set up a studio in the far end of the basement—nobody can find us. We call it the "Corvette skunk works" and that's where we're working on the new Corvette.

But our isolated studio location doesn't mean we're designing in a vacuum. Our Advanced Packaging group is right next door. We've had many discus-

sions already with Dave McLellan [Corvette chief engineer] and his guys. And the Marketing group has been over to give us the "voice of the customer"—how sports-car people feel and what they like and dislike about today's cars. And these discussions will continue. In the meantime, behind the locked doors of the "skunk works," a small family of our best designers, sculptors, and technical people are at work in a free, creative atmosphere. This is "bubble up" time—the time to explore, to reach. Walking through the door of that studio is like walking into a new era. The collection of ideas—the sketches, scale models, full-size drawings, and the interior buck—give you a "smell" of the new car—and I'll tell you, it blows your mind.

Now it may sound like this is a "play pen" where we're just having fun—and it is to a degree, but it's also serious business. This free atmosphere pro-

1986 Corvette Indy

duces some wild, imaginative design directions—but they have to be tempered with good judgment. In the end, we're only looking for one design—the right design for the next Corvette.

Ed: What about your Advanced Concepts Center in California?

Jordan: Yeah, they're working on the new Corvette design, too. Their first proposals look great—but we're going to keep them independent from our work here. It's basically the same approach we took with the California IROC concept car, where we asked the team in California to design a Camaro that would be a significant car in that market. We figure a car that can make a strong impact in California will be fine in, say, Wichita, Kansas. You know, they're pretty hard-nosed out there in California, and you've got to do some things differently from what you do in Warren, Michigan. So we're going to use their designs as another input for the final production design.

Ed: We've heard the California IROC looks very much like the next production Camaro.

Jordan: Yes, it does. It's close, but not exact line for line. We can't show *everything* we're planning. By the way, that Concept Camaro is a running car. It started out as a production model that got hit by a train at the Van Nuys [California] factory —you know, backing into the yard. We got it, took the old

body off and did the rest.

Ed: You've declared that the era of look-alike styling is over at GM, and that you want to establish greater brand identity among the five car divisions. How will this affect the Corvette, and what do you see as the biggest challenge in designing the next one?

Jordan: You're right, the era of "look-alikes" at GM is dead. Part of our new design philosophy has to do with strong images on the road. There's a pot full of car brands running around out there. An awful lot of them are just plain bland, dull, and boring design-wise. I think it's time to bring the excitement back—to make a bold statement and focus the image of the cars and trucks we produce. When you see a Buick, you've got to know it's a Buick. Not from some loud graphics or strange design elements but from its proportions, its shape —the "feel" of the car. And you shouldn't need 20/20 vision to recognize this.

The same thing applies to the Corvette. I suppose it's a little easier with the Corvette. It already has a strong image. We're going to make it stronger. There's a lot of competition out there in the sports car area and more coming. So we're not going to be timid.

You know, people don't buy Corvettes for basic transportation. It's an emotional car. Some people love it for its ride, handling, and performance. Others

are attracted by its image—the excitement of driving a distinctive sports car. We're dealing with a "total car" here—one that will perform the way it looks. And that's the exciting part for us, as designers. From our standpoint, our design will be new in proportion and shape—and beautiful from any angle. Our goal is to make the next Corvette as significant, design-wise, as the split-window Sting Ray when it came out.

Now that's easy for me to say—not so easy to do. I'm not talking about doing another split-window design. I'm talking about the feeling I had when I was younger, and we were designing the split-window coupe. I just couldn't believe that car would actually be on the road—it was so wild! We're doing it again right now in our basement studio. Some of the things I see down there scare the bejeezus out of me but, let me tell you, *it is exciting!*

Profile:
Jerry P. Palmer

Beginning with the 1984 model, the Corvette's future would be entirely in the hands of a younger, yet no less capable generation of General Motors professionals. Jerry Palmer is one of the most important of the new breed. In 1974 he became head of Chevrolet's Production Studio Three, where the 1984 Corvette would take shape. Though he has since been appointed executive head of GM's Advanced Design Studios under vice-president Charles M. Jordan, Palmer

Jerry P. Palmer

still has overall responsibility for the Corvette's exterior in the manner of his illustrious predecessor, William L. Mitchell.

When Mitchell retired as GM design chief in 1977, Palmer inherited an exciting yet formidable job, much as Dave McLellan did in taking over for Zora Arkus-Duntov on the engineering side. Both men and their respective teams faced the challenge of not only maintaining the tradition of America's sports car, but improving on it.

But though admirably suited for the job, Palmer did not find it easy. For one thing, this articulate, thoughtful, soft-spoken man took over for one of the most flamboyant and outspoken designers in the industry. Moreover, Mitchell had been the sole arbiter of Corvette styling for more than 20 years, itself a tough act to follow. And though the fifth-generation design had remained quite popular through its extraordinarily long production run, it was also quite dated by the

Jerry P. Palmer (left) and Chuck Jordan

mid-Seventies. Clearly, its replacement had to be more modern both in appearance and in function. Yet as development work proceeded on what would become the 1984 model, it was equally clear that any new Corvette would still have to be instantly recognizable as a Corvette. Palmer also faced the problem of providing a look that would remain fresh well in the 1990s, for the sixth generation would almost surely be in production for about as many years as its long-lived predecessor.

Finally, Palmer faced the thorny matter of "updating the future." GM had tantalized enthusiasts with numerous Corvette dreams over the years, notably the mid-engine experiments of the late Sixties and early Seventies, exemplified by the shapely Aerovette. In fact, Mitchell's stunning Aerovette was actually readied for 1980 production, only to be canceled at the last minute. Most of these concept cars still looked wild and exotic some 10 years later, and many Corvette devotees remembered them. Palmer's challenge was to come up with styling that would be just as eye-grabbing within the 'Vette's traditional format, yet practical for production.

That Palmer managed to reconcile these conflicting concerns testifies to his creativity and artistry, and that of his team. In fact, Palmer and his group produced what may well be the most handsome car of the Eighties. Certainly, few would disagree that the sixth

generation is one of the best-looking Corvettes ever.

Jerry Palmer claims to be one of the few designers in the domestic auto industry who is a native Detroiter. His experience with GM Design goes back to 1964, when he spent a summer there as a student. The following year, he graduated from Detroit's Center for Creative Studies, then joined GM permanently, completing the company's internship program before serving briefly in the Advanced Studios he would later head. After a hitch in the Army during 1966-67, he worked for Chevrolet except for brief tours at GM subsidiaries in Europe and Japan. His first Corvette assignment came in 1969, when he assisted Mitchell in creating several show models.

Palmer's affable, easy-going personality belies an intense enthusiasm for his work, about which he is uncharacteristically modest for such a high-ranking executive. He's always eager to talk Corvettes despite an always-hectic schedule. Below are excerpts from several conversations we've had with him since introduction of the 1984 model:

Editor: When did you first become involved with the Corvette?

Jerry P. Palmer: My first production involvement came in the '73 and '74 car. I was the assistant chief designer, and we were doing only the front and rear of the car.

Ed: What did you think of the 1968 generation?

Palmer: I thought it was an exciting car. I was really enamored by the show cars, such as the Mako Shark, that led into that body style. Even today you see an '81 or '82 on the road—I know they're dated, but they're still exciting and have a lot of personality. They are definitely Corvettes.

Ed: When did you start work on the '84?

Palmer: We're always working on new Corvettes. We started on [the sixth generation] in 1977, but there were designs before that which were part of the program. We literally laid out the package starting with a clean sheet of paper. The only thing that was a given was the engine and transmission and need for additional ground clearance. We really started with a package. There's a lot of time and effort spent finalizing the rest of the architecture.

Ed: At that point, were there any more thoughts of a mid-engine design?

Palmer: When the decision was made to go front-engine, the mid-engine responsibility went downstairs to the Advanced Studio. [Chevy Production Studio Three] had mid-engine responsibility until that time. We are the production studio, so when the decision to go front-engine was made, the mid-

engine design went downstairs to an Advanced studio.

Ed: Would you have preferred the mid-engine format?

Palmer: A mid-engine design offers different proportions, more unfamiliar proportions. Based on the components available at that time, we made the right decision. The P-car [1984-88 Pontiac Fiero] was essentially what we were looking at—V-6 powered. I also had [1982] Camaro responsibility, and we were going to come out with a pretty wild Z28 package. There's no way that a 60-degree V-6 Corvette in the form we were working on could compete with the Z28 we were working on. Then Porsche came out with their front/mid-engine [928] design. All those decisions made back in that late-Seventies time frame fortified Chevrolet's direction.

The mid-engine car is an exciting car, but the [latest] Corvette is a fantastic car for the money in handling, braking, performance. It's right there. We didn't have to apologize for anything. The car is very forgiving. It's hard to screw up in a Corvette. You can screw up in a Ferrari or a rear-engine Porsche very easily. Those considerations were very strong on the engineering side. Plus, the mid-engine car offers less packaging flexibility.

Ed: Tell us about your working relationship with Dave McLellan.

Palmer: We have a very good relationship. Dave knows enough about what we do to understand or challenge. We are very knowledgeable about each other's bailiwick and can challenge each other. I would say Chevrolet was very creative in helping us achieve the package we wanted.

To come up with the idea and make it look good is one thing; to make it work is another. There is more integration between the two [disciplines] than there was . . . years ago. We have a better understanding of what has to be done to make the product people are demanding out there. We're getting closer together.

Ed: The late Bill Mitchell criticized the 1984 Corvette in some respects. What was your reaction?

Palmer: We talked about it. Bill and I were still good friends. He really didn't like the car at first and said so. Then, after he saw the car out in the real world and saw it in motion, he called me up and said, "I gotta tell ya, that thing really looks aggressive. I still don't quite like the back end, but it looks like a Corvette" . . . It doesn't have the exaggerated statement that the previous Corvettes had, but I'm sure if Bill were running the studio . . . the Corvette would be a lot different than it is today. The shapes are Corvette, but the shapes are also aerodynamically tuned. We didn't conceive the design to aero, but we certainly had aero in mind. We had to meet targets.

Ed: Mitchell once told us he thought the '84 was more an engineer's car, not a stylist's car.

Palmer: I was not controlled at all by Engineering. In fact, Engineering bent over backwards to give us what we wanted. I think Bill would have probably done things a little differently. However, I don't think it would be a lot different. The 16-inch wheels, the 65-degree windshield—those things are all designer's wants, like the flip-open front end, the T-less T-top. Engineering didn't make those things. They made them happen, but the concepts originated here at Design Staff. For some of those design features we paid penalties . . . in cost and in mass. But the appearance or aura of that car is the thing we wanted. Engineering didn't back off. In fact, I can't think of anything Engineering demanded we have that we're not happy with. I think the days [are gone when Engineering compromises] what we want. They want as exciting a car as we do.

Ed: What is the limiting factor in production numbers with the current car?

Palmer: It gets down to how many people you want to employ at Bowling Green and how many shifts. We are very reluctant to go into a double shift until we are satisfied the demand is there, not an artificial demand because of the newness of the car. If the demand is there, I'm sure Chevrolet will consider another shift.

I feel with a double shift we can make 60,000 cars with the quality the car has to have. We will not pump out cars and detract from the quality. We are still gaining on the quality of the car. I see the car leveling out at around 40,000 units a year. That's a gut reaction.

Ed: The fifth-generation design lasted 15 years. How long do you think the current one will be around?

Palmer: I don't think it's going to last anywhere near that long. But I think it will take us into the Nineties; in fact, I *know* it'll take us into the Nineties. That's not to say the car will not be injected with new technology wherever possible or [if] we discover something better appearance-wise or function-wise. We'll implement that, but it won't be a total new design.

Ed: Do you have a favorite Corvette?

Palmer: Several. The 1956 [and] '57 are favorites of mine. Of course, the '63 split-window coupe has been identified as the classic Corvette, and I have to

agree with that. The '65 convertible, '68, [and] '69 cars. Didn't like the rounded-off rear end [on] the '61. I think the '80 car was an improvement over the 1974-79 car.

Ed: Do you keep an eye on the aftermarket to see what other people do with the Corvette?

Palmer: Sure, but there hasn't been anything that's gotten me to say, "Hey, look at what they've done here. Let's try that." We've been through this thing for so many years [and] we've tried a lot of things. I really get a kick out of seeing the competition cars, because [altering the design] becomes functional.

Ed: Do you foresee a V-6 Corvette?

Palmer: It's an interesting package. I'm sure it's one of the options we'll be looking at in the Nineties if the gas guzzler problem stays with us and we have to maintain or achieve higher performance levels.

Ed: Would a V-6 work in the current chassis, and what kind of styling options would that offer you?

Palmer: I really don't know, because when you get the V-6 to put out the kind of power needed to match or surpass the performance levels we know now, all that room vacated by the two cylinders will be absorbed by intercoolers. The secret to the V-6, obviously, is turbocharging. I don't think there's any question the V-6 is going to be the performance engine of the future. But we're not planning any styling changes around that possibility now.

Profile:
David R. McLellan

David R. McLellan succeeded Zora Arkus-Duntov as the head of Corvette engineering in 1975. Like so many others who have been involved with America's sports car over the years, McLellan is a unique personality. The 1984 was the first Corvette to fully reflect that personality—and his considerable expertise.

McLellan was born on Michigan's Upper Peninsula in the mid-Thirties, soon after Harley Earl had designed his first LaSalles and Cadillacs. McLellan grew up in Detroit, where he later attended Wayne State University, majoring in mechanical engineering. Fresh out of school, he went to work for General Motors in 1959 at the corporation's Milford proving grounds. McLellan spent the better part of a decade there, during which he earned a master's degree in engineering mechanics from Wayne State.

In 1968, McLellan was transferred to Chevrolet Division, where he worked on the second-genera-

tion "1970½" Camaro. He was also involved with John DeLorean's proposal for a common chassis shared by Camaro, the compact Nova, and possibly, McLellan says, the Corvette. It's perhaps fortunate for the two-seater that this idea came to nothing, though McLellan did contribute to a shared Nova/Camaro chassis.

Next came a year's sojourn at MIT in 1973 as a Sloan Fellow sponsored by Chevrolet. It was an important experience that gave McLellan a chance to learn about the automotive industry in other lands. He returned to Chevrolet in 1974, when he was given his first Corvette assignment as a staff engineer under Duntov. Just six months later, Duntov retired and McLellan was named chief Corvette engineer.

Though the proposed mid-engine production car derived from Bill Mitchell's Aerovette design was nearly ready at that point, McLellan favored the traditional front-engine/rear-drive configuration, and he carried the day with what ultimately became the sixth-generation Corvette. Significantly, a series of owner surveys supported his position. Also by that point, McLellan had established himself as a clever, capable designer—which he had to be. The challenge of engineering and overseeing development of the first all-new Corvette in some 20 years was formidable, to say the least.

The editors had several interviews with McLellan soon after the 1984 model was unveiled. What follows are excerpts from those conversations:

Editor: What was the first Corvette you worked on?

David R. McLellan: The first program I had any impact on was the '78. As chief engineer there are some aspects that are under my direct control, some things not under control. The engine and transmission were not under direct control. The '78 program involved many things besides moving on emissions and fuel economy. From a design

standpoint, we had devised a hatchback Corvette which was never approved. That was a hatch with a large frame around it. For '78 we reassessed why we were having problems getting stuff like that approved. The '78 design was originally conceived as a frameless hatch design. This was the one that appeared in the Collector Edi-

David R. McLellan

tion in 1982, its first production appearance.

Ed: When did you realize you would be able to build a new Corvette?

McLellan: We realized in that 1977-78 time frame [that] we had to do a new Corvette or the product would be in serious jeopardy. There was general recognition it was time to take a major step with the Corvette. The big issue was what should that step be? The options ranged from carrying out the midships V-8 Aerovette-based design to doing a V-6 midships car to taking the front/mid-engine design we had and doing a thorough reassessment of it. We started the process with the midships variation as our mainstream. It occurred to us only as we got into detailed assessment to look into the front/mid-engine design again. About that time, Porsche came out with the 928—a front-engine V-8 sports car. We looked again at the benefits and it emerged as a very strong candidate and . . . ultimately emerged.

Ed: What was the mid-engine design's downfall?

McLellan: When you get to a high-performance-engined car that carries two people and has some kind of creature comforts, the mid-engine gets very tough to deal with. . . . There is a certain amount of cubic volume that is consumed by all those functions to transport two people and achieve a level of creature comfort. To make the midships cars look so slick, we had been ignoring the people issue. There was no utility or luggage space at all in those cars. That's where you get into trouble with the larger engine. The front/mid-engine design offers more benefits at that point. Then it comes down to what can we do to reconfigure [it].

So we set about doing that by repackaging the details: putting the front suspension around the engine, putting the engine in at a completely different attitude, designing the rear suspension to configure it around the occupant requirements. Generally, we were able to make the car a little bit shorter and lower, though a little bit wider.

Ed: What changes did you deem most important?

McLellan: As we analyzed the old car, a lot of things, we felt, were right. . . . That was reflected in its performance in the marketplace. We really look at this new Corvette as an ultimate performance statement by Chevrolet. What I mean by that is, in all respects that are important to a Corvette, the car needs to be king of the hill. If it's worth doing, it's worth doing better than anybody else. With the old Corvette, we had kind of let things slip a little bit. We had not been pounding the table with our management as hard as we should have. We certainly are today. In fact, we are being pressed by our own management.

Ed: What changes in automotive technology have affected the Corvette?

McLellan: It has been updated year by year. It progressed dramatically in '81 and '82 when we moved production from St. Louis to Bowling Green. It was Jerry Palmer and the design team who worked closely together. One of the first things we laid down [for the '84 model] was the tire size. For the kind of performance we wanted, the only tire available in that size was a Pirelli P7. Much of the design was done around that tire. We brought Goodyear in early in [the program] and gave them the specifications, and they worked hard on it. We're very pleased with the results. The tires have been trouble-free. [Even with the wider footprint] they have better hydroplaning performance than previous tires. Goodyear is X-raying 100 percent of the tires for quality control and is testing a sampling using a holographic technique.

Ed: Why the unidirectional wheels on the '84?

McLellan: Basically for aesthetics. It's kind of a non-issue. If that is what the designer wanted and it's reasonable to give it to him, then we'll give it to him.

Ed: Is your relationship with Design Staff much like it was between Bill Mitchell and Zora Arkus-Duntov? Mitchell told us that he thinks Engineering is running the show more now than he let them when he was in charge.

McLellan: Certainly Bill Mitchell is a very flamboyant guy. The only way we really got our act together on this car was by waiting until Bill Mitchell retired. The previous car was never really accepted outside the U.S. The new car carries the cues that make people recognize it as a Corvette, but [are] not so exaggerated. As we got into the aero aspect of it, this car was really designed in the tunnel. [It] has a coefficient of drag of 0.34, and we know how to get it down to a 0.31 or even 0.30 in honest production trim.

Ed: How did the wind tunnel affect the '84 styling?

McLellan: Top speed and fuel economy have a lot to do with aero design. Probably the most critical piece of the car from an aero design standpoint was the backlight and the way the taillights were formed. We looked at a variety of ways to terminate the rear of the car.

I can't think of any great disagreements we had with Palmer. The only thing I recall was that we had to redo the taillamps without visible screws. Once we laid down where the engine and people were, it was Jerry fine-tuning the design. I think Jerry was very satisfied with the design, and so were we.

Ed: Why is the Corvette still as heavy as it is?

McLellan: I can't tell you how many pounds are tied up in open [Targa-roof body] design, but it's a lot. Structural integrity is important.

Ed: Was anything other than fiberglass considered for the sixth-generation body?

McLellan: We never considered anything other than reinforced plastic. It has the ability to absorb minor impacts, and is nearly as light as aluminum.

Ed: So why haven't more cars been made this way?

McLellan: It's expensive. But you are seeing more and more use of reinforced plastics. Cars such as the Pontiac Fiero and Honda CRX are using it.

Ed: Will the Corvette continue to employ plastic or fiberglass construction?

McLellan: Yes! I see the plastic family of materials evolving themselves. There's a great revolution going on in . . . composites.

Ed: The 1984 Corvette took a lot of criticism for being a hard-riding car. Why did you do it that way?

McLellan: There are two schools of thought in the press, and we obviously don't side with those who say the car is too harsh. It is a "tough" car. It was never intended as anything else. It was intended to allow you to get out on a race track and not wallow all over the place. It was intended to enable you to get out and set lap records, and the car has set a number of production lap records at various race tracks. That's one aspect of the car we wanted to optimize and —no question about it—we did.

When you get onto some of the terrible concrete we have in the frost zone, the car gets kind of tough. In response to those kind of inputs, we are looking into softening up the ride [accomplished starting with the '85 model—Ed.]. But we're doing it very carefully so as not to jeopardize the handling performance that is inherent there. It's going to be evolutionary, and it's going to be done without degrading the handling performance we've already demonstrated.

Ed: What's the rationale in having a separate export model for the first time?

McLellan: The car was designed not just for Canada and the U.S. market but for the export market from the ground up. The export requirements were taken into consideration very early in design, so changes were kept to a minimum. We're producing the export car in the Bowling Green plant so it doesn't have to be retrofitted at point of sale. The car is export-certified for—(and I think I'll get all the countries here, but I may miss a few)—Germany, France, Switzerland, Austria, the low countries, Sweden, England, Spain, Italy, Saudi Arabia and that whole Middle East area, and Japan.

Ed: Will we see much factory support of Corvette racing?

McLellan: Our support of racing is a technical support, a position we have taken for a long time. We won't be out there racing the car ourselves.

Ed: Is racing still important to maintaining Corvette sales?

McLellan: I think it's a very important adjunct to it. There's the overall statement on Chevrolet performance we're making with the Lola turbo V-6 GTP car project. That's a joint venture between ourselves and Ryan Faulkner, who is doing the turbocharged V-6 motors. We did the aero work. . . . That car . . . will be a test-bed development

tool to wring out the vehicle system as a competitive prototype vehicle. Then it's up to various private racers to take replicas of that car and turn them into successful racing cars. We're doing the part of that venture that we do best, which is supporting engine development and doing the aerodynamic development.

Ed: Will we see twin-turbocharged, aluminum-block V-6s in racing 'Vettes?

McLellan: That's certainly a possibility. But that's up to [the private racers] given the rules of the series. We really feel the production car is itself a viable competitor. . . . We're fairly comfortable that the [Corvette] just driven to the race track is competitive.

Ed: What's the reason for the bulge on the right of the dashboard? Was it originally designed to house an airbag?

McLellan: The car is designed around an interior concept to make the car more "friendly" to the occupant in the event of a crash situation. It was developed somewhat like the driver's side, where you have a steering wheel in front of you that absorbs some of that energy. That's why the instrument panel comes out in that padded area the way it does. It was not designed to house an airbag.

Ed: Will we see a different engine such as a V-6 anytime soon?

McLellan: Probably not. We're not going to see them in the short run, period. We'll see them only if we see a benefit. If we can see a V-6 turbo that would outgun the V-8 and had fuel economy and what other benefits it would need to have to be viable, we would consider it. Part of it is that we have such a damn good engine in the small-block V-8. Its evolutionary progress outstrips anything we can demonstrate in a competing alternative. . . . That engine in NASCAR form is putting out over 600 horsepower. We are continuing to evolve the engine. You'll see an evolutionary process over the next few years where you'll look back and say, step by step, "they radically changed that engine."

Ed: How long will the sixth generation be in production?

McLellan: You have to look at the viability of the configuration. As long as fuel prices do not become outrageous in terms of [buyer] income, and all other things being equal, the current configuration has a long potential life. We will continue to evolve the present configura-

tion. If there is some dramatic shift in consumer demand, we'll have to reconsider what we're doing.

Ed: What sort of Corvettes do you see further down the road?

McLellan: There may be turbine powerplants by then that are viable. That would open up dramatic new opportunities in terms of vehicle design.

Ed: Several manufacturers are looking at four-wheel drive for road cars. Is there a four-wheel-drive Corvette in the future?

McLellan: Duntov did a four-wheel-drive Corvette back in the Sixties [CERV II]. In fact, the first of the mid-engine production designs [XP-882] was conceived such that it could have a four-wheel-drive variation. It's not out of the question, [but] it's not very pertinent to the short term.

Ed: Why was the first sixth-generation Corvette designated a 1984 model and not an '83, leaving out a 30th anniversary model?

McLellan: Well, [then Chevrolet general manager Robert C.] Stempel said it. He had two choices: He could have the last '83 into the marketplace or the first '84. Everything we built [on an experimental basis] we called an '83. Bob made the decision that, nope, it's going to be the first '84. The government rule is that you can have only one January 1 in your model year. . . . Since we were not going to sell the cars to the public until March 24, we fell within that criteria.

We went out of production with the old one back in mid-October [1982]. We had shut down production and cleared the plant out and rebuilt the assembly facility to handle the '84 Corvette. The first production car that was a salable vehicle—VIN 00002—is in the Sloan Museum in Flint. VIN 00001, which is the lowest serial number, was raffled off by the National Council of Corvette Clubs for charity. It was car number one of '84 production, but it was not the first car built. It was built a couple days later, after they had the production line up and running smoothly. 00002 was part of a family of cars, about the first 70, we [weren't] selling because we use those cars to get the build of the vehicle up to standard.

David R. McLellan

Major Specifications: 1989 Corvette

Body/Chassis

Frame:	Unitized steel/aluminum "birdcage"
Body:	Glass-reinforced plastic, 2-seat coupe and convertible
Front suspension:	Independent; upper and lower A-arms, transverse fiberglass leaf spring, tubular hydraulic shock absorbers, (ZR-1 and FX3 options: variable-rate via electric actuators), anti-roll bar
Rear suspension:	Independent; upper and lower trailing arms, lateral arms, tie rods, halfshafts, transverse fiberglass leaf spring, tubular hydraulic shock absorbers (ZR-1 and FX3 options: variable-rate via electric actuators), anti-roll bar
Wheels:	Unidirectional cast alloy; 9.5 × 17-inch standard except ZR-1 (9.5 × 17-inch front, 11 × 17-inch rear)
Tires:	Goodyear Eagle ZR50; P275/40ZR-17 standard except ZR-1 (P275/40ZR-17 front, P315/35ZR-17 rear)

Dimensions

Wheelbase (in.):	96.2
Overall length (in.):	176.5
Overall height (in.):	46.7 coupe, 46.4 convertible
Overall width (in.):	71.0 (ZR-1 coupe: 74.0)
Track front/rear (in.):	59.6/60.4
Ground clearance (in.):	4.7
Curb weight (lbs):	3298-3333

Engines

	L98	LT5
Type:	90-degree ohv V-8, water-cooled	
Construction:	Aluminum heads/cast-iron block	All-aluminum
Valves per cylinder:	2	4
Valve actuation:	Pushrods, rocker arms	Pushrods, rocker arms, twin overhead camshafts per cylinder bank
Main bearings:	5	
Bore × stroke (in.):	4.00 × 3.48	3.90 × 3.66
Displacement (ci):	350	
Compression ratio:	9.0:1	11.25:1
Induction system:	Bosch multi-port fuel injection	
Brake horsepower @ rpm:	245 @ 4300	NA
Torque @ rpm (lbs/ft):	340 @ 3200	NA

Drivetrain

Transmission:	ZF 6-speed overdrive manual	GM 4-speed overdrive automatic
Gear ratios:	First—2.68:1	First—3.06:1
	Second—1.80:1	Second—1.63:1
	Third—1.31:1	Third—1.00:1
	Fourth—1.00:1	Fourth—0.70:1
	Fifth—0.75:1	
	Sixth—0.49:1	
Rear axle ratios:	Manual: 3.33:1; Automatic: 2.59:1/2.73:1 std. couple/convertible; 3.07:1 optional	
Steering:	Power-assisted rack-and-pinion, 13.0:1 overall ratio	
Turns lock-to-lock:	2.0	
Turning circle (ft):	40.0	
Brakes:	4-wheel ventilated discs, 12.0-inch diameter; Bosch ABS II 3-channel anti-lock braking system; 193 sq. in. effective lining area	

Performance*

	L98 manual	LT5 manual
0-60 mph (sec):	5.4	5.0
0-100 mph (sec):	14.42	11.0
Top speed (mph):	150 +	180 (est.)
Fuel consumption (mpg):	16-25	16-25

* Manufacturer data

CHAPTER 13

CORVETTES IN COMPETITION: A WINNING HERITAGE

Sports cars are supposed to be capable of racing, but the Corvette wasn't specifically conceived with that in mind. Harley Earl thought people might race it, since the '53 was fairly spartan, light, and pretty hot—for a six. As we've seen, though, the Corvette quickly became more of a boulevard sports car like the Kaiser-Darrin—albeit a very *fast* one. Even the original two-seat Ford Thunderbird had more racing success than the first-generation Corvette.

According to Sports Car Club of America (SCCA) records, the early six-cylinder 'Vettes did not win any races of importance. A '55 model with the new 265-cubic-inch small-block V-8 gave the Corvette its first major victory: a stock-car-class win at the annual Pikes Peak Hill Climb in Colorado in 1955. It was an unofficial triumph, however, because the body that would eventually sanction that event, the United States Auto Club, hadn't been formed.

But, of course, this was only the beginning of Corvette competition. The advent of the powerful and eminently "tunable" Chevy small-block tempted Corvette owners to tape the headlights, add numbers to the doors, and go racing in earnest for the first time. Once the urge was born, it took hold and grew.

Meantime, Chevrolet was looking for ways to make the Corvette more saleable and was persuaded by Zora Arkus-Duntov that winning cars often sell better than those that don't—or those that don't compete at all. At least that was the experience of other sports car builders. Duntov, as it happened, had done some racing himself, though he was by no means a distinguished driver. In fact, he'd twice failed even to qualify at Indianapolis. What he did have was the technical expertise to make the Corvette a serious track competitor, something he knew it could be once the high-winding V-8 arrived. Management told him to proceed. The rest, as they say, is history.

Small-block power made enthusiasts take note of Chevrolet passenger-car performance in 1955. It also made the Corvette seem really exciting for the first time—especially when Duntov himself set a record for the flying mile at Daytona in late 1955: a sterling 150.583 miles per hour. At that same venue the following January, Betty Skelton broke the existing American sports-car speed record and John Fitch drove a Corvette to class victory in the standing-start mile. These performances suggested that all the Corvette needed to become a top track contender was a little research and development, backed by plentiful aid from the factory.

But how far were Chevrolet and General Motors actually willing to go? David E. Davis, who'd later establish *Car and Driver* magazine and, later still, *Automobile*, was a copywriter for Chevy's ad agency in those days, and he reminisced on that question in the first issue of the division's *Corvette Quarterly* magazine (Spring 1988): "I saw the first Corvette show car at the 1953 General Motors Motorama. I saw my first production Corvette on the starting line for Michigan's 1954 Press On Regardless Rally—an event, incidentally, for which I was the rallymaster. I was awed at the notion that a giant like Chevrolet might actually be interested in our remote enthusiasts' corner

of the automotive universe, but not sure exactly how interested they were, judging from the [original] Corvette's Blue Flame Six powerplant, Powerglide transmission and sedan frame, which was probably as old as several of the spectators that summer.

"Two years later, at Pebble Beach, I discovered exactly how serious they were. I'd been invited to the 1956 Pebble Beach road races...as an honorary emergency control marshall....I had little to do but watch; and there, in the paddock, I spotted a familiar face. Frank Burrell, a friend from my Press On Regardless days, was laboring over a red and white Corvette....Burrell worked in research and development at Chevrolet Engineering, and he'd been a mechanic on Cadillac-powered Allard teams at Le Mans. His presence told me something was up. Dr. Dick Thompson [a Washington D.C. dentist] was listed as the car's driver, and I'd known Thompson—raced against him, in fact—when he drove a ratty-looking blue Porsche 356.

"Even with a bellowing Chevy small-block for power," Davis continued, "the red and white Corvette, with its hardtop, three-speed manual transmission and crude drum brakes, seemed overmatched. Jim Peterson, the West Coast's reigning production car driver, was there with an immaculately prepared Jaguar XK-140, and Rudy Cleye was entered in his factory-assisted Mercedes-Benz 300SL gullwing. These were not cars to be taken lightly in 1956. Frank Burrell told me that the Corvette's brakes were hopeless (for racing), and he said none of the crew was absolutely certain that Thompson was a real racer, but they were going to give it their best shot.

"I was on the far side of the track when the starter's flag sent the big production cars hurtling off through

Three milestone Corvettes (opposite): the silver XP-87 Stingray racer, the red SR-2, and the blue Grand Sport. The sixth-generation '84 Corvette (below) went racing in SCCA's Showroom Stock division.

This page: *The SR-2 (top and center) was created for Sebring. Two copies of this highly modified stock model were built during the summer of 1956. In racing form, its engine (bottom left) cranked out an impressive 310 bhp. A special racing SR-2 with a lower rear deck fin (bottom right) was built for Jerry Earl, Harley's son. Opposite page: When equipped with fuel injection, the '57 'Vette was a formidable road car.*

the dark and misty forests surrounding Pebble Beach. When the leaders reached the corner where I was standing, the Corvette, the Jaguar and the gullwing Mercedes were all wedged together, battling for the lead. Tweedy types around me nodded sagely and predicted that it would be different on the next lap, and it was. Not even the Corvette's fiercest partisans expected the heavy red and white car to keep up with the thoroughbreds for very long. But on the next lap the Corvette arrived at our corner in the lead, and continued to extend that lead two-thirds distance, when its brakes just couldn't stand the pace anymore and Thompson was forced to back off. He still managed to finish second overall (to Cleye's 300SL) and first in class—a fact Chevrolet was so pleased with that they prepared an ad stating this. A new era had dawned."

Obviously, the restyled '56 Corvette not only looked more purposeful than the '55 but was even more capable on the track, and the young dentist was a fiercely skilled driver. Aided by Duntov and Chevrolet, Thompson had been campaigning Corvettes in SCCA C-Production only since the spring, yet by season's end he was the class champion. The following year, an enlarged 283-cid small-block pushed the Corvette up into the B-Production category, but Thompson won that, too. A big part of his initial success was the special "Duntov cam" that had proved its mettle in the record-setting Daytona runs.

Other than the fabled 24 Hours of Le Mans, the most important international sports-car race of the mid-Fifties was the Sebring 12 Hours of Endurance. Duntov knew that a good showing at this event would be a tremendous boost to the Corvette's fortunes. To achieve this goal, Duntov won management approval to make an all-out assault on Sebring with a purpose-built Corvette-based racer that emerged as the Super Sport (SS), often referred to as the Sebring SS. The inspiration for this experimental project (XP-64) was the racing D-Type Jaguar, which would be one of its track competitors. The full story of the potentially great SS racer is told in Chapter 5. Suffice it to say here that an over-torqued bushing forced the SS out of the March '57 Sebring contest after only 23 laps. Although the car's considerable promise remained, it was never fulfilled, largely because of the anti-racing edict handed down in June 1957 by the Automobile Manufacturers Association, and a similar order from GM that preceded the AMA's by about a month.

With that, the Corvette competition spotlight shifted to privateers beginning with the 1958 season. As in the stock-car field, most Corvettes raced that year were the more competitive 1956-57 models, not the bulkier, heavier '58s. The production 'Vette repeated its triumph at Sebring when a near-stock example driven by Jim Rathmann and Dick Doane again placed 12th overall and first in GT, sprinting to the line 20 laps ahead of the nearest Mercedes-Benz 300SL. At the Pikes Peak Hill Climb, Ak Miller took his 'Vette to a first-place win in the sports car division with a time of 15 minutes, 23.7 seconds and a speed of 48.392 mph for the 12.42-mile course, which rises from 9402 feet through 230 curves to 14,110 feet. Jim Jeffords gave the 'Vette its second consecutive B-Production crown in SCCA with his "Purple People Eater," actually one of two SR-2 racing machines created for Sebring. Built during the summer of 1956, the car featured a rounded nose, a single central rear tail fin with faired-in headrest, and paint reminiscent of the kind used on racing airplanes. The People Eater was also raced by Dick Thompson, stockcar ace Curtis Turner, and Harley Earl's son Jerry before Jeffords acquired it. In 1959, Jeffords added a third B-Production championship to the Corvette's lengthening string.

It was mostly third-generation models that were carrying Corvette's competition banner by the 1960 season, which brought fresh successes for the plastic Chevy. The first was another GT-class win at Sebring, courtesy of drivers Chuck Hall and Bill Fritts. But the highlight was the moral victory at Le Mans that Duntov had sought with the SS back in '57. It came courtesy of Briggs Cunningham, himself no stranger to the French circuit, having competed there with various cars (including some of his own design) for about a decade.

Cunningham entered three modified production Corvettes plus a Jaguar prototype in the newly reinstated over-3.0-liter GT class. One of the 'Vettes spun out on the rain-soaked track and retired, but the John Fitch/Bob Grossman car came in eighth overall and first in GT, completing 3782 kilometers. At one point, Fitch was timed at over 151 mph down the long Mulsanne Straight. Although the winning Ferrari of Oliver Gendebien/Paul Frere was considerably faster at 170 mph, the Corvette had conclusively proven its staying power in the world's most demanding long-distance contest.

In another arena, Dr. Dick Thompson was cam-

paigning Bill Mitchell's Stingray Special, which would influence the shape of the next-generation Corvette being readied for 1963. In 1960, the Stingray breezed Thompson to the SCCA's C-Modified National Championship. As expected, modified showroom models picked up another national title in B-Production.

Corvette continued its winning ways in 1961. On July 4, Ak Miller repeated his '58 feat at Pikes Peak by hurtling up the mountain in 14:28.6 minutes for an average speed of 51.5 mph. Other Corvettes swept home in places three through six. The year also brought another first-in-class at Sebring and still one more B-Production championship.

Late in 1961, Duntov began work on yet another Corvette racer that he hoped would be a world-beater—the fearsome Grand Sport. Designed with assistance from chassis specialist Walt Zeyte and others, it was Chevrolet's reply to the Cobra—the lightweight rocketship created when ex-racer Carroll Shelby stuffed a British AC roadster full of Ford 289 V-8, an engine

had envisioned.

The fate of the Grand Sport demonstrated that full-scale racing programs are neither easy nor cheap. And it can be noted as an ironic aside that Corvette sales had become sufficiently healthy by the early Sixties that a competition image was no longer needed.

Nevertheless, numerous die-hard independents continued putting production Corvettes in victory circles all across the country. Dick Thompson took the 1962 A-Production championship with that year's newly homologated 327, which the SCCA considered too overwhelming for B-Production. Class B itself was dominated through 1964 by the 283-powered cars of Don Yenko and Frank Dominianni. And, after a dry spell in 1962-63, Corvette again ruled the GT class at Sebring.

Highlighting the 1963 season was Yenko's repeat B-Production championship and Roger Penske's prototype-class victory at Nassau with the Grand Sport. The following year, a Penske car ran first in GT at the Daytona Continental, driven by George Wintersteen, Dick Guldstrand, and Ben Moore. Such victories were heartening for Corvette fans, who had little else to cheer about now that the Cobras were claiming most of the truly important events. Although the Cobra was far from the production sports car Carroll Shelby said it was, it had the SCCA's blessing, and that's what counted. So it was that the Corvette's road-racing career was stymied for a few years.

Duntov knew the score: "It was clear as day to me that the Cobra had to beat the Corvette. The Cobra was very powerful and weighed less than 2000 pounds. Shelby had the configuration, which was no damn good to sell to the people, except a very few. But it had to beat the Corvette on the tracks." Cobra production would cease after 1967, and those Cobras that continued to race would be tired and worn out by the end of '68. Until then, Corvette pickings were slim.

But there were still a few bright spots even in the Cobra's heyday. For example, a Sting Ray entered by Roger Penske finished 12th overall and first in GT at the '66 Daytona Continental, then placed ninth

that quickly showed its muscle on the tracks. Duntov had hoped to complete at least 100 Grand Sports, the number needed to qualify as a production sports car under international racing rules. Because GM was still nominally abiding by the 1957 AMA anti-racing edict, the development program was carried out in great secrecy, far from disapproving managerial eyes.

As related more fully in Chapter 8, the Grand Sport project withered in early 1963 beneath an official GM policy statement that reaffirmed the company's non-involvement with racing. Only five (engineless) Grand Sports had been built when this axe fell, all quickly ended up in private hands. Although these cars saw action at Watkins Glen, Nassau, Sebring, and else-where as late as 1966, the results were variable and far from the world-beating performance that Duntov

overall and first in GT at the Sebring 12-Hours. Don Yenko teamed up with Dave Morgan for another GT-class win at Sebring the following year. At Le Mans in 1967, the Corvette of Bob Bondurant and Dick Guldstrand ran a strong first in class until its engine failed toward the end of the marathon. That year also saw a little-reported triumph at the Bonneville Salt Flats in Utah, where Bob Hirsch ran to a record-setting 192.879 mph. Nineteen sixty-eight brought more class wins at Sebring and Daytona.

With Cobras being retired from competition to car-collector garages, the Corvette reasserted its SCCA dominance in 1969. Chevy engineer Jerry Thompson (no relation to the racing dentist) and driver Tony DeLorenzo teamed up to take that year's A-Production national championship, ending the six-year drought that had begun in 1963. Allan Barker captured the '69 B-Production title, which his Corvette would own through the next three seasons. After 1972, Barker sold his car to Texas racer Bill Jobe, who won the class with it in '73 and again in '74, giving this car six consecutive national B-Production titles. It was still being campaigned as late as 1978.

Corvette repeated as A-Production champ in 1970, with a young John Greenwood doing the honors. He won again in 1971, then teamed up with entertainer Dick Smothers to come home first in GT at Sebring in 1972. At that year's 24 Hours of Daytona, DeLorenzo and Yenko scored yet another GT victory while finishing a surprising fourth overall. Greenwood went on to Le Mans, where he qualified faster than any other GT contender. He led the class for hours

during the race itself until a blown engine forced him out. Jerry Hansen filled in as 1972 A-Production national champion.

The energy crisis put a temporary damper on racing in 1974, but things were more or less back to normal the following year. Like the Sting Rays before them, the fifth-generation Corvettes were too big and heavy to compete effectively against the likes of Porsche and BMW in international endurance events. And Corvette campaigners couldn't hope to match the large sums of money spent by the European companies. So the 'Vette's greatest success continued to come in SCCA racing. America's sports car was A-Production champion from 1973 to '78, and B-Production titleholder in 1973-74 and from 1976 through '79. Corvettes also did well in the new sport of autocross, winning the B-Stock Solo II crown for 1973-74 and 1976-79.

Seventies competition in the SCCA's Trans-American Championship road-racing series saw many great Corvette performances. In 1973, J. Marshall Robbins,

John Greenwood, and Jerry Thompson brought their Corvettes to third, fourth, and fifth in overall points. Greenwood won the championship outright in 1975, with Babe Headley, Jerry Hansen, and Paul Misuriello bringing their 'Vettes in second, third, and fourth. After two lean years, Corvette claimed the Trans-Am's Category II title in 1978, thanks to Greg Pickett's wild racer. That same year, Headley finished a distant second in Category I to Bob Tullius' Jaguar, which was heavily backed by the British firm's U.S. subsidiary.

But Jaguar was not so fortunate in 1979, when Gene Bothello's Corvette won Category I, and Frank Joyce and Gary Carlen finished third and fourth. Pickett was runner-up in the consolidated 1980 series. For 1981—a season described as one of the most exciting and competitive in Trans-Am history—Eppie Wietzes ended up the point leader.

More recent Trans-Am seasons have been ruled by Capris, XR4Tis, Camaros, and Nissan ZXs, but a Corvette has usually finished near the top of the points

Opposite page: *Some racing Corvettes: at the SCCA Nationals at Mid-Ohio in 1966 (top); a '63 Grand Sport (center left); competing at Riverside in 1962 (bottom left); "Don Steves Chevrolet" car 00 (bottom right).* This page: *A 1963 B-Production racer (top); a 1965 L-88 big-block 'Vette (center); a 1967 Le Mans competition Corvette (bottom).*

This page: More racing Corvettes: J. Marshall Robbins' car at the SCCA Trans-Am at Road Atlanta, 1973 (top left); a 427 'Vette at Daytona. For the last few years, Chevrolet has been involved in the role of providing technical assistance for an exciting mid-engine prototype racing car, the Lola-based, Chevy-powered Corvette GTP that competes in IMSA's Camel GT series. An '84 edition (this page) and an '86 (opposite page) are shown, along with a cutaway that reveals the location of its turbo V-6 engine and other major components.

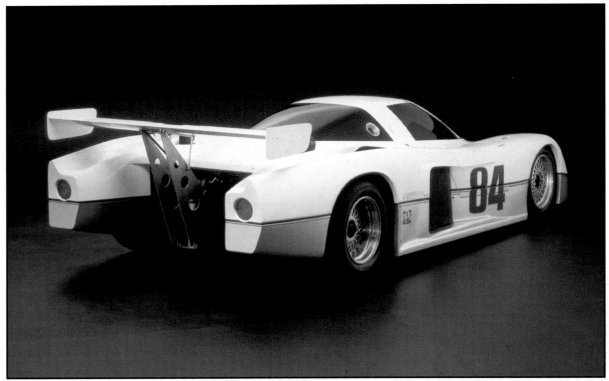

standings. For example, Phil Currin ran third in points in 1982, though he never won a race outright—another example of Corvette consistency and staying power. Two years later, Darin Brassfield and David Hobbs ran sixth and eighth in points in a season highlighted by Brassfield's outright wins at Road America and Riverside.

Corvette has done even better in the SCCA's Showroom Stock Endurance Series. Despite tooth-and-nail battles with Porsche 944 Turbos, the sixth-generation cars went undefeated four years in a row, winning every race on the card from 1984 to '87—four events that first year, six in the second, and seven each in 1986-87. After that, the 'Vette was retired to give other cars a shot at victory.

Being barred from Showroom Stock after '87

suggested that the Corvette was in a class by itself—which, of course, it was. But there were still plenty of SS competitors who wanted to run the cars, so Chevy and the SCCA got together on a special series just for Showroom Stock Corvettes. Called the Corvette Challenge Series, it harked back to the original idea of the International Race of Champions (IROC) of the 1970s—a limited number of races open to a set number of identically prepared cars. This made for closer, more exciting competition, with driving skill rather than technical tricks being the key to victory. Chevy built 50 specially equipped Challenge Corvettes for the 10-race 1988 inaugural, only this time the cars were sold to the individual drivers and teams rather than being retained by the manufacturer. As principal sponsors, Chevy, Goodyear, and Bilstein put up a

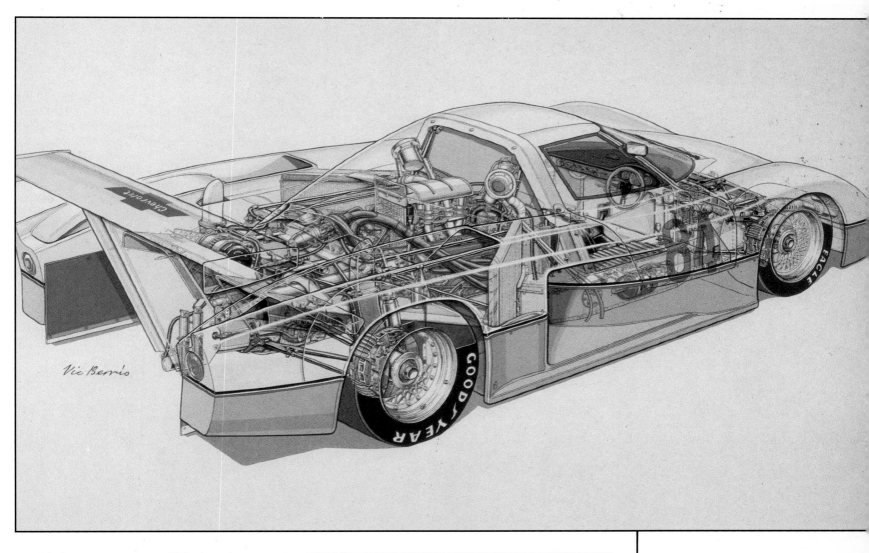

Vic Berris

Bilstein driver-adjustable shock absorbers [same as those on the latest Formula 1 Lotus] and six-speed ZF manual transmission."

As before, noted a Chevy press release, "Challenge [Corvettes] may be purchased through Chevy dealers after the driver's credentials are approved by the Powell organization and SCCA. Except for the addition of roll cages and other required safety equipment, all [the] cars are just like production Corvettes....Engines and transmissions will be tested, equalized and sealed at the factory. The General Motors Computer Aided Maintenance System (GM-CAMS) will be utilized throughout the season to insure that all cars stay within specifications." This sophistication is a far cry from the rough-and-ready days of Dick Thompson at Pebble Beach '56, but who'd have thought way back then that the Corvette would one day have its own series?

Over at the SCCA's rival organization, the International Motor Sports Association (IMSA), the Corvette has been a consistent contender and frequent winner in the GTO division (GT cars over 2.5 liters). Corvette brought home the All-American GT Manufacturers Championship in 1978 and finished the 1984 season in second spot.

Even more exciting is the advent of a mid-engine prototype racer designed for IMSA's Camel GT series and supported by Chevrolet. This Corvette GTP is built around a long-tail monocoque structure made mainly of a Kevlar and aluminum honeycomb, and is easily identified by "ground effects" skirting, a big rear wing riding high on slim support struts, and a low, rounded nose vaguely reminiscent of that on the sixth-generation production car. The sophisticated chassis was engineered by Lola of England under Eric Broadley; in fact, the initial car was designated Lola T-710.

Powering the GTP is a turbo-intercooled 90-degree V-6, essentially the division's stock 229-cid production unit with a 0.26-inch larger bore and 0.73-inch shorter stroke; the resizing is necessary to meet the maximum displacement limit of 209 cid. A Chevy flyer on the GTP took pains to point out that "although the differences between [the] production and race engines are considerable, the [racing] V-6 incorporates as many off-the-shelf components as possible...[many] available through *Chevrolet Power*, the combination heavy-duty parts catalog and Chevy performance 'bible.'" Chevy says some 300 hours went into the engine's preparation, building, and testing. The payoff was dynamometer readings of up to 775 horsepower at 8500 rpm at the maximum boost pressure of 20 psi. Typical torque output was quoted at 556 pounds-feet at 7000 rpm.

Usually seen with Sarel Van Der Merwe and Doc Bundy behind the wheel, the Corvette GTP proved its potential its first year out, setting a new IMSA lap record at Daytona in 1985. It started that race on the grid and went on to capture a record seven pole positions in 1986 and another four in '87. Although it's won a good number of races for the Hendrick Motorsports racing team and its sponsor, GM's "Mr. Goodwrench," the GTP has yet to record its first championship season, bowing to the likes of Porsche's 962 and Nissan's ZX GTP.

But consistent race-winners aren't built in a day, and the mere existence of the GTP, as well as the continued success of production-based Corvette racers, is heartening, especially given less overt factory support than one finds in Porsche and Ferrari efforts. As has been true for more than three decades now, a winning tradition on the racetracks of the world is part of what makes Corvette the American sports-car legend it is.

With the Corvette barred from Showroom Stock racing after 1987, Chevy and the SCCA got together to form the Corvette Challenge series. Fifty identically (and specially) equipped Corvettes (both pages) were sold to individual drivers and teams for the 10-race 1988 inaugural season, which had a total purse of a million dollars. At least 10 races were planned for '89.

million dollars in total prize money—$500,000 distributed among the top 24 drivers eligible for points and another $500,000 in individual-event purses. Canadian John Powell produced the whole thing in cooperation with SCCA as an offshoot of SS competition.

When the dust cleared after a hard-fought 1988 season, Walt Hayner of Yorba Linda, California, a two-year veteran of the earlier Escort Endurance Series, was top point-earner and took home nearly $143,000 for his efforts. "This is a lot of money," Hayner said, "but I've never worked so hard to win anything. This may be the richest Showroom Stock race series, but it's also the most competitive." Runner-up (at $115,300) was none other than Argentina's Juan Manuel Fangio II, son of the immortal Grand Prix driver of the Forties and Fifties. Indy veteran Johnny Rutherford also competed; he finished only 20th in points but received the Series' $7500 Sportsman Award.

Important from Chevy's point of view, the Corvette Challenge was a great promotional success as well as an exciting addition to the SCCA calendar. The Series seems destined for a long run. At least 10 races were planned for 1989, most to be staged in conjunction with Indy-car events, and with all first-season sponsors continuing their participation. SCCA was to again sanction the series, and the ESPN cable-TV sports network was slated to provide same-day coast-to-coast coverage.

But if Hayner hopes to repeat as Challenge champion in '89, he'll have to buy another Corvette, since the '88 cars were ineligible. The competition will be tougher, too. "The '89 cars will be too strong," John Powell stated. "Among [their] new features are

Corvette Racing Highlights

1955	Stock car record for Pikes Peak Hill Climb
1956	Record 150-mph run, Daytona Beach SCCA C-Production champion Ninth overall, Sebring 12-Hours Second overall, Pebble Beach road race
1957	First in class, Sebring 12-Hours SCCA B-Production champion SCCA B-Sports/Racing champion
1958	First in class, Sebring 12-Hours First in class, Pikes Peak Hill Climb SCCA B-Production champion
1959	SCCA B-Production champion
1960	First in class, Sebring 12-Hours Eighth overall, Le Mans 24-Hours SCCA B-Production champion SCCA C-Sports/Racing champion
1961	First in class, Sebring 12-Hours First in class, Pikes Peak Hill Climb SCCA B-Production champion
1962	First in class, Daytona Continental SCCA A-Production champion SCCA B-Production champion
1963	First in Prototype class, Nassau Speed Weeks SCCA B-Production champion
1964	First in class, Daytona Continental First in class, Sebring 12-Hours SCCA B-Production champion
1965	SCCA Midwest Division A-Production champion SCCA Midwest Division B-Production champion SCCA Southwest Division B-Production champion
1966	First in class, Sebring 12-Hours First in class, Daytona Continental
1967	First in class, Sebring 12-Hours
1968	First in class, Sebring 12-Hours
1969	SCCA A-Production champion SCCA B-Production champion
1970	SCCA A-Production champion SCCA B-Production champion
1971	First in class, Daytona 24-Hours First in class, Sebring 12-Hours SCCA A-Production champion SCCA B-Production champion
1972	SCCA A-Production champion SCCA B-Production champion First in class, Sebring 12-Hours
1973	First in class, Sebring 12-Hours SCCA B-Production champion SCCA B-Stock Solo II champion SCCA B-Prepared Solo II champion
1974	SCCA A-Production champion SCCA B-Production champion SCCA B-Stock Solo II champion
1975	First overall, SCCA Trans-Am series SCCA A-Production champion
1976	SCCA A-Production champion SCCA B-Production champion SCCA B-Stock Solo II champion
1977	SCCA A-Production champion SCCA B-Stock Solo II champion SCCA B-Prepared Solo II champion
1978	First overall, SCCA Trans-Am Category II SCCA A-Production champion SCCA B-Production champion SCCA B-Stock Solo II champion SCCA B-Prepared Solo II champion SCCA B-Stock Ladies Solo II champion IMSA All-American GT champion
1979	First overall, Riverside Vintage Car Races (Grand Sport #003) First overall, SCCA Trans-Am Category I SCCA B-Production champion SCCA B-Stock Solo II champion SCCA B-Prepared Solo II champion SCCA B-Stock Ladies Solo II champion
1980	Second overall, SCCA Trans-Am series
1981	First and third overall, SCCA Trans-Am series
1982	Second overall (tied), SCCA Trans-Am series
1984	Two wins, SCCA Trans-Am SCCA Showroom Stock Endurance Series champion (won all four races) SCCA Showroom Stock GT national champion
1985	First in class, Laguna Seca IMSA GTO SCCA Showroom Stock Endurance Series champion (won all six races) SCCA Showroom Stock national champion IMSA GTP Corvette on pole at Daytona 24-Hours, lap record
1986	SCCA Showroom Stock Endurance Series champion (won all seven races) First at Road Atlanta IMSA Camel GT Two wins, Corvette GTP Seven IMSA pole positions (record), Corvette GTP
1987	First in all seven SCCA Showroom Stock Endurance events Four IMSA pole positions, Corvette GTP
1988	Million-dollar Corvette Challenge Series inaugurated for SCCA Showroom-Stock models; Walt Hayner champion Second overall in IMSA GTO

CHAPTER 14

CORVETTE SHOW CARS: SHAPING THE FUTURE

Harley Earl's excitingly prophetic Buick Y-Job of 1938 gave the public a privileged glimpse of a "dream car,"a new concept from America's leading automaker. Detroit soon came to appreciate the value of "sneak previewing"—an appreciation that was borne out by the expensively mounted, always well-received Motorama shows of 1949-61.

The term "show car" can mean most anything, from a beautiful body shell bereft of engine and drivetrain to a fully functional, one-of-a-kind prototype. It's not likely—nor does anyone expect—that a show car will make an immediate leap to local showrooms. But as we've seen, the Corvette—which made a smashing debut at the 1953 Motorama—was a vivid exception, a car that was promptly offered to the public with only minor deviations from show-car form.

But show cars aren't simply glamorous toys designed to excite buyer interest in particular marques. For Corvette, particularly, show cars have been invaluable tools utilized to test new concepts in design and engineering—to expand the definition of what the Corvette should be.

Sorting out the various Corvette-inspired show cars of the past 35 years is sometimes as difficult as tracking changes in the production models. That's especially true of the 1968-77 period, when GM tantalized us with a profusion of not only mid-engine experiments but more conventional front-engine designs related to the production "Shark." Although equally important to the evolution of the Corvette, the front- and mid-engine show cars were designed with significantly different technology and goals. For that reason, these show-car developments will be discussed separately. We'll look first at the front-engine designs.

As noted earlier, the fifth-generation Corvette was, in essence, a less exaggerated version of the Mako Shark II, initiated in 1964 as a follow-up to the supercharged XP-755 show car of 1961. The earlier exercise was originally called Shark, then retitled Mako

Shark I when the Mako II debuted in 1965. Both were executed by Larry Shinoda from Bill Mitchell concepts as sneak previews of upcoming production Corvette styling: Mako I previewed the '63 Sting Ray and Mako II forecast the '68 model. Although the show cars differed markedly in appearance, they shared a dramatic paint treatment inspired by their nautical namesake—an inky blue-black graduated to silver on the lower extremities, suggesting a white "underbelly."

Unlike XP-755, there were two versions of Mako II (officially designated project "X-15," after the experimental aircraft that first broke the sound barrier). The first was a nonrunning mock-up distinguished by square-section side exhaust pipes that exited paired vents on each front fender, all trimmed with fine chrome bars, plus a futuristic interior featuring an aircraft-style rectangular steering wheel. After October 1965, the "pushmobile" was pushed aside for a fully functional Mako II. This lacked the side pipes but sported a more vivid shark paint scheme, plus a round steering wheel in a mostly similar cockpit.

Innovations abounded on the running Mako II. For example, its pointy nose held twin banks of square, European-style headlamps hidden behind "clamshell" covers. Out back was a rudimentary square-tube bumper that extended electrically for extra body protection. A retractable "whaletail" spoiler was also provided, forecasting that of the Porsche 911 Carrera 4 that would appear more than 20 years later. Equally predictive was the use of digital displays.

Borrowed from the Jaguar E-Type and Triumph Spitfire was a one-piece front-hinged forward body section that tilted up to expose a 427 Mark IV engine, then being phased in as an option for production Corvettes. (The pushmobile carried "Mark IV 396" lettering on the prominent hood bulge.) This drove through a three-speed Turbo-Hydra-Matic transmission, offered at that time on full-size Chevys but not on Corvettes until 1968.

Opposite page: The front end of Bill Mitchell's 1960 Corvette XP-700 show car didn't make it to a production Corvette, but the rear styling (along with the Stingray racing car) inspired the rear styling of the 1961 'Vette. This page: The XP-87 Stingray (right) rode the 1957 SS chassis. It is seen here in silver, the color it was painted for the 1961 auto shows. Mitchell's racing Stingray from 1959 led directly to the XP-755 Shark of 1961 (left), which was later renamed Mako Shark I. Both cars influenced the design of the '63 Sting Ray.

Having served its purpose, the Mako II should have been retired. But at GM, even show cars can be facelifted, and for the 1970 season the working Mako was transformed into the Manta Ray. Aside from more extensive lower-body "silvering" and the return of side exhausts that recalled the nonrunning Mako II, most changes involved the roof. Contour was unchanged, but the backlight louvers were exchanged for a slim vertical rear window just behind the cockpit, making for a dramatic "sugar scoop" treatment. Flanking the "boattail" was a third pair of taillights that popped-up to supplement the existing quartet in the back panel—an idea that predicted the mandatory center high-mount stoplamp required on today's cars. Motive power was changed to the brawniest ZL1 version of the Chevy big-block.

The Manta Ray *would* be retired—to Bill Mitchell's garage, where it joined his original Stingray racer and the Mako I. Also among his "pets" for a time was the Aero Coupe. This was a lightly customized '69 Corvette with 1970-style crosshatch grille and front-fender vents, plus big side exhausts and a modest rear spoiler flared around and forward into the rear fenders, a treatment also seen on 1970-1972 early Camaro Z28s. The production car's twin T-tops were replaced by a one-piece roof section that led to a slightly higher windshield. Like Mako II, the Aero Coupe would also be "facelifted," becoming the Mulsanne of 1972. Updates included the "soft" body-color front and rear ends destined for 1973-74 production, exposed headlamps, high-set door mirrors, and a fixed roof with a wide rear-facing periscope.

A more curious variation on fifth-generation styling themes appeared not long after the new '68 Corvette itself. Named Astro-Vette, it was a super-slick roadster first shown in the spring of that year. Author Karl Ludvigsen describes it as "looking as though it was already halfway to Bonneville to break all speed records, but it was strictly a motor show special....Its main styling features were all in the interest of reduced aerodynamic drag: fully enclosed rear wheels, a long, tapering tail, narrow wheels and tires, flush discs for the front wheels, and an extended nose with air inlets of minimum size." Toward the same end, partial belly pans were fitted front and rear, as well as a low racing-type windscreen that wrapped around into the doors. Behind and just above the mostly stock cockpit was a low-profile spoiler-cum-rollbar faired down to a pointed tail. With its cigar-like shape and pearlescent white paint, the Astro-Vette was nicknamed "Moby Dick" by GM stylists—which may help explain why it was never seen again.

The last major front-engine exercise of the fifth-generation's first decade was the XP-898 of 1973, a smooth Corvette-like "glassback" on suspension and running gear from the twincam Cosworth version of Chevy's subcompact Vega hatchback coupe. This car was built to study the feasibility of a new approach to fiberglass construction: a unit body/chassis made entirely from a GRP shell injected with liquid polyurethane foam. The thickness of the "sandwich" was varied throughout the structure to achieve the desired cross-section and hence stiffness—something like the later VARI (variable resin injection) process of

future GM subsidiary Lotus in England.

A retrospective in the May 1975 *Car and Driver* cited simplicity and low weight as the main advantages of the XP-898 structure, though it was also said to be "particularly good at absorbing both crash energy and normal engine and road noises." By Corvette standards, the car was a featherweight—just 2285 pounds at the curb—and *C/D* projected that an XP-898 with five-speed manual transmission "would have little trouble delivering 1975 Corvette performance levels" even with the four-cylinder, 111-bhp Cosworth engine.

Despite its Vega base, the XP-898 was rumored as late as 1981 to be the shape of the "next" Corvette, which is its main historical significance. Though its resemblance to the sixth generation is slight to be sure, it is there, especially in the crisp roofline with its compound-curve hatchback.

Midships engine positioning, like front-wheel drive, doesn't necessarily make for a better car than some other configuration, but it's long been the most appealing for "car people." Born of racing, with all the charisma that carries, and with inherently good mass balance as its principal advantage, it's always seemed ideal for a roadgoing sports car, especially for an image-leader, as Corvette has been for Chevrolet. Moreover, the layout presents several technical and packaging challenges of the sort that designers and engineers love to tackle, and it tends to result in a more "interesting" car with higher appeal (if not practicality) for enthusiasts.

This, in a nutshell, explains the various efforts toward a mid-engine Corvette that began in the early Sixties—efforts always overruled by the firm's infamous "bean-counters" after enormous expenditures of time, effort, and money. By the late Sixties, though, several factors had combined to make the mid-engine dream seem a real possibility for the first time.

As ever, Zora Arkus-Duntov and others who had the ear of top GM brass were pushing for a more sophisticated, no-compromise Corvette to counter Europe's best sports cars. But now, they pointed out, the midships configuration was spreading from expensive exotics like the Lamborghini Miura to very affordable sports cars like the Lotus Europa and Porsche 914. How, asked Duntov and his supporters, could the Corvette be America's performance and technological standard-bearer with an old-fashioned front-engine/rear-drive format?

The same question was asked by Ed Cole, father of the Corvair and an engineer long attracted to advanced concepts—and, as of 1967, GM's new president. Faster than you can say "show car," we began seeing a parade of tantalizing mid-engine experiments that evidently pointed to the next Corvette, each prominently displayed before the public, whose reactions were carefully evaluated. Significantly, the first of these was a Corvair-powered exercise that appeared the year Cole became president.

Called Astro I, it was a wild-looking two-seat fastback coupe with smooth, muscular contours and a fiberglass body with only two sections: a front unit comprising fenders and wraparound windshield, and a rear assembly combining cockpit canopy, rear fenders, and deck. Because it stood a mere 35.5 inches high—too low for conventional seats—the Astro I had something called "pushbutton positioning." After raising the aft-hinged rear section (which also provided engine access), you stepped inside and touched a center-console button to move the seat to a racing-style semi-reclining posture, then lowered the canopy once you settled in. Power came from a Corvair flat six enlarged to 176 cubic inches and given overhead camshafts, hemispherical combustion chambers, and twin triple-throat carbs. Double-wishbone suspension and disc brakes were used all-round. Performance was never measured, but the Astro I would likely have been impressive on S-curves and straightaways alike. A 160-mph speedometer and 9000-rpm tachometer hinted at its potential.

Ford's successful GT enduro racers and mid-engine Mach 2 show car prompted the Astro II, essentially a less extreme version of Astro I. Designated XP-880, it looked producible—and quite pretty—but its Lotus-style "backbone" monocoque and a bulky rear-mounted powerteam (the ohc Corvair engine and Pontiac Tempest transaxle) would have sent showroom prices out of sight.

Duntov, meantime, had found a way around the expensive, purpose-built transaxle that had always kept a mid-engine 'Vette from production. It wasn't particularly elegant, but he thought enough of his answer to have it patented.

Again starting with the V-8 he knew would be expected, Duntov mounted it sideways rather than "north-south." To one side and also sitting crosswise was a stock Turbo-Hydra-Matic driven directly from

Opposite page: *The Corvette (top) first appeared at GM's 1953 Motorama, and went into limited production later in the year. The 1954 Motorama spotlighted a fastback Corvette show car called the Corvair (bottom left). Charming models always enhanced the Corvette's appeal (bottom right). This page: The design of the XP-700 looks a bit cluttered today, but it turned heads in 1960.*

407

the crankshaft by chain. The transmission connected to a normal Corvette differential via a short driveshaft that negotiated a right angle up front to align with the "east-west" transmission; the driveshaft was encased in a tube and passed through the engine's oil pan. Essentially the same arrangement used on Oldsmobile's big front-drive Toronado, the system was more complex than a rear transaxle but a lot cheaper, since it made greater use of more off-the-shelf components. Even better, it was easily adaptable to *four*-wheel drive, which Duntov had begun working with in the CERV II, a midships Can-Am-type car developed in 1964 as a follow-up to the experimental rear-engine CERV I.

This so-called "split" drivetrain was investigated as Project XP-882, for which two running chassis were completed by early 1969. One was bodied as a neat fastback coupe bearing a low, squarish, hidden-headlamp snout; trim midsection; prominently bulged rear fenders; and a louvered, "boattail" rear that recalled the Mako Shark II. The entire body section behind the cockpit was unitized and rear-hinged to tilt up for engine access. There was room behind the power package for a small trunk, which had a separate external lid.

Suspension was much like that of the production Sting Ray, but tighter dimensions (wheelbase was a tidy 94.5 inches) and careful weight-watching brought the XP-882—even with air conditioning—to just 2595

pounds, about 400 pounds lighter than a stock '68 Corvette. Significantly, the chassis could accommodate both big- and small-block V-8s, and Duntov had worked out a manual transmission based on the Turbo-Hydra-Matic.

But the project stalled when John Z. DeLorean, who came in as Chevy general manager just as the prototype was finished, shelved XP-882 as impractical and too costly. A year later, when Ford announced its intention to import the mid-engine DeTomaso Pantera for U.S. sale, DeLorean resurrected the XP-882 for the 1970 New York Auto Show. It was soon hailed as "The 1973 Mid-Engine Corvette," as *Road & Track* headlined its January 1971 feature story, but we wouldn't see a consumer version in Chevy showrooms in that or any other year. However, we would see more of the XP-882.

And that's because president Ed Cole had become intrigued with the innovative trochoidal-rotor engine developed in Germany by NSU's Felix Wankel—so intrigued that he pushed GM to develop its own. Although initially targeted for small cars like Chevy's new 1971 Vega subcompact, the developing General Motors Rotary Combustion Engine (GMRCE) offered advantages that made it a natural for a new Corvette: greater compactness, fewer moving parts, and most of all, high specific output. The new engine also pointed the way to solutions to several packaging problems that are inherent in mid-engine design.

The Mako Shark I (top) took some inspiration from its name. Note the "gills" on the front fenders ahead of the wheels and the shark-like grille opening (mouth) under the elongated snout. The characteristics are even more striking on the rendering being completed in March 1961 (bottom).

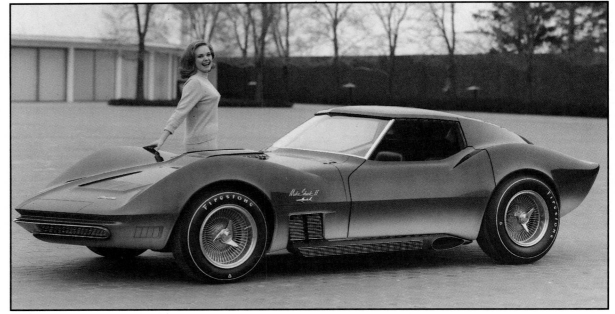

Cole's enthusiasm for the rotary led to two different mid-engine 'Vette proposals. The first, internally known as XP-897GT, got going in early 1971 under Clare MacKichan, then chief of GM's Advanced Design area and the stylist who'd helped finalize the original '53 Corvette. The actual design work fell to Dick Finegan of the Experimental Studio. XP-897 wasn't conceived as a Corvette per se. Rather, it was seen as a possible successor to GM Germany's two-seat "mini-'Vette," the Opel GT coupe, and, at the same time, as a sporty addition to the Vega line for 1975 or '76—hence its informal name "Chevrolet GT." Bill Mitchell, in fact, thought it might become the first "world" sports car. Although Opel would do nothing with it, the project did lead to the production Chevy Monza 2+2—without the GM rotary, of course.

To save time, XP-897GT was built on a modified Porsche 914 platform frame. Bodywork was entrusted to Italy's Pininfarina, who went from drawings and full-size plaster models to finished shell in a mere 12 weeks. "We'd played with different designs for small

sports cars with the rotary engine," MacKichan later told Karl Ludvigsen, "with front-wheel drive and other layouts—on paper. But our real love was always the mid-engine car. We kept it down to the absolute minimum size that we could...because there was a feeling the Corvette had gotten too big and heavy." The result was dimensionally quite close to the production Ferrari Dino 246GT. Unit-steel construction with aluminum hood, doors, and deck kept curb weight to a svelte 2600 pounds.

Significantly, Duntov's chief chassis engineer, Walt Zeyte, was on hand to adapt the Porsche underpinnings for their new role. Of course, the 914's anemic four-cylinder piston engine was removed. In its place went a two-rotor version of the "Generation I" GMRCE, designated RC2-266, producing an estimated 180 horsepower at 6100 rpm from 399 cubic inches total displacement. It drove to a three-speed torque-converter automatic transmission in an aluminum case. A train of helical gears between the converter and the planetary gearset took the drive down and slightly to the right of

the differential. A Corvair-type four-speed manual gearbox was also developed to fit this driveline.

XP-897GT was not only pretty but surprisingly practical for a midships two-seater. Pedals moved instead of the seats, although the latter could be pivoted for height/back-angle adjustment. There was more than enough passenger and cargo room, and even outward vision was good. Still, the "2-Rotor Car," as press reports typically termed it, never had a shot at production. In the December 1973 *Motor Trend,* writer Ludvigsen reported that when the car was first shown to top GM managers in June 1972, chairman Richard C. Gerstenberg asked, "What do you want a new Corvette for? You're selling all the cars you can make right now!" That was hard to argue with. Goodbye, XP-897GT.

But hello again, XP-882—or rather the second chassis from that project, soon to be the "Four-Rotor Car." Duntov didn't really like the Wankel engine, believing that any new Corvette should retain the traditional V-8. But if he had to take a rotary to get a mid-engine model, as Cole seemed to be dictating, then he'd have a

real rip-snorter. It was as "simple" as bolting together a pair of two-rotor jobs—early-1971 RC2-195 engines—and substituting this for the original V-8 in the second XP-882 chassis. By July 1972 the engineers had a 585-cid screamer producing some 350 bhp at 7000 rpm (output was never officially measured).

Bill Mitchell needed little persuading to get his Design Staff to do a completely new body for the "Wankelized" XP-882. Reason: He was miffed at DeLorean, who, as Mitchell later revealed, was "going to let [designer] Georgetto Giugiaro do it." According to Ludvigsen's *Motor Trend* story, work was underway in Henry Haga's studio by January 1973, though the decision to marry the new body with the four-rotor chassis wasn't made until April. Tellingly, the car was referred to at one stage as "197X M.E.V.," meaning a mid-engine vehicle for possible production sometime before 1980. The designers soon faced a more imminent deadline: the October 1973 Paris Auto Show, where management had decided to unveil the car. They finished in time, and the Four-Rotor simply stunned all who saw it.

"Stunning" really described it. Executed under Haga's

Opposite page: The XP-897 GT project got underway in early 1971. It was a mid-engine two-rotor job built by Pininfarina (top). The XP-882 (center) bowed in New York in 1970. It had a transverse V-8 mounted between the rear wheels. The Aero Coupe was a 1969 effort (bottom left), which evolved into the Sirocco (right). This page: The Corvette Four-Rotor (top) debuted at the 1973 Paris Motor Show. The Mulsanne (bottom left) was yet another modified production 'Vette; the Astro II, XP-880 (bottom right), was shown in 1968.

413

This page: The Astro-Vette (top) made the show circuit in 1968. The fender skirts were hinged at the top to allow access to the rear wheels. XP-898 (bottom) was a 1973 exercise based on the suspension and running gear of the Cosworth Vega to test an all-fiberglass unit/body chassis. Opposite page: Although a one-off, the 1984 Corvette-based Bertone Ramarro (top) was fully driveable. The Turbo Vette 3 (bottom) looked very much like a production Corvette except for graphics.

direction by Chuck Jordan (newly returned from a stint at Opel and destined to become GM's design vice-president in the late Eighties), the Four-Rotor was ultra-clean and dramatically different, yet unmistakably Corvette. A distinctive "mound" profile left no doubt where the engine was, and unique "bi-fold" gullwing doors cleverly one-upped Mercedes' experimental C-111. Mitchell later termed the Four-Rotor "my example of the opposite of Giugiaro. His cars are full of angles....[They] look like they've been cut from cardboard. You want to stick Tab A into Slot B....But [this one] had nice contours, soft curves and still a certain sharpness. It had really good balance...a design [that looked good] from any angle."

It was good in the wind tunnel, too. Recalling Sting Ray development, the Four-Rotor was evaluated in scale-model form at Cal Tech's GALCIT facility. The tests showed a drag coefficient of only 0.325, sensationally low for that time and still not bad today.

But once more, forces were conspiring against a mid-engine 'Vette. To the sales argument that weighed against the Two-Rotor was now added the OPEC oil embargo, which began almost simultaneously with the Four-Rotor's unveiling and revealed the Wankel to be a relative drunkard next to piston engines of comparable size or output. This hardly boded well for sales—it nearly wiped out Mazda of Japan, the only automaker besides NSU then selling showroom Wankels—so GM dropped its rotary program like a hot potato and put the intriguing Four-Rotor in

cold storage. But it would have a final burst of glory as the Aerovette, refitted with a conventional Chevy V-8 as the template for a proposed 1980 production Corvette (see Chapter 10,).

The first XP-882, the prototype coupe that *Road & Track* had predicted as the '73 Corvette, was reincarnated, too—as project XP-895. Initiated in 1972, this effort explored the possibilities of steel/aluminum and all-aluminum unit construction for a future production Corvette. Because of its weight-saving advantage, the latter gained new impetus once the energy crisis hit in late '73. A new body was crafted with help from Reynolds Aluminum but the unique "split" powertrain with cast-iron 400-cid Chevy V-8 was retained. Styling was neat and purposeful, more balanced than that of the original XP-882 body, if not as arresting as the Four-Rotor design.

Although undoubtedly valuable as a research tool, XP-895 was unceremoniously tossed into the corporate wastebasket after 1974. It would have remained there, too, had it not been for several history-minded GM engineers, who discovered it wasting away and decided to refurbish it on their own time and with whatever help they could get from various Tech Center departments.

Thus did XP-895 turn up unexpectedly in late 1988 as part of Chevrolet's 1989-model long-lead press review at California's Riverside Raceway. It was just an exhibit and not meant to suggest that a mid-engine 'Vette was imminent. But it was good to see it, even if it wasn't quite as pristine as it once was. (Restoring an experimental car isn't easy—even if you work for the company that built it!)

In the end, the mid-engine dream that seemed so achingly near in the Seventies was ever far from reality and for one simple reason: The traditional fiberglass-bodied, front/V-8 Corvette was still selling well enough to make a replacement unnecessary—never mind one that would certainly have cost a lot more to build. But the dream still burns brightly for many 'Vette fans, as it did at GM until 1978. And as GM has lately rekindled the flame with the high-tech Corvette Indy, it looks like a midships model will finally arrive in Chevy showrooms come 1993. So you see, dreams can come true. Some just take longer than others.

INDEX